CANADA ALWAYS

The Defining Speeches of Sir Wilfrid Laurier

Edited by
ARTHUR MILNES

McCLELLAND & STEWART

Library and Archives Canada Cataloguing in Publication is available upon request

ISBN: 978-0-7710-5977-3
e-book ISBN: 978-0-7710-5978-0

Library of Congress Control Number is available upon request

Published simultaneously in the United States of America by McClelland & Stewart, a division of Penguin Random House Canada Limited, a Penguin Random House Company

Printed and bound in USA
Typeset in Bembo by M&S, Toronto

McClelland & Stewart,
a division of Penguin Random House Canada Limited,
a Penguin Random House Company
www.penguinrandomhouse.ca

1 2 3 4 5   20 19 18 17 16

Penguin
Random
House

For my part, when the hour for final rest shall strike, and when my eyes shall close forever, I shall consider that my life has not been altogether wasted, if I shall have contributed to heal one patriotic wound in the heart even of a single one of my fellow countrymen and to have thus promoted, even to the smallest extent, the cause of concord and harmony between the citizens of the Dominion.

Wilfrid Laurier, 1887
Somerset Quebec

CONTENTS

PART IV: THE OLD CHIEFTAIN, 1911–1919

SIR WILFRID LAURIER: "A RULER OF MEN"

BY ARTHUR MILNES

As Canadians enter the 175th anniversary year of the birth of their first French-Canadian prime minister, Sir Wilfrid Laurier, it is an opportune moment to re-acquaint ourselves with his public words and story.

In his famous eulogy of Sir John A. Macdonald, Laurier said the Father of Confederation's life was "the history of Canada." As Canada cemented its place in the post-Macdonald era, few would disagree that Laurier's life, too, became in so many ways "the history of Canada." That is why his public words, even today, remain so crucial to understanding our nation.

Writing during Laurier's lifetime, journalist John Willison captured these thoughts:

"There is more of the history of Canada in Sir Wilfrid Laurier's speeches than in those of any other public man of his generation, and his remarkable historical equipment lends steadiness and sobriety to his."[1]

Laurier, born on November 20, 1841, devoted almost his entire adult life to the business of politics. First elected to the House of Commons in 1874, he was still an MP when he died in 1919. By that time he had served as a cabinet minister under Alexander Mackenzie, and had risen to become leader of the Liberal Party and leader of the Opposition, prime minister from 1896 until 1911, and then leader of the Opposition once again.[2]

It was a remarkable journey, one that can be followed today in his wealth of public addresses, delivered both in the Commons and on platforms across Canada.

Alberta and Saskatchewan joined Confederation, national railways were built, and Laurier followed in Macdonald's footsteps by encouraging, more successfully, immigration to the West from Europe.

In Laurier, Canadians also had for the first time a prime minister widely celebrated on the world stage. Many of the addresses in this collection are drawn not only from Canadian newspapers, but from those in Australia, across the United States, and in Europe.[3]

Laurier's life and career is a story of confidence, national optimism and success. But it is also one of a Canadian leader continually buffeted by racial and religious intolerance from French and English, Protestant and Catholic. His career culminates in the brutal realities of the 1917 conscription campaign.

At the train station in what is now Thunder Bay, Ontario, in December 1917, Laurier receives the evening telegrams reporting on the election results. It is dark. The former prime minister of Canada has just turned seventy-six. As he walks along the station platform, a small group of friends gather around him protectively. He is defeated and will never face Canadians at the polls again. His white plume no longer led to victory.

A reporter, whose name has been lost to history, described the scene:

"The tall figure of the Liberal chieftain was surrounded by his special party as he scanned the figures that meant so much to him. He stood hatless as he absorbed the details of his defeat, and if his emotions were not well under control his closely surrounding friends sheltered any display he made from the crowd on the platform outside."[4]

One wonders what would have become of Canada had Laurier given up and returned to his native Quebec and his nationalist roots. Had that happened, I submit, there would be no Canada as we know it today: both in office as prime minister or in Opposition, he was that significant.

In his lifetime Laurier was well aware of the leading place he had already earned in Canadian history.

"In 1916 an artist painted a portrait of Laurier to hang in the Legislative halls of Quebec, where the sound of his magic voice had first been heard in parliamentary speech," it is recorded. "The artist began to paint the Laurier of 'the sunny ways.' The old man corrected him. 'No, if you please,' he said gravely, 'paint me as a ruler of men.' It was the Cardinal speaking; the man who had disciplined more Cabinet politicians than even Macdonald, the master of Cabinets; the old man who remembered the power of an earlier day."[5]

Still, that Northern Ontario train station in 1917 was a long way and years removed from the days when Laurier had electrified friend and foe alike with his brave defence of Louis Riel, had taken the Queen's Diamond Jubilee celebrations of 1897 by storm, and modernized Canadian politics by holding the first-ever post-Confederation party convention on the road to power.

In his collected speeches is found the entire story. For Canadians of today, including those who have lulled themselves into thinking that the pull of Quebec separation is gone forever, Laurier's words should be required reading. His speeches remind us that Canada requires vision, constant care, concern mixed with optimism, and more than a little luck. Laurier's life's work will therefore be important to recall as we prepare to mark our nation's 150th anniversary in 2017.

It is with this belief in Laurier's continued importance in mind that I turned to a variety of distinguished Canadians from across the political spectrum, inviting them to write a commentary essay, in their own areas of expertise, to accompany a specific Laurier address. Thus, for example, readers will find former prime minister Kim Campbell, who has spent many years living and working in the United States, commenting on Laurier's interest in Abraham Lincoln; Alberta premier Rachel Notley reflects on a speech delivered by Laurier in her province in 1910; British Columbia premier Christy Clark discusses the often difficult issues surrounding Asian immigration in her province's history; and past Ontario premier Dalton McGuinty considers the legacy of Laurier's close colleague Sir Oliver Mowat of Ontario. Another former prime minister, John N. Turner, compares the House of Commons today with that of yesteryear, while Joe Clark and Brian Mulroney comment, respectively, on Laurier's role in the creation of Alberta and on his famous tribute to Sir John A. Macdonald. Paul Martin uses a speech by Laurier delivered in his father's hometown of Pembroke, Ontario, to reflect on the roots of his own Liberalism. Finally two other former prime ministers, Jean Chrétien and Stephen J. Harper, close the book with separate essays. From the United Kingdom, former prime minister Tony Blair has also graciously contributed an essay from a nation that meant so much to Laurier.

Past prime ministerial chiefs-of-staff Thomas S. Axworthy (whose title when he served Prime Minister Pierre Trudeau was principal secretary), Derek H. Burney, Nigel S. Wright, Edward Goldenberg, and Hugh Segal have also provide commentaries. In doing so they are joined by veteran political speechwriters David Lockhart and Scott Reid, and retired Senator Lowell Murray.

Distinguished academics and legal scholars Professor Patrice Dutil of Ryerson University, David Asper of Winnipeg, Mr. Justice Thomas Cromwell of the Supreme Court of Canada, historian Dr. Christopher McCreery, and Thomas S. Harrison of Queen's University Law School have also contributed essays to this volume.

They are joined by past provincial premiers Jean Charest (with his son Antoine), Bob Rae, Alison Redford, and Roy Romanow.

Journalists like André Pratte – himself a biographer of Laurier – Lawrence Martin, Russell Mills, Steve Paikin, Jane Taber, Bruce Yaccato, Jacques Poitras, and Andrew Cohen have also penned commentaries that help bring Laurier into present-day discussions.

From the United States, David Mitchell, Michael A. Meighen, and David Jacobson of Chicago, who represented his nation in Ottawa as ambassador, has provided his own unique insight, as has Canada's high commissioner to the United Kingdom, Gordon Campbell, a past premier of British Columbia.

Each was invited to comment on a specific Laurier address in his or her area of expertise. This method was chosen because Laurier's primary instrument in shaping Canada was his oratory. And in those speeches, I believe, are found valuable lessons and insights that remain relevant to Canada and Canadians today. Readers themselves, of course, must render the final verdict.

Sources have been provided for each speech, unless delivered in the House of Commons, in which case readers are encouraged to visit the Parliament of Canada's impressive website at http://parl.canadiana.ca to further explore debates of the Laurier era.

Laurier's speeches are divided into four chronological sections: The Young Politician, which takes Laurier from his earliest days to his assumption of leadership of the Liberal Party; Party Leader, which follows him as leader of the Liberal Party until he becomes prime minister in 1896; Prime Minister, which covers his years as head of the country; and The Old Chieftain, which brings together Laurier's addresses from his defeat in 1911 to his death in 1919. This section also includes tributes to Laurier delivered after his death by other leaders. Footnotes have been kept to a minimum so as not to detract from the flow of Laurier's oratory.

From a very young age Wilfrid Laurier was celebrated for his public addresses. So a word on his method and style is in order. John

Willison, again, provides the following overview, written at the height of the Laurier era, of his subject as speech-maker:

"His speeches have much of the beauty and simplicity of Lincoln's addresses and State papers, with more of imaginative quality and oratorical intensity. He is more diffusive than Bright, but far less so than Gladstone. He lacks Gladstone's energy and is doubtless less ready to invite combat, less eager in his impulses, less restless in his environment. But once he has made his decision he is bold, resolute, wary, and sagacious in the pursuit of his end. He has an infinite patience under attack and a thorough contempt for the mere tattle of partisan controversy. He seldom corrects the smaller misrepresentations of his objects and motives, and much that is said by a hostile press he wholly sets aside as of no practical account in the serious discussion of public questions."[6]

In 1890, six years before he even entered the Prime Minister's Office in the East Block, journalist Ulric Barthe gathered and published a collection of Laurier's major addresses.[7] (Barthe's collection, in fact, is the basis for the first parts of this book and I wish to acknowledge the late journalist's contributions to both my work and to all those who have studied Laurier and who will do so in the future). He too, through his book's contributor L.-O. David,[8] described his subject as speech-maker:

"Mr. Laurier enjoys the advantage of being a born orator, but he has the merit of having cultivated this splendid natural gift, of having respected it, and of having understood that the orator must be an honest and a good man," David wrote in his essay, "The Man: Wilfrid Laurier," which opens Barthe's book. "Listen to him and it is at once seen that this language is the echo of conviction, of correctness of mind, and of a noble heart. And the impression which he created upon his auditory constitutes the greatest and best part of his force and his merit."[9]

In reading Laurier's addresses, also keep in mind that he was one of Canada's greatest politicians. As he was a ruthless partisan when necessary (like Macdonald and all successful prime ministers who followed) and a master of the political craft, some caution is advised before delving into this volume.

Historian Richard Clippingdale describes why this is necessary:

"One word of warning may be appropriate for the uninitiated in Laurier land," he wrote in his own study of Laurier in 1979. "Sir Wilfrid is awfully hard to resist once you get to know him at all. As the jaunty journalist Edward William Thomson said of him in 1911: 'He bamboozles me most sweetly, often. I know when he does it, and he knows I know. Still I am bamboozled, which is the main thing'."[10]

For the record, readers should be aware that I consider myself fully "bamboozled" by Laurier. But today it is hard not to be. For decades Canadians, like citizens of most western nations, have been told by their leaders what a government and people cannot accomplish. In contrast, a study of Laurier reminds us of a time when Canada's future was limited only by the imagination of a prime minister and the peoples he led.

Laurier, like Sir John A. Macdonald, challenged the Canadians of his day to look beyond themselves. At Toronto's Massey Hall in 1904, he gave young people advice that is relevant today:

"Remember from this day forth never to look simply at the horizon as it may be limited by the limits of the province, but look abroad all over the continent and let your motto be Canada first, Canada last, Canada always."[11]

To round off this book, I have included a selection of tributes to Laurier delivered after his death. If political leaders and partisans of any party in Canada today could read only one passage in this book, my hope is that it will be Sir Robert Borden's speech about his fallen opponent. Borden delivered his tribute on Parliament Hill on a summer day in 1927. The occasion was the unveiling of Laurier's commanding statue:

"He had a remarkably thorough grasp of constitutional practice and procedure which were always safe in his hands," Borden said. "His attitude to the party in Opposition was not only fair, but generous and considerate. His profound faith in the high destiny of Canada never faltered for a moment. The years of his Premiership were attended with many events and developments of the greatest importance, and with questions of exceptional difficulty. All these he approached with a keen sense of public trust, and when the storm of war burst upon the Empire in 1914 he gave to the Administration of the day his unstinted support in making Canada's effort worthy of the cause and our country."

Sir Robert concluded:

"To me the House of Commons was never the same after his gracious presence no longer moved among us. Without distinction of race or party his countrymen hold him in happy memory, and accord him a final fame that will overcome [and] . . . overbear reluctant time."[12]

At a time when partisans of all stripes often act as if they view political opponents as personal enemies, it would do all Canadians well if a return to the days of mutual respect between politicians, as embodied in Sir Robert Borden and Sir Wilfrid Laurier, and by Laurier and Macdonald before that, were on our nation's agenda.

We ignore their examples at our peril.

Finally, and with the greatest respect and admiration, this book is dedicated to my friend Jimmy Carter of Plains, Georgia. President Carter, like Laurier before him, has spent his life building bridges between peoples and always appealing to our better angels along the way.

Arthur Milnes
Kingston and Scarborough, January 2016

ACKNOWLEDGEMENTS

I have incurred many debts these last number of years while exploring the life and public words of Sir Wilfrid Laurier. Firstly, I wish to extend my profound gratitude to Canada's seven living past prime ministers for each sharing with me many hours of discussion about Laurier, Sir John A. Macdonald, and other facets of Canadian history. While I owe all of them, I want to recognize in particular the Rt Hon. Stephen J. Harper. For much of the period during which I was working on this volume, he was Canada's sitting prime minister. Despite his onerous duties, he gave me the one thing a prime minister has little of – personal time – to discuss Laurier (and Macdonald) with me.

While I owe an additional debt to all those who submitted essays to this volume, Thomas Axworthy, Bob Rae, Thomas Harrison, and Patrice Dutil have spent many, many hours with me over many years and passed onto me their own infectious enthusiasm for Laurier and Canadian history. I also owe much to fellow political speechwriters like Scott Anderson, Rebecca Staley, Scott Reid, and David Lockhart for all they have done to improve our craft and, along the way, encourage my interests in Canadian history. They are joined by my other friends and mentors Jeremy Hunt, Kathy Brock, Peter O'Malley, Kate Malloy, Ben Harper, Claude Scilley, Steve Serviss, Jan Murphy, Robert P. Tchegus and Dr. Deborah Berry, Clyde Smith, Gavin Cosgrove, Myles Atwood, the Ransom family, George F. Henderson, Mike Fraser, Jonathan Rose, Derek and Joan Burney, Jimmy and Rosalynn Carter, Brian and Mila Mulroney, Paul E. Martin, Joe and Catherine Clark, John N. Turner and family, Kim Campbell, Steve Paikin, Cynthia Beach, Bryan Paterson, Anthony Wilson-Smith, Brad Duguid, Lawrence Martin, Andrew Cohen, Sandy Berg, Kerry Sammon, Christina Spencer, Mel Wiebe, Julie Burch, and so many others.

John Honderich of the *Toronto Star*, joined by Marilyn Hertz of the *Globe and Mail*, helped me greatly with arranging permissions from their newspapers. At the Tony Blair Faith Foundation, Anthony Measures facilitated the essay contributed by the Rt Hon. Tony Blair, while Alberta MLA Craig Coolahan (from my hometown of Scarborough, Ontario) and Carissa Halton assisted in arranging for Alberta premier Rachel Notley's essay. Mrs. Therese Horvath, William Pristanski, Bruce Hartley, Michele Cadario, Maclean Kay, Sheila Graves, Tracey Sobers, and Steve Dyck helped me with other contributions. Ann Prince Stevens assisted greatly with inputting and early edits, and Michel W. Pharand performed incredible service as copy editor and as advisor on all matters technical.

My thanks to Kimberlee Hesas, Joe Lee, Aoife Walsh, and everyone at McClelland & Stewart, and in particular to Doug Pepper, who has been in my corner for many years.

Finally, I owe my wife, Alison, the greatest debt of all, as she too has spent countless hours with me and Sir Wilfrid.

Arthur Milnes

PART I:

THE YOUNG POLITICIAN

1864–1884

Laurier's oratorical story begins on a stage at Montreal's McGill University in 1864. He is a young man, only twenty-two. This section ends with him speaking to an audience at the offices of the newspaper *La Patrie*, again in Montreal. By this point he is forty-two. The name of Laurier is now well known across the entire country.

In the first speech presented here, he is speaking at the convocation ceremonies upon his graduation from the McGill law school. At this English institution, the young Laurier chooses to deliver his remarks in French. This is noticed. "A valedictory address was read in French by one of the members of the graduating class," reports the Montreal *Gazette*.[13]

Historian Joseph Schull later described the young man who turned heads at McGill and in Montreal that day.

"He was just over six feet tall and he looked almost bulky in a long, square-cut coat that hung to his knee-joints, and trousers of some wrinkled homespun stuff that had never known an iron. The effect was an illusion created by a country tailor. The body tapering up to the wide shoulders was in reality frail, with a grace that would be set off by elegance in dress long before he was able to afford it. One of the sharpest pangs of three hard student years in Montreal had been the lack of suitable clothes for many functions he would have liked to attend. The head was striking, with the broad front swept by a mass of chestnut hair, thick and inclined to curl. The nose was aquiline and strong. . . . About the eyes, concentrated though they were at the moment on the effort to deliver carefully prepared phrases, there was a hint of something melancholy and detached. They were the eyes of an observer as well as an actor."[14]

Seven years later we follow along as Laurier, a new member of the Quebec Assembly, rises to make his maiden address. His speech is eagerly anticipated by party elders on both sides of the Quebec House. They are not disappointed. "[His] first appearance . . . caused a sensation," wrote the poet Louis Fréchette. "Who was this junior member . . . who spoke on . . . major political issues with such freedom and authority?"[15]

Then the damn bursts. We next see Laurier in the spring of 1874. He is now a Liberal member of the House of Commons. Tensions are running high in political Ottawa as Laurier rises in the chamber. Métis leader Louis Riel, fresh from the events of 1870–71 in Manitoba, has been elected to the House. A future prime minister, Mackenzie Bowell, now on the Opposition benches like his leader Sir John A. Macdonald, has proposed that Riel be expelled from the Commons before he takes his seat. In a move that makes history – and inflames his critics – Riel has shown himself to the clerk of the Commons and asked to be sworn in.

Laurier bucks English-Canadian public opinion and argues against Riel's expulsion. Even his critics take note. It is soon apparent that while one might agree or disagree with the youthful MP, one could only admire his oratorical skill and political bravery. This Laurier could not so soon be ignored.

Laurier cements this reputation three years later. We now find him at the Academy of Music in Quebec City, speaking before the Club Canadien. He again bucks the winds of elite opinion and stakes out his ground, defining his liberalism in a Quebec dominated by the Roman Catholic Church. He dares oppose the views of the elites. This address is destined to follow Laurier through history.

We also, in 1881, meet the party man. Laurier introduces and praises his leader, Edward Blake, before a meeting of Quebec Liberal youth in Montreal. Back in Ottawa, Laurier has been acting as Blake's personal secretary in the Commons. This night in Montreal,

Quebec's most important Liberals assemble and hear from both men. The past, present, and perhaps the future. It is Laurier's job to reply to the meeting's toast to the House of Commons.

This section closes, again in Montreal, with Laurier delivering a non-partisan lecture about parliamentary life. He describes the social and political atmosphere on the Hill with a skill befitting a former journalist (which he was), drawing verbal sketches for his audience of the performances he witnesses daily back in Ottawa. By now he has spent ten years as MP. Known far and wide as "silver-tongued Laurier," he will soon be his party's leader.

Questions, often whispered, still remain. He's considered too bookish, sickly, even a bit lazy. A great speaker, yes, but could he really lead a national political party? Would Wilfrid Laurier really be up to the job?

VALEDICTORY ADDRESS

McGILL UNIVERSITY, MONTREAL, QUEBEC

MAY 4, 1864[16]

To the Students of McGill University, Faculty of Law.

Gentlemen: Of all the missions entrusted to man living in society, I know none greater than that of the man of law. The mission of the man of law is found in this one thought: to make justice prevail. Nothing on earth is as precious as justice, and nothing perhaps is as difficult to obtain. Such is the unthinkable blend of good and evil comprising man's nature that the true and the false are found in all his works. As this state of affairs is evidenced by everyday experience, one can appreciate that to dispense justice to its members is for society at once an arduous task and a terrible responsibility. Moreover, as soon as civilization began to spread, the administration of justice, until then held fast in the arbitrary hands of power, was entrusted to a class of men specifically devoted to that purpose.

Knowing how to distinguish the true from the false; knowing, amidst the most intricate complexities, how to differentiate between right and wrong; knowing how to preserve and share the rights of citizens; knowing how to keep the general peace; knowing how to safeguard for families their forefathers' legacy, to maintain the individual's honour when assailed, to justly suppress offenses for public morals; knowing how to stem the temerity of the powerful and relieve the misery of the weak without violence to the one, without impunity to the other, and finally to render to each according to his deeds:[17] that is the mission conferred upon the man of law.

And I am aware of nothing greater; I admire the man who, on a battlefield, knows how to die and save his homeland; I admire the man who knows how to bind entire generations to the creations of his genius; I admire the man who devotes a lifetime to relieving humanity; but I admire even more the one who has chosen as the purpose of his life, his studies, and his labours, to render to each according to his deeds.

All glories and all merits pale before these simple and great thoughts: to render to each according to his deeds, to make justice prevail. And yet from those who devote themselves to administering justice, society demands hard and heavy labour.

Aside from arduous preliminary studies, the man of law must possess a profound knowledge not only of the laws of his country, but also of those that have been the most authoritative and influential; he must possess not only these unwavering principles of eternal truth, but know how to trace the transformations and changes of the centuries and the needs of his own era; finally, he must possess a depth of knowledge that would enable him, in all human endeavours, to distinguish evil from good and to render to each according to his deeds.

That is what society expects and demands of the man of law. Yet I will admit that this is not how the profession is seen. Still, the actual state of the profession does not destroy the truth of what I have said, and we would all benefit, I believe, from seeing these ideas increasingly disseminated.

The more these ideas are developed, the more the mission of the man of law will be magnified and dreaded: one will see in it something other than a mere livelihood; something more than an art, more than a science; one will see in it a great duty to accomplish; fewer will be its devotees and more zealous, more active, and more earnest in our work will we be, we who will embrace this career.

Aside from this general mission to dispense justice, the man of law, in a free country, sees another mission open to him. It is a remarkable and proven fact that in a free country, the first place belongs to the men of law.

Thus in England we have seen the Eldons, the Erskines, and many others, after starting at the bottom of the social ladder, by means of the study of law take their place among the highest political luminaries of their day.[18]

Thus it is that nowadays, one has seen the illustrious Lord Brougham, to whom England owes so many helpful and judicious reforms, begin at the bar a career that closed on the benches of the House of Lords.[19]

Thus it is again that only yesterday, when a modicum of freedom was granted to France, we saw the outcome of country's fate debated and determined by the Jules Favres, the Olliviers, the Billaults, the Rouhers – all of them men of law.[20]

Ah! But we need not seek out foreign examples: history will show that in our country, the most illustrious men were men of law. Nothing could be more natural: things could not be otherwise under the rule of freedom.

Freedom is not the power to say and do everything: freedom is the right to act and to move about agreeably and without hindrance within the circle of the constitution drawn by the people, without that circle being expanded or contracted at the whim of a despotic hand. Thus freedom assumes law, and that is the lawyer's domain.

The prerogatives and the duties of the people and of the executive branch must be maintained within the limits of the constitution, and the man of law, by his very studies, is in the best position to meet the requirements of this situation, whether he acts at the executive level and claims the rights of authority, or whether his voice emerges from among the people, to maintain its prerogatives or restrain the encroachment of power.

While in the political arena, the man of law does not change missions; there too, he will have to render to each according to his deeds, to make justice prevail; he merely extends his sphere of action: henceforth he will address the court of public opinion; his theme will be the rights or the duties of an entire nation, and his audience will comprise all the echoes of publicity.

If I speak this way, it is not because I wish to arouse anyone's ambition; no, but there are lessons that one must never lose sight of. In the words of an eminent jurist, we live in an age when each must contribute to the social fabric. This truth, everywhere enacted, will produce no more considerable results than in this country.

Indeed, in the nineteenth century, when most societies are already well advanced in age, this country has existed for barely a few centuries. While today in the ancient world one can only work to make reforms, on this new continent everything is still new, everything is yet to be shaped.

In taking advantage of the experience of other parts of the world, this country can thus avoid groping about as did modern societies when they were formed. To the vivid might of youth, it can join the light of centuries.

However, as I have tried to show earlier, if one loves his country and sincerely wishes to help it, the most effective way he will do so is by the study of law.

Moreover, in this country the law plays another role, a tremendous role found nowhere else. Today, two races share Canadian soil. As that day has vanished, I can say it here: the French and English races have not always been friends; but I hasten to say, and I do so to our glory, racial struggles on our Canadian soil have ended; there is no other family here but the human family, no matter what language we speak, or at which altars we kneel.

Each day we find the happy effects of this sacred work, – and in this solemnity we have yet another proof; you have heard here French and English names listed on the honour roll, you have heard someone speak to you in English, and I who now speak to you do so in my mother tongue, I speak to you in French. There is in this fraternity a glory of which Canada cannot be too proud, for many a powerful nation could find here a lesson in justice and humanity.

Gentlemen, to what do we owe this happy state of affairs? There may be more than one cause, but the primary one is the study of law. Two different laws govern this country: French law and English law. Each of these affects not only its particular race, but each governs both races simultaneously – and it is worth noting that this introduction in the same country of two entirely different legal systems was accomplished without violence, without appropriation, but only by the effect of the laws of justice.

Indeed, it was natural that, in passing under British rule, the inhabitants of this county should have continued to be governed by their ancient laws, amidst all the disputes that stem from life's common transactions; but it was equally fair that the new Government should have suppressed, according to its own laws, offences against public order. These two different laws, applying as they do to two different races and both to each race in particular, affected the first *rapprochement*. If we imagine on this soil two nationalities each subject to its own laws, there would have been no cordiality or union. Why? Because we would have carefully avoided transactions that could have resulted in having citizens judged by laws other than their own.

The study of laws has maintained that *rapprochement*; we have come to know the lawyers of France and England, our motherlands; we meld the genius of these great nations; we take reason and wisdom wherever they are found, no matter the language in which they are expressed.

As a result, and as proof of what I advance, here is a fact that each of you can verify: union among races is found to no greater extent in any class of Canadian society than among men of law.

Gentlemen, such is the career open in this country to men of law; I affirm that in no other place has man ever had before him a career as expansive and as productive.

In short, the mission of the man of law in Canada encompasses the following: justice as the most noble of all human perfections; patriotism as the most noble of all social virtues; union among peoples, the secret of the future. Now, gentlemen, we see the goal; it is up to us to ensure that our efforts are worthy of it.

To our professors, to those who initiated us into the first secrets of the science of law, to those who generously opened for us the treasures they had acquired by arduous study, we now say adieu and thank you. Thanks to them, we have avoided long and painful research; their hand has traced the route through the complex maze of our laws. The most noble acknowledgement we can offer them is to carry out the precepts they have given us. To our fellow students we say goodbye; we will see each other again in the professional arena.

Having arrived at the uttermost limits of our life as students, contemplating the path now open before us, a path filled with uncertainties, where we can count only on our own strength, where there will no longer be hands ready to extract thorns and make our work easier, and thinking back upon these days, of which this is the last one, on these days where studying was easy, guided as it was by knowledgeable hands, recreated by everyday friends – this comparison alone, failing other reasons, would be enough to make us count these student days among the most beautiful of our life. Whatever fate the future has in store for us, we will always find it

sweet to recall the time of our youth and its teachers and companions, and henceforth we may now say, like Aeneas to his companions, "Forsan et haec olim meminisse jubavit."[21]

By the Honourable Thomas Cromwell

*Laurier's first major speech, his 1864 valedictory address at the McGill law
school, initially repels, then attracts, and ultimately persuades. It exemplifies
"that combination of naïveté and idealism that would always be his"[22] and
remarkably sets out a political vision deeply rooted in the ideals of justice
and tolerance.*

*As the speech opens, one sees little to admire. The young lawyer serves
up a time-bound understanding of the pre-eminent place of the legal profession in the social order, an unpalatable concoction made with equal measures
of professional arrogance and entitlement. The idea that to the "man of law"
belongs the "first place" in a free country is discordant with contemporary
understandings of the role of lawyers — let alone of women — in society. This
paean of praise for patriarchy and professional entitlement is long past its best
before date. We know that men and lawyers do not always know best and
we are repelled by the reminder that it was once thought to be otherwise.*

*Laurier then changes the focus from the legal profession's prerogatives to
its responsibilities. He concedes that his idealistic vision does not reflect contemporary reality but rather describes a goal towards which the profession
should strive: "this is not how the profession is seen . . . [and the] more these
ideas are developed . . . one will see in it a great duty to accomplish." Who
can quarrel with the vision of lawyers as persons called to the "hard and
heavy labour" of making "justice prevail"? And who cannot be encouraged
by the thought that the study of law will nurture the conviction that "there
is no other family here but the human family, no matter what language we
speak or at which altars we kneel"? What we may have condemned too
quickly as professional chauvinism emerges as a plea for enhanced professional contribution to national harmony. As the focus shifts, repulsion gives
way to attraction.*

Then comes the convincing core of Laurier's message. Justice is the "most noble of human perfections." Patriotism for the new country, "yet to be shaped," is "the most noble of all social virtues." And the "union among peoples [is] the secret of the future." Here is the foundation of Laurier's political beliefs. He hoped that Canadian patriotism, mutual respect, compromise and adherence to the deep principle of justice would overcome linguistic, religious and regional divisions.[23] As he would say forty years later, his object was "to bring our people long estranged from each other, gradually to become a nation." This, for him, was "the supreme issue" to which everything else was subordinate."[24] We see in this early speech how Laurier enlisted the professional ideal of justice – of giving to each according to his due – into the service of his larger, persuasive vision for Canada.

Our national life together is, we hope, a never-ending work in progress. And so we will never be able to say, once and for all, that Laurier's vision was right. But we do know that it has not yet been proven to be wrong.

The Honourable Thomas Cromwell served as justice of the Supreme Court of Canada from 2008 until his retirement in 2016.

PARLIAMENTARY DEBUT

The Honourable Members, who have proposed the address, have drawn a most attractive picture of the situation of the country. They have vied with each other in efforts to dazzle us with what they have been pleased to pompously term our wealth, prosperity and happiness. If they are to be believed, Canada is a real land of Cocayne,[26] where everything is lovely and there is nothing left for us to do but to return thanks to Providence and to the Ministry.

But does this picture really portray the truth? I, for one, cannot accept it in that light. All who have studied the situation of the country otherwise than on paper and in the seclusion of their own homes, who have had the opportunity of a nearer view of our backward system of agriculture, our timid and vacillating trade and our blighted industry, know full well that the brilliant image evoked by the hon. Members, who proposed the address, is not the reality, but a deceptive mirage.

If the purely political and social aspect of the situation were the only question, I would accept without reserve all that has been said by the Honourable Members. Undoubtedly, our situation, viewed from the merely political and social standpoint, is excellent, thanks to the fundamental principle of our constitution the principle of free and representative government. It is due to this principle that the diverse elements, which compose our population, have been enabled to unite and form a compact and homogeneous whole, yet leaving to each its character and its autonomy. Certainly, the fact is one of which we can be justly proud, that so many different races and so many opposite creeds should find themselves concentrated on this little corner of earth and that our constitution should prove broad enough to leave them all plenty of elbow room, without friction or danger of collision and with the fullest latitude to each to speak its own tongue, practise its own religion, retain its own customs and enjoy its equal share of liberty and of the light of the sun. I myself have the honour to represent a county in which are grouped all shades of race and creed and am happy to be able to bear testimony publicly to this state of things.

But there is another side to the situation; there is the economic side and I do not hesitate to say that it seems to me dark, very dark, indeed.

We have been told that we are rich and prosperous. But is this the case? Question all classes of society, the merchant, the banker, the shop-keeper, the member of the liberal professions, the farmer, the simple mechanic, and among all, without exception, you will find the same story of hard times, of uneasiness, of suffering and languor, denoting that there is something wrong somewhere.

It might be almost said that this country is placed under an immense pneumatic machine and that it is writhing and struggling in vain to get to its lungs a few particles of an air which is becoming more and more rarefied. This is the truth! This is the true situation! He is blind who does not see it, and he is guilty, who, in seeing, does not admit it.

Still, it is being constantly dinned into our ears that we have mines, timber, resources of all kinds that we are rich, in fact. Sir, there are riches and riches.

Tantalus[27] was rich. He had always an abundantly, a sumptuously served table spread before him; but the trouble was that, in sight of all this abundance, he was eternally starving.

Our position very much resembles that of Tantalus. An infernal hand seems to be always withdrawing our riches whenever we strive to grasp them. The man, who found a bag of gold dust in the desert, considered himself rich. But shortly afterwards, when he was dying of hunger over his treasure, he no doubt exclaimed in bitterness of spirit that a simple piece of bread would have been preferable, as it would have saved him.

We also are expiring over our treasures and year after year the flood of those who are leaving our riches and going to the United States to seek the morsel of bread that will save them goes on steadily increasing.

Once more, I say, this is the real situation. God forbid that I should hold the Ministry alone responsible for it! Its causes are multiple and all of them are not under its control. But what I blame the Ministry for is not seeing the situation or, if they see it, for not having the courage to face it.

I was disappointed yesterday on hearing the Speech from the Throne. His Excellency[28] had done us the honour to summon us for the despatch of business; we come, we listen with respectful attention, and we find that the only business which His Excellency invites us to despatch is what, to congratulate the Government on the happy labours of the last Parliament; and that's all. Not one measure proposed; not one reform suggested.

Yes, I repeat, I was grievously disappointed: I had expected that the Ministry had studied the situation and that it would indicate both the source of the ill and the remedy.

The principal source of the evil from which we suffer is that thus far the production of this country is not equal to the consumption. The Ministry might all the more easily have admitted this, seeing that it does not alone bear the responsibility which weighs upon the entire nation. It is a humiliating confession to make that, after three centuries of existence, this country is still unable to supply its own wants and that it is still obliged to have recourse to foreign markets, though nature has lavished upon it all the gifts necessary to render it a manufacturing country.

It is now, Sir, a good many years since the great Patriot, whom we recently lost, Honourable L.J. Papineau,[29] casting about for a remedy for the ills of the time, summed up his policy on the subject in this simple precept: "We should buy nothing from the metropolis." My opinion is that this policy is even more urgent today than it was when first formulated.

It is a duty, especially for us Canadians of French origin, to create a national industry. We are surrounded by a strong and vigorous race who are endowed with a devouring activity and have taken possession of the entire universe as their field of labour.

As a French Canadian, Sir, I am pained to see my people eternally excelled by our fellow countrymen of British origin. We must frankly acknowledge that down to the present we have been left behind in the race. We can admit this and admit it without shame, because the fact is explained by purely political reasons which denote no inferiority on our part.

After the conquest, the Canadians, desirous of maintaining their national inheritance intact, fell back upon themselves, and kept up no relations with the outside world. The immediate result of this policy was to keep them strangers to the reforms which were constantly taking place beyond their boundaries and to fatally shut them up within the narrow circle of their own old theories. On the other hand, the new blood, which was poured into the colony, came from the most advanced country under the sun in point of trade and industry. They brought with them the civilization of their native land and their strength was ceaselessly renewed by a constant current of immigration, which added not only to their numbers, but to their stock of information and their ideas.

We need therefore have no shame in admitting that we were beaten by such men and under such circumstances. But the times have changed and the hour has struck to enter the lists with them. Our respective forefathers were enemies and waged bloody war against each other for centuries. But we, their descendants, united under the same flag, fight no other fights but those of a generous emulation to excel each other in trade and industry, in the sciences and the arts of peace.

I have already stated that the Government of the Province of Quebec is not alone responsible for the stagnation of our industry. It is sufficient to say that alone it can neither create nor develop it, but it can contribute powerfully thereto by the kind of immigration which it introduces into the country. Thus far it seems to me that the Government has been moving in the wrong direction. The Government has devoted itself to recruiting an exclusively agricultural immigration and its efforts will end in nothing. The agricultural population of this country will never be increased from outside. Our climate is too severe and the development of our lands too costly and difficult.

The children of the soil will not be deterred by these obstacles; but the stranger will simply pass through our territory and locate on the rich prairies of the west. Moreover, wherever our agents set their foot, they find themselves forestalled by American agents, by American books and pamphlets, and, above all, by American prestige.

We can, however, introduce here with good results, I think, an industrial immigration. I do not mean simple workmen, but master mechanics and small capitalists such as are to be found in all the cities of Europe. The inducement, which would lead them to invest their labour and their capital in our midst is that we can produce twenty-five per cent cheaper than any other part of the American continent what we need is the master-miners of Wales and the north of England, the mechanics of Alsace, the Flemish weavers and the German artisans of all kinds. Such an immigration, it seems to me, would give an extraordinary impulse to our industry.

In addition to this purely economic question, there are political reforms which we hoped to have seen announced in the Speech from the Throne. Among these reforms, there are two, which have been urgently demanded by public opinion for a long time past, in our election law and in education.

Our election law is deplorably behind that of the other provinces and even of the Dominion. Public opinion has long demanded a law modelled on that of Ontario, where the elections are all held on the same day. Our law has opened the door to lamentable abuses and to the direct intervention of the Government in the exercise of the popular suffrage. At the last elections, the Government was thus enabled to first issue the writs for such of the counties as it considered safe, and afterwards, thanks to this tactic, to bring all its strength to the assistance of its friends whom it deemed in danger. Such conduct is an abuse. If we are a free people, the popular suffrage must be freely exercised and the exact expression of the popular will must be secured.

I shall only refer incidentally to the question of education upon which we have been long and are still waiting for the Premier's action. When the Honourable Premier[30] assumed the reins of power in 1867, he had been for twelve years Superintendent of Education and had just returned from a trip to Europe undertaken for the express purpose of studying on the spot the different educational systems of the Old World. It was our hope that, on his return, he would have embodied in legislation the results of his observations and experience. But for the last four years, like Sister Anne on the tower top,[31] we've have been looking for something to come, but it has not yet appeared.

I have heard it said elsewhere: "But what is the good of these reforms? Will they increase the public wealth? Will they enhance in the slightest degree the prosperity of the country?" Sir, in a free state, everything is connected and linked together legislation, trade, industry, art, sciences and letters, all are members of a same body, the body social.

When one of the Members suffers, the entire body is affected; when there is an abuse anywhere, the entire body social is more or less paralyzed; when there is anywhere something left undone which should be done, the normal order is thereby disturbed.

England has become great because she has thoroughly understood this principle. No question there has ever been allowed to languish. No sooner has an abuse been noted and a reform demanded, than the Government of the day, whatever it might be, Whig or Tory, has at once given the subject attention and taken the initiative, never dropping it until the abuse has been destroyed and the reform accomplished.

We, on the contrary, only know how to pander to our own prejudices and our self-love; we never have the courage to admit that we are not perfect or that there is anything we should do.

I grant, Sir, that, underlying this conduct, there may be a thought or rather an excess of patriotic affection. But this is far from being a proper patriotism and it is certainly not mine. My patriotism consists rather in telling my country hard truths, which will help to arouse it from its lethargy and to direct it at last into the path of true progress and true prosperity.

By Antoine Dionne Charest and the Honourable Jean Charest

Laurier's reply to the Speech from the Throne in the Parliament of Quebec, in 1871, reminds us of a situation best described by the Greek word "triptych" with his description of the three most crucial aspects of Canadian society. The first two, our political and social institutions, do not pose many problems for the young Quebec parliamentarian that was Laurier. For him, his age's political institutions, like the constitution and representative government, had already allowed Canadians and Quebecers to unite under one flag. These principles were – and remain today – the bedrock of our democracy. They have preserved both the character and autonomy of Canada's communities, regions, and national minorities.

It is rather the third facet, the economy, which poses problems. Canada, according to Laurier in his maiden address of 1871, was a wealthy country. But it was still one incapable of providing for itself. Despite an abundance of natural resources, Canada remained, precariously in Laurier's view, dependent upon foreign markets.

It appears that Laurier's concerns are still relevant today. First, all three facets remain, even today, closely intertwined. When Laurier says that "in a free state, everything is connected and linked together," this means that when one facet is weaker all parts are affected. If Quebec's economy is underdeveloped, as Laurier believed it was during that period, then her political and social institutions will also be affected: the government, for example, may not be able to offer certain public goods, such as social benefits, health care, etc.

Conversely, if Quebec's social and political institutions are weak, this may threaten the viability of the French language. But in both areas these points are secondary. Neither will improve without the existence of strong economies for Quebec and Canada. This argument remains true today. We have made formidable progress since Laurier's time. We have signed free trade agreements, notably NAFTA, CETA, and the TPP. Interestingly, Quebec has always supported and defended these agreements when other provinces did not. That being said, Canada's and Quebec's economies continue to lag behind others in crucial areas such as innovation and productivity. So if there were only one thing to remember from Laurier's reply, it would be the following: there is no triptych without a strong domestic economy. Otherwise put: the economic challenges Canada and Quebec faced during Laurier's time remain our challenges today.

Antoine Dionne Charest is a Ph.D. student in philosophy at the Université de Montréal and works in the office of the Minister of Labour and Employment of Quebec. His father, the Honourable Jean Charest, was Quebec's twenty-ninth premier.

PLEA AGAINST LOUIS RIEL'S EXPULSION FROM THE COMMONS

HOUSE OF COMMONS, OTTAWA, ONTARIO
APRIL 15, 1874[32]

Mr. Speaker: Although this debate has been prolonged beyond the limits of human patience, I shall nevertheless take the liberty of putting the indulgence of the House to the test. At first, it was not my intention to take part in this discussion, but it has taken such an unexpected turn that it seems to me that I would not properly do my duty towards myself and towards my constituents if I contented myself with giving a silent vote.

I have listened, Sir, with the greatest attention to all the arguments which have been advanced in support of the main motion, and, although some of these arguments have been urged by men whose opinion I greatly respect, I must frankly admit that I have found it impossible to be convinced by them; I have not been convinced that, at the point reached by the proceedings taken against the Member for Provencher [Louis Riel] and with all that has been proved thus far against him, we would be justified or have the right to expel him.[33]

The conclusion to which, in my opinion, the House should come is that there have been too many facts raked out of oblivion and laid to the charge of the Member for Provencher to permit of his being absolved; it is not the less true that too many other facts have been overlooked to warrant his expulsion. . . .

But, before going further, I must apologize to the House for using a language with which I am only imperfectly acquainted; really, I should claim a complete amnesty, because I know only too surely that, in the course of the few remarks I wish to make, I shall frequently murder the Queen's English. I am perfectly conscious of the disagreeable task which I impose on the House when I force it to listen to a man so unfamiliar with the language he uses, but I can assure you that if it is a task for the House, it is much more disagreeable for myself.

I am so convinced, so thoroughly convinced, that the adoption of the Honourable Member for Chateauguay's[34] amendment is the only course that the House should pursue that I consider that I would be guilty of an act of cowardice if, for any motive whatever, I allowed myself to be turned away from the defence of the opinions which I regard as the soundest and safest on this subject.

As I have already stated, I would not have had the presumption to take part in this debate, but I think that I am warranted in intervening, because it seems that the true question before the House has not been treated. Many secondary considerations have been raised, but the real question has not been touched.

The question has been treated as if the facts on which the main motion is based had been proven and proven beyond all doubt. Now, I maintain that the facts alleged in the motion have not been established in a way to warrant this House in voting the expulsion.

I desire to state at once that I have no side taken on the question now before us against the Member for Provencher, I have not the slightest prevention and, on the other hand, I have no predisposition whatever in his favour. I have never spoken to him; I have never seen him; I have never had any relations with him either directly or indirectly. He belongs to no political party and between him and me there is no bond of sympathy; I am as impartial as if I was in the jury box. And we should all act as if we were jurors, because the functions we exercise at this moment are judicial functions. It is quite true that the object in view is to protect the honour and purity of this House; but it is equally true that the effect might be to deprive one of our fellow citizens of what rightfully belongs to him, to strip the Member for Provencher of his title and privileges as a Member of this House, and to rob the county of Provencher of the services of the man whom it has chosen as its representative.

I maintain that we are exercising judicial functions and, without going farther, I base this opinion on the words uttered by Lord Granville in the English House of Commons in 1807.[35] A similar case to this one was in question, and the opinion referred to was later on quoted approvingly by the Attorney General for Ireland in the celebrated Sadleir affair already so many times cited in the course of this debate.[36] Here is what he said:

"We are now acting in our judicial capacity and we are consequently obliged to base the judgment we are about to render not on our desires or prepossessions, but on specific facts alleged and proved according to the ordinary rules of our procedure."

This opinion of Lord Granville's, corroborated and approved as it was by the Attorney General for Ireland in the Sadleir affair, gives us the true basis on which we should regulate our decisions and confirms in a conclusive manner my contention that we are exercising judicial functions and that we should follow the rules of judicial proof. This point being established beyond all doubt, let us examine the facts that have been alleged and those that have been proven:

The Honourable Member for North Hastings[37] has based his motion on three facts. He asserts:

1) That Louis Riel, Member for Provencher, was indicted before the Court of Queen's Bench for Manitoba, in the month of

November last, for the murder of Thomas Scott[38] and that a bill was returned against him;

2) That thereupon a warrant was issued for his arrest, but that, since that time, he has systematically eluded justice and that he is consequently contumacious;

3) That he disobeyed the order of this House, commanding him to appear in his seat on the day fixed.

I contest the Honourable Member for North Hastings's first assertion and I maintain that there is not a shadow of proof that an indictment was laid against the Member for Provencher and that a true bill was returned against him; I mean to say that there does not exist the slightest judicial proof which would justify this House in taking action. There was only one way to prove this precise fact: it was by producing the indictment, but nothing of the sort has been done.

Singular to say, too, in the evidence given by the Attorney General of Manitoba, there is not one word to prove that an indictment was returned against the Member for Provencher. I will take the liberty of referring the House to the evidence of the Attorney General, at page 16 of the Votes and Proceedings:

QUESTION: Did an indictment of Louis Riel take place before the Court of Queen's Bench, in Manitoba?

ANSWER: At the extra term of the Court of Queen's Bench for Manitoba, in November last, Louis Riel was indicted.

And that's all. There is not a word to indicate that a true bill was returned. If I make this remark, it is not because I attach any great importance to this omission, for, from my point of view, the indictment could not be proven except by the production of the document itself or of a certified copy of it.

I have made this remark for the sole purpose of showing how weak is the proof, even from the most favourable point of view as regards the motion. But it will be said, perhaps, that we have ample proof that a true bill was returned, in the warrant which was issued against Mr. Riel and which has been produced. This argument cannot be accepted.

I will remind the House once more that we are exercising judicial functions and that we should be guided entirely by the rules of judicial proof. Is the rule admitted by Lord Granville when the question was to deprive a man of his property not just enough that we should obscure it in the present case?

Wherefore I again insist on the necessity, the absolute necessity, of deciding this question according to the rules of judicial proof and not otherwise.

The first of these rules is that, when the best proof can be furnished, secondary evidence is never admitted. Now, I note that this principle, which I have just laid down, has been admitted and recognized by the Honourable Member for North Hastings himself. In fact why did he bring the Attorney General of Manitoba to the bar of the House?

Simply, to get official judicial proof regarding the charges which he has made against the Member for Provencher. It was not to bring any new facts to the knowledge of the Members of this House. We are acquainted with all the unfortunate events that have occurred in Manitoba before and since the entry of that province into the Confederation.

Every one of us knows these facts as well as the Attorney General of Manitoba himself and when he appeared at the bar, not a single Member learned a fact that he had not previously known.

Why then did the Honourable Member for North Hastings bring here the Attorney General of Manitoba and get him to repeat what we already knew as well as the witness?

It was because he admitted and recognized the principle which I am defending at this moment. It was because he recognized the fact that the complete knowledge which each of us possessed was not sufficient to permit the House of Commons to act; because he recognized that we are exercising judicial functions and that it was essential for him to establish judicially and by the best evidence the charges he has made against the Member for Provencher.

Since he admits this principle, he should be consistent and furnish literal proof of his charges; but in this he has completely failed. He was bound to produce an indictment, but he has failed in this duty and I can safely conclude that there is no proof that the Member for Provencher was indicted and that a true bill was found against him.

It will be argued, perhaps, that the reasons which I advance are pure legal subtleties. Name them as you please, technical expressions, legal subtleties, it matters little; for my part, I say that these technical reasons, these legal subtleties, are the guarantees of British liberty.

Thanks to these technical expressions, these legal subtleties, no person on British soil can be arbitrarily deprived of what belongs to him. There was a time when the procedure was much simpler than it is today, when the will alone of one man was sufficient to deprive another man of his liberty, his property, his honour and all that makes life dear.

But, since the days of the Great Charter [Magna Carta] never has it been possible on British soil to rob a man of his liberty, his property or his honour except under the safeguard of what has been termed in this debate technical expressions and legal subtleties.

It will be further objected, perhaps, that the admission of this principle will have the effect of preventing this House from reaching a man accused of an abominable crime. This objection simply evades the question, for the point which remains to be decided is whether it is true that such a charge exists against the Member for Provencher. I maintain that, as long as we have not before us the literal proof, we have no proof.

It is perfectly true that in matters of this kind, we exercise a sovereign authority. No power can alter what we shall do, no matter how unjust or arbitrary it may be. We can, if we like, take no account of the precedents cited for our guidance, pay no attention to the sacred laws established for the protection of the citizen, act upon incomplete evidence or upon none at all, but will we do so?

We undoubtedly have the power, but have we the right to arbitrarily set aside the rules which constitute the security of society and of the citizen? If the House forgets this today, it may perhaps, obtain a temporary satisfaction, but it will create a precedent which will be a perpetual danger for our constitution and which in the future will serve as a pretext for more crying acts of injustice.

I submit to the consideration of the House that he who has to apply the law should not try to show himself wiser than the law. I submit that there is no practice more dangerous than to try to violate the law to obtain any result, no matter how desirable it may be.

I will be further told, perhaps, that these are lawyers' objections. This remark may have some force, but what is still more forcible is that these objections command the respect of every man who respects the laws of his country.

I repeat that these objections are not mere subtleties. While we have not the indictment here before us, we have only an incomplete proof, a part of the proof.

If we had had the indictment, we might have questioned the Attorney General and then we would have succeeded in bringing out an important fact, namely, that that indictment was obtained by a conspiracy between the Attorney General and a packed jury. In any case, we could have cross-questioned the Attorney General in regard to his strange conduct.

We would have learned how it was that he, with zeal enough to turn simple constable with a bench warrant in his pocket, did not seek before today to capture the man whom he calls a murderer;

how it was that to that man, whom he now calls a murderer, he for years applied the title of friend.

Now, we cannot cross-question the witness on these important points, while we have not before us the proof of the principal fact, which would have opened the door to important developments.

Mr. Speaker, nobody has forgotten that the Honourable Member for North Hastings, in making his motion, laid stress chiefly on the precedent furnished by the English House of Commons in the Sadleir case. That precedent, I accept not only on this, but on all the other points, and I will call the attention of the Honourable Member to one thing, which was that the first step taken against Sadleir was to prove the indictment found against him, by laying on the table an authentic copy of the same.

I now pass to the second allegation of the motion of the Honourable Member for North Hastings, which states that the Member for Provencher has systematically eluded the pursuit of justice and that he is at present guilty of contempt.

If there is no proof before the House of an indictment against the Member for Provencher, it is impossible, legally speaking, to pretend that he is a fugitive from justice and this, of itself, is enough to destroy the assertion of the Member for North Hastings.

Without, however, adopting this, perhaps, extreme way of looking at it, let us face and examine the question squarely: is the Member for Provencher a fugitive from justice or is he not? Is he or is he not contumacious?

I have already repeated that we have no legal proof of an indictment; it is true that we have before us that a bench warrant was issued by the Court of Queen's Bench in Manitoba against the Member for Provencher and that so far that warrant has not been executed. This is all the proof before this House in support of the motion of the Honourable Member for North Hastings. Well, I do not hesitate to say that, in law as well as in justice and equity, it cannot be concluded from this simple fact that the Member for Provencher can at this present hour be considered as contumacious.

In point of fact, that warrant was issued at the term of November last. Now there is nothing very extraordinary in the fact that it could not be executed in time to bring the accused before the court before the close of the term; the Member for Provencher might have been absent from Manitoba at that period. It is notorious that, since the unfortunate events of 1869–70, he has almost constantly resided abroad.[39] It is very possible that the news of his indictment may not have reached him until after the close of the term. But, it may be said, why did he not give himself up then? Simply because it was better for him to remain at liberty until the next term. If he had given himself up at once, he would have been obliged to remain a prisoner for six or seven months, perhaps, awaiting his trial.

Who can say, however, that he will not appear even tomorrow before the court, if it required his presence tomorrow? Who can say that he will not eagerly seize the occasion to stand his trial if that occasion be given him?

But I hear it said: there was quite recently a term of the court and he did not give himself up to answer to the charge standing against him.

Sir, this object is worthless, because if you pretend that the court has sat, then where are the proceedings which have been taken to establish that he is a fugitive from justice? Where is the report of the sheriff of the province attesting that he tried to execute the warrant issued against the Member for Provencher, but that he could not succeed in doing so?

In the face of this proof or rather of this absence of proof, where is the English subject, with respect for English law, who will dare to rise in this House and maintain that the Member for Provencher is contumacious?

But there is more than all this. The Member for Provencher has always asserted that the old Administration had promised him an amnesty for all the acts in which he had taken part in Manitoba prior to the admission of that province into the Confederation. He has reiterated this assertion twenty times, perhaps. His friends have made the same assertion and the old Administration has never been willing to speak out on the subject. Called upon over and over again to declare what there was in this alleged promise of amnesty, to state simply yes or no, it has never been willing to say yes or no.

I regard this obstinate silence of the old Administration as an absolute confirmation of the pretension of Mr. Riel and his friends – it is a case of silence giving consent.

Well, if this be the case, if the Member for Provencher was promised an amnesty for all the acts which he may have committed in Manitoba while at the head of the provisional Government, is it surprising that he should not want to submit to those who now wish to drag him before the courts for those same acts? Is he not warranted in so acting? Is he not right in so doing in order that the promise of amnesty made to him, in the Queen's name, may be carried out? Who can say that, under the circumstances, he is a fugitive from justice, that he is contumacious?

No, Sir, as long as this question of the amnesty has not been cleared up I, for one, shall never declare that this man is a fugitive from his country's justice. Moreover, this question will be soon elucidated, as no later than last week we named a committee to enquire into it. This committee is sitting at this moment and the House, in my opinion, would do not only a culpable, but an illogical and inconsistent act, if it came to any decision affecting this question from near or far, until it has received the report of the committee.

In addition, Sir, from the legal point of view alone, at the stage reached by the proceedings taken against the Member for Provencher before the Court of Queen's Bench, in Manitoba, it is impossible to say that he is contumacious.

I have already stated that I was ready, in all respects, to follow the rules laid down by the House of Commons in the Sadleir affair: now, the principal rule adopted in that affair is that a man cannot be declared guilty of contempt unless all the opportunities of standing his trial have been exhausted and that he has not sought to take advantage of them.

When the Sadleir affair came up for the first time before the House of Commons the motion for expulsion was rejected, because Sadleir could still come before the court to stand his trial and because it would have been premature to declare him contumacious.

The Attorney General for Ireland said on the subject "that, if he had an advice to give to the House, he would recommend it to let the motion stand over until the next session; in the interval, the proceedings begun would be continued and Mr. Sadleir would be brought before the court and stand his trial or he would be outlawed."

The House of Commons adopted this wise suggestion and, as I have already had the honour to state, the motion of expulsion was rejected on that occasion.

There, Sir, is an example already traced out for us: for my part, as I have already remarked, I am ready to follow it in all respects. I do not know whether the Honourable Member for North Hastings is prepared to say as much.

I come now to the third point of the motion; that the Honourable Member for Provencher has disobeyed the order of this House commanding him to appear in his seat on a fixed day.

I maintain that this fact does not exist. The Member for Provencher could not disobey, for the simple reason that he could not have regularly had knowledge of this order, since it was never signified to him.

Mr. Bowell: Hear, hear.

Mr. Laurier: I hear the Honourable Member for North Hastings cry: "hear, hear!" Well, I again refer the honourable Member to the Sadleir precedent upon which he claims to rest his case and which nevertheless he is always forgetting. He will see there that the House of Commons had caused to be served on Sadleir the order commanding him to appear in his seat and that it had sent one of its messengers expressly to Ireland for the purpose. I again quote the words of the Attorney General:

"He could inform the House that on Monday last one of its messengers had gone to Ireland and, on the next day, had served upon Mr. Sadleir, at his domicile in the county Tipperary, the order commanding him to be in his seat: that, on the same day, he had left a copy of the order at a house in Dublin, in which Mr. Sadleir had formerly resided, and that he had left another copy with Mr. Sadleir's lawyers."

I now expect to hear the Honourable Member for North Hastings tell us that it was useless to try to serve the order of the House on the Member for Provencher, since nobody knows where he is at this moment. But, if it was impossible to serve the order personally on the Member for Provencher, it was easy to have served it at his domicile, as in the Sadleir affair. Is there not an absolute similarity between the two cases? And look at the minute precautions taken by the English House of Commons to notify Sadleir and to call upon him to defend himself against the motion of expulsion!

Here, nothing of the same kind has been done, absolutely nothing. I therefore contend and I defy contradiction on this point that the House cannot take into consideration the motion of the Honourable Member for North Hastings as long as it has not served on the Member for Provencher the order commanding him to appear in his seat, as long as it has not challenged him to defend himself. For it is the privilege, the right, in fact, of every British subject that he shall be stripped of nothing which belongs to him, without first being called upon to defend himself.

But it will be said, perhaps, on the other side of the House: What is the good of all these purely abstract objections? What purpose would it serve to notify the Member for Provencher of the motion to be made against him? Are not all the facts charged against him true? Is he not guilty?

Even though he were the greatest culprit in the world, the law should be followed and respected. Even though he might not have a word to say in his own defence, he should not the less be notified. The fundamental principle of all justice is that nobody shall ever be condemned, without having been heard in his own defence, or without having been called upon to defend himself. In numerous cases decisions, just in themselves and perfectly equitable, have been reversed by the higher courts in England, solely because the party condemned had not been notified to defend himself.

I may be permitted to here cite the language of Judge Bailey in a case reported in volume 12 of the Law and Equity Reports, p. 242:

"I know of no case," he said, "in which a power exercising judicial functions can deprive a man of any fraction whatever of his property, without his having been previously called upon to present his defence. He who decides a case without having heard the other side, has not done what is just, even though his decision should be just."

As for me, Sir, I am of French origin and my education has been French, but I have this of the Briton in me: an ardent love of fair play and of justice. Now, I assert and nobody can contradict me that the Member for Provencher has not on this occasion had either justice or fair play. The House is asked to come to an unjust and illegal decision; but, for my part, I shall never consent, in this instance or any other, to deprive a man of the smallest particle of his rights or property without first having given him the benefit of all the legal forms to defend himself.

I therefore believe that, on this point as on the preceding ones, I can conclude in all safety that the allegations on which rests the motion of the Honourable Member for North Hastings are not supported by sufficient proof.

These reasons are certainly conclusive in favour of the amendment of the Member for Chateauguay. To that amendment, my Honourable Friend, the Member for Bagot [Joseph-Alfred Mousseau] has proposed a sub-amendment, demanding purely and simply an amnesty on the spot, without waiting for the report of the committee of enquiry. It is difficult to conceive a reason to warrant this demand of the Honourable Member.

A member on the ministerial side told the Honourable Member for North Hastings yesterday that his object in making his motion was much less to expel Mr. Riel than to try to embarrass the Government. I suspect that the object of the Honourable Member for Bagot, in proposing his amendment, is absolutely the same. There seems to be an intimate alliance between the Honourable Member for North Hastings and the Honourable Member for Bagot, (extremes meet:) both are on the war path and both are assailing a common enemy; one directs his attack against the right flank and the other against the left, and both hope that, if the enemy escapes from the blows of the one, he will fall under those of the other and that they will succeed in each planting his flag on the fortress top.

Sir, I have not the honour to know the Honourable Member for North Hastings, and I would not wish to suspect his motives; I do not . . . .

Mr. Bowell: Oh! Don't hesitate: I have no scruples.

Mr. Laurier: But I have. Once more, I say, I have not the advantage of knowing the Honourable Member for North Hastings. I do not want to suspect his motives; I would rather believe in their sincerity. But as for my honourable friend, the Member for Bagot, I know him too long and too well to not read his game clearly and I do not hesitate to say that he is far less anxious for the amnestying of Mr. Riel than he is for compromising the administration, if possible. I think that when the Honourable Member for Provencher learns what is happening here today he will exclaim: Lord save me from my friends!

As a matter of fact, could the Honourable Member for Bagot seriously hope that the House would adopt his amendment? Why then did he propose it? It was only last week that the House unanimously named a committee to enquire into the whole question of the amnesty, and, at this very hour, this committee is sitting and Mgr Taché is giving his evidence before it.[40]

Now, Sir, this committee is useful or it is not. If it has no utility whatever, why did not the Honourable Member oppose it when it was asked for? Why did he not propose a sub-amendment, recommending the immediate granting of the amnesty? Why did he not save to the country the enormous expense that the enquiry will entail?

If, on the other hand, the enquiry made by the committee may be useful for the amnesty, why not wait until Mgr Taché and Father Ritchot have given their evidence? Does the Honourable Member for Bagot imagine that he is doing a service to Mr. Riel in striving to deprive him of the benefit of the evidence of Mgr Taché and Father Ritchot? Does the Member for Bagot think that the evidence of Mgr Taché and Father Ritchot will have less effect towards obtaining the amnesty than his sub-amendment?[41]

Well, if all that has been said about the promises made by the ex-Government to Mr. Riel be true, I am in favour of the amnesty, and for this reason I shall not hesitate for an instant about voting against this sub-amendment. And, if my honourable friend will permit me, I will tell him that his sub-amendment will not have in the province of Quebec the effect he anticipates from it. Because, Sir, I tell the Honourable Member that from this day forward the province of Quebec will know who are the pretended friends of Mr. Riel and what they are aiming at in shouting so loudly in his behalf. I also trust that Mr. Riel will understand that he has been made the tool of a few intriguers, who, in the name of friends, have endeavoured to make him the instrument of their machinations; in time, I trust that he will understand that his best friends are not those who most pretend to be such.

Yea, I am in favour of the amnesty, and when the time comes, that is to say, when the committee has made its report, when the proof which has been begun has been closed, I will not be the last to demand it. I am in favour of the amnesty for two reasons: the first is that given, last night, by the Honourable Member for South Ontario [Malcolm Cameron], that the Canadian Government received the delegates of Mr. Riel's government and treated them him as one power treats with another power.

If this reason exists in fact, the conclusion is inevitable: the amnesty must be granted. Yesterday, the Honourable Member for South Bruce, (Mr. Edward Blake), replying to the Member for South Ontario, seems to have admitted the legality of the proposition emitted by the latter, because he gave for sole answer that the proposition did not exist as a question of fact, that Mr. Riel's delegates had ever been received by the Canadian Government as delegates of Mr. Riel, but as delegates of the people of Red River. Certainly, I would think it an honour under almost all circumstances to adopt the Honourable Member for South Bruce's way of thinking, but I cannot do so in this instance the proof he offered us in support of his opinion being anything but conclusive to my mind.

In fact, what proof did he give us? Only an extract from a speech delivered in some part of Ontario by the Honourable Member for Kingston [John A. Macdonald], in which the latter appears to have stated what I have just repeated, namely: that the delegates sent by Mr. Riel had not been received as the delegates of Mr. Riel, but as the delegates of the people of Red River.

Once more, I say, this proof cannot convince me. For I have yet to learn that the delegates were informed of this distinction at the time of their reception; if such a distinction was made, it must have consisted of a mental restriction by which the Honourable Member for Kingston said to himself, while ostensibly receiving the delegates of Mr. Riel, that, in reality, he only wished to deal with the delegates of the Red River people.

Whatever may be the case, if the Honourable Member for Kingston received the delegates of the people of Red River, his colleague, Sir George Cartier,[42] received the delegates of Mr. Riel and they presented to him, as the representative of the Canadian Government, their letters of credit signed with Mr. Riel's own hand. If this be the case, and it will probably be established by the evidence before the committee then the logical consequence of this act must follow and the amnesty be granted.

I am in favour of the amnesty for still another reason – because all the acts with which Mr. Riel is charged are purely political acts. It was said here yesterday that the execution of Scott was a crime; granted, but it was a political act. The reason of this seems evident; Mr. Riel, in signing the warrant for Scott's execution, did nothing but give effect to the sentence of a court. However illegal may have been that court, however iniquitous may have been the sentence rendered by that court, the fact alone that it was rendered by a court and that that court existed de facto was sufficient to impart an exclusively political character to the execution.

It has also been said that Mr. Riel was only a rebel. How was it possible to use such language? What act of rebellion did he commit? Did he ever raise any other standard than the national flag? Did he ever proclaim any other authority than the sovereign authority of the Queen? No, never. His whole crime and the crime of his friends was that they wanted to be treated like British subjects and not to be bartered away like common cattle? If that be an act of rebellion, where is the one amongst us, who, if he had happened to have been with them, would not have been rebels as they were? Taken all in all, I would regard the events at Red River in 1869–70 as constituting a glorious page in our history, if unfortunately they had not been stained with the blood of Thomas Scott. But such is the state of human nature and of all that is human: good and evil are constantly intermingled; the most glorious cause is not free from impurity and the vilest may have its noble side.

Yes, once more, I say that to ask for the amnesty now will simply render it more difficult to obtain it eventually.

Before sitting down, I may be allowed to sum up in a single word: we have no proof of the facts on which the motion of expulsion rests and to adopt that motion would be not only to commit an arbitrary act, but to establish a precedent which will be a perpetual danger to our free institutions.

By the Honourable Bob Rae

There is in the life of every successful parliamentarian and politician a fight that makes his opponents see him in a special way. A young, diffident, even languid lawyer from Quebec made his way from the Quebec assembly to the House of Commons in the early 1870s, and in his first days made little impression.

An opponent of Confederation in 1867, like many other liberal "Rouges" of his day, Laurier made his first major speech on the Manitoba question in April of 1874. A motion before the House, moved by the Conservatives, called for the expulsion of Louis Riel as a Member of Parliament on the grounds that he had been charged with the murder of Thomas Scott.

Laurier's argument was quite simple: the facts in the motion had not been proven. A warrant for Riel's arrest was not proof of his guilt.

"His whole crime and the crime of his friends was that they wanted to be treated like British subjects and not to be bartered away like common cattle? If that be an act of rebellion, where is the one amongst us, who, if he had happened to have been with them, would not have been rebels as they were?"

A full ten years later, as the repression of the "rebellion" was being debated in the House, Laurier used the same argument – a profound difference of interest and opinion in the northwest and in the rest of the country was being portrayed as an affront to authority and the Crown. Macdonald argued that a rebellion had only one solution, a military crackdown to restore "law and order." Laurier insisted that this repression had nothing to do with justice, and that by acting in this way Macdonald was creating a generation of rebels:

"This I do charge upon the Government: that they have for years and years ignored the just claims of the half-breeds of the Saskatchewan, that for years and years these people have been petitioning the Government and always in vain. I say they have been treated by this Government with an indifference amounting to undisguised contempt, and that they have been goaded into the unfortunate course they have adopted, and if this rebellion be a crime, I say the responsibility for that crime weighs as much upon the men who, by their conduct, have caused the rebellion as upon those who engaged in it."

Laurier understood that the conflict in Manitoba and Saskatchewan was no purely local affair, that it was an extension of the battle for real understanding between English and French, for the rule of law, and for democratic government founded on the principles of pluralism and justice. He identified with the "rebels" in this important sense – just as violence and division in Quebec ended with a recognition of rights and self-government, so too would the same happen in Manitoba and Saskatchewan. Absent such reconciliation, bitterness and hard feeling would continue.

The parliamentary battle, and indeed the passionate argument across the country, came to a head with Macdonald's decision to execute Louis Riel. In Laurier's eloquent argument, Riel's uprising was a political event. Thomas Scott was killed on the orders of a government-created court, and, in addition, Riel was not of sound mind. The vindication of rights was met with a brutal sword:

"But if it be expected of me that I shall allow fellow countrymen unfriended, undefended, unprotected and unrepresented in this House, to be trampled underfoot by this Government, I say that is not what I understand by loyalty, and I would call that slavery."

It can fairly be said that it was Laurier's long fight for justice for the Métis and French-Canadian population of western Canada that made his reputation as an orator not afraid of the wall of English Canadian opinion against him. He rallied his party in Opposition, something for which he was warmly remembered in the Liberal Party for generations. He would draw on this courage as he fought his final political struggle in the conscription fights of the First World War.

While we remember Laurier now for his "sunny ways," his willingness to fight for his beliefs was even more important. He was prepared to court unpopularity in the name of justice, and in so doing turned many heads and won even more hearts.

The Honourable Bob Rae was Ontario's twenty-first premier and later served as interim leader of the federal Liberal Party.

ON POLITICAL LIBERALISM

ACADEMY OF MUSIC, QUEBEC CITY, QUEBEC

JUNE 26, 1877[43]

I cannot conceal the fact that it was with a certain feeling of pleasure that I accepted the invitation to come before you to explain what are the doctrines of the Liberal Party and what the word "Liberalism" means as regards the Liberals of the province of Quebec.

I say that it was not without a certain feeling of pleasure that I accepted; but I would certainly have refused if I had looked only to the difficulties of the task. However, if the difficulties of that task are numerous and delicate, on the other hand I am so imbued with the importance for the Liberal Party of clearly defining its position, before the public opinion of the province, that this consideration was to my mind far above all the others.

In fact, I do not deceive myself with regard to the position of the Liberal Party in the Province of Quebec and I have no hesitation in immediately saying that it occupies a false position from the standpoint of public opinion. I know that, in the eyes of a large number of my fellow countrymen, the Liberal Party is a party composed of men of perverse doctrines and dangerous tendencies, pressing knowingly and deliberately towards revolution. I know that, in the eyes of a portion of my fellow countrymen, the Liberal

Party is a party of men with upright intentions, perhaps, but victims and dupes of principles which are leading them unconsciously, but fatally, towards revolution. In fine, I know that, in the eyes of another, and not the least considerable portion, perhaps, of our people, Liberalism is a new form of evil, a heresy carrying with it its own condemnation.

I know all this and it is because I know it, that I have accepted the invitation to come here. I have not the presumption to believe that anything I might say here tonight will have the effect of dissipating any of the prejudices existing at present against us; my only ambition is to lead the way in the hope that it will be followed by others and that the work thus begun will be fully carried out; my pretensions go no farther than this.

And let no one say that this manifestation is useless or untimely. It is neither useless nor untimely to combat the prejudices which have been raised like a barrier everywhere between us and public opinion; it is neither useless nor untimely to clearly define our position as it really is.

It is quite true that we have been already long enough before public opinion to give it full opportunity to know and appreciate us. But it is equally true that if we have had our enemies like every other political party, we have been more assailed than any other political party. Of our enemies, the one has systematically slandered us; the others have in good faith calumniated us. Both have represented us as professing doctrines, the effect of which, foreseen and calculated by some of us, not foreseen by, but fatal for the others, would be the overthrow of our society, the revolution with all its horrors. To reply to these charges and to defend our position is the object of the demonstration of this evening organized by the Club Canadien.

To my mind, the most efficacious, the only way, in fact, to defeat these charges, to defend our ideas and principles, is to make them known. Yes, I am convinced that the exposure alone of our principles will be their best and most eloquent apology. And when we shall have made ourselves known as we are, when we shall have made known our principles as they are, we shall have gained, I believe, a double point. The first will be to rally to our side all the friends of liberty, all those, who, before 1837 or after it, laboured to secure for us responsible government, government of the people by the people, and who, on the establishment of that form of government, separated from us through fear that we were in reality what we were represented to be, and that the realization of the ideas ascribed to us would lead to the destruction of the government which they had had so much trouble in establishing.

The second point will be to force our real enemies, all who at bottom are enemies more or less disguised of liberty, to no longer appeal against us to prejudices and fear, but to come forward frankly as we do before the people with their ideas and their acts.

And when the fight takes place on the ground of pure questions of principle according to the thought by which they are inspired, when people will be no longer afraid to accept the good and reject the bad under the impression that in accepting the one and rejecting the other, strength will be only given to a party of perverse doctrines and dangerous tendencies, it matters little to me on which side victory will then perch.

When I state that it matters little to me on which side victory will perch, I do not mean to say that I am indifferent to the result of the struggle. I mean this: if the struggle turns against us, the opinion expressed will be the free expression of the people; but I am convinced that a day will come when our ideas, planted in the soil, will germinate and bear fruit, if the seed is sound and just.

Yes, I am confident, I am certain that if our ideas are just, as I believe they are, if they are an emanation of the eternal and immutable truth, as I believe they are, they will not perish; they may be rejected, reviled, persecuted, but a day will come when they will germinate, spring up and grow, as soon as the sun shall have done its work and prepared the ground.

I have already noted some of the charges made against us; I shall return to the subject, as it is the most important point. All the charges made against us, all the objections to our doctrines, may be crystallized into the following propositions:

1. Liberalism is a new form of error, a heresy already virtually condemned by the head of the Church;

2. A Catholic cannot be a Liberal.

This is what our adversaries proclaim. Mr. President, all who honour me with their attention at this moment will do me the justice of recognizing that I put the question as it is and that I exaggerate nothing. All will do me the justice of admitting that I reproduce faithfully the reproaches which are day after day cast up to us. All will acknowledge that it is well and truly the language of the Conservative press.

I know that Catholic Liberalism has been condemned by the head of the Church. But I will be asked: what is Catholic Liberalism? On the threshold of this question I stop. This question does not come within the purview of my subject: moreover, it is not of my competence. But I know and I say that Catholic Liberalism is not political Liberalism. If it were true that the ecclesiastical censures hurled against Catholic Liberalism should also apply to political Liberalism this fact would constitute for us, French by origin and Catholics by religion, a state of things, the consequences of which would be as strange as they would be painful.

In fact, we, French Canadians, are a conquered race. This is a melancholy truth to utter, but it is the truth. But, if we are a conquered race, we have also made a conquest: the conquest of liberty. We are a free people; we are a minority, but we have retained all our rights and all our privileges. Now, what is the cause to which we owe this liberty? It is the constitution which was conquered by our forefathers and which we enjoy today. We have a constitution which bases the Government on the suffrage of the citizens and which was granted to us for our own protection. We have not more rights or more privileges, but we have as many rights and as many privileges as the other elements, which go to make up the Canadian family. But it must not be forgotten that the other members of the Canadian family are divided into two parties, the Liberal Party and the Conservative Party.

But if we, who are Catholics are not to have the right to have our preferences, if we are not to have the right to belong to the Liberal Party, one of two things must happen, either we would be obliged to abstain completely from taking any share in the management of the affairs of the State and then the constitution, that constitution which was granted to us for our own protection, would be no longer in our hands only a dead letter; or we would be obliged to take a part in the management of the affairs of the State under the direction and to the profit of the Conservative Party and then, our action being no longer free, the constitution would again be in our hands a dead letter and we would in addition have the ignominy of being regarded by the other members of the Canadian family composing the Conservative Party as tools and slaves.

Do not these absurd consequences, the strict accuracy of which nobody can question, conclusively show how false is the assertion that a Catholic cannot belong to the Liberal Party?

Since Providence has united together on this corner of earth populations of different origins and creeds, is it not manifest that these populations must have together common and identical interest, and, that, in all that affects these interests, each one is free to follow either the Liberal Party or the Conservative Party, according to the dictates of his conscience?

For my part, I belong to the Liberal Party. If it be wrong to be a Liberal, I accept the reproach: if it be a crime to be Liberal, then I am guilty of it. For my part, I only ask one thing: that we be judged according to our principles. I would be ashamed of our principles, if we were afraid to give expression to them and our cause would not be worth the efforts for its triumph, if the best way to secure that triumph was to conceal its nature. The Liberal Party has been for twenty-five years in Opposition and let it remain there for twenty-five more, if the people have not yet been educated up to accepting its ideas, but let it march proudly with its banners displayed in the full face of the country!

Before all, however, it is important to come to an understanding upon the meaning, value and bearing of the word "Liberal" and that other word "Conservative."

I maintain that there is not one thing less understood in this country by its assailants than Liberalism and there are several reasons for this.

It is only yesterday that we were initiated into representative institutions. The English element understand the working of these institutions in some way by instinct, as well as by long experience. On the other hand, our people hardly understand them yet. Education is only beginning to spread among us and, in the case of the educated, our French education leads us naturally to study the history of modern liberty, not in the classic land of liberty, not in the history of old England, but among the peoples of the continent of Europe, of the same origin and faith as ourselves. And there, unfortunately, the history of liberty has been written in letters of blood on the most harrowing pages which the annals of the human race, perhaps, contain. In all classes of educated society may be seen loyal souls, who, frightened by these mournful pages, regard with terror the spirit of liberty, imagining that it must produce here the same disasters and the same crimes as in the countries I have just referred to. In the eyes of such well-meaning people, the very word "Liberalism" is fraught with national calamity.

Without blaming altogether these fears, but without allowing ourselves to be frightened by them, let us go back to the fountain-head itself and calmly examine what is at the bottom of those two words: *Liberal, Conservative!* What idea is hidden under this word Liberal that it should have called down upon us so many anathemas! What idea is hidden under the word Conservative that it should be modestly applied to everything that is good? Is the one, as is pretended and, in fact asserted every day, the expression of a new form of error? Is the other, as it seems to be constantly insinuated, the definition of good under all its aspects? Perhaps the one means revolt, anarchy, disorder, and is the other the only stable principle of society? These are questions which people are putting to themselves daily in our country.

These subtle distinctions, which are constantly appearing in our press, are nevertheless not new. They are only the repetition of the fancies of certain French writers, whose horizon is bounded by the narrow limits of their sanctums and who, only looking to the past, bitterly criticize everything existing in the present for the simple reason that nothing now existing resembles anything that existed formerly.

These writers proclaim that the Liberal idea, is a new idea but they are mistaken. The Liberal idea is no more a new idea than is the contrary idea. It is as old as the world and is found written on every page of the world's history, but it is only in our days that we have come to know its force and its law and to understand how to utilize it. Steam existed before Fulton, but it has only been since Fulton that we have learned all the extent of its power and how to make it produce its marvellous effects. The combination of the tube and piston is the instrument by which we utilize steam and the system of representative governments is the instrument which has revealed to the world the two principles, Liberal and Conservative, and by which we get from that form of government all its effects.

Upon any subject whatever, within the range of human things, the truth does not manifest itself equally to all intellects. There are some whose gaze pierces further into the unknown, but takes in less at a time; there are others whose gaze, even if it be less penetrating, perceives more clearly within the sphere which it embraces. This primordial distinction at once explains to a certain extent the Liberal idea and the Conservative idea. For this sole reason, the same object will not be seen under the same aspect by different eyes; for this sole reason, the one will take a route which the others will avoid, although both propose to arrive at the same end. But there is a conclusive reason which clearly explains the nature and the why and the wherefore of the two different ideas. Macaulay, in his *History of England*, sets forth this reason with admirable clearness. Speaking of the meeting of the Houses for the second session of the Long Parliament, the great historian says:

"From that day dates the corporate existence of the two great parties which have ever since alternately governed the country. In one sense, indeed, the distinction which then became obvious had always existed and always must exist; for it has its origin in diversities of temper, of understanding, and of interest, which are found in all societies and which will be found until the human mind ceases to be drawn in opposite directions by the charm of habit and by the charm of novelty. It is not only in politics, but in literature, in art, in science, in surgery and mechanics, in navigation and agriculture, nay, even in mathematics, we find this distinction. Everywhere there is a class of men who cling with fondness to whatever is ancient and who, even when convinced by overpowering reasons that innovation would be beneficial, consent to it with many misgivings and forebodings. We find also everywhere another class of men sanguine in hope, bold in speculation, always pressing forward, quick to discern the imperfection of whatever exists, disposed to think lightly of the risks and inconveniences which attend improvements and disposed to give every change credit for being an improvement."[44]

The former are the Conservatives; the latter are the Liberals. Here you have the real meaning, the true explanation, of the Liberal principle. They are two attributes of our nature. As Macaulay admirably expresses it, they are to be found everywhere: in the arts, in the sciences and in all the branches open to human speculation; but it is in politics that they are most apparent.

Consequently, those who condemn Liberalism as a new idea have not reflected upon what is transpiring every day under their eyes. Those who condemn Liberalism as an error have not reflected that, in so doing, they condemn an attribute of human nature. Now, it should not be overlooked that our form of government is a representative monarchy. This is the instrument which throws into relief and brings into action the two principles, Liberal and Conservative.

We, Liberals, are often accused of being Republicans. I do not note this reproach for the purpose of taking it up, for it is not worth taking up. I merely state that the form matters little; whether it be monarchical or republican, the moment the people exercise the right to vote, the moment they have a responsible government, they have the full measure of liberty. Still, liberty would soon be no more than an empty name, if it left without control those who have the direction of power. A man, whose astonishing sagacity has formulated the axioms of governmental science with undeviating accuracy, Junius, has said: "Eternal vigilance is the price of liberty."[45] Yes, if a people want to remain free, they must like Argus have a hundred eyes and be always on the alert.[46] If they slumber, or relax, each moment of indolence loses them a particle of their rights. Eternal vigilance is the price which they have to pay for the priceless boon of liberty.

Now, the form of a representative monarchy lends itself marvellously much more, perhaps than the republican form to the exercise of this necessary vigilance. On the one hand, you have those who govern and, on the other, those who watch. On the one hand, you have those who are in power and have an interest in remaining there, and, on the other, those who have an interest in getting there.

What is the bond of cohesion to unite each individual of the different groups? What is the principle, the sentiment, to range these diverse elements of the population either among those who govern or those who watch? It is the Liberal principle or the Conservative principle. You will see together those who are attracted by the charm of novelty and you will see together those who are attracted by the charm of habit. You will see together those who are attached to all that is ancient and you will see together those who are always disposed to reform.

Now I ask: between these two ideas which constitute the basis of parties, can there be a moral difference? Is the one radically good and the other radically bad? Is it not evident that both are what are termed in moral philosophy *indifferents*, that is to say, that both are susceptible of being appreciated, pondered and chosen? Would it not it be as unfair as it would be absurd to condemn or to approve either the one or the other as absolutely bad or good?

Both are susceptible of much good, as they are also of much evil. The Conservative, who defends his country's old institutions may do much good, as he also may do much evil, if he be obstinate in maintaining abuses, which have become intolerable. The Liberal, who contends against these abuses and who, after long efforts, succeeds in extirpating them, may be a public benefactor, just as the Liberal who lays a rash hand on hallowed institutions may be a scourge not only for his own country, but for humanity at large.

Certainly, I am far from blaming my adversaries for their convictions, but for my part, as I have already said, I am a Liberal. I am one of those who think that everywhere, in human things, there are abuses to be reformed, new horizons to be opened up, and new forces to be developed.

Moreover, Liberalism seems to me in all respects superior to the other principle. The principle of Liberalism is inherent to the very essence of our nature, to that desire of happiness with which we are all born into the world, which pursues us throughout life and which is never completely gratified on this side of the grave. Our souls are immortal, but our means are limited. We constantly gravitate towards an ideal which we never attain. We dream of good, but we never realize the best. We only reach the goal we have proposed to ourselves, to discover new horizons opening up, which we had not before even suspected.

We rush on towards them and those horizons, explored in their turn, reveal to us others which lead us on ever further and further. And thus it will be as long as man is what he is, as long as the immortal soul inhabits a mortal body, his desires will be always vaster than his means and his actions will never rise to the height of his conceptions. He is the real Sisyphus of the fable: his work always finished has always to be begun over again.[47]

This condition of our nature is precisely what makes the greatness of man, for it condemns him irrevocably to movement, to progress: our means are limited, but our nature is perfectible and we have the infinite for our arena. Thus, there is always room for improvement of our condition, for the perfecting of our nature, and for the attainment by a larger number of an easier life. Here again is what, in my eyes, constitutes the superiority of Liberalism.

In addition, experience has established that insensibly, imperceptibly, abuses will creep into the body social and end by seriously obstructing its upward march, if not endangering its existence. Experience has further established that institutions which, at the outset, were useful because they were adapted to the state of society at the time of their introduction, often end by becoming intolerable abuses owing to the simple fact that everything around them has changed. Such was the case in our own midst with the seigniorial tenure. It is unquestionable that, in the infancy of the colony, that system greatly facilitated the settlement of the soil. But, in 1850, everything had changed so much amongst us that the system would have eventuated in deplorable complications, if our Legislature, upon the initiative of the Liberals, had not had the wisdom to abolish it.

As a consequence of the law which I have indicated as the determining cause of the Liberal and Conservative ideas, there will be always men found, who will attach themselves with love to these abuses, defend them to the bitter end, and view with dismay any attempt to suppress them. Woe to such men, if they do not know how to yield and adopt proposed reforms! They will draw down upon their country disturbances all the more terrible, that justice shall have been long refused. History, alas! superabundantly shows that very few of those who govern have been able to understand these aspirations of humanity and satisfy them. Indeed, more revolutions have been caused by Conservative obstinacy than by Liberal exaggeration.

The supreme art of government consists in guiding, directing and controlling these aspirations of human nature. The English are, in a high degree, masters of this art. Look at the work of the great Liberal Party of England! How many reforms has it not brought about, how many abuses corrected, without shock, disturbance and violence! Understanding the aspirations of the oppressed and the new wants created by new situations, it has carried out, under the sanction of the law and without other aid than the law, a series of reforms which has made the English people the freest people and the most prosperous and happy of Europe.

On the other hand, look at the continental governments! The

most of them have never been able to grasp these aspirations of their peoples. No sooner do the sufferers raise their heads to catch a few breaths of air and of freedom, than they are brutally crushed back again into a circle which is ever growing more and more hermetically restricted.

But the day comes when the obstacles are shivered to pieces, when these peoples break forth from their paralyzing restraints, and, then, in the holy name of liberty, the most frightful crimes are committed. Is there reason to be surprised at this? Are we astonished when the storm clouds, rolling over our heads, burst forth in hail and lightning? Are we surprised at the explosion of the steam-boiler, when the engineer neglects to open the safety valve and relieve it of its superabundant pressure? No, because we see in these events the working of an inevitable law which is always attended with the same effects, as well in the moral as in the physical system.

Wherever there is compression, there will be explosion, violence and ruin. I do not say this to excuse revolutions, as I hate revolutions and detest all attempts to win the triumph of opinions by violence. But I am less inclined to cast the responsibility on those who make them than on those who provoke them by their blind obstinacy. I say this to illustrate the superiority of Liberalism, which understands the aspirations of human nature, and, instead of doing violence to them, seeks to direct them. Can it be believed, for instance, that – if England had persisted in refusing emancipation to Catholics; if it had persisted in refusing the fullness of their civil and political rights to the Catholics, the Jews and the other Protestant denominations not forming part of the established church; if it had persisted in keeping the suffrage limited to a small number; if it had persisted in refusing free trade in breadstuff; if it had persisted in refusing the right of suffrage to the working classes – a day would not have come when the people would have risen in arms to do themselves the justice that would have been obstinately denied to them?

Do you think that riot would not have raised its hideous head under the windows of Westminster and that the blood of civil war would not have reddened the streets of London, as it has so often reddened the streets of Paris? Human nature is the same all over, and there, as elsewhere, compression would have produced explosion, violence and ruin. These terrible calamities, however, were obviated by the initiative of the Liberals who, understanding the evil, proposed and applied the remedy.

What is grander than the history of the great English Liberal Party during the present century? On its threshold, looms up the figure of Fox, the wise, the generous Fox, defending the cause of the oppressed, wherever there were oppressed to be defended.[48] A little later, comes O'Connell, claiming and obtaining for his co-religionists the rights and privileges of English subjects.[49] He is helped in this work by all the Liberals of the three kingdoms, Grey, Brougham, Russell, Jeffrey and a host of others.[50] Then come, one after the other, the abolition of the ruling oligarchy, the repeal of the corn laws, the extension of the suffrage to the working classes, and, lastly, to crown the whole, the disestablishment of the Church of England as the State religion in Ireland.

And note well: the Liberals, who carried out these successive reforms, were not recruited from the middle classes only, but some of their most eminent leaders were recruited from the peerage of England. I know of no spectacle that reflects greater honour on humanity than the spectacle of these peers of England, these rich and powerful nobles, stubbornly fighting to eradicate a host of venerable abuses and sacrificing their privileges with calm enthusiasm to make life easier and happier for a larger number of their fellow beings. While on this head, permit me to cite a letter of Macaulay's written to one of his friends on the next day after the vote on the famous Reform bill, which put an end to the system of rotten-boroughs.[51] I ask pardon for making this quotation, as it is somewhat long:

"Such a scene as the division of last Tuesday I never saw, and never expect to see again. If I should live fifty years, the impression of it will be as fresh and sharp in my mind as if it had just taken place. It was like seeing Caesar stabbed in the Senate-house, or seeing Oliver taking the mace from the table; a sight to be seen only once, and never to be forgotten. The crowd overflowed the House in every part. When the strangers were cleared out, and the doors locked, we had six hundred and eight Members present – more by fifty-five than ever were on a division before. The ayes and noes were like two volleys of cannon from opposite sides of a field of battle. When the Opposition went out into the lobby, an operation which took up twenty minutes or more, we spread ourselves over the benches on both sides of the House; for there were many of us who had not been able to find a seat during the evening. When the doors were shut we began to speculate on our numbers. Everybody was desponding. 'We have lost it. We are only two hundred and eighty at most. I do not think we are two hundred and fifty. They are three hundred. Alderman Thompson has counted them. He says they are two hundred and ninety-nine.' This was the talk on our benches. The House, when only the ayes were in it, looked to me a very fair House – much fuller than it generally is even on debates of considerable interest. I had no hope, however, of three hundred. As the tellers passed along our lowest row on the left-hand side the interest was insupportable – two hundred and ninety-one – two hundred and ninety-two – we were all standing up and stretching forward, telling with the tellers. At three hundred there was a short cry of joy – at three hundred and two another – suppressed, however, in a moment, for we did not yet know what the hostile force might be. We knew, however, that we could not be severely beaten. The doors were thrown open, and in they came. Each of them, as he entered, brought some different report of their number, it must have been impossible, as you may conceive, in the lobby, crowded as they were, to form any exact estimate. First we heard that they were three hundred and three: then that number rose to three hundred and ten; then went down to three hundred and seven. We were all breathless with anxiety, when Charles Wood, who stood near the door, jumped up on a bench and cried out, 'They are only three hundred and one.'

"We set up a shout that you might have heard to Charing Cross, waving our hats, stamping against the floor, and clapping our hands. The tellers scarcely got through the crowd; for the House was thronged up to the table, and all the floor was fluctuating with heads like the pit of a theatre. But you might have heard a pin drop as Duncannon read the numbers. Then again the shouts broke out, and many of us shed tears. I could scarcely refrain. And the jaw of Peel fell; and the face of Twiss was as the face of a damned soul; and Herries looked like Judas taking his neck-tie off for the last operation. We shook hands, and clapped each other on the back, and went out laughing, crying, and huzzaing into the lobby. And no sooner were the outer doors opened than another shout answered that within the House. All the passages and the stairs into the waiting-rooms were thronged by people who had waited till four in the morning to know the issue. We passed through a narrow lane between two thick masses of them; and all the way down they were shouting and waving their hats, till we got into the open air. I called a cabriolet, and the first thing the driver asked was, 'Is the bill carried?' 'Yes, by one.' 'Thank God for it, sir!'"

And Macaulay concludes with a sentence strongly indicative of the Liberal: "And so ended a scene which will probably never be equalled till the reformed Parliament wants reforming."[52]

The man, who wrote in these cheery terms, had just come from voting the abolition of the system by virtue of which he held his own seat. Macaulay owed his seat to the generosity of an English peer, Lord Lansdowne, who had him returned for the rotten borough of Calne. I know of few pages that do more honour to humanity then this simple letter which shows us these English natures, calm but steadfast in the fight and only kindling into emotion when the battle has been won, because an act of justice has been accomplished and an abuse uprooted from the soil of old England.

Members of the Club Canadien, Liberals of the province of Quebec, there are our models! there are our principles! there is our party!

It is true that there is in Europe, in France, in Italy and in Germany, a class of men, who give themselves the title of Liberals, but who have nothing of the Liberal about them but the name and who are the most dangerous of men. These are not Liberals; they are revolutionaries: in their principles they are so extravagant that they aim at nothing less than the destruction of modern society. With these men, we have nothing in common; but it is the tactic of our adversaries to always assimilate us to them. Such accusations are beneath our notice and the only answer we can with dignity give them is to proclaim our real principles and to so conduct ourselves that our acts will conform with our principles.

Now, at this stage of my discourse, I shall review the history of the Liberal Party of this country. I am one of those who do not fear to scrutinize the history of my party. I am one of those who think there is more to be gained by frankly stating the truth than by trying to deceive ourselves and others. Let us have the courage to tell the truth! If our party has committed mistakes, our denials will not change matters; moreover, if our party has committed faults, we shall always find in the other party enough of faults to balance ours, and, even if the other party were immaculate, our principles would not, for that reason, be either better or worse. Let us have the courage to tell the truth and let it prevent us from falling into the same faults in the future!

Down to 1848, all the French Canadians were of but one party, the Liberal Party. The Conservative or rather the Tory Party, as it was called, only represented a feeble minority. But, from 1848, date the first traces of the two parties, which have since disputed power. Mr. Lafontaine had accepted the regime established in 1841.[53] When Mr. Papineau returned from exile, he assailed the new order of things with his great eloquence and all his elevation of mind. I shall not here undertake to enter into a criticism of the respective policies of these two great men. Both loved their country ardently, passionately; both had devoted to it their lives; both, in different ways, had no other ambition than to serve it; and both were pure and disinterested. Let us be content with these souvenirs, without seeking which of the two was right and which wrong!

There was at this time a generation of young men of great talent and still greater impetuosity of character. Disappointed at having come on the scene too late to stake their heads during the events of 1837, they threw themselves with blind alacrity into the political movement of the day. They were among the foremost of Mr. Lafontaine's partisans in his glorious struggle against Lord Metcalfe. They afterwards abandoned him for the more advanced policy of Mr. Papineau, and, though taking their places among his following, as was natural, they soon went beyond him.

Emboldened by their success and carried away by their enthusiasm, they one day founded *L'Avenir* in which they posed as reformers and regenerators of their country. Not satisfied with attacking the political situation, they boldly attacked the social situation. They issued a programme containing not less than twenty-one articles commencing with the election of justices of the peace and ending with annexation to the United-States, and, taken as a whole, practically amounting to a complete revolution of the province. If, by the wave of some magic wand, the twenty-one articles of this programme had been realized in a single night, the country in the morning would have been no longer recognizable, and the person, who should have left it the evening before and returned the next day, would not have known where he was. The only excuse for these Liberals was their youth. The oldest of them was not more than twenty-two years of age.

Gentlemen, I am stating facts. I have no intention of reproaching anyone. Talent and sincere convictions are entitled to respect. Moreover, who is the one amongst us, who, if he had been living at that time, could flatter himself that he would have been wiser and that he would not have fallen into the same mistakes? Everything was favourable to such exaggerations: the situation of our own country and the situation in Europe.

The wounds of the country from the insurrection were not yet healed: we had been granted, it is true, a free constitution, but the new constitution was not being applied in good faith by the Colonial Office. There was at the bottom of every soul a discontented spirit, which was alone kept down by the recollection of the vengeance for which the insurrection had furnished the opportunity. Moreover, from all sides, the effluvia of democracy and revolt came pouring in upon us. Society was already shivering in the first blasts of that great storm, which was to break forth a few years later over the whole civilized world and which for a moment caused society to stagger.

The years preceding 1848 are frightful to contemplate. One feels a thrill of honour at the contemplation of the sinister work which was being everywhere done and which at one time drew into revolt upwards of eighty millions of men. This state of things naturally made a powerful impression on young, ardent and inexperienced imaginations, and, not satisfied with wanting to revolutionize their own country, our young reformers greeted with transports each fresh revolution in Europe.

However, hardly had they taken two steps in life, when they perceived their immense error. In 1852 they brought out another newspaper. They abandoned *L'Avenir* to the demagogues and sought in a new paper, *Le Pays* – without, however, finding it, it is true – the new path which should be followed by the friends of liberty under the new constitution.

One cannot help smiling today on reading over again *L'Avenir*'s programme; one cannot help smiling at finding, mixed up with so much good sense occasionally, so many absurd or impossible propositions. It would be tiresome to review one by one all the incongruous propositions which *L'Avenir*'s programme contained. I shall take one at random: Annual Parliaments.

I am satisfied that each of the young Reformers of that day, who is today in Parliament, is firmly convinced that an election every five years is quite sufficient. And moreover is it not obvious that annual Parliaments would be a constant obstacle to all serious legislation and a permanent source of agitation?

Still, the harm was done. The clergy, alarmed at these proceedings which reminded them of the revolutionaries of Europe, at once declared merciless war on the new party. The English population, friendly to liberty, but also friendly to the maintenance of order, also ranged themselves against the new party, and during twenty-five years that party has remained in Opposition, although to it belongs the honour of having taken the initiative in all the reforms accomplished during that period. It was in vain that it demanded and obtained the abolition of the seigniorial tenure; it was in vain that it demanded and obtained judicial decentralization, and it was in vain that it was the first to give an impetus to the work of colonization; it was not credited with these wise reforms; it was in vain that those children, now grown into men, disavowed the rashness of their youth; it was in vain that the Conservative Party made mistake after mistake: the generation of the Liberals of 1848 had almost entirely disappeared from the political scene ere the dawn of a new day began to break for the Liberal Party. Since that time, the party has received new accessions, calmer and more thoughtful ideas have prevailed in it: and, as for the old programme, nothing whatever remains of its social part, while, of the political part, there only remain the principles of the English Liberal Party.

During all this time, what was the other party doing? When the split between Mr. Papineau and Mr. Lafontaine became complete, the fraction of the Liberal Party, who followed Mr. Lafontaine, wound up, after some groping, by allying themselves with the Tories of Upper Canada, and then, to the title of Liberal which they could not or dared not yet avow, they added that of Conservative. The new party took the name of Liberal–Conservative. Some years elapsed and fresh modifications ensued. I know no longer by what name we call this party. Those who today seem to occupy leading positions in it will call themselves the Ultramontane Party, the Catholic Party. Its principles, like its name, have been modified. If Mr. Cartier were to come back to the earth today, he would not recognize his party. Mr. Cartier was devoted to the principles of the English constitution. Those who today take the lead among his old partisans openly reject the principles of the English constitution as a concession to what they term the spirit of evil. They understand neither their country, nor their time. All their ideas are modelled on those of the reactionists of France. They go into ecstasies over Don Carlos or the Comte de Chambord just as the Liberals admired Louis Blanc and Ledru-Rollin. They shout: long live the King! as the Liberals shouted: long live the Republic! In speaking of Don Carlos and the Comte de Chambord, they affect to always say only His Majesty the king Charles VII, His Majesty the king Henry V, just as the Liberals, in speaking of Napoleon III always said only Mr. Louis Buonaparte.

I have too much respect for the opinion of my adversaries to ever insult them; but I reproach them with understanding neither their time nor their country. I accuse them of judging the political situation of the country, not according to what is happening in it, but according to what is happening in France. I accuse them of wanting to introduce here ideas, which are impossible of application in our state of society, I accuse them of laboriously and, by misfortune, too efficaciously working to degrade religion to the simple proportions of a political party.

In our adversaries' party, it is the habit to accuse us, Liberals, of irreligion. I am not here to parade my religious sentiments, but I declare that I have too much respect for the faith in which I was born to ever use it as the basis of a political organization. You wish to organize a Catholic Party. But have you not considered that, if you have the misfortune to succeed, you will draw down upon your country calamities of which it is impossible to foresee the consequences?

You wish to organize all the Catholics into one party, without other bond, without other basis, than a common religion; but have you not reflected that, by the very fact, you will organize the Protestant population as a single party and that then, instead of the peace and harmony now prevailing between the different elements of the Canadian population, you throw open the door to war, a religious war, the most terrible of all wars? Once more, Conservatives, I accuse you in the face of Canada of not understanding either your country or your time.

Our adversaries also reproach us with loving liberty and they term the spirit of liberty a dangerous and subversive principle. Is there any justification for these attacks? None whatever, except that there exists in France a group of Catholics who pursue liberty with their imprecations. Assuredly, it is not true enemies of liberty in France alone who regard it with terror. The most ardent friends of liberty often contemplate it with the same feeling. Recall Madame [Marie-Jeanne Phlippon] Roland's last words [before the guillotine in 1793]. She had warmly loved liberty, she had ardently prayed for it, and her last word was a sorrowful one: "Oh! Liberty, how many crimes are committed in thy name!" How often have the same words been as sincerely uttered by fully as sincere friends of liberty!

I can readily conceive, without, however, sharing them, the feelings of those Frenchmen, who, regarding how much liberty has cost them in tears, blood and ruin, have sometimes favoured for their country a vigorous despotism; I can conceive their anathemas, but that these anathemas should be repeated in our midst is a thing I cannot understand. What? Is it a conquered race, who should curse liberty? But what would we be without liberty? What would be today if our forefathers had cherished the same sentiments as the Conservatives of the present time? Would we be other than a race of pariahs?

I frankly admit that liberty, as it has been generally understood and practised in France, has nothing very attractive about it. The French have had the name of liberty, but they have not yet had liberty itself. One of their poets, Auguste Barbier, has given us a pretty correct idea of the kind of liberty which is sometimes in vogue in France and which was last seen at work in 1871. He represents it as a woman

> *À la voix rauque, aux durs appas,*
> *Qui, du brun sur la peau, du feu dans les prunelles,*
> *Agile et marchant à grands pas,*
> *Se plaît aux cris du peuple, aux sanglantes mêlées,*
> *Aux longs roulements des tambours,*
> *À l'odeur de la poudre, aux lointaines volées*
> *Des cloches et des canons sourds;*
> *Qui ne prend ses amours que dans la populace,*
> *Qui ne prête son large flanc*
> *Qu'à des gens forts comme elle, et qui veut qu'on l'embrasse*
> *Avec des bras rouges de sang.*[54]

If liberty was well and truly this sinister virago, I could understand the anathemas of our adversaries and I would be the first to join in them. But it is not liberty. An English poet, Tennyson, has sung about liberty, the liberty of his country and of ours. In his poem *In Memoriam*, Tennyson addresses himself to a friend who enquires why he does not seek a milder climate in the South Sea islands and why, notwithstanding his impaired health, he persists in remaining under the foggy skies of England? And the poet replies:

> It is the land that freemen till,
> That sober-suited Freedom chose,
> The land, where girt with friends or foes
> A man may speak the thing he will;
>
> A land of settled government,
> A land of just and old renown,
> Where Freedom slowly broadens down
> From precedent to precedent;
>
> Where faction seldom gathers head,
> But, by degrees to fullness wrought,
> The strength of some diffusive thought
> Hath time and space to work and spread.[55]

This is the liberty we enjoy and defend and this is the liberty which our adversaries, sharing in its benefits, attack, without understanding it. Jean-Baptiste Rousseau, in one of his odes, speaks of barbarous peoples, who, one day in a moment of inconceivable folly, fell to insulting the sun with their cries and imprecations. The poet, in a word, characterizes this stupid piece of impiety:[56]

> *Le dieu, poursuivant sa carrière,*
> *Versait des torrents de lumière*
> *Sur ses obscurs blasphémateurs.*

In the same way liberty has its assailants among us. Liberty covers them, floods them, protects them and defends them even in their imprecations.

But, while reproaching us with being friends of liberty, our adversaries further reproach us, with an inconsistency which would be serious, if the charge were well founded, with denying to the Church the freedom to which it is entitled. They reproach us with seeking to silence the administrative body of the Church and to prevent it from teaching the people their duties as citizens and electors. They reproach us with wanting to hinder the clergy from meddling in politics and to relegate them to the sacristy.

In the name of the Liberal Party and of Liberal principles, I repel this assertion. I maintain that there is not one Canadian Liberal who wants to prevent the clergy from taking part in political affairs if they wish to do so. In the name of what principle, should the friends of liberty seek to deny to the priest the right to take part in political affairs? In the name of what principle, should the friends of liberty seek to deny to the priest the right to have and express political opinions, the right to approve or disapprove public men and their acts and to instruct the people in what he believes to be their duty? In the name of what principle, should he not have the right to say that, if I am elected, religion will be endangered, when I have the right to say that if my adversary is elected, the State will be endangered? Why should the priest not have the right to say that, if I am elected, religion will be inevitably destroyed, when I have the right to say that, if my adversary is elected, the State will go into bankruptcy? No, let the priest speak and preach, as he thinks best; such is his right and no Canadian Liberal will dispute that right.

Our constitution invites all citizens to take part in the direction of the affairs of the State; it makes no exception of any person. Each one has the right not only to express his opinion, but to influence, if he can, by the expression of his opinion, the opinion of his fellow citizens. This right exists for all and there can be no reason why the priest should be deprived of it. I am here to speak my whole mind and I may add that I am far from finding opportune the intervention of the clergy in the domain of politics, as it has been exercised for some years. I believe on the contrary that, from the standpoint of the respect due to his character, the priest has everything to lose by meddling in the ordinary questions of politics: still his right to do so is indisputable and, if he thinks proper to use it, our duty, as Liberals, is to guarantee it to him against all denial.

This right, however, is not unlimited. We have no absolute rights amongst us. The rights of each man, in our state of society, end precisely at the point where they encroach upon the rights of others. The right of interference in politics finishes at the spot where it encroaches on the elector's independence.

The constitution of the country rests on the freely expressed wish of each elector. It intends that each elector shall cast his vote freely and willingly as he deems best. If the greatest number of the electors of a country are actually of an opinion and that, owing to the influence exercised upon them by one or more men or owing to words they have heard or writings they have read, their opinion changes, there is nothing in the circumstance but what is perfectly legitimate. Although the opinion they express is different from the one they would have expressed without such intervention, still it is the one they desire to express conscientiously, and the constitution meets with its entire application. If, however, notwithstanding all reasoning, the opinion of the electors remains the same, but that, by intimidation or fraud, they are forced to vote differently, the opinion which they express is not their opinion, and the constitution is violated. As I have already said, the constitution intends that each one's opinion shall be freely expressed as he understands it at the moment of expression, and the collective reunion of the individual opinions, freely expressed, forms the government of the country.

The law watches with so jealous an eye the free expression of the elector's opinion as it really is that, if in a constituency the opinion expressed by a single one of the electors is not his real opinion, but an opinion forced from him by fear, fraud or corruption, the election must be annulled. It is therefore perfectly legitimate to alter the elector's opinion by argument and all other means of persuasion, but never by intimidation. As a matter of fact, persuasion changes the elector's conviction; intimidation does not. When, by persuasion, you have changed the elector's conviction, the opinion he expresses is his own opinion; but when, by terror, you force him to vote, the opinion he expresses is your opinion; remove the cause of his fear and he will then express another opinion, which is his own.

Now, it will be understood, if the opinion expressed by the majority of the electors is not their real opinion, but an opinion snatched from them by fraud, by threats or by corruption, the constitution is violated and you have not the government of the majority, but the government of a minority. Well, if such a state of things continues and is repeated, if, after each election, the will expressed is not the real will of the country, once more you do violence to the constitution, responsible government is no longer an empty name and, sooner or later, here as elsewhere, the pressure will culminate in explosion, violence and ruin.

But people are not wanting who say that the clergy have a right to dictate to the people what are its duties. I simply answer that we are here under the government of the Queen of England, under the authority of a constitution which was granted to us as an act of justice, and that, if the exercise of the rights which you claim is to have for effect the impeding of the constitution and our exposure to all the consequences of such an act, then the clergy themselves would not want it.

I am not one of those who parade themselves as friends and champions of the clergy. However, I say this: like the most of my young fellow countrymen, I have been reared among priests and among young men who have become priests. I flatter myself that I have among them some sincere friends and to them at least, I can and I do say: see, if there is under the sun a country happier than ours; see, if there is under the sun a country where the Catholic Church is freer or more privileged than it is here. Why, then, should you, by claiming rights incompatible with our state of society, expose this country to agitations, of which it is impossible to foresee the consequences?

But I address myself to all my fellow countrymen without distinction and I say to them:

We are a free and happy people; and we are so owing to the liberal institutions by which we are governed, institutions which we owe to the exertions of our forefathers and the wisdom of the mother country.

The policy of the Liberal Party is to protect those institutions, to defend and spread them, and, under the sway of those institutions, to develop the country's latent resources. That is the policy of the Liberal Party and it has no other.

Now, to properly estimate all the value of the institutions by which we are ruled today, let us compare the present state of the country with what it was before these were granted to us. Forty years ago the country was in a state of feverish commotion, a prey to an agitation which, a few months later, broke out in rebellion. The British crown was only maintained in this country by powder and ball. And yet what were our predecessors seeking? They were asking for nothing more than the institutions which we have at present; those institutions were granted to us and loyally applied; and see the result; the British flag floats over the old Citadel of Quebec; it floats tonight over our heads, without a single English soldier in the country to defend it, its sole defence resting in the gratitude, which we owe it for our freedom and the security which we have found under its folds.

Where is the Canadian who, comparing his country with even the freest countries, would not feel proud of the institutions which protect him? Where is the Canadian who, passing through the streets of this old city and reaching the monument raised a few steps from here to the memory of the two brave men, who died on the same field of battle while contending for empire in Canada, would not feel proud of his country?

In what other country, under the sun, can you find a similar monument reared to the memory of the conquered as well as of the conqueror? In what other country, under the sun, will you find the names of the conquered and the conqueror equally honoured and occupying the same place in the respect of the population?

Gentlemen, when, in that last battle which is recalled by the Wolfe and Montcalm monument the iron hail was spreading death in the ranks of the French army; when the old heroes, whom victory had so often accompanied, saw at last victory snatched from them; when, stretched on the ground with their life-blood fast ebbing away, they saw, as the result of their defeat, Quebec in the hands of the enemy and the country forever lost; no doubt, their last thought was of their children, whom they were leaving without protection and without defence; no doubt, they pictured them as persecuted, enslaved, and humiliated, and then, it is reasonable to believe, they drew their last breath with a cry of despair.

But, if, on the other hand, Heaven had lifted the veil of the future from their dying eyes and enabled them for an instant, before these closed forever, to pierce what was hidden from their sight; if they could have seen their children free and happy, marching proudly in all spheres of society; if they could have seen, in the old cathedral, the seat of honour of the French governors occupied by a French governor; if they could have seen the church steeples rising in every valley from the shores of Gaspé to the prairies of the Red River; if they could have seen this old flag, which recalls the

finest of their victories, carried triumphantly in all our public ceremonies; in fine, if they could have seen our free institutions, is it
not permissible to think that their last breath would have been
exhaled in a murmur of gratitude to Heaven and that they would
have died consoled?

If the shades of these heroes still hover over this old city, for
which they laid down their lives; if their shades hover tonight over
the hall in which we are now assembled, it is free for us, Liberals,
to think – at least we cherish the fond illusion, – that their sympathies are all with us.

By André Pratte

*During the second half of the nineteenth century, members of the Liberal
Party in the Province of Quebec did not have it easy. At nearly all provincial
and federal elections, they found themselves on the losing side. In addition
to their Conservative adversaries, the Liberals faced an even more formidable
opponent: the ultramontane wing of the Catholic Church, led by the powerful and zealous Archbishop of Montréal, Ignace Bourget.*

Encouraged by Pius IX's Quanta Cura Encyclical *condemning liberalism, the bishops of Quebec had published a* Programme catholique *in
1871, followed by a* Lettre pastorale *in 1875, both affirming the Church's
right to have its say in political matters. And it was a right they did not
hesitate to avail themselves of, asserting that it was the Catholics' "duty to
loyally support" the Conservative Party. That party, they explained, was
the only one offering "serious guarantees for religious interests." Furthermore,
quoting the encyclical, the prelates of Quebec warned "it cannot be permitted,
in conscience, to be a liberal catholic."*

*The bishops' message was relayed from the pulpit in all the parishes of
the province. The curés made sure their flock understood the message: voting
for the liberals, thundered some, was nothing less than a mortal sin.*

*This is the period Quebec City liberals chose to position their friend,
young MP Wilfrid Laurier, as the future star of the party in the province.*

Having spent three years in Quebec's Legislative Assembly, he had been elected to the House of Commons in 1874. Since then, Laurier had been noticed as a serious study and a talented orator. His friends thought the time ripe for him to take the next step: a major speech, in front of a large and distinguished audience.

And so the Club Canadien sent Wilfrid an invitation to speak at the Quebec Music Hall, the city's largest theatre (over one thousand seats), on June 26, 1877. The topic, certainly agreed to in advance by both parties, was Political Liberalism – Definition of the Liberal Idea. The speech could only be foreseen as a rebuttal to the ultramontane hierarchy's positions. A bold young man he must be, this Laurier: taking on the bishops! The mayor was on hand, so were many of Laurier's colleagues in Parliament. "The audience," reported The Morning Chronicle, *"crammed the building to its utmost capacity."*

★ ★ ★

Weighing the speech's impact on Laurier's career and the ascent of the Liberal Party in Quebec, we must be wary of the stories told by the great man's many contemporary admirers. As Laurier's reputation grew, every significant event of his life became momentous. So it was for the speech on political liberalism: the crowd at the Music Hall grew larger, the applause got louder, and the address grew so powerful that it alone struck down the ultramontane dragon.

It certainly was a clever and erudite speech. For many Quebec liberals, it confirmed that Laurier was fated to become their leader. However, the MP's performance did not prevent his defeat in a by-election four months later. As for overcoming the Ultramontane Church, it obviously took more than one speech, as brilliant as it was.

As a matter of fact, around that time, the Ultramontanes' knees buckled. It was not Laurier, but moderates inside the Church, the courts (condemning the clergy's undue influence in elections), and the Vatican (ordering the local church to stop meddling in politics) that had thrown the hard punches. To the point where, a few months before Laurier's speech on liberalism, Ignace Bourget resigned as Bishop of Montreal, a post he had held for thirty-nine years.

That being said, leaving the Music Hall, Quebec liberals were understandably ecstatic. A new leader had emerged, who dared to respond to the Church's attacks, and doing it in an enlightened manner and a cool tone. A heretic, Wilfrid Laurier? A revolutionary? Come on!

Therein lay the genius of that address: it made its points forcefully enough to impress the audience, yet so subtly that adversaries would find it hard to criticize (although of course they did). Should the clergy intervene in politics? The Church answered yes, the radical liberals (the Rouges) no. Let's listen to Laurier's answer:

"Why should the priest not have the right to say that, if I am elected, religion will inevitably be destroyed, when I have the right to say that, if my adversary is elected, the State will go into bankruptcy? No. Let the priest speak and preach, as he thinks best; such is his right and no Canadian liberal will dispute that right."

One of the Ultramontanes' main charges was thereby defused. Of course, that was not the end of Laurier's reasoning. The priest could preach politics, but for him as for any other individual, there were limits. And those limits were in the interest of . . . the Church!

"The right of interference in politics finishes at the spot where it encroaches on the elector's independence. . . . Now, it will be understood, if the opinion expressed by the majority of the electors is not their real opinion, but an opinion snatched from there by fraud, by threats or by corruption, the constitution is violated and you have not the government of the majority, but the government of a minority. Well, if such a state of things continues and is repeated, if, after each election, the will expressed is not the real will of the country, once more you do violence to the constitution, responsible government is no longer anything but an empty name and, sooner or later, here as elsewhere, the pressure will culminate in explosion, violence and ruin."

By imposing their will on the people, the young MP cautioned, the conservative bishops would eventually provoke the very troubles they wished to avoid, repeating the errors of the European regimes that had given liberals on the Continent no other avenue for change but insurrection.

It was the events on that side of the Atlantic Ocean that had brought Pius IX to condemn "catholic liberalism." So Laurier spent much of his 1877 address discussing the situation in Europe. The audience gasped at the breadth of his knowledge. Very few politicians, if any, in Canada at the time could quote British historian Macaulay, the pamphleteer Junius, the English poet Alfred Tennyson, his French contemporary Auguste Barbier, and Madame Roland ("O Liberté! Que de crimes on commet en ton nom!"). Liberal supporters were discovering part of the Silver Tongue's recipe: his intimate knowledge of both languages and cultures, augmented each day since his childhood by voracious reading of every book and newspaper he could get his hands on.

We come to the crux of Laurier's argument that evening. The Church attacked the liberals because if feared that what had happened in France, Germany, Austria, and Italy in the middle of the century could happen here. That fear was unfounded, Laurier assured his audience: Canadian liberals were not the same as their European namesakes.

"It is true that there is in Europe, in France, in Italy and in Germany, a class of men, who give themselves the title of Liberals, but who have nothing of the Liberal about them but the name and who are the most dangerous of men. These are not Liberals; they are revolutionaries: in their principles they are so extravagant that they aim at nothing less than the destruction of modern society."

Quebec liberals found their inspiration not on the continent, but across the English Channel:

"What is grander than the history of the great English Liberal Party during the present century?" Laurier names the great leaders: Fox, O'Connell, Brougham, Russell, Jeffrey. . . . "Then come, one after the other, the abolition of the ruling oligarchy, the repeal of the corn laws, the extension of the suffrage to the working classes, and, lastly, to crown the whole, the disestablishment

of the Church of England as the State religion in Ireland. . . . Members of the Club Canadien, Liberals of the province of Quebec, there are our models! There are our principles! There is our party!"

Could the Catholic Church of the province of Quebec, which had so often preached loyalty to the Crown, condemn Canadian liberals for following in the footsteps of the British?

★ ★ ★

It took years to reverse the Liberals' electoral misfortunes in Quebec. But once the wind turned, it blew in their backs for decades. In Quebec, beginning in 1887, the Liberal Party was in power for 80 of 127 years. It governs the province at the moment of this writing. It is by far the oldest political organization of the province. At the federal level, the Liberal Party of Canada has dominated the province's representation in the House of Commons, from Laurier's first victory in 1896 to 1957, and from 1962 to 1980. The party won a majority of seats in Quebec in the general election of 2015.

Canadians from other regions might not see it that way but Quebec is a deeply liberal society. When, in its final report published in 2008, the Bouchard-Taylor Commission rejected the hardline approach that many wished taken against accommodation requests by members of religious minorities, it based its recommendations on the fact that Quebec is a "liberal democracy." In fact, the word "liberal" appears some fifty times in the report.

Of course, Quebec's liberalism is not the one Laurier espoused. Like all liberal societies, the province evolved under the influence of the "new liberalism" that, from the early twentieth century onwards, understood the State to have a duty to help the disadvantaged. Quebec has gone a little further down that road than other regions in North America, with mixed results. Yet the province still has much more in common with Ontario and New Brunswick than it does with France or Sweden.

How profoundly liberal Quebecers are – perhaps unknowingly – is buried by the noise made by those who are less so. To come back to the issue of religious signs: under then Premier Pauline Marois, at the head of a minority government (2012–2014), the Parti Québécois proposed a "charter of values" that would have prohibited government employees from wearing religious symbols. The policy was responding to the noisily expressed wishes of many Québécois: "In Rome, do like the Romans do." The PQ leaders were certain that they had hit a political home run, all but guaranteeing a majority at the following election. Yet when voting day came, in April 2014, as they have done so often in the past, the majority of Quebecers quietly chose the moderate, tolerant, generous way of doing things. The liberal way.

Already in Laurier's time, that moderate temperament was becoming part of the French-Canadian character. Especially amongst members of the elites, French-Canadians admired the capacity of nineteenth-century British society to evolve without the violence and radical turns that shook the Continent. That is why when Laurier proclaimed that French, Italian, and German liberals were "revolutionaries," whereas the authentic liberals, "our models," were the English liberals, the crowd rose to its feet, forgetting, at least for that evening, whatever resentment they might have felt towards the victors of the battle fought 118 years ago, a few hundred metres from where the Music Hall now stood, on the Plains of Abraham.

Animosity and respect. How could a people feel such contradictory emotions towards a nation which, less than forty years before, had explicitly tried to assimilate it? Laurier knew why:

"In fact, we, French Canadians, are a conquered race. This is a melancholy truth to utter, but it is the truth. But, if we are a conquered race, we have also made a conquest: the conquest of liberty. We are a free people; we are a minority, but we have retained all our rights and all our privileges."

Like all minorities, French-Canadians had suffered unfair treatment and policies over the years. But thanks to the traditions and institutions that they extracted from the British, and that rubbed off on them, they began to see the possibility of thriving as a distinct society, enjoying a good quality of life, living peacefully within a greater ensemble.

Which is why, 140 years after the young MP from Drummond-Arthabaska brought tears to the eyes of his listeners with the closing part of his speech, a modern reader is moved by the same words: "Gentlemen, when, in that last battle, the old heroes, whom victory had so often accompanied, saw at last victory snatched from them. . . ."

And, suddenly, today's reader understands why this speech on political liberalism became famous. And why his "silver tongue" made Wilfrid Laurier one of Canada's greatest leaders.

André Pratte is a member of the Senate of Canada. He was a journalist for more than thirty-five years. His latest book is a biography of Wilfrid Laurier, published in 2011 by Penguin Canada as part of its Extraordinary Canadians series.

TRIBUTE TO EDWARD BLAKE

YOUNG MEN'S REFORM CLUB, MONTREAL, QUEBEC
MARCH 29, 1881[57]

There have been few occasions in my life on which I have felt so much genuine satisfaction as in sitting down at this table tonight. You have called upon me to reply to the toast of the House of Commons and I comply with the greatest pleasure, for it enables me to give expression to the sentiments with which my heart is overflowing.

The immense satisfaction I feel does not come from the fact that the City of Montreal, the city which our adversaries have been pleased to ever regard as their stronghold, has been the first to hail the new leader of the Liberal Party; nor does it arise even from the very legitimate emotion of the personal and political friend at the spectacle of this enthusiastic public expression of sympathy for the great ability and the not less eminent character of Mr. Blake.[58]

No, this intense satisfaction rather springs from the fact that this demonstration is the inspiration and work of our young men, that the youth of this country are the first to hail the new leader of the Liberal Party, and that that youth, true to the generous instincts of their years, thus proclaim their adhesion to the ideas of the Liberal Party on the very morrow of a session during which, in Parliament, those ideas were crushed by the weight of a compact majority.

You have proposed the health of the House of Commons. We are the party of reform and I drink to the reformation of the present House of Commons, in the hope that, when it passes though the crucible of another election, the signal note sounded here tonight by the young men of Montreal will find an echo and that, in the new House of Commons, Mr. Blake's policy will be triumphant.

This, however, is only a hope. Those present here this evening do not hesitate to believe that that policy is the policy of the future. But should it be victorious at the next elections or should it even not be victorious in our day is another question – a question which is only of secondary importance for us. We do not concern ourselves to know whether we shall gather the fruits of the seed we are now sowing or whether they shall be gathered by our success. For the moment, we only see one thing, that the cause which is dear to us all, the cause which we believe just and true, is, despite the transcendent ability and character of our chief, in a disastrous minority among the representatives of the people. Once more, this is not what concerns us. Be that cause strong or weak numerically, it is the cause of right and justice. The young men who hail Mr. Blake on the morrow of the session, do not look to what was the success of his efforts. Moreover, it is the nature of onerous souls, of youth especially, to not prize success, but rather the cause and we can proudly exclaim with the ancient poet:

Victrix causa diis placuit, sed vicla Catoni.[59]

Young men of the Montreal Liberal clubs, young English Canadians, young French Canadians, you all, the organizers of this demonstration, it would be, perhaps, misplaced on my part to offer you thanks. Still I cannot resist the pleasure of doing so. In this age of universal egotism, when even the young do not always escape the contagion, it is consoling to see that you at least have remained faithful to the enthusiasm and the disinterestedness which from time immemorial have been the glorious appanage of youth.

I am happy to note this fact, for, to my mind, the first duty of the Liberal Party is to regenerate the public sentiment of the country. Nothing could be more deplorable or more disastrous than the state of degradation into which politics have fallen. As I speak, there is in this province a great party in which each act done or word spoken is only done or spoken in view of the personal benefit of the doer or speaker. If they go beyond these walls, the views which I am now expressing will, perhaps, be furiously assailed and their truth angrily disputed; and my statements, perhaps, will be treated as a slander. I nevertheless reiterate what I have asserted and for their truth, I appeal not to you, gentlemen, but to our adversaries themselves; I make this appeal, not to what is uttered publicly, not to what is printed for the galleries, but what is fearlessly and frankly admitted in the secrecy of friendship, and there, Gentlemen, you know, for we have all heard it repeated ten, twenty, a hundred times, those who still regard political honour as something, those who still believe that patriotism is not a word without meaning, those whose hearts are touched and strongest emotions aroused by the word *country*, are treated as simpletons, the true policy, in the opinion of the strong, positive minds, who look down upon them for their guilelessness, being to always speak and act in view of the profit derivable from each word or act.

Gentlemen, I have no need to tell you that if in politics we only keep in view our individual interests, if each act, each word, has to be measured according to the benefits derivable therefrom, then we are not worthy to be a free people. Alas! if those who laid down their lives on the battlefield or this scaffold had shared the views of the contemporary school, had calculated their acts and their words according to the new rule, instead of dying as they died, they would have lived on the favours and largesse which the bureaucracy of their day would have been only too glad to shower upon them, and our people would still be a people of slaves.

Alas! The times are greatly changed, but is it necessary to repeat that there is no salvation for a country unless its citizens remain faithful to it and place the public over private interest. The party, which has governed us almost without interruption for twenty-five years, has forgotten these great truths. It has ruled by pandering to cupidity and by putting personal over general interests. Its appeals unhappily have found only too wide an echo. The policy of this province has been shaped not in view of the public interest, which should alone be the pole star of the true patriot, but in view of individual interests. And now, look at the result. We are on the brink of an abyss, the depth of which is unfathomable, and it is evident that, in a few years, the country will find itself face to face with a frightful financial situation.

What will be the upshot of this fatal state of things? We see the evil well enough, but where are we to look for the remedy? With a debt of many millions, a limited asset, an exhausted credit and not even the honour, which is the last resource of those who have none, what remains to us with which to confront the situation? I trust I may be mistaken in predicting that the province will probably have to pay with the loss of some of its constitutional liberties for the crime, with which I charge the party in power, of not having governed for the country, of not having alone consulted the public interest, and of having sacrificed the public cause to personal cupidity.

For our part, we, who claim to continue the work of the men who conquered the constitutional liberties which we today enjoy, we, who claim to be following the path traced out by those grand figures who still shine out in our history, by those who loved their country to the extent of dying for it; we only seek, like them, in the share we take in public affairs the greatest possible sum of good for the country.

What we have to contend against at present is this dissolving tendency to only consider personal interest, which leads to venality, to the debasement of consciences, to all those infamies of the recent past and to all the dangers which are looming up in the near future. Once more, I say that, if the public cause is not worth the greatest efforts of which we are capable, we are not worthy of being a free people.

The Liberal Party has nothing to hold out to those who march in its ranks. We are in the minority, and we have no favours, honours, lucrative places or high-sounding titles to distribute. We cherish a legitimate ambition to triumph and to see Mr. Blake at the head of this country, but, if we hope for its gratification, it is not for the individual profit which each of us may derive from the circumstance, but for the good of the country at large.

I do not pretend to be indifferent to the possession of power. Under our system of government, the possession of power and its accompanying advantages are the legitimate reward of the victorious; but the first and the principal object is to struggle for what we believe to be just and true, whatever may be the upshot of our efforts.

The heroism of those who died on the battlefield simply for the honour of their country is remembered with emotion. The last charge made at Reischoffen by [Marshal Patrice de] MacMahon's cuirassiers, riding to their certain and, so to say, useless death, is recalled with emotion, because it was a last sacrifice to the fortunes of France.[60] Well, if the soldier gives up his life for his country, is it too much to expect the citizen to sacrifice a few material advantages for the sake of fidelity to what he believes to be his country's cause?

As for us, once more I repeat that our leaders have nothing to offer individually and we look for nothing from them. Our adversaries may not know it, but we know what the noble pride of being honourable in our own eyes is worth, and we also know the worth of the proud pleasure of owing nothing except to ourselves, of expecting nothing except from ourselves, and of being patriots in deed as well as in name.

By Scott Reid

Plus ça change.

Setting aside nineteenth-century formalities, this brief address from a young Wilfrid Laurier reminds us that superior political oratory has always rested on the exploration of timeless themes. In fact, much of what is said here could be ripped from the front pages of today's newspapers. Unapologetically partisan, Laurier leverages the occasion to tear into the government-of-the-day for its fiscal recklessness while lamenting the, "state of degradation into which politics have fallen." Toss in a hashtag and this text could slip effort-lessly into contemporary political discourse. Nevertheless in these few words, there are historical hints of the remarkable leader who would go on to complete Macdonald's task of Confederation and singlehandedly create the modern Liberal Party of Canada.

Laurier's appeal to party youth (all young gentlemen, of course, this being long before the political talents of women were thought worthy of harnessing) also echoes with particular familiarity to anyone who has ever attended a modern campus rally. The future prime minister flatters his audi-ence, as leaders today might also, by suggesting that their energy and unblem-ished motives hold the power to "regenerate the public sentiment of the country." It falls an inch short of proclaiming "you are this nation's future." But only an inch.

It is especially illuminating to place these remarks in the context of their times and their speaker. In 1881, the Liberal Party was a devastated mess, one year away from suffering its second of four consecutive majority defeats. Laurier, not quite yet forty years old, was regarded by his Opposition peers as talented, but insufficiently diligent. A full fifteen years before he would emerge as a prime minister of ferocious and lasting importance, the young

Laurier was seen as something of a dilettante. An able speaker. An adequate mind. An acceptable parliamentarian. But a man whose promise would likely go unfulfilled.

Hints of future success can be detected, however, in the words that Laurier assembles for this audience. With obvious skill, he excites the crowd and displays a style that we now unmistakably identify as his and his alone. When he concludes that "we know what the noble pride of being honourable in our own eyes is worth," Laurier has hit full stride. It is a seize-the-high-ground put-down that shrewdly exploits the deficiencies of his opponents. Over the course of his career, the wily master would utilize this trick of oratory often, employing his "sunny ways" to gather together the country while simultaneously forcing his political foes to the ineffective margins.

More than 130 years later, what Laurier had to say that March evening in Montreal not only holds up, it resonates with currency. In its subject matter, its shape, and its speaker, this isn't just a speech. It's a sign of things to come. For Laurier. And for Canadian politics.

Scott Reid is a CTV political analyst and principal at the strategic communications and speechwriting firm Feschuk.Reid. From 2003 to 2006 he served as director of communications to former prime minister Paul Martin.

A LECTURE ON
PARLIAMENTARY LIFE

IN THE ROOMS OF *LA PATRIE*, MONTREAL, QUEBEC
MAY 19, 1884[61]

. . . . For the present, I propose to go outside of politics, though I may, perhaps, fail to keep very far away from them.

I propose to speak to you of parliamentary life, not of public life, for the latter is already well enough known. During the three months of the session, which is its usual duration, what is said and what is done are published daily, commented upon, criticized, approved, blamed, by all the voices of modern publicity. I could say nothing on this subject which is not already well known by everybody. But there is another aspect to the session: the inner or domestic aspect, which the press disdains to notice, which can only be observed on the spot and which is also not without instruction. It is this aspect to which I desire to call your attention.

It may, perhaps, not be misplaced, at the start, to say a word relative to the capital. The subject is a delicate one; I would not wish to say anything disparaging of the capital, but it is hard to say anything good of it. Ottawa is not a handsome city and does not appear destined to become one either. There is, however, in it one point of great beauty, the site of the Parliament Buildings, on a cliff rising up from the bed of the river, not far from the falls which have been rendered famous by the accounts of every traveller since Champlain. This is Ottawa's only natural beauty. Behind the cliff, the land sinks into a monotonous plain, with a flat horizon unbroken by a single line.

The Parliament Buildings are in the Gothic style, and, in the opinion of connoisseurs, entitled to rank with the best architecture of Europe. They certainly have an admirable effect either when they break upon the sight bathed in the brilliant light of the summer sun or when seen on a dark winter's night illuminated from within by the floods of light, which shine in capricious arabesques through their many ogival windows.

But despite their unquestionable beauty, these buildings are badly adapted to the purpose for which they were intended. The Gothic style, always admirable in outward effect, renders the interior dark and cold, and it may be said that this style was badly suited to the kind of buildings in which air and light should circulate as freely as possible. As Mr. Mackenzie[62] said one day, these buildings were splendidly adapted for a monastery, but never for a legislative assembly.

However, therein once a year meet the Senate and Commons of Canada. The opening of Parliament is always a great event for Ottawa. It invariably excites the whole population, but they by no means monopolize the excitement, as the city is always crowded on such occasions with strangers from all parts of the country.

The official ceremonies are announced to take place at three in the afternoon. But, from eleven in the forenoon, the crowd begins to gather on the grounds and by three o'clock the latter are completely filled. In 1879, as early as ten o'clock in the morning, the doors of the Senate Chamber were besieged by a crowd anxious to get a good view of the Princess Louise.[63]

Moreover, these opening ceremonies are not lacking in grandeur and are certainly curious to behold. These old customs and antique solemnities, transplanted from another world to our modern and democratic midst, and connecting the middle ages with our contemporary epoch, open up all the pages of history from the day on which William the Conqueror landed on the shores of England down to the day on which a royal princess, descended from the blood of William, comes to take her place in these old ceremonies, which were carried by the Conqueror from Normandy into England and imported from England to this continent, in the midst of a population a large portion of whom have themselves been detached from the land which was the cradle of William the Conqueror.

It is to the Senate Chamber goes the Governor. This chamber is very fine and of the same size and architecture as that of the Commons, but the draperies and furniture are in excellent taste and give it a stamp which is altogether missed from the Commons chamber. On this occasion, however, the Senate Chamber is resplendent. Ladies are admitted to the floor and appear in full dress; the judges of the Supreme Court are present in their scarlet robes bordered with ermine; and the Cabinet Ministers attend in their gold-laced uniforms. I do not admit, however, that all this scarlet and gold lace is to my taste. I would prefer to see the judges in the ordinary silk robes, which are plain, it is true, but not wanting in dignity, and, as for the gold-laced uniforms, they may be suited to Westminster, but, in this democratic country, the simple black coat unquestionably appears better.

I have already said that the ceremony is fixed for three o'clock, and, between the official hour and the practical hour, the old Senators attempt to indulge in innocent flirtations with their fair guests. At last, the Governor has arrived amid the usual enthusiastic cheering and taken his seat on the Throne. He desires the presence of his faithful Commons.

And, during this time, what are the faithful Commons doing? Having nothing to do, they have endeavoured to be as noisy as possible.

Nothing resembles a school more than Parliament. Nothing is more like the reopening of the classes than the opening of Parliament. Despite the ten months of confinement to follow, the day of reopening of the classes is always a gay one, and the same may be said of the day of the opening of the session. The pleasure of meeting each other again, the almost ceaseless handshaking, the exchange of more or less spicy jokes, all are to be found in Parliament just the same as in school, on opening day.

But, hark! to the three knocks at the chamber door. The Sergeant-at-Arms goes to see what's the trouble, just as if he was not quite well aware beforehand. He returns grave and solemn to announce to the Speaker that a messenger from the Senate is waiting at the door, and with no less gravity and solemnity the Speaker answers: "Let the messenger enter!"

The messenger enters. It is the Usher of the Black Rod, the chief officer of the Senate, who comes to announce that the Governor General desires the presence of the Commons in the Senate Chamber. Before opening his mouth, he advances nine steps, making three bows as he proceeds, and, having delivered his message, he backs out, repeating the same number of steps and of bows, wheels on his heels and disappears, invariably accompanied by a formidable clapping of hands from all parts of the chamber. John Bull seems to take a perennial pleasure in seeing these bows made by a man paid to make them, and the same remark is repeated every year: "Well, it is worth the money!"

Then, like so many unruly boys, the Members run in a troop to the Senate Chamber. Their least anxiety, however, is to listen to His Excellency's speech. They leave that duty to the Speaker, who discharges it most religiously.

I have used the term Speaker in alluding to the president or chairman of the House of Commons. I am not ignorant of the long controversy, which took place in the press over the rendering into

French of the English word "Speaker," but it is not my intention to mix myself up with it, as I have no desire to add another to the list of snarling critics to whom the country has given birth. It is simply wonderful how many literary critics we have, when we have so little literature.

But, in spite of all the snarling critics, I persist in translating the word "Speaker" by the French word "Orateur"; to translate the word "Speaker" by the word "President" reminds me of the time when I was a student here and when it was said that an eminent lawyer, who came across the word "by-and-by" in a letter, vehemently maintained that it meant "tomorrow."

The reason assigned for translating the word "Speaker" by the word "President" is that it would be a counter-sense to call him the Speaker, since he takes no part in the debates and since his functions consist in presiding over the chamber. But those who take this ground do not reflect that, if it was a counter-sense in French to say *Orateur*, it would also be a counter-sense in English to say "Speaker." In the English language, there is an absolute equivalent for our word *President*; it is the word "president" and, if they do not use it to designate the person presiding over the House of Commons, there must be a reason for it.

I have noticed that those affected puritans who persist in calling the Speaker president usually belong to the school which makes a great display of its principles and systematically curses modern France. I naturally conclude that they must at least have read the good authors of the age of Louis XIV. They are well aware that, on every page, there is an allusion to the sovereign of what was then the Duchy of Bavaria, and who nevertheless is never styled the "Duke," but the "Elector" of Bavaria.

Would it not be also a counter-sense, in the eyes of our critics, to designate the sovereign of this duchy as an elector? But the reason for it is that the sovereign of the Duchy of Bavaria was at the same time an elector of the Holy Empire and that this quality took precedence over the other. Under the old organization of the Empire, there was in Germany a crowd of small principalities, whose rulers, like the Duke of Bavaria, had the title of Elector as their principal title.

This title of Elector formerly carried great weight in Germany, and even yet the word has an imposing sound in German ears, if we are to credit the capital joke which Henry Labouchère[64] lately played on them and which those worthy Germans seem to have unhesitatingly swallowed. Arriving in one of the German towns, the name of which I cannot now recall, the editor of *Truth* boldly entered himself in the hotel register as Henry Labouchère, Elector of Middlesex.

I cannot say whether it was from force of historical reminiscence or from extravagant admiration for the parliamentary system which Bismarck[65] never doles out except with a niggardly hand to the subjects of King William, but it is certain that the title of Elector won for Mr. Labouchère a host of little attentions, which the German innkeepers are not in the habit of wasting upon travellers.

If the English give the title of Speaker to the President of their legislative assemblies, there is also a good reason for it, namely, that the President of the House is at the same time the interpreter with the Sovereign of the body over which he presides. He speaks for the Members. He is their Speaker.

Thus, suppose that general elections have taken place. The House of Commons has no Speaker as yet. The Members proceed to the Senate Chamber to hear the opening Speech from the Throne; but His Excellency causes it to be intimated to them that he does not deem it advisable to make known the causes for which he has summoned Parliament until the Commons have elected a Speaker.

Summoned again on the following day to the Senate Chamber, the Members troop back to it pretty much in the same disorderly fashion as on the previous day. The newly elected Speaker alone wears an air of gravity, because he has a speech to make and nothing conduces so much to seriousness as to make a speech in those vast halls, and whose severe architecture chills one to the marrow. It is now that we get the opportunity to understand why the English, who are noted for their practical good sense, apply the name of Speaker to the president of the House of Commons. He is, in fact, the speaker of those who have elected him. In their name he addresses the Sovereign and his speech is both respectful and dignified. Here it is:

"May it please Your Excellency: The House of Commons have elected me as their Speaker, though I am but little able to perform the important duties thus assigned to me. If, in the performance of those duties, I should at any time fall into error, I pray that the fault may be imputed to me and not to the Commons, whose servant I am, and who, through me, the better to enable them to discharge their duty to their Queen and country, humbly claim all their undoubted rights and privileges; especially that they may have freedom of speech in their debates, access to Your Excellency's person at all reasonable times, and that their proceedings may receive from Your Excellency their most favourable interpretation."

At the prorogation of the House, the Speaker again addresses the representative of the Sovereign, in presenting the Supply Bill, and the following is the language which he uses on that occasion:

"May it please Your Excellency: The Commons of Canada have voted the supplies required to enable the Government to defray the expenses of the public service. In the name of the Commons, I present to Your Excellency a bill entitled 'An act to grant to Her Majesty certain sums of money to defray certain expenses of the public service during the fiscal year commencing on the _____ and to which I ask Your Excellency's assent.'"

The reply is in these terms: "In Her Majesty's name, His

Excellency the Governor General thanks her loyal subjects, accepts their benevolence and assents to this bill."

All these old ceremonies may seem absurd; but in reality they are not. The most of them have a deep meaning and possess historical value, recalling as they do a triumph over absolutism and the progression towards that complete liberty now involved in our parliamentary system. Thus, when the Speaker of the Commons presents the Supply Bill to the Sovereign, he recalls the fundamental principle of the people's right to govern themselves and to permit none other to tax them but themselves.

It may be urged, perhaps, that these old ceremonies are only the expression of principles which are not questioned by anyone at present and that the time has arrived to adopt simpler methods of parliamentary procedure and more in keeping with the modern spirit. I am not too sure of this. I am Liberal in principle, but Conservative in sentiment. I confess to this weakness. I cherish a respect for these old solemnities, which are not harmful in themselves and which have only the demerit of having outlived their time.

Nevertheless, my words only apply to the Federal Parliament. I have already said that, at Ottawa, these ceremonies are not without a certain grandeur. The Legislature there is numerous enough and the pomp rich enough to impart to them a certain splendour. But, at Quebec, the same ceremonies have always seemed to me very grotesque. Moreover, the legislative body of twenty-four Members, which is supposed to there represent the House of Lords, the house at Spencer Wood,[66] which is supposed to represent the royal castle of Windsor, and all those attempts of Local Government to ape royalty, appear to me very comical, to say the least.

I am certainly far from wishing to belittle our local legislatures. Quite the contrary. The attributes of the local legislatures are of the highest importance. But at the same time their resources are small and their revenues very limited, and, from this standpoint, it seems that the local legislatures should glory rather in plebeian simplicity. To imitate royalty at Ottawa is in keeping with the fitness of things; to ape it at Quebec is absurd.

Setting aside all political preferences and leaving out Mr. Letellier's grand figure, I hold that, of all our lieutenant-governors, Sir Narcisse Belleau was the one who came nearest to perfection.[67] During the five years in which he was called to discharge the functions of chief magistrate of the province, Sir Narcisse Belleau never sought either to pose as a king or to dazzle the ninnies. He would never consent to reside at Spencer Wood. He said, perhaps, rightly, that Spencer Wood was too expensive for the means of a private citizen and he disdained to throw the cost of its maintenance on the State. He lived on St. Louis Street like a worthy bourgeois of the good city of Quebec. In the morning he made a tour of the markets; in the evening, he went to breathe the fresh air on the Terrace. Like the king of Yvetot,[68] rising late and lying down early, he lived very well without glory.

These democratic ways remind one of the governors of the New England States who spend the forenoon at the Government house despatching the public business and the afternoon at their own offices attending to their own affairs.

Sir Narcisse committed only one mistake during his administrative career and that was in going to open the session in a hat decorated with cock's feathers, and a gold-laced coat, between two files of policemen stationed at least thirty feet from each other and supposed to represent a hedge for the protection of his person. In my opinion, he would have been perfect, if on opening days he had had the courage to button up his overcoat, take his cane in his hand, and walk to the Buildings to read to the two Houses the lesson which in parliamentary language is styled the Speech from the Throne.

But I am straying pretty far from my subject. I return to it.

The Governor has opened the session by a speech to the two Houses, and they reply by an address, so that there is an exchange of courtesies. Before the address is presented to the Sovereign it must be adopted by each of the two Houses. In the House of Commons the task of proposing and seconding the address is usually entrusted to the youngest Members. I have just used the word "second." Here again is a word which grates on the nerves of a certain class of critics. They want us to say *"appuyer"* (support). I call their attention to the fact that the English verb "to second" comes from the French verb *"seconder"* and that there assuredly cannot be a better translation than the etymological meaning of the word to be translated. I would ask them to also note that all those expressions: address, seconded, Speech from the Throne, motion, found their way into the parliamentary language of England at a time when the official language of England was the French language and that later when the Saxon race had absorbed the conquerors and that English once more became the language of the nation, all these expressions were literally translated from French into English.

By a strange fortune, while these expressions have lost in France their technical meaning owing to the disappearance of the institutions to which they were adapted, the descendants of France on this continent are destined to restore them to the language. In fact, is it not a labour of love to revive these old expressions as they were conveyed from France to England by the Normans?

The moving and seconding of the address is an honour alike desired and feared. Indeed, there are few more ungrateful tasks. The speaker has to comment on the Speech from the Throne, which is his text, so to say, and it would be difficult to find one more dry or barren — it being one of the usages of Parliament to place in His Excellency's mouth a tissue of commonplaces dressed up in the dullest style imaginable. His Excellency is happy to meet again the Members of the Senate and the Commons; he thanks Providence for the bountiful harvest with which the country has been blessed; the Ministerial policy is yielding satisfactory results; bills will be submitted for this or that purpose; the public accounts will be laid before the Commons, and lastly His Excellency invokes the blessings of Heaven on the labours of his Parliament. The drafting of this masterpiece is always a subject of joking at the Council board, and when the Premier lays before his colleagues the draft he has elaborated, they are always in humorous vein and it is a contest between them to see who will make the most laughable remark.

The unlucky young man, to whom this outline is handed, does not feel quite so much pleasure and despairingly asks himself what he can find to say on such a subject. He can, however, always count upon an indulgent audience. The old Parliamentarians naturally look for some rambling on his part and some soaring from the earth into the clouds, and smile a little in advance at these ambitious flights; but, if the substance of his remarks be sensible and if he eschew the pompous and the trivial, he wins a legitimate success and is sincerely applauded.

Is it now the turn of the Opposition leader to speak – his task being to review the Government's policy as set forth in the Speech from the Throne. He invariably begins by complimenting the movers of the address. This is sometimes difficult, as the movers are not always successful. I have always, however, admired this delicate portion of the Opposition leader's speech, whether the speaker was Sir John, Mr. Mackenzie or Mr. Blake, each of them seeming to know how to award delicate praise without falling into improper flattery.

On ordinary occasions, the Opposition leader's tone is one of banter. He does not give battle, but merely contents himself with harassing the enemy and affecting to be a good fellow; he lays bare the Government's weak points, but does so without bitterness, seeming to say to the majority: Look at the Government you are supporting; see it as it is and make the most of it; there is plenty [of] room to do so. His own supporters are jubilant; they laugh and applaud and every fresh shaft tickles and cheers them. On the other hand, the Ministerialists begin by smiling, but end by thinking that they are getting too much of that sort of thing.

At last, the Premier's turn comes and he replies in the same tone. The laughter and fun are now on the Ministerial side. Still, on both sides, the weapons on that day are blunt, unless, indeed, the Opposition leader deems the occasion opportune to offer an amendment.

In that case, the voices become sharp and the weapons are cutting. At Ottawa, since Confederation, there has been only one amendment proposed to the address and that was by Mr. Mackenzie in 1873 relative to the Pacific scandal, when the fall of the Government ensued.[69]

I have just referred to the manner in which the leaders of the two parties are greeted. Among the many qualities which render them so apt in parliamentary government, the English possess one of rare merit for the application of that form of government. They know how to listen and to be tolerant. It is not in the ardent temperament of the French to respect the convictions of others. What the Frenchman conceives, he conceives with so much intensity that he cannot admit the possibility of others thinking differently from him.

This is not the case with the Englishman. He has his own convictions, but he is neither astonished nor irritated because you differ from him. On the contrary, he is prepared for this eventuality and expects that the diversity of opinions will be as great as the diversity of intellects and of faces. He would cordially despise you if he thought you had no opinions of your own. In fact, while the Frenchman wants you to have his opinions, the Englishman wants you to have opinions of your own.

See what happens in the legislative body in Paris! There is an orator in the tribune! His adversaries cannot keep quiet. From all points of the Chamber arise interruptions and protests and frequently the confusion becomes so great that the President cannot control it.

Look on the other hand at our House of Commons! It supports the most furious attacks without wincing and no one dreams of interrupting, unless the orator permits interruption. Nevertheless, the attack is keen, violent and often bitter. The orator's friends applaud; his adversaries do not budge; when they believe that the attack is fair warfare and that, from his standpoint, he is right, they endure without wincing; but if he exaggerates they emphasize the exaggeration by ironical applause. If he falls into misstatement, the faces relax as there is nothing to fear, and if, lastly, he grows paradoxical, he receives every latitude and the House listens with the feeling which the English characterize as "amused wonderment."

This is what happens at Ottawa, where the House is in great part English, but also in part French. Still even in the House of Commons, we French Canadians do not know how to bear contradiction like our fellow citizens of British origin.

But, after all, we are in this respect superior to our cousins across the sea. We can listen to an adversary and sit still, but we cannot listen to him with complete coolness. We can occasionally, but rarely, acknowledge his talents; but we can never render justice to his thesis. According as he speaks in favour or against our opinion, his utterances are absurd or sublime.

The English are more sober in expression. When we have heard one of Mr. Blake's speeches, we give vent to our enthusiasm in metaphors; but the great orator's warmest admirers among his own countrymen content themselves with saying: "that was a great speech of Blake's."

On the other hand, if an adversary has made a successful hit, instead of saying that his statements were absurd, they simply say: "that was well put from his standpoint."

If the French were gifted with this frankness of expression and tolerance of opinion, the courtesy of their discussions would be marked. It is not so with the English. Their discussions are never vulgar, but on the other hand they are never gracious and always lack that urbanity which respects your feelings as your life.

The Englishman respects your opinions; but he never thinks of your feelings. The capital point on which we differ from our fellow citizens of British origin is our idea of politics. For us, sons of France, political sentiment is a passion; while, for the Englishmen, politics are a question of business.

The only thought of the English Members in going to Ottawa is that they are called there to discuss and decide the affairs of the country, just as the shareholders of a bank are called to discuss and decide the affairs of the bank. I say the affairs of the country, and I purposely use this unusual expression in our language. When I say the affairs, I use the word in its restricted sense, as the equivalent of the word "business."

According to the English notion, the affairs of the country, like those of a private individual, comprise the revenue, expenditure and all the cognate questions; and it is needless to remind my hearers that these questions of revenue and expenditure fill the largest place in our Federal politics.

We of French origin understand politics quite otherwise. Tariff and revenue questions are not our chief preoccupation. We rather incline towards the speculative and have a fondness for theories.

Now look at the different results in the case of the two races! Take an ordinary man in any rank whatever of English society! He knows the figure of the public expenditure, and of the receipts; he can tell you the yield of the customs and excise, and he is conversant with every item of the tariff.

Now, how many are there among us, even among those who shout loudest at election time, who have taken the slightest trouble to post themselves on these heads? We know, however, that they are thoroughly acquainted with all the discussions on the school question, on the relative value of the different forms of government, on the theories of divine right, on the union of Church and State, and on a host of other abstract questions, which have no application to our politics and which have never been discussed in any of our legislative assemblies.

The House of Commons is, above all, a meeting of business men and business questions are there treated. At least three fourths of the proceedings are carried on by means of conversations exchanged across the floor of the House, without preparation, and without effort of eloquence. The strangers, who come to the capital to hear the debates, are usually disappointed. They expect to hear great eloquence; they simply hear business discussions.

Nevertheless, some of these discussions are really eloquent. For instance, a Ministerial question of great importance is to be treated. Sir Charles Tupper is to explain the Government's policy.[70] He will be followed by Mr. Blake and the fight will then become general. Unconsciously, the House takes on a particular physiognomy. Every Member is at his post. There is not a vacant seat. The galleries are full and, on every face, sits a look of expectation.

The debate is opened by two master speeches, as diametrically different from each other as are the orators themselves and yet visibly of the same school and of a unique style of eloquence. This style of eloquence is what we term English parliamentary eloquence.

What we, of French race and education, appreciate and enjoy the most is that nervous, magnetic eloquence which stirs the soul and brings a choking sensation to the throat and water to the eyes, or, again that academic eloquence, pure in language and elegant in diction, which fills the ear with a music that tends more to charm than to convince. French eloquence is above all aesthetic. English eloquence is above all practical.

The great aim of the English orator is to go straight to the point. He has a proposition to uphold and he piles up arguments, figures, comparisons, quotations, everything, in fine, that is calculated to bolster it up. He does not seek to please, but if he succeeds in dazzling your reason, in inundating it with a flood of light, and rendering luminous what was obscure, he has won the success he coveted. This eloquence is not soul-stirring and possesses none of those oratorical movements which strike the hearer like an electric shock; but when an orator like Mr. Blake carries you on with him into the intellectual realms, lifts you to inaccessible heights, and unfolds to your eyes new horizons, which are immediately replaced by others still higher, emotion slowly, gradually creeps upon you, takes possession of you and finally subjugates you altogether.

My hearers may, perhaps, be curious to learn something of the leading orators of the House. I have just mentioned the name of Mr. Blake. The Leader of the Opposition is beyond question the foremost orator of the House. His eloquence borrows nothing from the ordinary means of the orator; it emanates entirely from a single source: intellectual force. Mr. Blake has without doubt one of the most extraordinary mental organizations that are to be found at present in the world. His powerful intelligence takes in everything. His grasp covers the whole as well as the details. All the outlines of the vastest political problem are perfectly clear to him; not one of the microscopic points of the most difficult legal problem escapes him. When he treats a subject, he exhausts it; when he leaves it, there is nothing more to be said or even to reply, and when at length he resumes his seat, his partisans are jubilant and even his adversaries cannot help expressing their admiration.

Sir John Macdonald's style is quite different. Singular to say, in the case of so alert a mind, he lacks happiness and movement of expression. He hesitates, stammers and repeats himself; he is incorrect, but, in all his speeches, there is always a nail that goes straight home. He excels in seizing upon an adversary's weak point. His highest art, however, consists in saying exactly what should be said to produce the most effect on his own supporters. He knows all their weaknesses and their prejudices and all he says is perfectly adapted to them.

Sir Charles Tupper's chief characteristics are force and, above all, audacity. He is the Danton of the House.[71] He speaks with all the abundance, vehemence and rush of the torrent. The more desperate is the cause he has to defend, the greater is his audacity. He asserts the most untenable propositions with coolness and an imperturbability which no question, no interruption, can discountenance. Far from that, if an interruption to the point demolishes on the spot an over risky assertion, instead of beating a retreat even to the extent of a hair's breadth, he invariably exclaims: "I am thankful for the interruption, as it proves exactly what I have just said." And then he goes on to repeat all he has already said, with redoubled energy, argument and vigour.

Mr. Mackenzie's voice is, unhappily, no longer heard.[72] This is an immense loss for the country and an irreparable one for the Liberal Party. Mr. Mackenzie had all the force of Sir Charles Tupper, without his fire; but, for that reason, his eloquence was, perhaps, not less effective. In all his words, there was a concentrated power which went to the very marrow. Let us pray that this valiant mind, this blameless character, may soon be restored to health and resume the leading position which he has filled and which belongs to him of right in his country's legislature. There is no man less known than Mr. Mackenzie and there has been none more slandered. While in power he was systematically represented as a fanatic and as a man with narrow and intolerant views. Nothing could be false. Mr. Mackenzie is a Liberal with the greatest breadth of ideas. I believe that, while he was Premier, he was somewhat embittered by the systematically unfair attacks of which he was the victim and by his superhuman and self-imposed labours, but I can state from a personal knowledge extending over a number of years that there are few men easier and more agreeable to deal or associate with. The savage man, as he was represented to the public, is on the contrary full of humour and always has a laughing word on his lips.

Like Mr. Mackenzie, Sir Richard Cartwright[73] is a man whom the tongue of slander has represented under false colours. In private life, Sir Richard is one of the most accomplished gentlemen it is possible to meet, affable, polite and distinguished by a regular Attic grace. As may be imagined, however, his adversaries do not like him. His tongue is the most formidable in the whole House. On the other hand his eloquence is, perhaps, the most classic. His language is always correct, precise, clear, and eloquent, but at the same time biting and cutting. I said a moment ago that the English know how to listen without wincing, but it is nevertheless not rare to see the British phlegm unable to resist Sir Richard Cartwright's attacks and I have often seen his adversaries writhing with anger under his elegant lash.

Is it not generally known that Sir Richard Cartwright is a lettered man. Indeed, he is not only a lettered man, but a literary dilettante. During the long sittings of the House, when the debate does not interest Sir Richard, a messenger brings him a select volume from the library, and then, with his hat down over his eyes, he becomes absorbed in its perusal and as indifferent to what is going on around him as if he was in his own study.

Mr. Blake is also a lettered man; in fact, he may be said to be even a glutton in the matter of literature. Notwithstanding the Herculean work he undertakes during the session, he keeps himself regularly posted in current literature and reads everything that is published. Said one of the officials of the library to me last session: "Mr. Blake is an omnivorous reader; we lend him everything that comes in." "Tell me," I said to him, "where does he find the time to read?" "It is a mystery, Sir, but he reads everything."

What I have thus far stated has shown you that, although there are about fifty French members in the House of Commons, it is exclusively an English assembly. French is its official language as well as English, but French is being less and less spoken in it. The reason for this is that it is impossible to take an effective part in the debates unless you use the language of the majority. This fact was only lately thrown up to me by a man of great talent, great sense and ardent patriotism, but I do not admit the reproach. Things must be taken as they are.

Our parliamentary laws, usages, and customs come to us from England. Moreover, the English are better adapted than we are for that system of government. In no matter what deliberative assembly they may find themselves, they are more at home than are the French, and, where they are in the majority, their language must necessarily prevail.

On the other hand we, of French origin, are essentially an artistic people, and if I had an advice to give to my fellow country-men, it would be to remain true to their origin and to cultivate that taste for the arts and letters which we inherit from France and in which we ought to take on this continent the place filled by France in Europe.

The force of circumstances is such that in America the English tongue will always be the language of the million and our ambition should be to make French, here as elsewhere, the language of pre-dilection, good company and polite society.

By the Right Honourable John N. Turner

In reading Laurier's lecture on parliamentary life it is important to recall that he had only been a Member of Parliament for a decade when it was delivered. The young Quebec MP who gave this impressive lecture still had almost thirty-five years of service in the Commons ahead of him.

Laurier was one of Canada's greatest parliamentarians, perhaps the greatest in our history. And in saying that, one must keep in mind some of the parliamentary giants of both parties of the day, with whom he served.

Along with the atmosphere of the nineteenth-century House, Laurier's address also brings to life parliamentary legends from history, such as Sir John A. Macdonald, Edward Blake, Sir Richard Cartwright, Sir Charles Tupper, and others. Had this address been delivered towards the end of his long life of public and parliamentary service, I am confident that names like Arthur Meighen's would have been added to this list.

During my own service in the House of Commons, where it was my very great privilege to represent ridings in Quebec, Ontario, and British Columbia, I too bore witness to towering parliamentarians who had mastered the ways of the Commons. As a young MP, first elected in 1962, I watched John Diefenbaker on his feet, first as prime minister and later as leader of the Opposition. He was a masterful parliamentary performer and to see him up against fellow masters of the House like Paul Martin Sr., Tommy Douglas, Réal Caouette, or Allan J. MacEachen, are memories I cherish still.

Laurier's address, with his non-partisan tributes to men who opposed him, also reminds me of a different time in politics, a better time. While the issues in my day could be just as divisive and passions as easily enflamed as they are today, MPs carried within themselves a fundamental respect for their opponents. While one might disagree strongly with a fellow MP's viewpoints, you respected him or her, as they, too, had been sent to the House to do the people's business. Today, I note sadly, partisanship often clouds House debates, and cross-party respect among MPs for all viewpoints is a thing of the past.

Finally, this address by Laurier, and so many others collected by Arthur in this fine volume, remind us that Parliament truly mattered in days gone by. Party discipline was not as strong, and the role of the MP – in caucus, committee, and in the House itself – was much more important than it is today. In allowing MPs to be diminished as we have, we diminish Parliament and, by doing so, Canada itself.

John Napier Turner was Canada's seventeenth prime minister.

PART II:

PARTY LEADER

1887–1896

As this section opens, Canada's Liberals have again been defeated by Sir John A. Macdonald and his Tories. From the ashes of the Pacific Scandal and five years in the wilderness while Alexander Mackenzie (who had brought Laurier into his cabinet) governed, Macdonald has by now vanquished Mackenzie and his successor, Edward Blake. The latter leader falls twice to Macdonald, in 1882 and 1887.

Laurier, supposedly with great reluctance, accepts the invitation from caucus to replace Blake. In the run-up to his section, he has again electrified friend and foe with his speeches attacking Macdonald and his government's handling of Louis Riel and the Métis, this time in Saskatchewan. Laurier has even ventured into English Canadian cities such as Toronto – where Orange feelings run high – and bravely taken up Riel's cause again.

So we catch up with the leader of the Opposition at a massive party picnic at Somerset, Quebec, where thousands have gathered with special trains bringing many to the event from afar. Quebec's premier attends, as do other leading Liberals from across the province. It is a resoundingly successful debut for the rookie party leader.

We then follow Laurier as he begins his climb to power. In Quebec City, he makes powerful appeals for unity and cultural understanding. In Ottawa, he eulogizes his fallen foe, Sir John A. Macdonald, after the grand old man of Canadian politics and history, his body worn and tired after fifty years on the campaign trail, gives out on June 6, 1891.

We also join Laurier as he builds, renews, and grows his party. In 1893 he calls the first-ever convention of a political party and rallies the rank and file and leadership equally. He also lays out policy positions on issues such as tariffs and taxation in addresses delivered in outlying communities such as Pembroke, Ontario. And he takes his first trip to the Canadian West, a part of Canada already crucial to his reputation because of his responses to Riel. It is also an area of Canada that Laurier will, as prime minister, play a crucial role in developing and fostering.

Lastly, we see a mature and wily politician develop. While Macdonald's successors implode over racial and cultural divides brought to the forefront nationally by the Manitoba Schools Crisis, we travel with Laurier to Morrisburg, Ontario. There he promises Canadians a "sunny way" approach – though no one really knows what that means – to solving the crisis and restoring racial peace in the land.

The section ends with the hapless Conservatives still floundering over the issue in front of Laurier in the House, and Laurier promising that the sunny way will bridge the crisis.

A few months after his Commons address, Laurier is Canada's seventh prime minister.

THE NEW PARTY LEADER

PICNIC AT SOMERSET, QUEBEC

AUGUST 2, 1887[74]

. . . . My friends, you all congratulate me upon my selection to henceforward guide the destinies of the Liberal Party of Canada. You congratulate me, gentlemen, on this circumstance, but I deplore it and you also, I am sure, deplore the sad event which has deprived the Liberal Party of the leadership of a man like the Honourable Edward Blake. The loss of Mr. Blake, Gentlemen, is an irreparable loss to the party which he directed with so much wisdom, grandeur and brilliancy, irreparable to the party which followed him with so much devotion and affection, and irreparable to the country to whose interests he gave his intelligence, his health and his time and which, I must say, repaid the sacrifice so badly.

You congratulate me, Gentlemen. I must, however, acknowledge that it was with the greatest repugnance that I accepted the position which was offered to me by my friends in the House of Commons. As heaven is my witness, Gentlemen, I never sought or coveted that position; my friends, deeming me worthy of it, gave it to me; but, for my part, I never desired it, not feeling in myself the qualifications for it; I would have much preferred to continue in the role which I had until then filled, that of a free-lance of the Liberal

Party, taking part in the fight when my feelings impelled me in that direction, rather than to accept the heavy responsibility which I must now bear as leader.

Nevertheless, I stifled my objections, believing it to be my duty to accept the post since my friends insisted on it. I considered that the services which we owe to one another made it a duty for me to take in my party the most exposed post, since the most exposed post was assigned to me.

You congratulate me, gentlemen, while you congratulate the French Canadians on the election of a French Canadian as leader of the great Liberal Party of the Dominion of Canada. I must do this justice to my honourable colleagues of the English tongue in the House of Commons, to Sir Richard Cartwright . . . and to a host of others, who had more claims than I had to the position of party leaders; I must do them the justice to say that they do not seem to remember that we are not of the same origin or, if they do remember it, it is only to affirm, by their acts as by their words, that, in the ranks of the Liberal Party, there is no question of race, but that all are equal.

Undoubtedly, gentlemen, I am a man, and men, as you know, have their sympathies and their preferences. But I will say with the Latin poet [Terence]: "Homo sum et humani nihil a me alienum puto"; "I am a man and I should be a stranger to nothing human." And, as a friend in the crowd said a moment ago, I am a French Canadian, with all the pride of my race, but all the rights of the British constitution are as dear to me as those of my race and, if the occasion ever arose that the rights of our separated brethren were assured, I would defend them with as much energy and conviction as I would those of my own race.

The manner might, perhaps, not be the same, but the impulse most assuredly would be. It may seem idle to enunciate truths as certain as this one, but there is now more than ever occasion to recall it, because I regret to say that between us – and I do confine my remarks to the Province of Quebec, but apply them to the entire Confederation – the prejudices of race and creed have increased in bitterness since the tragic events which have ensanguined the North-West. With a zeal worthy of a better cause, a certain portion of the Ontario press has been doing its best to divide the Catholics from the Protestants, and I regret to say that in our own province these attacks are often repelled by means fully as reprehensible.

Whether they come from the Catholics of Quebec or from the Protestants of Ontario, appeals to prejudice are equally deplorable. For my part, I have as much aversion for the man who appeals to Catholic prejudices in the province of Quebec, as for the man who appeals to Protestant prejudices in the province of Ontario.

The true patriot, Gentlemen, is a stranger to flattery – he only knows justice. The true patriot always uses the same language, whether he addresses himself to the Protestants of Ontario or to the Catholics of Quebec. The true patriot has only one measure, that of justice, to whom justice is due.

Has not this more than anything else characterized the political career of the Honourable Edward Blake? Neither for the possession of power, nor for any other motive, did Mr. Blake ever stoop to appeal to prejudices; if he had a defect, it was the defect of great souls and grand characters, but we do not call it a defect, but a sovereign quality, and it dominated his nature.

The cause of the weak and the oppressed attracted him, so to say, instinctively. Where is the man of our race who has defended with more energy and vigour than Mr. Blake the cause of the half-breeds driven to revolt and crime by the injustice of a perverse Government? Where is the son of Ireland on this continent who has defended the cause of that unhappy country with more eloquence and logic?

French Canadians, I ask you one thing: that while remembering that I, a French Canadian, have been elected leader of the Liberal

Party of Canada, you will not lose sight of the fact that the limits of our common country are not confined to the Province of Quebec, but that they extend to all the territory of Canada and that our country is wherever the British flag waves in America. I ask you to remember this in order to remind you that your duty is simply and, above all, to be Canadians. To be Canadians! That was the object of Confederation in the intention of its authors; the aim and end of Confederation was to bring the different races closer together, to soften the asperities of their mutual relations, and to connect the scattered groups of British subjects. . . .

But are the divisions ended? The truth is that after twenty years' trial of the system, the Maritime provinces submit to Confederation, but do not love it. The province of Manitoba is in open revolt against the Dominion Government, gentlemen, not in armed revolt, like the revolt of the half-breeds, but in legal revolt. The province of Nova Scotia demands its separation from the Confederation. In fact, carry your gaze from east to west and from north to south, and everywhere the prevailing feeling will be found to be one of unrest and uneasiness, of discontent and irritation.

Such, Gentlemen, is the picture which unrolls itself today to our eyes after twenty years of the regime of Confederation. It will be said, perhaps, that this picture is overdrawn. I appeal to the sound good sense of my present hearers; unfortunately, the picture is only too realistic. And yet, it is perfectly true that, if this be the painful state of things which we have to note, the fault does not rest with the institutions, but with the men by whom we are governed.

The fault does not rest with the institutions under which we are governed, because they are excellent, and, for my part, I at once declare, in my quality as leader of the Liberal Party, that I propose to do all in my power to inculcate love and respect for the institutions under which we live; those institutions, Gentlemen, are excellent. I am a British subject; I am of the French race; I have proclaimed the fact in the Province of Ontario and I am happy to proclaim it again today before countrymen of my own race and mother tongue. I am proud of my allegiance.

I shall not stop to discuss the question so often a subject of controversy among ourselves as to the manner in which we became British subjects. Did we become British subjects by conquest or by cession? There is no difficulty in the matter for me, and no more, on history than on contemporary events, have I any desire to conceal my way of thinking. If Montcalm had not lost the battle of the Plains of Abraham, the Chevalier de Lévis would not have capitulated and the Treaty of Paris would never have been signed.[75]

That is the position. But I state here before my brethren of the French language and before my brethren of the English tongue that we have made a greater and a more glorious conquest than any territorial conquest; we have conquered our liberties, and, if the event of today has any meaning, we can affirm without fear of mistake that we owe it to the acquisition of our civil and political liberties.

We form part of the British Empire, we are British subjects; and remember, gentlemen, all the dignity and pride that were involved in the title of a Roman citizen, at the beginning of the Roman era when St. Paul, loaded with chains and on the point of being subjected to unworthy treatment, had only to exclaim: "I am a Roman citizen" to be treated with the respect to which he was entitled.

We are British subjects and should be proud of the fact: we form part of the greatest empire on the globe and are governed by a constitution which has been the source of all the liberties of the modern world. I even go further and make bold to say that I am an admirer of our constitution. Undoubtedly, it is not perfect; it has serious defects which my friend, the Honourable Mr. Mercier, will be called upon to soon correct at the interprovincial conference. And, speaking as I do, I state my personal ideas. For my part, I have no hesitation in saying that the principle of our Confederation, that is to say, the principle of the separation of the legislative powers, is a source of privileges for us if we know how to properly avail ourselves of it. . . .

Nobody can view without alarm the present state of things in this country, the sullen discontent, the growing irritation, at the system under which we have been ruled for close upon twenty years, and I submit to my fellow countrymen of every origin and race that it is high time to put an end to the policy which has provoked this irritation, which has no other aim than the triumph of a party, and which sacrifices the country's dearest interests to a party triumph.

I submit to all my fellow citizens that it is time to strive for the establishment of a policy which will make all the inhabitants of Canada feel happy to belong to this country. I submit to my fellow countrymen that it is time to restore to the Maritime provinces all their rights, that is to say, their natural market. I submit that it is time to give to the Province of Manitoba the exercise of all its privileges, and that it is time to give to all the provinces their complete legislative autonomy, so that they may exist in fact as they exist in law.

It is time to endeavour to obtain, if possible, for all the people of this country the most natural and at the same time the most profitable market. Now, I state in concluding as I stated in commencing: I have faith in my country's institutions and I believe that, if they were well administered, they would engender a prosperity, the like of which we have not yet known.

For my part, I may say that as long as I shall occupy a place in the confidence of my party, as long as I shall fill a seat in the Legislature and as long as, by word and example, I can preach this doctrine, I shall devote my political life to spreading among my fellow countrymen, the love of our national institutions.

I know that the task is a great one, and that I dare not hope to carry it to a successful issue myself. The most I can do is to trust that I may advance it a step – but at least the work is worthy of our efforts. And for my part, when the hour for final rest shall strike, and when my eyes shall close forever, I shall consider, gentlemen, that my life has not been altogether wasted, if I shall have contributed to heal one patriotic wound in the heart even of a single one of my fellow countrymen and to have thus promoted, even to the smallest extent, the cause of concord and harmony between the citizens of the Dominion.

By Arthur Milnes

Laurier's speech at Somerset allows us the opportunity to pause, ever briefly in a book about the seventh prime minister, to consider the position of Sir John A. Macdonald in 1887.

With the advent of Laurier, the Old Chieftain finally had an opponent worthy of his concern. Laurier, then all of forty-five, enjoyed in abundance what Sir John A. no longer possessed: youth. Equally important was the fact that from 1887 onward Macdonald had, as leader of the Opposition, what he had never faced before: a true threat.

While Macdonald's past opponents Alexander Mackenzie and Edward Blake were solid, accomplished men and leaders, they had little chance when facing a master politician like the Father of Confederation. Mackenzie had indeed defeated Sir John A., but that loss was of Macdonald's own doing: a justified spell in the wilderness brought on by the Pacific Scandal. When given the first opportunity, in 1878, Canadians returned power to Sir John A.'s hands.

It is fascinating to note that at Somerset, Laurier was emulating a revolutionary political tactic that Macdonald had pioneered: the political picnic.

This would not be the first time Laurier would emulate the Old Chieftain he had watched wield power for so long. After Macdonald's death, Lady Macdonald herself grew to recognize that some of Laurier's success was due, in part, to the lessons he had learned from her husband. "Laurier has taken in the strangest way, not only the policy but also the personality of Sir John," she told a man who knew both men well, Sir Joseph Pope.[76]

Sir John A.'s greatest modern-day biographer (to whom Canada owes a great deal), Richard Gwyn, makes the following perceptive observations about the relationship between his subject and Laurier:

"At the very moment when the old lion was showing that none of his powers had diminished, a sleek young lion had entered the arena," he writes. "Thereafter, they would circle each other warily, but always with mutual respect. About their relationship there was always a sense of a might-have-been: near to his end, when Macdonald discussed Laurier with . . . Joseph Pope, he remarked, 'If I were twenty years younger, he'd be my colleague.' When Pope suggested this might still happen, Macdonald replied, 'Too old, too old.'"[77]

Laurier and Macdonald only battled directly in one general election, in 1891. While Sir John A. proved the victor, it was Canada and Canadians who benefitted most from this clash of titans. They did so because in defeat the young Liberal leader, who had first taken the stage at Somerset, Quebec, in 1887, learned the hard lessons and began his final march to power.

Arthur Milnes is co-editor, with Sarah Katherine Gibson, of *Canada Transformed: The Speeches of Sir John A. Macdonald. A Bicentennial Celebration* (McClelland & Stewart, 2014).

THE NATIONAL FESTIVAL OF
THE FRENCH-CANADIANS

JACQUES CARTIER HALL, QUEBEC CITY, QUEBEC

JUNE 24, 1889[78]

I have often thought, and the idea has been impressed on me more than ever by the brilliancy of this day's festivities, that there should be only one celebration of the St. Jean Baptiste in this country and that that celebration should take place in the good old city of Quebec: I have often thought and I now think more than ever that Quebec should be for French Canadians what Mecca is for Arabia, the city *par excellence*, the holy city among all.

It may be said, perhaps, that I am partial towards Quebec, but to this my simple answer is that I have many reasons for being so and that, far from being ashamed of the fact, I glory in it.

For, it must be conceded, there is only one Quebec. Our Montreal friends, who are with us tonight and who are with good reason proud of their own city will, perhaps, protest; but I do not allow their protests. This continent swarms with cities like Montreal, and I call to witness our friends here present from the United States. I am far from wishing to say anything disparaging of Montreal, but there is only one Quebec.

Cities like Montreal, with wide, straight, regular streets, are, as an Irishman would say, to be found at every door. These things have their value, certainly, but I repeat that there is only one Quebec. What constitutes the great charm of Quebec is its variety, the unexpectedness of its aspects; at each step you make, the scene changes and a new panorama as ravishing as the previous one, but of a different style, unrolls itself to your sight. This charm of Quebec everyone can enjoy: strangers enjoy it as well, and, perhaps, more than we do, because men are so constituted that they do not know how to sufficiently appreciate what they have themselves.

But Quebec possesses another charm, which can be enjoyed in all its plenitude only by us, French Canadians; it is the charm of memories. Men of Quebec, you are privileged beings. Antiquity has preserved for us the memory of a famous epitaph, calling on the passer-by to stop, as he was treading on the ashes of a hero, but you, men of Quebec, you breathe, live and have your being among the dust of heroes.

At each step you make in your city, a monument, a building, a stone, a glimpse of the sky at the end of a narrow street calls to mind a whole world of heroic events. Today, you have raised another monument, which will forever perpetuate the memory of the cross planted by the envoy of the King of France, when he took possession of this country in the name of his royal master.

This country, however, has not remained French soil. Still we have remained true to the memory of our old mother country. Although separated from France for over a century and differing from her at present in several ways, we have always worshipped her in our hearts, watching from afar, but with ceaseless interest, all the vicissitudes of her agitated career and sharing in her joys and triumphs, as well as in her disasters and sorrows, still more, indeed, in her sorrows than in her joys.

Adversity is the test of affection and I appeal to you all if it is not true that we never realized how dear France was to us as we realized it during the period of her reverses, during the fatal years of 1870 and 1871, when the telegraph brought us the news of defeat instead of the victories which we had looked for.[79] And when there was no longer room for doubt, when, having hoped against hope, we had, in order to convince ourselves, to read over and over again the text of the harsh law imposed by the conqueror and when Alsace and Loraine were violently severed from French territory, I ask you, if we had been deprived of one of our own limbs could we have suffered keener anguish?

. . . . Our separation from France has imposed new duties upon us, has created new interests and opened new affections to us. We are French Canadians, but our country is not confined to the territory overshadowed by the citadel of Quebec; our country is Canada, it is the whole of what is covered by the British flag on the American continent, the fertile lands bordered by the Bay of Fundy, the Valley of the St. Lawrence, the region of the Great Lakes, the prairies of the West, the Rocky Mountains, the lands washed by the famous ocean where breezes are said to be as sweet as the breezes of the Mediterranean. Our fellow countrymen are not only those in whose veins runs the blood of France. They are all those, whatever their race or whatever their language, whom the fortune of war, the chances of fate, or their own choice have brought among us, and who acknowledge the sovereignty of the British Crown.

As far as I am concerned, loudly do I proclaim it, those are my fellow countrymen. I am a Canadian. But I told it elsewhere, and with greater pleasure, I repeat here this evening, among all my fellow countrymen, the first place in my heart is for those in whose veins runs the blood of my own veins. Yet I do not hesitate to say that the rights of my fellow countrymen of different origins are as dear to me, as sacred to me, as the rights of my own race, and if it unfortunately happened that they ever were attacked, I would defend them with just as much energy and vigour as the rights of my own race.

I say I: should I not say you, we, all of us? Yes, we are too much the sons of France, of that generous nation which has so often shed her blood for the defence of the weak, of the oppressed, not to be ever ready to defend the rights of our fellow countrymen of different nationalities to the same extent as our own. What I claim for us is an equal share of sun, of justice, of liberty; that share we have it; we have it ample, and what we claim for ourselves we are anxious to grant to others.

I do not want French Canadians to domineer over anyone, nor anyone to domineer over them. Equal justice. Equal rights. It is written that the sands and seas are numbered. It is written that not a hair falls from one's head without the permission of an Eternal Providence, eternally wise. Can we not believe that in that supreme battle here, on the Plains of Abraham, when the fate of arms turned against us, can we not believe that it entered into the decrees of Providence that the two races, up to that time enemies, should henceforth live in peace and harmony, and henceforth should form one nation? Such was the inspiring cause of Confederation.

When the British provinces were united under the same constitution, the hope now acknowledged was to give to all the scattered elements therein a national ideal, to present to the world the spectacle of a nation diverse in its origins and retaining in all its groups the respect for family and race traditions, but giving thenceforward to all one and the same aspiration. I have not forgotten that, at its inception, Confederation was not accepted without fear by [a] number of Canadians of French origin, but there is nevertheless one thing for which the French Canadians are entitled to: universal admiration. The fault of democracies is usually to flatter the mob. I do not know how to flatter and I shall never stoop to play the part of the flatterer, either to crowds or to individuals; but it is an act of simple justice to note the admirable pliability with which the French Canadians have adapted themselves to the different regimes through which they have passed, the constitution of 1775, that of 1791, that of 1841 and lastly that of Confederation.

I am not ignorant of the fact that there can be no nation without a national pride, nor am I unaware that in almost all cases national pride is inspired by those tragic events which bring suffering and tears in their train, but which at the same time call out all the forces of a nation or of a race, and on this head it has been correctly said that the happiest people are those without a history. Our history under Confederation presents none of the dramatic facts, which make us so attached to the past; it has been calm and consequently happy. But peace has also its glories and its heroes.

Canada under Confederation has produced men of whom any nation might justly feel proud. I will not speak of the Canadians of French origin . . . but I will allude to the Canadians of British origin and mention two as examples. The first name I shall recall is that of a man from whom I differ, *toto coelo*, but I am too much a French Canadian not to glory at all times in doing justice to an adversary. I refer to Sir John A. Macdonald. I will not astonish [those present] . . . if I state that I do not share Sir John Macdonald's political opinions; I may even add that I condemn almost all of them; but it must be acknowledged that, in his long career, Sir John Macdonald has displayed such eminent qualities that he would have made his mark on any of the world's stages and that, with the single exception, perhaps, of Mr. Mercier,[80] no one on this continent has excelled as he has in the art of governing men.

The other name is that of a man who has been to me not only a friend, but more than a friend. I mean the Honourable Edward Blake. Some years ago, speaking here of Mr. Blake, I declared that, in my opinion, America, at that moment, did not possess his equal and Europe could not show his superior. That opinion has been confirmed by all that I have since seen of Mr. Blake. I have enjoyed the advantage of very close relations with him and have learned that his heart, soul, and character are in keeping with his splendid intellect.

Besides these, many other names, the names of men of the highest eminence occur to me; but I shall pass over them in silence in order to remind you of an event which sums up in itself all that I could say and which will show you that, while remaining French Canadians, we are Canadians in the broadest acceptance of the term. Only a few weeks have elapsed since St. Sauveur was destroyed by fire. On that occasion, a man came forward to fight the scourge and check the spread of the conflagration.

With all the smartness, zeal and intrepidity of the true soldier, he rushed into the thick of the danger and found his death there. On the following day, the whole French population of Quebec filled the streets as they filled them today, but, instead of a feeling of joyfulness, the feeling in their hearts was one of deepest grief for the gallant Major Short, whose mutilated remains they had congregated to reverently salute on their way to the grave.[81]

Major Short did not belong to our race; but he was our fellow countryman; and I would ask which one of you, French Canadians, in the midst of the still smoking ruins of your city and the presence of the dead hero, did not feel proud of being a Canadian?

Gentlemen, let us have the pride of our race! Let us be just to all our fellow countrymen, without distinction of race or creed! Let us know how to be not alone just, but generous, and let all our actions in the Confederation be characterized by that generosity which has marked the career of France in Europe.

By Antoine Dionne Charest and the Honourable Jean Charest

For Laurier to have said that Quebec City is the national capital of Quebec is a truism. But to further describe it as the "holy city" of French-Canadians is a rather bold statement.

Laurier's boldness, however, is not gratuitous. His speech reminds us of a few important features about French-Canadian society and, ultimately, about Canada itself.

Regarding French-Canadians, it says that there is such a thing as a distinct French-Canadian people, with a unique history, culture, and language. And though French-Canadians have faced adversity numerous times, notably when they were separated from France, they have remained loyal to their roots. They have preserved and enhanced their distinctiveness. And nowhere is this truer and more visible than in Quebec City.

As for all Canadians, it is understood that French-Canadians, and especially Quebeckers, would not have joined the Canadian federation unless the other founding partners recognized and respected those fundamental characteristics. This is why Laurier speaks of "Equal Justice" and "Equal rights": in order to form a single Canadian nation, Quebec had to be recognized as an equal partner. This was, in other words, a matter of equal respect, something that is, at least in Laurier's eyes, at the very heart of this country. When this condition is met – and Laurier believed it had been – then French-Canadians will see themselves as Canadians. They will also view other Canadians of non-French-Canadian extraction as their fellow countrymen. Hence, Laurier's speech has the wonderful merit of demonstrating the compatibility and complementarity of French-Canadian patriotism and Canadian patriotism. We strongly believe that this is still true today. But we also believe that these ideas must be constantly promoted, especially in times of doubts about Quebec's future, as that future necessarily determines Canada's future as a whole.

ON THE DEATH OF
SIR JOHN A. MACDONALD

HOUSE OF COMMONS, OTTAWA, ONTARIO
JUNE 8, 1891

Mr. Speaker: . . . . I fully appreciate the intensity of the grief which fills the souls of all those who were the friends and followers of Sir John Macdonald, at the loss of the great leader whose whole life has been so closely identified with their party; a party upon which he has thrown such brilliancy and luster. We on this side of the House who were his opponents, who did not believe in his policy, nor in his methods of government, we take our full share of their grief – for the loss which they deplore today is far and away beyond and above the ordinary compass of party range.

It is in every respect a great national loss, for he who is no more was, in many respects, Canada's most illustrious son, and in every sense Canada's foremost citizen and statesman. At the period of life to which Sir John Macdonald has arrived, death, whenever it comes, cannot be said to come unexpected. Some few months ago, during the turmoil of the late election, when the country was made aware that on a certain day the physical strength of the veteran Premier had not been equal to his courage, and that his intense labour for the time being had prostrated his singularly wiry frame, everybody, with the exception, perhaps, of his buoyant self, was painfully anxious lest perhaps the angel of death had touched him with his wing. When a few days ago in the heat of an angry discussion the news spread in this House, that of a sudden his condition had become alarming, the surging waves of angry discussion were at once hushed, and everyone, friend and foe, realized that this time for a certainty the angel of death had appeared and had crossed the threshold of his home.

Thus we were not taken by surprise, and although we were prepared for the sad event, yet it is almost impossible to convince the unwilling mind, that it is true, that Sir John Macdonald is no more, that the chair which we now see vacant shall remain for ever vacant; that the face so familiar in this Parliament for the last forty years shall be seen no more, and that the voice so well known shall be heard no more, whether in solemn debate or in pleasant and mirthful tones.

In fact, the place of Sir John Macdonald in this country was so large and so absorbing, that it is almost impossible to conceive that the political life of this country, the fate of this country, can continue without him. His loss overwhelms us. For my part, I say with all truth, his loss overwhelms me, and it also overwhelms this Parliament, as if indeed one of the institutions of the land had given way. Sir John Macdonald now belongs to the ages, and it can be said with certainty, that the career which has just been closed is one of the most remarkable careers of this century.

It would be premature at this time to attempt to fix or anticipate what will be the final judgment of history upon him; but there were in his career and in his life, features so prominent and so conspicuous that already they shine with a glow which time cannot alter, which even now appears before the eye such as they will appear to the end of history. I think it can be asserted that for the supreme art of governing men, Sir John Macdonald was gifted as few men in any land or in any age were gifted; gifted with the most high of all qualities, qualities which would have made him famous wherever exercised and which would have shone all the more conspicuously the larger the theatre.

The fact that he could congregate together elements the most heterogeneous and blend them into one compact party, and to the end of his life keep them steadily under his hand, is perhaps altogether unprecedented. The fact that during all those years he retained unimpaired not only the confidence, but the devotion – the ardent devotion and affection of his party, is evidence that beside those higher qualities of statesmanship to which we were the daily witnesses, he was also endowed with those inner, subtle, indefinable graces of soul which win and keep the hearts of men.

As to his statesmanship, it is written in the history of Canada. It may be said without any exaggeration whatever, that the life of Sir John Macdonald, from the date he entered Parliament, is the history of Canada, for he was connected and associated with all the events, all the facts which brought Canada from the position Canada then occupied – the position of two small provinces, having nothing in common but a common allegiance, united by a bond of paper, and united by nothing else – to the present state of development which Canada has reached.

Although my political views compel me to say that, in my judgment, his actions were not always the best that could have been taken in the interest of Canada, although my conscience compels me to say that of late he has imputed to his opponents motives as to which I must say in my heart he has misconceived, yet I am only too glad here to sink these differences, and to remember only the great services he has performed for our country – to remember that his actions always displayed great originality of views, unbounded fertility of resources, a high level of intellectual conceptions, and, above all, a far-reaching vision beyond the event of the day, and still higher, permeating the whole, a broad patriotism – a devotion to Canada's welfare, Canada's advancement, and Canada's glory.

The life of a statesman is always an arduous one, and very often it is an ungrateful one. More often than otherwise his actions do not mature until he is in his grave. Not so, however, in the case of Sir John Macdonald. His career has been a singularly fortunate one. His reverses were few and of short duration.

He was fond of power, and, in my judgment, if I may say so, that may be the turning point of the judgment of history. He was fond of power, and he never made any secret of it. Many times we have heard him avow it on the floor of this Parliament, and his ambition in this respect was gratified as, perhaps, no other man's ambition ever was. In my judgment, even the career of William Pitt can hardly compare with that of Sir John Macdonald in this respect; for although William Pitt, moving in a higher sphere, had to deal with problems greater than our problems, yet I doubt if in the intricate management of a party William Pitt had to contend with difficulties equal to those that Sir John Macdonald had to contend with.[82]

In his death, too, he seems to have been singularly happy. Twenty years ago I was told by one who at that time was a close personal and political friend of Sir John Macdonald, that in the intimacy of his domestic circle he was fond of repeating that his end would be as the end of Lord Chatham – that he would be carried away from the floor of Parliament to die. How true that vision into the future was we now know, for we saw him to the last, with enfeebled health and declining strength, struggling on the floor of Parliament until the hand of fate pinned him to his bed to die. And thus to die with his armour on was probably his ambition. Sir, death is the law – the supreme law. Although we see it every day in every form, although session after session we have seen it in this Parliament striking right and left without any discrimination as to age or station, yet the ever-recurring spectacle does not in any way remove the bitterness of the sting. Death always carries with it an incredible sense of pain; but the one thing sad in death is that which is involved in the word separation – separation from all we love in life. This is what makes death so poignant when it strikes a man of intellect in middle age.

But when death is the natural termination of a full life, in which he who disappears has given the full measure of his capacity, has performed everything required from him, and more, the sadness of death is not for him who goes, but for those who loved him and remain. In this sense I am sure the Canadian people will extend unbounded sympathy to the friends of Sir John Macdonald – to his sorrowing children, and above all, to the brave and noble woman, his companion in life and his chief helpmate.

Thus, Mr. Speaker, one after another we see those who have been instrumental in bringing Canada to its present stage of development, removed from amongst us. Today, we deplore the loss of him who, we all unite in saying, was the foremost Canadian of his time, and who filled the largest place in Canadian history.

Only last week, was buried in the city of Montreal another son of Canada, one who at one time had been a tower of strength to the Liberal Party, one who will ever be remembered as one of the noblest, purest, and greatest characters that Canada has ever produced, Sir Antoine Aimé Dorion.[83] Sir Antoine Aimé Dorion had not been in favour of Confederation. Not that he was opposed to the principle; but he believed that the Union of these provinces, at that day, was premature. When, however, Confederation had become a fact, he gave the best of his mind and heart to make it a success.

It may indeed happen, Sir, that when the Canadian people see the ranks thus gradually reduced and thinned of those upon whom they have been in the habit of relying for guidance, that a feeling of apprehension will creep into the heart lest, perhaps, the institutions of Canada may be imperilled.

Before the grave of him who, above all, was the Father of Confederation, let not grief be barren grief; but let grief be coupled with the resolution, the determination that the work in which the Liberals and Conservatives, in which Brown and Macdonald united, shall not perish, but that though United Canada may be deprived of the services of her greatest men, still Canada shall and will live.

By the Right Honourable Brian Mulroney

Sir Wilfrid Laurier's masterful Commons tribute to his fallen foe Sir John A. Macdonald has stood the test of time. It remains, 125 years after its delivery, perhaps the finest such address ever heard by Canadian parliamentarians.

What is not often discussed when Laurier and Macdonald are considered is their lengthy personal and professional relationship. It is also important to recall that Laurier carefully watched the Old Chieftain for almost twenty years, learning the lessons of party leadership the entire time.

Remember that Laurier first sat opposite Sir John A. in the Commons in 1874. Macdonald was then at the lowest point in his political career, having resigned office due to the Pacific Scandal and been relegated to the Opposition benches. This decision was confirmed by voters who quickly elected Alexander Mackenzie and his party to power.

Laurier's first address in the House, delivered when he was only thirty-three, quickly caught Macdonald's attention. Prime Minister Mackenzie, eager to showcase new talent, wisely tapped the young Quebec MP to lead off from the Government side during that year's debate on the Speech from the Throne.

As preserved in early Hansard, *Macdonald was impressed. "It looked well for the future of Canada when they saw her young statesmen on their first entrance into political life take a course so satisfactory to the majority of the people of this country, satisfactory to the majority of the representatives of the people, and certainly most satisfactory to himself (Right Hon. Sir John A. Macdonald)."*

Laurier then watched as Sir John A. achieved the impossible by returning to power four years later. And once back in the Prime Minister's Office in East Block, Macdonald would own it until the end.

For the next seventeen years, until Sir John A. died in 1891, Laurier continued his study of Macdonald's leadership. Political differences aside, he watched carefully – and with great admiration – how Macdonald crafted cabinets and held a disparate caucus together, navigating the ever-difficult issues of race, religion, and region in nineteenth-century Canada.

Laurier noted Macdonald's careful attention to the organization of a national political party and drew lessons from the Old Chieftain he never forgot. He also studied Macdonald during debate, developing a respect and admiration for the older man's style and skill – lessons he too would eventually bring to the office of prime minister.

In 1884 Laurier described Macdonald's debating skills during a lecture he delivered in Montreal:

"In the case of so alert a mind, he lacks happiness and movement of expression," Laurier said, describing Sir John A. "He hesitates, stammers and repeats himself . . . but, in all his speeches, there is always a nail that goes straight home. He excels in seizing upon an adversary's weak point. His highest art, however, consists in saying exactly what should be said to produce the most effect on his own supporters. He knows all their weaknesses and their prejudices and all he says is perfectly adapted to them."

Towards the end of his life Sir John A. gave strong indication of the high regard in which he held his Liberal opponent.

Sir Joseph Pope, in The Day of Sir John A. Macdonald, described the scene:

"About a month before Sir John Macdonald died Mr. Laurier came to his office in the House of Commons to discuss some question of adjournment," wrote Pope, who served both prime ministers. "When he had gone, the chief said to me, 'Nice chap that. If I were twenty years younger, he'd be my colleague.' 'Perhaps he may be yet, sir,' I remarked. Sir John shook his head. 'Too old,' said he, 'too old,' and passed into the inner room."

I have often reflected on that scene and image, one so ably captured before history by Joe Pope. Here were Canada's two greatest prime ministers, fierce opponents to be sure, but united in the common cause of Canada, with the older of the two only weeks from death.

The dream of every prime minister that has followed both Laurier and Macdonald is in fact the dream and challenge both these prime ministers first bequeathed Canadians: that Canada would one day live up to her full potential as a country.

And when that day comes it will arrive because of the foundations laid so long ago by Sir John A. Macdonald and Sir Wilfrid Laurier.

The Right Honourable Brian Mulroney was Canada's eighteenth prime minister.

TRUE TO THE DOUBLE BLOOD

QUEBEC CITY, QUEBEC

JANUARY 4, 1894[84]

I am of French origin, a descendant of that great nation, which, as remarked by a thinker,[85] has provoked enthusiasm, admiration, hatred, envy or pity, but never indifference, because it has ever been great, even in its faults. I acknowledge that I am of French origin, but if I recognize the fact, I also recognize the position in which my race have been placed by the battle which was fought on the Plains of Abraham, and which is commemorated by a monument reared by you to the memory of the two commanders who there lost their lives. There are some amongst us who forget this state of things, who affect to believe that a small French republic or monarchy – I hardly know what they want – should be established on the banks of the St. Lawrence.

I cannot accept this idea, because those who use this language speak like slaves who would break their bonds if they dared, but who do not do so because they are cowards. For my part, I believe myself to be a free man, and this is why I am in favour of the actual regime. . . .

Is there a man amongst us who forgets that when Papineau was struggling for the rights of his race and for the constitutional liberty which we today enjoy, his principal coadjutors were John Neilson, the Scotchman, and O'Callaghan, the Irishman?[86] Is there a man who can forget that, when the constitutional voice was useless, when our representations and our remonstrances remained for years and years unanswered, and when the peasants of St. Denis took up arms and faced the veterans of Waterloo, their commander was not a Canadian, but an Englishman named Wolfred Nelson?[87] And, three days afterwards, when these same peasants were swept with the leaden hail at Saint-Charles,[88] can it be forgotten that the man who again led them was an Englishman named Thomas S. Brown?[89] How can these men or their descendants – English, Scotch, Irish, and French – who shed their blood to win for us the liberties we enjoy today, make use of the same liberties to tear each other to pieces? Far be from me the thought; let us be more broad-minded, and say that those who shared in the labour shall also share in the reward. . . .

But in politics we cannot hold a candle to them [Conservatives] on the score of religion. The moment politics are in question they become terribly religious. Discuss any question with them of protection, free trade, finance or railways, and immediately their great argument amounts to this: "Ah! we are religious, we are; but those other fellows opposite have not much religion."

I do not boast about my religion. It sometimes happens to me, however, to go to church, and, when I do go there, the only thing I can do on entering is to say to the Lord, "Pardon me, a poor sinner." And when I raise my eyes I see close to the altar rails, almost on the very steps of the altar itself, Mr. So-and-So and his friends, whom you know very well, and who are saying: "I thank you, O! God, that I am not like unto that publican there."

I have always proclaimed, and again I repeat, that in politics we belong to the British Liberal school, to the school of Fox and Gladstone.[90] In religion I belong to the school of Montalembert and

Lacordaire, of the men who were the greatest perhaps of their age in loftiness of character and nobility of thought. I know of no grander spectacle than the spectacle of Montalembert and Lacordaire, two adolescents, two children almost, undertaking to conquer in France freedom of education, and succeeding in their object after many years of struggle.[91]

I know of no finer spectacle than that furnished by Montalembert confronting the French bourgeoisie, impregnated as they were with that dissolving materialism, the Voltairian skepticism of the eighteenth century, and exclaiming, "We are the sons of the Crusaders, and shall not retreat before the sons of Voltaire."

I know of no grander or more beautiful spectacle than that of Lacordaire proclaiming from the pulpit of Notre Dame the truths of Christianity to the incredulous crowd, and teaching them that life is a sacrifice and is only rendered worthy by duty accomplished. These are our models, and whether we be assailed or approved, we shall endeavour to imitate these models without fear and without reproach to the end. Unfortunately these men who rendered so much service to Christianity and struggled so much in its holy cause, were attacked and denounced as bad Catholics and as heretics by the men who, fortunately, did not constitute a school, for, if they had, they would have rendered Catholicism impossible.

We have such men in our midst today; we have intolerant and extravagant Catholics who understand neither the times, the country, nor the surroundings in which they live. I mention these things, which you may think do not apply here, but which, on the contrary, have an immense application, for this reason: because if we have amongst us men who try to prostitute the Catholic religion to the ends of politics, there are also men in the Province of Ontario who are endeavouring to play the same game with the Protestant religion.

There has just been formed in that province an organization called the Protestant Protective Association,[92] whose object is to exclude all Catholics from the civil government on the pretence that they cannot be loyal citizens to the State, and that they are compelled by their faith, even in temporal matters, to obey the authority of the Pope. Gentlemen, standing here in the Province of Quebec, and in the city of Quebec, you know as well as I do that these theories are positively false. Nevertheless, they are constantly repeated in Ontario. . . .

You are aware that in the 11th century certain men started out from Normandy, Anjou, Brittany, and Angoulême to capture England. Duke William of Normandy was their leader, and our present sovereign is the last scion of a royal race that dates back to William the Conqueror. In the sixteenth century men started from the same province of Normandy, Anjou, Brittany and Angoulême to colonize the fertile lands on the banks of the St. Lawrence.

In the next century the men of both races met here and you know what happened. Well, is it not permissible to hope that a day will come, when, instead of facing each other on hostile purpose intent, the men of the two countries, the descendants of the Britons, Angevins, and Normans, who invaded England in the eleventh century, and the descendants of the Angevins, Normans, and Britons, who peopled Canada in the sixteenth, will meet together, not to fight, but to hold the grand assizes of peace and commerce?

I may not live long enough to see that day, but if my career should be sufficiently extended to allow me to take part in these assizes, it will be a happy day to me. I shall attend them bearing with me my Canadian nationality, and I believe that I shall continue the work of Mr. Lafontaine and Sir George-Étienne Cartier, and that the result will be all to the advantage of French Canada.

Gentlemen, our situation as a country is full of difficulties, and those difficulties are no doubt immense. Still, there is nothing desperate about them. What this country needs above all else is peace, concord, and union between all the elements composing its population. Let us show the world that if we reverence the past, we also have a regard for the future. Let us show to the world that union does not mean absorption, and that autonomy does not mean antagonism.

Victor Hugo,[93] recalling his double origin, used these fine words:

'Fidèle au double sang qu'ont versé dans ma veine,
Mon père, vieux soldat, ma mère, Vendéenne.'

("True to the double blood that was poured into my veins by my father, an old soldier, and my mother, a Vendean.")

Let us also be true to our double origin, true to the memory and the reverence of the great nation from which we have sprung, and true also to the great nation which has given us freedom. And in all the difficulties, all the pains, and all the vicissitudes of our situation, let us always remember that love is better than hatred, and faith better than doubt, and let hope in our future destinies be the pillar of fire to guide us in our career.

By Nigel S. Wright

It has become a commonplace among opinion elites in Canada since the mid-1960s that the symbols and artifacts of the British stream of our lineal descent as a nation are divisive, alienating to many Canadians, and ought to be removed from the public face of Canada. It is true that these symbols and artifacts were used too exclusively and insensitively to suggest a mono-culture that has never existed in Canada. But perhaps the public policy response should have been to bring about a more inclusive approach rather than to denigrate this portion of our inheritance and replace it with ahistorical substitutes. Interestingly, Sir Wilfrid Laurier piloted this alternative approach almost a century earlier.

Sir Wilfrid Laurier hewed consistently throughout his public life to his passion for concord between the French- and English-speaking inhabitants of Canada and for Canada to become a stronger, greater, more autonomous political entity. In his embrace of the whole spectrum of Canada's political and philosophical inheritance, and the fact that he so clearly and consistently believed his own identity to be informed by the completeness of that inheritance, he argued against the precept, now so embedded in fifty years of public policy, that Canada's British political and cultural roots are alien, and alienating, to its French-Canadian population.

Laurier was a proud son of Quebec and fought to ensure that Québécois, and French-Canadians more broadly, could play a leading role in our public, social, and economic life. Equally, his political identification was with the school of British liberalism, as was that of the political movement he led, and in no way would or could he have considered that its British roots made it less authentically or indigenously Canadian, for his adherence to it sprung also from the particular political and religious culture of Quebec and from the common ground to be found with classical liberals in other parts of Canada.

In his first speech in the House of Commons, in March 1874, Laurier extolled the concept of liberty in the constitutional principles that Canada inherited from Britain, and in June 1877, to Le Club Canadien in Montreal, he added a singular ode to British liberals, celebrating their reforms and the freedom and happiness flowing from them. In January 1894, in Quebec City, Laurier declared that "in politics we belong to the British Liberal school, to the school of Fox and Gladstone," and spoke glowingly of the Empire, and in October 1916, in a speech given in London, Ontario, towards the end of his public career, Laurier again declared himself a "British Liberal."

Laurier was sometimes extravagant in his praise for Britain and its political system, but just as this cannot be mistaken for acquiescence to a concept of the British Empire that would have limited Canada's political maturation, so it cannot be dismissed as simply pragmatic rhetoric from a politician whose success depended on votes outside Quebec and other heartlands of the French-Canadian population. Rather, he saw Canada as a confluence of two streams, as an inheritor of two great traditions, and the better for it. Today, we might describe it as four streams, recognizing belatedly *the bequest of the original inhabitants and of immigrants coming from around the globe.*

That would be faithful to Laurier's understanding of Canada. He laid it out in December 1886 to the Young Men's Liberal Club of Toronto:

"We may not assimilate, we may not blend, but for all that we are the component parts of the same country. We may be French in our origin – and I do not deny my origin, I admit that I pride myself on it. We may be English, or Scotch or whatever it may be, but we are Canadians; one in aim and purpose; and not only Canadians, but we are also members of the same British Empire. This fact, that we are all Canadians, one in our objects, members of the British Empire, proud of being British subjects and Canadian, is evidence that we can keep pride of race without any detriment to the nation."

Laurier understood and celebrated the various streams that contributed and still contribute to the Canadian national identity and would never have contemplated that one could understand Canada without understanding them. It is the diminution of one of those streams through the insistent public policy choices of the past fifty years that is inconsistent with the Laurier dream. As a man inspired by ideas more than by ethnic identity, Laurier would find foreign the notion that it was and is necessary to erase from the historical understanding of children in our educational system, of immigrants seeking to understand the country to which they have come, and from the symbols through which we understand our nationality, the British political and philosophical inheritance that did so much to shape the country we have become. Locke, Adams, and Gladstone, and even Burke, Disraeli, and Wilberforce: all were part of Laurier's Canadian identity. And I think he would have understood that it would be a weakening of our identity, a weakening of our understanding of why we are and need to remain a society different from the nation that lies to our south, to let go of any part of the history that made us.

Nigel Wright is active in business and has served on staff to two Canadian prime ministers. He lives in London, England.

CANADA'S FIRST POST-CONFEDERATION NATIONAL PARTY CONVENTION

OTTAWA, ONTARIO
JUNE 21, 1893[94]

I would vainly seek to find, even though I attempted to do so, words adequate to convey to you a sense of the gratitude of myself and those entrusted with the fortunes of the Liberal Party toward you for the kindness with which you have responded to the appeal which I made a few weeks ago in my capacity as official head of the Liberal Party of the Dominion of Canada.

It is most encouraging that there should be such numbers present, and not only that there should be such numbers present, but that we should have upon this platform the leaders of Liberal thought in so many provinces of the Dominion, from the veteran of Ontario to the young fighting Premier of Prince Edward Island.

Sir, if you would allow me a personal thought upon this occasion, I would say that, proud as I am today in the presence of Sir Oliver Mowat, Premier of the Province of Ontario; of Mr. Fielding, the Premier of Nova Scotia; of Mr. Blair, the Premier of New Brunswick; of Mr. Peters, the Premier of Prince Edward Island, and of Mr. Sifton, of the Manitoba Government; if you will allow me here to speak of myself, I would say that I value still more, from a personal point of view, the presence amongst us of my old friend, Mr. Joly de Lotbinière, under whose leadership it was my good fortune a good many years ago to serve my apprenticeship when I had the honour to sit in the Local Assembly of the Province of Quebec, when he was leader of the Opposition.[95] He has told you here today that he has retired from politics, but when he heard the sound of the bugle, and got the smell of the powder, he had to fall into the ranks like an old soldier.

I am proud to tell you, gentlemen, that we have today representatives from nearly all parts of the Dominion of Canada – from the Provinces by the Atlantic, from the valley of the St. Lawrence, from the region of the Great Lakes, even from the prairies of Manitoba and the North-West. The only province which is not represented today officially is the Province of British Columbia, and yet to some extent it is, for this morning the Chairman of the Convention received the following telegram:

"Although not represented, British Columbia takes warm interest in the proceedings of the Liberal Convention. Sentiment here favours a policy of freer trade relations with Great Britain and her colonies, especially Australia, and reciprocity of trade with all other nations."

Nothing like this convention has yet taken place since Confederation, and to find anything of the kind or approaching it you must go back to the days of old Canada – to the famous Liberal Convention which met in Toronto in 1859. And, Mr. Chairman, you will allow me the pleasure of saying that this meeting is presided over by one of the leaders of that convention in that year. Sir Oliver Mowat was one of those who helped on that occasion to shape the policy which afterwards prevailed. Sir Oliver Mowat belongs in more senses than one to the school of that Grand Old

Man who today, under the gaze of an admiring and wondering world, is struggling against many odds to relieve a country from a regime of oppression, and to give it good government of the people. With Sir Oliver, as with Mr. Gladstone, age seems to have made no impression on his faculties; his mental activity seems to increase with years.

Sir Oliver Mowat better than any of us remembers that the convention of 1859 had for its object the meeting of difficulties then prevailing. Canada was suffering from severe ills at that time. These ills, however, were of a constitutional nature. For years an imperfect constitutional system had prevailed in Canada. There was the union of Upper and Lower Canada, an English and a French Province, with all the disadvantages of a federal and a legislative union, and without any of the advantages of either form.

You know that the principle which was then adopted as a solution of the woes which Canada was then suffering was representation by population. This principle was gradually extended until it became the origin of Confederation, until it became the means whereby the four Provinces of British America were united into a Confederation under the sanction of the Mother Land, with the object that it was to extend all over the British portion of the continent.

We, the Liberals, at this late day, are again assembled in order to discuss the present position of the country. I am glad to say that, though Canada is suffering many ills and woes, they do not arise from constitutional defects. I am glad to say that the constitution, though not perfect, still is such that it should command the respect and love of all Canadians.

I want it to be known at the very outset of our proceedings that, while coming here from all parts of the Dominion to discuss the political situation of the country, to remedy, if possible, the ills from which our country is suffering, we do not come here in any carping spirit, with any revolutionary words. I say, we come here with our hearts full of love for our Canadian country, with pride for its past and hope for its future.

Mr. Chairman, it is undeniable that today the position of Canada is not what it ought to be. In the eyes of many of us – I should say in the eyes of all of us – the position is such as to make a good many of the people of Canada feel anxious for the fate of the country. We are here to discuss the situation of our country. Whenever we meet, as we do upon this occasion, to discuss the situation of our country, we are met by our opponents with a very singular objection. If we speak of the situation of the country, and if we do not represent it in roseate colours, we are told at once by the Conservative Party that we are decrying the country.

This is a very strange objection. It would mean that the party in power have the right to do anything they please, and the only thing left to the Opposition is approbation. The position of the Opposition under this rule would be a slavish one, and it would never dare to speak the truth. There is but one answer to make to this, and it is that the truth, whatever it is, must be told.

It were a crime undoubtedly – it were a national crime – for anyone to speak ill of his country if he spoke falsely. It would be a crime, and a great crime, if the colour under which the country is presented were not true; but I submit that it would be more a crime to conceal the truth for fear of causing fear or shame. There is but one thing to do, sir, and it is to speak the truth on every occasion. It is not perhaps within the bounds of human nature to expect that every page of the history of a people should be free from blots, but I assert that a people's history will be freest from blots where you find a strong and healthy public opinion to denounce every crime and outrage. I submit the only possible condition of the success and grandeur of a people is that all moral offences should be denounced, that all crimes should be denounced, and that the truth should be spoken upon every occasion without fear or favour.

If anyone were to look at the history of the country for the last twenty-six years, that man must admit (and I may say here to begin with, that Canada has made great and substantial progress) that our progress has not reached the legitimate expectations of the Canadian people. No man can say, I do not care to what party he belongs, that Canada has realized in these twenty-six years the hopes that we had twenty-six years ago. If our hopes had been realized, the population of Canada would be at least seven million souls. It is today about five million. If our hopes had been realized, we would today have upon the soil of Canada one million of our fellow Canadians who are now to be found in a neighbouring country.

It is not too much to expect that in a country like Canada, with so many resources of every description, every child born upon the soil should remain a citizen of Canada for all his life. When the Ministers of the Crown speak of this matter they elect to treat it very lightly. I submit to you that there is nothing of greater importance than this very question.

Why, Sir, it is a well-known fact that the growth of population is the measure in many instances of the development of a people. Not only that, but so important is it considered, that, not satisfied with the natural growth of our population, we have spent thousands and millions of dollars in the last fifteen years in order to bring in immigrants. It is a matter of regret to think that, though we are spending . . . every year in order to bring in immigrants, we cannot keep our own people amongst ourselves. Is it to be supposed, is it to be expected, that if those born on the soil cannot remain attached to the soil, this foreign population will become attached to it?

Is it to be expected that if we cannot keep our own people, those we bring from abroad will remain? There is only one conclusion to be arrived at, and it is this, that if a country like Canada, which can maintain a hundred millions of men, cannot keep a paltry population of five million, there must be something wrong with the policy and with the Government. The conclusion is irresistible. When the Ministers of the Crown deal with this question, they do not impugn the conclusion, they simply deny the facts. They tell you that the country is prosperous and that there is very little emigration, that the statement that there is large emigration is a Grit lie.

There was a few days ago a meeting in Orangeville, which is situated in the county of Cardwell, and you know it has been rumoured that the Government were contemplating rewarding one of the faithful, that the Government were contemplating removing Mr. White, the representative of Cardwell, to another sphere of usefulness, to make him the collector of customs in Montreal.[96] But before they came to that conclusion, they had heard that perhaps it would not be safe under the present circumstances to open Cardwell. Therefore, they made a descent upon the faithful of Cardwell. One of the Ministers who was taken up for his eloquence, and perhaps for something else, was Mr. Clarke Wallace, the Controller of Customs.[97] He opened his remarks by expressing his great admiration for the beauty of the surroundings of Orangeville. He spoke in glowing terms of the appearance of prosperity of the farm houses, and of the farms, which he saw in all directions.

I have no doubt Mr. Wallace had good reason to speak thus. Orangeville is one of those localities which, like many others, claims to be the garden of Ontario and of Canada. Mr. Wallace said that if the "Grit croakers," as he called them, had been there, they would find evidences of the error of their statements regarding the condition of the country.

But if the "Grit croaker" had been there he would have told Mr. Wallace what was a fact, that every one of those farms had decreased in value thirty or thirty-five per cent, during the last fifteen years, He would have told Mr. Wallace: Yes, this is a fine country. The sun does not shine upon a better in its course. Yet on every one of those farms they deplore the loss of a son or daughter who has gone to the United States to find what his own native country does not give him. This is the strongest possible arraignment of the policy of the present Government, that, with the undoubted advantages we have, these people of Orangeville and surrounding country cannot keep their own children at home.

The Minister of Finance also said on that occasion that the country was prosperous to a degree, and the story of the exodus was invented simply by the Grits. There might be, he said, a few emigrants now and then, and what, think you, was the cause Mr. Foster[98] told them of these people leaving the country? You who have not read the speech could not possibly divine it. What little exodus there may be out of the country is caused, according to Mr. Foster, by the articles in the *Globe* newspaper. According to Messrs. Foster and Wallace, those who leave the country leave it simply because they read the *Globe* newspaper.

Well, sir, the *Globe* is a very good paper in many ways. I commend the *Globe* and I commend the editor of the *Globe*, who is on the platform tonight. I am glad to see a compliment paid by an opponent, but I am a Frenchman, and must show the chivalry which is credited to my race. I must stand up for the Conservative press. It is not fair for Mr. Foster to discount its influence. If the people around Orangeville read the *Globe*, is it possible they do not also read the *Empire*? If the *Globe* tells them they are not prosperous, is it possible they do not read the *Empire*, which tells them they are prosperous? Is it possible the people of Orangeville and vicinity are so stupid as to believe the *Globe*, when it tells them they are not prosperous, when they are? Are they such geese as not to know their own circumstances, but must rely upon the Grit papers to tell them?

Sir, such arguments do not deserve any answer. There was another meeting held elsewhere. At the present time there is a roving commission going from place to place to find flaws, if flaws there be, in the National Policy. A few weeks ago they were in the city of Saint John, N.B., and his admirers gave Mr. Foster a banquet. To this I have no objection. At this banquet, a fellow countryman of mine, who happens to be Minister of Agriculture, Mr. Angers, made a speech.[99] He proved that he could be, on any occasion, the equal of an Englishman, that he could be equal to his predecessor, Sir John Carling.[100] He gave figures to his hearers, and spoke of the exodus and prosperity of the country, and told the people assembled that the exodus "was not of a very great size."

He spoke in a city which in ten years has not increased in population, but has actually lost two thousand souls. The population of Saint John under Mackenzie's regime exceeded forty thousand; by the last census the population was reduced to under forty thousand. That is to say, that the whole of the natural increase had been swept away, and two thousand souls more. He spoke in a Province in which the whole increase during the ten years was thirty-seven; that is, that the whole of the natural increase had been swept away, together with every immigrant except thirty-seven. Yet Mr. Angers said the exodus was not of a very great size.

We read in the Sacred Book that the Lord one day sent His angels to smite the first born of a people to punish them for their cruelty. But here not only the first born are swept away, but the whole issue of the people is extinguished. Yet Mr. Angers says that the exodus is not of a very great size. The newspaper report did not say that this statement was received with any cheers, but if they did not they did not do him that justice to which he is entitled, because it must have been something new to them to know that the exodus was of no great size.

What would be the condition of New Brunswick and of the city of Saint John if the exodus had been of a great size? There would have been nothing left of the city; the whole population would have been swept away. Under Mr. Mackenzie the city of

Saint John was swept by a disastrous fire.[101] I assert in your presence, without fear of successful contradiction, that the National Policy has done more to injure the city of Saint John than that great fire, and, in the face of this, Mr. Angers could tell them that the exodus was of no great size.

Once a missionary went to preach the good news to a heathen city. From the first house which he passed he received the contents of a pot of boiling water. He did not go further, he thought he had gone far enough, and went back and told his friends what had occurred. He was asked: "What did you say?" and replied, "I thanked them." "For what?" "Because," he answered, "they did not send the pot as well as the water."

Well, sir, the people of Saint John must thank Mr. Angers for knowing that the exodus was not of a great size. The statement was made at a dinner given in honour of Mr. Foster, who, as you know, is, or was, a cold-water man. He is still a cold-water man, I believe, yet of not the same degree of intensity as in former days. In former days I remember, in the House of Commons he wanted every man to be a cold-water man like himself. He seems to have changed his view, but for that I have no remark to make, save this: that the statements of Mr. Angers require a good deal of cold water to wash down, and perhaps something stronger as well.

But, Sir, the ills of Canada today are not constitutional; they are altogether of an economic nature. In my humble opinion we should set it down at once that this is an assembly of plain and practical men, met together to deal with plain and practical questions. I agree with every word of the Chairman of today. We might be tempted, and the occasion would be a tempting one, to enlarge the political horizon, to enter new fields, and perhaps direct a policy to the future destiny of Canada. Some people – perhaps they are represented here – favour closer union with the Mother Country; some want Canada to take rank with the other nations of the earth; and there are some today who would favour the union of the two great branches of the Anglo-Saxon race on this continent.

Sir, I respect all these opinions; but listen to me when I say that we should not indulge in speculative politics. This Convention ought to be confined to plain and practical questions. It is not when the house is on fire that we should think of needed improvements. Our first duty is to arouse the people to a sense of their immediate danger, and the immediate danger is the tariff which now oppresses Canada.

There is, as you well know, a universal consensus of opinion among all classes, nay among all parties in this country, that the tariff which now prevails in Canada is a burdensome tariff, that it is an oppressive tariff, and that what was known at one time as the National Policy has been found to be a fraud and a failure. I say there is this universal consensus of opinion amongst us that the tariff has to be reformed.

What do you see in Ontario today? A large section among the rank and file of the Conservative Party openly declaring that they want to undo the evil they helped to establish in former years. Look in the ranks of the faithful, those who are ministerial to the backbone. Last session we saw man after man rising in his place in Parliament and proposing amendments to the tariff, men like Messrs. Cleveland, of Richmond, Pope, of Compton, and others, proposing to take one brick here and another there, until the wall was threatened with destruction.

Sir, the feeling became so unanimous among the Conservatives themselves that the Government had to come forward and promise that they would deal with the question and reform the tariff. That was the promise extracted from them, but what reform can you expect from men who tell you that the country is prosperous and that there is no exodus; who tell you that their system is perfect and hardly in need of modification?

Look at what took place a few months ago. Sir John Thompson,[102] at the Board of Trade banquet in Toronto, told a large audience that the Government would be prepared next session to lop off some mouldering branches. When we came to the session we were fully prepared to see the Government lop off these mouldering branches; but we found that the Government had changed their view, and what were mouldering branches in January, like the rod of Moses, became towering boughs in March. They had no alteration to make.

Gentlemen, you have nothing to expect from them. Apart from the logic of events, you have the word of Mr. Foster himself, who has declared again and again within the last few weeks that tariff reform would consist in this, that there might be a few changes here and there, but that the principle of protection in the National Policy would be maintained. This simply means that the Government are going to scratch off the paint, and put on a new coat of varnish, and call it tariff reform. Mr. Chairman, again upon this occasion, I want it to be well understood that we take direct issue here and now with the Government. The Government tells us that the principle of the National Party they are going to maintain, and we answer to the Government that the principle of the National Party is vicious and must be taken off – not only the branches.

Sir, you remember what took place previous to the defeat of Mr. Mackenzie. At that time we had for Premier, as you well know, a man of unbending rectitude. There never was a purer or a greater man in my estimation in Canada than Alexander Mackenzie. He would not stoop to pander to what he supposed to be popular prejudice. He thought that the country could not be made prosperous by high taxation. The people believed otherwise. I have no fault to find with anybody, and no criticism to offer. The time for recrimination is gone. But I appeal to your judgment in the face of the experience of the last fifteen years under the system which was introduced by the Conservative Party, which was dubbed the National Policy, to say if that system is not vicious in principle, iniquitous in its terms and dangerous in its consequences. I say that it is vicious in principle.

I want to know – and I put the question so as to be heard through the length and breadth of this country – by virtue of what principle will you tax a man to enrich his neighbour? By virtue of what principle will you tax the farmer in order to give work to the workingman? On what principle will you tax the workingman in order to give better prices to the farmer?

We were told in 1877 and 1878 that by adopting a policy of high taxation we should create labour, and if we created labour, those who bore the burden would be recouped in some way. All these promises have been found to be fallacious. If the principle had been true that by high taxation we would create labour, we would see the result today, our population would be increased. And you were told that you would have a population of teeming thousands in the cities of Canada.

What are the results? I am going to give you just a few figures which are, in my estimation, a most eloquent arraignment of the National Policy. During the period from 1871 to 1881 in the Province of Ontario there was an increase of 342,071 souls. In the following period, from 1881 to 1891, the increase of population fell from 342,071 to 151,553, a decrease of more than fifty per cent. In Quebec during the previous period the increase of population was 167,511, and in the following period the increase was 130,035, or a decrease of 37,000.

In Prince Edward Island in the former period the increase was 14,870; in the following period the increase was how many? Not even 1,000; not even 500, nor even 200, but simply 189. In Nova Scotia the increase was in the previous period 52,772, while in the following period it was 9,920. In New Brunswick the increase was in the former period 33,639, while in the second period it had fallen off to just thirty-seven. The whole increase was swept away.

Such figures as these are the strongest possible arraignment of the National Policy. It is true there has been an increase in Manitoba in some respects, but Manitoba has been peculiarly situated. The fine prairies of the west have, to some extent, attracted immigration, but we know by the figures of the census, which have been taken from time to time, that not more than fifty per cent of the immigrants who went to Manitoba remained there. There is not, I may say, a single Province throughout the Dominion which clamors so much and so loudly to be freed from the incubus of the National Policy.

I appeal to the farmers who are now before me if it is not true that the most difficult period for the farmer is the period following the first settlement. This is the period when, if the farmer is to be favoured, he should be assisted, but the farmers of Manitoba have been forced to pay tribute to the manufacturers of the East. Manitoba would hail with joy the day when it would be freed from the incubus of the National Policy. We are told that we cannot say that the National Policy has been the cause of the exodus, because when the people leave the country, they go to the United States, which has also a protective tariff. The argument is a captious one. It is true that the National Policy is nothing but a servile copy of the American system of protection.

The Conservative Party, the loyal party, left the example of the Mother Country and went over to the other side for a policy, and they brought it back singing "God Save the Queen." They advocated that policy in 1878. In 1879, after they were returned to power, they introduced an American nostrum and gave it to the loyal people of Canada. When they were told by people like myself, who claim to be as loyal as they are, but whose loyalty is in the heart, and not on the lips, "You are endangering British connection," they said. "So much the worse for British connection." They adopted the policy, but the result was not what they had expected. The policy did not stop the exodus, as they said it would. The exodus under their policy doubled and trebled.

What is the reason the policy prospered comparatively in the United States and not in Canada? The reason is that the great variety of climate to the south of the line, their increasing population and the great accumulation of wealth, were a protection against protection. They had free trade amongst an ever-increasing community, and were saved by free trade notwithstanding the high protection. But there was more. You know very well that this wisdom which was borrowed by our Government from the United States has been condemned by the American people.

You know very well that this Yankee system has been condemned by a majority of the states and a majority of the popular vote. Last year there was a Democratic convention, and on that occasion they declared: "That we condemn Republican protection as a fraud and a robbery of the great majority of the American people for the benefit of a few." That condemnation was endorsed by the American people at the first opportunity following, and they declared in the most emphatic language that the system of protection over there was a fraud and a robbery.

Mr. Chairman and Gentlemen, I submit to your judgment that the servile copy of the American system which has been brought amongst us by the leaders of the Conservatives, is, like its prototype, a fraud and a robbery, and I call upon you one and all to pronounce at once and give your emphatic support to the proposition that we shall never rest until we have wiped away from our system that fraud and robbery under which Canadians suffer.

But, Sir, there is something more. We pronounce today in favour of tariff reform, and our opponents have borrowed the word from us. You know it has been the system of the Conservative Party more than once, whenever their clothes became dilapidated, to steal the clothes of their opponents, and present themselves before the people decently attired. This is what they want to do again, and on this occasion I do not object to their stealing our clothes, but I do object to their appearing before the country in false colours. They want to reform the tariff and still to retain the principle of protection. I submit to you that the ideal fiscal system is the British system of free trade.

Sir, my loyalty, as I stated, does not ooze from the pores of my body, but I do want to go for an example to the Mother Country, and not to the United States, much as I respect and love the people on the other side of the line. I say the policy should be a policy of free trade, such as they have in England, but I am sorry to say that the circumstances of the country cannot admit, at present, of that policy in its entirety. But I propose to you that from this day henceforward it should be the goal to which we aspire. I propose to you from this day, although we cannot adopt the policy itself, to adopt the principle which regulates it; that is to say, that though it should be your misfortune for many years to come to have to raise a revenue by custom duties, these duties should be levied only so far as is necessary to carry on the business of the Government.

I submit to you that not a cent should be extracted from the pockets of the people, except every cent goes into the treasury of the people and not into the pockets of anybody else. I submit to you that no duty should be levied for protection's sake, but levied altogether and only for the purpose of filling the treasury to the limits required. I submit to you that every cent that is levied should be levied first and foremost upon the luxuries of the people. I submit to you, therefore, that the system of protection which is maintained by the Government, that is to say of levying tribute upon the people not for the legitimate expenses of the Government but for a private and privileged class, should be condemned without qualification.

Let it be well understood that from this moment we have a distinct issue with the party in power. Their ideal is protection, our ideal is free trade. Their immediate object is protection; ours a tariff for revenue only. Upon this issue we engage the battle from this moment forward, and I ask you once more never to desist until we have achieved victory, until we have freed this country from the incubus which has been weighing it down for fifteen long years.

Nothing is more difficult – that is one of the evils of protection – than to wipe away protection, because under it interests have been established which every man who has at heart the interest of all classes must take into consideration. It is always easy to increase the tariff, because by so doing you increase the private fortunes of certain individuals; but whenever you decrease the tariff it has always to be done with careful consideration, and I am sure that when the Liberals are in power they will not be indifferent to this primary truth.

Anyone in this audience, any Conservative in the country, if I ask: Do you crave more markets for your produce? would answer: "Yes." If I were to tell him: There is on the other side of the line a nation of sixty-five million of the Anglo Saxon race, that is the greatest commercial race in the world, would you not like to trade with them untrammeled and unfettered? he would answer "Yes."

Years ago we had a treaty of reciprocity with the United States confined to natural products, it is true, but under it trade developed rapidly, and you know that was the golden era in the history of the trade of Canada. Again and again the wish has been expressed that we should obtain that market if possible, but it has become a settled fact with both the great parties in the United States that they will not renew the treaty of 1854, that is to say, a treaty confined to natural products, but manufactures have to be included as well. In 1888 we adopted a policy of untrammelled trade with the United

States. This policy was distorted by the wicked perversions of our opponents. They asserted on the platform and in the press that what we wanted was unrestricted reciprocity, and nothing else, and that we would not take anything else, whereas the fact was that we were prepared to negotiate upon a basis of unrestricted reciprocity, but we would have been happy to obtain any possible measure of reciprocity in natural products and manufactures.

The Liberal Party, when it formulated the policy of unrestricted reciprocity, never disguised that there were difficulties in the way, and that when we came to negotiate the treaty, several lines of manufactured goods would have to be eliminated, but what we wanted was to send a commission to Washington to lay down a basis of negotiations for a treaty. We would have supported our opponents in any similar policy, but, while professing a willingness to go to Washington and negotiate a treaty, they never had any such intention, and while with one breath they told the people they wanted to negotiate a treaty, with the next they said we were disloyal because we wanted to negotiate a treaty.

You know the part disloyalty played in the last election. I am loyal to the British crown. I have often stated in the Province of Quebec, and I am happy to repeat it today when so many of my fellow countrymen of French origin are present, that we owe a debt of gratitude to the British Crown for the way it has treated us in the last fifty years. Loyal although I am, I do not think it would be my part to say that the interests of a colony are the interests of the Empire. Take the best families in the land, there is often a diversity of interests between the members of that family, and there is a diversity of interests between the members of an empire.

The commercial interests of England are not the interests of Canada, and the commercial interests of Canada are not the commercial interests of England; and there is no Conservative who can gainsay this doctrine, for the fact that England is free trade and the

Canadian Conservatives protectionist shows that there is in their opinion a diversity of interests between England and Canada.

Sir, I want now to say this, if the interests of Canada clash with the interests of England, is it in any part of my loyalty or yours that we should make the interests of Canada give way to the interests of Great Britain? What is the reason, I want to know, that my ancestors left the shores of France to come to this then savage country? Simply because they were not satisfied with their condition in France and thought they would better it in Canada. What is the reason your own fathers left the shores of Great Britain, of England, Ireland and Scotland? Simply because your own fathers were not satisfied with their condition upon their native soil, but believed that by coming to this country they would build up for themselves and their families a better and more prosperous condition of things. And are we, their descendants, to be told when we find our interests clashing with those of the Mother Land, we must stand by the Mother Land? I do not admit any such loyalty as that, and I am quite sure of the position that would be adopted in any part of Great Britain. I would not hesitate to go upon any platform there and state the same thing that I say tonight, I am a British subject, and if it were my lot to have been a member of the British House of Commons I would speak like an Englishman and stand up for England in preference to Canada every time. But I am a member of Her Majesty's House of Commons of Canada, and I leave it to Englishmen who represent the interests of Her Majesty's subjects in the Imperial Parliament to deal with the interests of the English nation, and I call upon the people of Canada to stand up for the interests of Canada. And if there be any man in this audience – no there is no one in this audience, but if there be any man outside of this audience – who says he stands up in preference for the interests of England, I tell him "Go back to England, that is your home."

And, in speaking as I do, I claim I am perfectly loyal, because Her Majesty the Queen does not expect that any of her Canadian subjects should abase themselves or should refuse to stand up for the interests of their country; but she expects from us upon every occasion that the interests of Canada shall be paramount. Again I say, this is loyalty such as I understand it. But there is more than this to satisfy the conscience, the supercilious conscience of those extreme Conservatives who, I am afraid, will not be satisfied with anything except the possession of power. Let me tell them this, that if a treaty is negotiated by Canada with a foreign country, that treaty will have to be ratified by the Government of Her Majesty the Queen in England, and if the British Government object that we should make such a treaty, then, Sir, and not sooner, it will be time to raise objections.

What I claim is that upon this policy of reciprocity, it should be well known and well understood that, while claiming to do the best for our country, we know full well that our action is subject to the approbation of the Government of Her Majesty the Queen. These two questions, in my judgment, ought to constitute mainly the programme of the Liberal Party. The battle in which we are engaged at this moment is a battle for the welfare of Canada, and the welfare of Canada depends upon her fiscal policy.

But there are other questions still. One of the evils of the National Policy and the system of protection has been here, as everywhere else, to lower the moral level of public life. It is a subject, however, into which I do not desire to enter at length. I speak of it more in sorrow than in anger; but I tell you this, if you want to purify the political atmosphere not a cent is to be levied except what is necessary to carry on the legitimate expenses of the Government economically administered. I speak of this subject more in sorrow than in anger, but there is not a man who has in his bosom a patriotic heart who does not see with shame that the name of Canada has become the by-word of corruption among the civilized nations of the earth.

There are other questions, but we have not time to take up too many. One or two, however, ought not to be forgotten. We should endeavour to retain in every election an honest expression of the public mind and of the public will. We must be governed by the majority. I do not say that the majority is always right, but until we have something better we must abide by the rule that the majority must govern. What I want is a true and honest expression of the public mind. I object, therefore, to those laws which have been placed on the statute book by the men in power, not to have an honest expression of the public mind but to distort the true expression of the public will. I denounce it to you as infamy. I say that the best and safest principle is to revert to the old policy we had in former years of having a Provincial franchise.

This system prevailed for eighteen years after Confederation and I never heard a single complaint against it. In 1885 this infamous Act was passed. So infamous is it that the men who promoted it dare not put it in force because the law requires that there should be revision of the list every year. But a revision every year costs so much that the Government are begged by their followers not to put that expense upon them. But the Act is put in force on the eve of an election because it gives to the party in power an unfair advantage.

Again I denounce this other infamy, the system of gerrymander. Under our own system it is necessary that there should be after every census a redistribution of seats. There is but one basis to adopt, the basis of the Mother Land. There have been redistributions in the Mother Land, but there has never been a word of complaint, because the redistribution takes place upon a well-known basis and principles, and that is that the boundary of no county should be interfered with. That is a principle which ought to be adopted here, and I hope that upon this we shall have a most emphatic expression from this Convention.

There are other questions, and it would not be fair on my part not to deal with them. Within the last fifteen days I have received several applications from different parts of the country asking me, "What are you going to do about Temperance?" "What are you going to do about Prohibition?" I ought to speak frankly upon this. I don't pretend at this moment to give you any more than my views. On a former occasion I already announced that this was a free, democratic Convention, in which no cut-and-dried resolutions are to be placed before you. You are free to move upon Prohibition or anything else that you choose, but I ask you simply to allow me to give you my view.

You are aware that two years ago, against our protest, however, the Government of the day appointed a commission to investigate the liquor question, not only in this country, but in other countries as well. This was done against our protest. We believed – I still believe, for my part – that we have all the information we require on which to form an opinion upon this subject. The Dominion Alliance, which is the great Prohibition Parliament of the country, has a representative to speak for it upon the floor of the House of Commons. That gentleman is Mr. Dickey.[103] You know very well that not upon one occasion, but during two sessions – the sessions of 1892 and 1893 – the Dominion Alliance, by the mouths of its spokesman and the other members of the Alliance upon the floor of the House of Commons, declared that until that commission had reported the question of prohibition it should be left in abeyance, so far as the Dominion Parliament is concerned.

Well, Sir, for my part, I do not see how, as long as his report is to come, as long as this investigation is to proceed and as long as the Dominion Alliance professes to be satisfied with it, the Liberal Party in Parliament can deal with it. Let me go one step further. As far as

I am personally concerned, I am prepared to give my views now and at once upon this question, and as soon as it is removed from the state it is in now I shall not hesitate to give my views with no uncertain sound. It would be premature to say how I would speak or vote, but my mind is made up and I will be prepared to give my advice to the Liberal Party for them to act upon it or not, just as they please. As long as the commission is deliberating it would be impossible for us to frame a policy. If they did the Government would go to their friends and say: This is not fair towards us, who are seeking information at your request, and therefore do not ask us to have an issue on this. We could not have issue on this subject and, gentlemen, I want to have an issue with the Government on every question that comes up.

Now it is my duty to refer to another matter which is an irritating subject because it touches questions of creed and race. I refer to the Manitoba school question. I have received several communications urging me to take a course upon that question. Different persons in the various Provinces have asked me to take opposite courses. To them I have given no answer. I give it now, Gentlemen. I wish the question were in any other condition. Those of you who follow political events know that last session Mr. Tarte on the one hand and Mr. Dalton McCarthy on the other agreed that the Government were a pack of cowards, that they did not deal with that subject in a manly way.[104] For my part I spoke in the same sense, and I now say that the Government acted in a cowardly way and did not dare to speak either one way or the other. It was their burden and duty to say one thing or the other, but instead of acting like men of courage they allowed passion to be inflamed in Manitoba and Quebec and never dared to stand up like men and put an issue of the question. They are to be blamed for this. They shunted the question to the courts, where it is now. The Opposition are not in a position to take any action until such time when a report has been given by the courts, and until the courts have decided whether or not the Government have the right to interfere. Then, Sir, it will be time for us to say we will act or not. In my estimation it is not prudent now that the question is before the court, to deal with it, because it would be appealing to prejudices which it would be better should be left aside. For my part, on the temperance question, I say it is possible the time may never come to speak on this subject again in Parliament, because, if the courts decide that the Government have no right to interfere, that will be an end of the question forever.

One word more. It is now twenty-six years since Confederation. It was openly said at the time that the object of those who framed the constitution was to make this Canada of ours a nation under progressive British institutions. For my part I have always regretted that, upon that occasion a Province was trampled on, instead of an appeal being made to the best instincts of their hearts. Such an appeal made to the people of Nova Scotia would have reconciled them long ago to a system, in my estimation, which is a noble one, because it has a great aim. Now and forever, whether we are in Opposition or in power, it will ever be our aim upon every occasion to appeal to the generous heart of the people and not resort to force or coercion.

We are divided in this country as to race and creed, but I am glad to see that in the high aim we have the view there is no creed or racial division. There is nothing broader and more lasting upon which we desire to build up a nation. But is it sufficient to [merely] have a moral basis for a people? We must have material prosperity, and the prosperity of the people depends upon our fiscal policy. We are probably on the eve of a general election. When it will come is among the secrets of the gods whose Olympus is upon Parliament Hill yonder. It is possible we may have a repetition of the decade of the last dissolution and it, therefore, behooves us to be henceforth prepared for the fray, whenever it comes. Let us resolve, here and now and henceforward and for every moment from this day until the battle has been won, that we will never cease our efforts, and for my part in this struggle I will endeavour to do my duty to the best of my ability, and I hope, and I am sure, that every one of you, general, colonel, captain and private, whenever it comes, will always be found at his post. . . .

The Chairman: – So far as I know this is the last resolution to be put to the meeting and there can be no happier one with which to conclude the convention than one which will call for a response from our esteemed and honoured leader. Those who are minded that this resolution shall pass will please signify their assent by rising. *The resolution was carried unanimously by a standing vote amidst enthusiastic applause.*

Laurier: – Mr. Chairman and Gentlemen: Once more we part. I must tender you my thanks, my very hearty thanks, for the numberless acts of kindness with which you have overwhelmed me on this occasion. I had hoped from the first that this convention would be a success. Still, while hoping, I was not without doubt. In fact I may say I was tossed between hopes and doubts, but in my most sanguine moments I never anticipated the success it has turned out to be. It has surpassed all my expectations, and I believe all the expectations of my most sanguine friends. I owe you thanks, Gentlemen, thanks to all. I cannot thank you each personally, but let me take this opportunity of tendering thanks more especially to the leaders from the several Provinces who have helped us in this convention, first and foremost, to our old friend Sir Oliver Mowat; next to our young, active and able friend, Mr. Fielding, of Nova Scotia; to Premier Blair, to Premier Peters, and last but not least, to my good friend, Honourable Mr. Joly.

You have been, Gentlemen, altogether too kind to me. You have, in the kindness of your hearts, attributed to me a character and traits I do not claim to have. Were I as good and great as you

174

have described me in your speeches I would have reason to feel proud, and I do not feel proud at all. I would feel proud if under my leadership the Liberals had won. The Liberals have once gone to the country since I took the reins of power. Did I say "power"?

A delegate: Prophetic.

Mr. Laurier: Since I took the lead, and we lost. Those around me in the House of Commons know full well that it was with the greatest possible reluctance I accepted the duties on the withdrawal of Mr. Blake from the leadership. I did not want the position. I, for many reasons into which it is not proper for me to enter at this moment, would have preferred to serve in the ranks of the party, as I had done in the past, and it was my hope that the health of Mr. Blake would be restored, and that before many months he would come back to the position which his great talents and many fine qualities fitted him for. Unfortunately our expectations were not realized. Mr. Blake, for reasons of his own, could not or would not resume the leadership.

Since that time I have been discharging the duties to the best of my ability, but I do not claim for myself the credit of whatever measure of success we have obtained. I attribute it to the able lieu-tenants by whom I am surrounded in the House. I give the full share of praise and of merit to our friend, Sir Richard Cartwright, a man whose mental qualities are well known to you all, but whose qualities of heart are well known also; to our friend, Mr. Mills, who knows everything, who has read everything – and I can tell you, in the position I occupy, it is always pleasant, instead of having to go to the library for books, to turn to Mr. Mills for the knowl-edge required; to our friend, Mr. Davies, a brave of the brave, a man who is ready whenever the call of duty comes; to our friend, Mr. Charlton, who, on questions of trade and commerce, has more theoretical and practical knowledge than any man in the House; to our friend, Mr. Paterson, who is a power whenever he chooses to be a power; to our friend Mr. Mulock, who, though young in the House, is already one of the most effective debaters we have; to our friend Mr. Edgar, whose qualities are well known to you.[105]

Well, Gentlemen, I will stop here, because if I go on I shall have to name the whole Liberal Party in the House. In the last election we were defeated. We are on the eve of another election, and, if I am not mistaken the result may be different. But let me tell you this, that though we hope for victory, still, you know that victory does not always come to those who expect it. Let me tell you that, whatever may be the result of the next election, even if it be defeat, I will never know what discouragement is. We are here to fight, and fight we will until these principles of truth and justice we have proclaimed today have won. It may be that it will not be the first time. You know that to politicians, as to others, very often reverses come when victory is expected, but let us say that whatever be the result of the next election, if we do not triumph we will go on fighting to the end.

Gentlemen, as you know I have the honour to be of French origin and I am proud of my origin. They say the French are a fickle race, but I do not pretend to be French in that respect. I claim something of the British tenacity and in matters of importance when my mind is made up I never vary in it, and my mind is made up that we shall fight this battle; and I can only repeat: "Let every man be at his post and every man do his duty."

The National Anthem was sung and the convention adjourned.

By Dr. Thomas S. Axworthy

The political gods had begun to smile on Wilfrid Laurier and the Liberal Party in 1893. Sir John A. Macdonald, the merry destroyer of Liberal hopes, had died in 1891 and the successor Conservative administration was floundering. Edward Blake, the former leader of the Liberal Party who had turned on Laurier a day after the 1891 campaign in his famous West

176

Durham letter questioning the Liberal platform of "unrestricted reciprocity" with the United States, had left Canadian politics to enter the British House of Commons in 1892. His predecessors' long shadow no longer put Laurier in the shade. It was finally time for Laurier to shape events himself.

And shape them he did: in a master stroke, Laurier called a national convention of Liberal delegates to meet at the Rideau Rink in Ottawa in June 1893 to heal party divisions, demonstrate new talent, and prepare a platform. The result was the largest, most representative, and successful political convention yet seen in Canada, and by employing this mechanism, Laurier not only helped himself politically in the short term but he set a precedent for party members and delegates to join the caucus and the leader as political decision makers. Building on the 1893 precedent, in 1919, following Laurier's death, the Liberal Party was the first to call delegates together, not only to shape a platform but to choose a new leader. Ever since, political conventions in Canada have made and unmade the leaders of our parties.

Political party conventions were an American invention (like so many political innovations adopted by Canada, such as polling, attack ads, direct mail, and social media). In 1831, the National Republican Party met in Baltimore to nominate Henry Clay, and the Democrats soon followed suit to nominate Andrew Jackson. Previously, candidates had been chosen in the congressional caucus of the two main parties, but in the 1830s American parties opened their doors to non-elected partisans. As Kenneth C. Davies writes in The Smithsonian, "King caucus was dead."

George Brown's Grit Party[106] had organized the first political convention in Canada in 1859 when 600 delegates from across Ontario met to debate and endorse the new idea of a federal Canada (and condemn the tricks of Sir. John A., something Liberals were still doing in 1893). But the idea had not been tried in the post-Confederation era, and no one had yet attempted to organize a national convention with delegates from across the country. Laurier candidly told the convention, "I had hoped from the first that this convention would be a success. Still, while hoping I was not without doubt." But urged on by J.S. Willison, editor of the Globe (Brown's old newspaper, which had equally promoted the 1859 Reform Party convention), the Liberal members of the House of Commons passed a resolution calling for a national meeting. The call for the convention established the federal parliamentary constituency as the basis for representation. "Each Electoral District shall be represented by the Liberal member sitting for the same, or the Liberal candidate defeated in the last election held therein, and by five delegates appointed by the Liberal Association for the district." Delegates from federal constituency associations have dominated every political convention since then.

The 1893 Liberal meeting had 1,800 delegates from every province except British Columbia (Liberals there sent a telegram), the talents of a batch of Liberal premiers, in particular Sir Oliver Mowat, premier of Ontario, who was chairman of the convention. More than sixty reporters were in attendance. Laurier also used the conventions to heal his divided party: in his speech he again affirmed the sacred cause of free trade, saying it was his long-term goal (thus keeping faith with the 1891 platform); but for now, he said, Canada needed revenue, and the only way to attain it was to keep tariffs, "duties only so far as necessary to carry on the business of the Government" (thus appeasing the Blake wing of the party). He was rewarded with a resolution overwhelmingly endorsing his leadership – not bad for someone who had lost the 1891 election!

Laurier had always been known as an orator. Beginning with the 1893 convention he also showed that he was no ordinary political manager. He had pulled off an organizational feat by having Canada's first national convention, brought rank and file party members into the decision-making mix, showcased talent for a new cabinet, and united the party with an artful compromise on the issue of free trade. His focus now was power as well as ideals: as he told Liberals on the eve of the convention, "it is not enough to have good principles; they must have organization. Principles without organization may lose but organization without principles may often win." Laurier had learned that political ideas without organization, money, and *communications to gain power to put them into effect are only aspirations. It was a lesson the Liberal Party took to heart.*

Dr. Thomas S. Axworthy is a senior fellow at both the Munk School of Global Affairs and Massey College in the University of Toronto.

TARIFFS AND TAXATION

PEMBROKE, ONTARIO

MAY 14, 1894[107]

I have no fault to find with the man who votes either Grit or Tory, but I would be better pleased if the conscience of the man impels him to vote Grit rather than Tory. But men, whether they be Grit or Tory, too often forget the Government exists for the people and not the people for the Government; too often men are carried away by prejudices or party bias or passion. They forget that questions with which they have to deal do not mean merely the advancement of Mr. So-and-So, but that these questions affect the material interests of the people of this country.

I claim no merit nor any extraordinary virtue, though virtue is to be depended upon and maintained, but I speak to you for a more common thought when I say to you, "follow the dictates of your own conscience and nothing else," because I am sure that if you do that, upon the questions now dividing the parties you will be overwhelmingly on the side of the Liberals; you will vote Liberal, whatever you may have done in the past. (Applause)

I affirm here [in Pembroke] this principle, that the only measure of taxation that is legitimate before the eyes of God or man himself is that which is limited to the necessities of revenue, and not one cent more. (Cheers) This is the principle upon which we contend on the side of politics to which I belong. On the other hand, the Conservative Party have a different policy. The Government at Ottawa tells you that they are levying taxation upon the people of the country for the necessities of revenue, not to carry on the administration, not to dispose of the business of this country, but they maintain that their principle is to levy taxation upon the people in order to take the money from the pockets of some and put it in the pockets of others.

I speak here to the Conservatives [in the audience]. I do not address myself to the Liberals. The Liberals are of the same mind that I am. If I have left my duties at Ottawa it is not to reach the just, but to save the sinner. The Minister of Finance has told you that the principle of the Conservative Party is to levy taxation upon the people, not for the necessities of revenue, but in order to create works, to develop the industries of the country to be extended at the expense of your or my pocket. (Hear, hear) If they are to be developed by duties, well and good, but I object to taking money out of one class of people and putting it into the hands of another class. The Conservative Party calls this protection; the Liberal Party and the moral law calls it robbery – legalized robbery – which can have no justification before God or man.

I do not object that the tariff has enriched the manufacturers, and they benefit by it; but let the manufacturer hear my words: I object that they should go to Ottawa and force the Government to levy taxation upon the people, not for the necessities of revenue, but in order to put money in their own pockets. . . .

No sane man will deny that it would be an infinite blessing if we had the freedom of the American market, which is our natural market, but, unfortunately, the same political heresy prevails over there as we have here. When we appealed to the country on the issue of reciprocity [in the 1891 election] the Tories first accused us of being disloyal, but later on they did not fail to observe the trend of public opinion, and while still adhering to the loyalty cry where it could be of service to them, they announced that an offer of reciprocity in natural products had been made by the American government.

As a Canadian of French origin, I say here boldly that I love England as much as any man, because under the flag of England I enjoy more freedom than I would under the flag of old France. Men are prone to love most the flag that gives them most freedom, but much as I love England I love Canada more. I am first, last and all the time a Canadian, and if it should so happen that English and Canadian interests clash then I am going to stand by Canadian interests.

I stand here as a man, erect and fearing nobody, in the cause of what I believe to be the path of rectitude, but let my tongue adhere to the roof of my mouth if ever it has to utter falsehoods, whether it be the price of power or anything else.

I appeal to you all, my fellow countrymen, to band yourselves together for the supreme struggle. I appeal to you all without regard to nationality, race or creed; I appeal to you Scotchmen, who have led in the van of freedom; to you Englishmen, Irishmen, Germans who come from lands less free in another continent; I appeal to you my fellow countrymen of French Canadian origin; rise up to the occasion for the supreme struggle to maintain principle. I call no man in question. It is a great principle for which we are struggling. I ask for your assistance, one and all. (Cheers)

You have an election in the Province of Ontario, and we ask you for your support for that little giant, Sir Oliver Mowat. Stand firm by the man who has given to the Province of Ontario a Government which is the envy of all civilized nations, a Government which has existed for twenty-two years, and a Government against which you cannot bring a breath of scandal. I ask for your support for that Government, and then I go back to ask that when the greater struggle shall come you will give us your assistance in the cause of freedom of trade. (Great cheers)

By the Right Honourable Paul Martin

It was while growing up in Pembroke that my father first became attracted to the Liberalism of Sir Wilfrid Laurier at a very young age. My grandfather had moved his family to this Ottawa Valley community shortly after dad was born.

Grandfather Martin worked in the general store operated by his brother-in-law, Isidore Martin, a legendary Liberal who went on to serve as mayor of Pembroke.

Uncle Isidore was a Laurier man from early on, even attending, as a delegate from the Valley, the first-ever national political convention in post-Confederation history, called by then Opposition leader Wilfrid Laurier, in Ottawa in 1893.

I therefore have no doubt that uncle Isidore was in the audience on May 14, 1894 – an address Arthur has wisely chosen to include in this volume – when Laurier visited Pembroke.

It would therefore surprise no one that my father was one of Sir Wilfrid Laurier's youngest supporters. Dad was all of nine years old when his father took him to see Sir Robert Borden speak at the O'Brien Opera House during the 1917 election.

"I knew nothing about the election except what I had heard from my father, who was a great supporter of Sir Wilfrid Laurier, Borden's opponent," my father later wrote.

How many times did I hear my father tell the story that, as a scholarship student at Collège Apostolique Saint-Alexandre de la Gatineau – he came from a very poor family and could never have afforded the tuition – he somehow got a ride into Ottawa to be one of the thousands lining the streets for Sir Wilfrid Laurier's funeral. Let there be no doubt that for all of his life my father remained a Laurier Liberal.

For me, it was in Pembroke where I, too, was to spend some of the best moments of my own childhood with my aunts, and I learned about Laurier at their knees.

Public life has taken me many places and to many communities, both at home and abroad, but I have no finer memory than that of the day I returned to Pembroke while serving as minister of finance.

It was 1994 and I was asked to unveil the street sign for Paul Martin Sr. Drive. It was a wonderful day and I thought of my father and his favourite quotation of Sir Wilfrid's: "But, men, whether they be Grit or Tory, too often forget the Government exists for the people and not the people for the Government." It would not hurt if we remembered that today.

I, like my father, am proud to be a Laurier Liberal.

And it all began in Pembroke.

The Right Honourable Paul Martin was Canada's twenty-first prime minister.

FIRST VISIT TO MANITOBA

WINNIPEG, MANITOBA

SEPTEMBER 3, 1894[108]

Mr. Chairman, Ladies and Gentlemen, I could not certainly indulge in the pretension that these ringing cheers are evoked by any poor merits of my own. I rather believe that they are an encouragement to a Canadian who has done his best for the development and the fortune of his country, who has done his humble, sincere and earnest share to promote and to maintain her honour, to enhance her dignity, to advance her welfare and to make it a country in which it would be the pride of the humblest citizen to live, and even to die. (Applause)

Let me tell you that I never felt prouder than I felt this day of being a Canadian. When I was met at the station by the throng of sympathetic faces who had come to welcome me here I may say in all sincerity my heart was deeply touched. I felt that I was amongst fellow countrymen and brothers indeed. (Applause)

I have now visited almost all parts of Canada. I have seen the tempestuous shores of Nova Scotia, the dyke lands of the Bay of Fundy. I am familiar with almost every inch of my own native Province of Quebec; I am familiar with the region of the great lakes of Ontario; I have now seen the picturesque shores of Lake Superior.

I now come to the plains of Manitoba. I stand on my native land. I could not but feel a sentiment of pride when I saw this great city of Winnipeg, with its buildings and monuments where scarcely thirty years ago there was nothing here but the silent tread of the fur trader over the trackless prairie. This progress is due to the energy, activity, courage and pluck of the early pioneers of this city and province.

But let me ask you, great as has been your development, great as has been the success of this city and province, am I beyond the mark when I say that your expectations have not been realized. Is it not a fact that after thirty years of the life of this province . . . the goal which you had set up for yourself has not yet been attained? [Our previous speaker] has spoken to you about the predictions made at one time by a gentleman who occupied a high position, and who said that at the end of 1891, Manitoba and the Northwest Territories would produce 640 million bushels of wheat and the same gentleman predicted that by the end of 1891 the Government of Canada would sell enough land to pay for the construction of the Canadian Pacific Railway. You know how far from the truth these predictions have been. The sale of land has barely been sufficient to pay for the cost of administration.

What is the cause? Again I ask, what is the cause? The Government has told us that from a term of years commencing in 1881 and terminating in 1891 we should have 850 thousand people [in Manitoba] . . . we have scarcely 850 thousand from the boundaries of Ontario to the shores of the Pacific. We have, as you are aware, a Minister of the Interior from Manitoba.[109] This gentleman initiated his regime by stating in plain language that he was about to inaugurate a vigorous immigration policy. (Hear Hear) Where it is to be found and where are the results? We have heard from the gentleman a "vigorous verbosity" and that is about all. What is the cause of this?

Is the cause to be found in the soil? It would be blasphemy on it to attribute their cause to the soil. It would be a blasphemy on this fruitful soil of Manitoba to attribute the cause to it. There is not wheat that will rank higher than that of Manitoba, as it takes the front place in the markets of the world. Manitoba hard is a name familiar all over the broad world.

Then if the cause is not to be found in the soil, where is it? Is it in the climate? We have here a climate to make a strong and dominant race of the world. The cause is not be found in the climate. Can it be attributed to the institutions of the country? We must claim that some of these are very lax, but if it is not attributed to this, what can it be attributed to? What is the cause? I repeat. It is not in the soil, it is not in the climate and not in the institutions. Then, where is it to be found?

I must confess to admitting that it is to be found in the vicious policy followed by the Canadian Government for that last fifteen years. I do not come here to say things which will hurt the feelings of anyone, but I come here to speak to my fellow countrymen in all frankness, and to let them know the real position of affairs. I come here in the name of Liberal Party to present to you the policy of the Liberal Party. It has been represented by Conservative speakers and the Conservative press that the Liberal Party is the enemy of the Northwest. I repel the assertion with all the energy I am capable of. I do not want to impute motives, but perhaps by repeating it they have come to believe it themselves. But it is not consistent with history. I am prepared to prove by the records that the assertion is a slander upon the name and fame of the Liberal Party.

Who was the man who even before Confederation urged upon the Canadian Government the duty of acquiring this immense territory? I am proud to say, for the honor of the party to which I belong, that the man who deserved honour as the first promoter of the acquisition of these territories was the Honourable George Brown. (Applause) Now it has been said again and again that in later days my friends in the House of Commons – Sir Richard Cartwright,

Mr. Mills and others – have been enemies of the Northwest, have opposed legislation for its advancement and that the Conservative have been the friends of Manitoba and the Northwest. Sir, I defy any man in this audience to show that Sir Richard Cartwright, Mr. Mills or any other Liberal leader has opposed any legislation calculated to do good to the people of the Northwest. I say this without hesitation; on more than one occasion our friends in the House of Commons have opposed legislation which was really in the interest of monopoly. I believe there are few men but will admit that if the advice of such men as Edward Blake, Sir Richard Cartwright and other leaders of the Liberal Party had been followed the interests of the country would have been better served.

I come to expose to you the policy of the Liberal Party. Let me tell you that policy may be summed up in the good Saxon word, freedom. Freedom in every sense of the term. Freedom of speech, freedom of trade. The task of the Liberals of the province in particular, has been to prove to the world and to our countrymen the benefits which are to be derived from the principles of free trade. I come before you tonight to preach to you this new gospel of freedom of trade, new, yes, new to this country, new on this continent, new on the other side of the line in the American Republic, but not new on the other side of the water, and in the old land (Applause), not new in the small island which has been the cradle of all freedom and civilization, not new in that land from which we Liberals are proud to derive our inspiration.

You have the line of cleavage which exists between the Liberal Party and the Conservative Party: the question of free trade. We stand for freedom, they stand for restriction, they stand for servitude, we stand for freedom. I denounce the policy of protection as bondage, not in the same degree, perhaps, but in the same manner. The slave in the American Confederacy had no freedom: he grew tobacco for his master; he grew cotton or sugar, worked day and night in rain and in the sun, but he never derived a cent of profit from his labour; the greed of his master would take away from him all freedom, giving him only such a pittance as you give to your horses. In this same manner the people of this country, the inhabitants of the city of Winnipeg especially, are toiling for a master who takes away not every cent of profit from you but a very large percentage, a very great portion of your earnings, the earnings for which you toil and sweat. You have to toil and sweat for privileged masters.

You know that the Minister of Finance has his moments of weakness as every other man, but he has also his moments of frankness. Some years ago I was told by the Minister of Finance that in one of his moments of weakness he had advocated prohibition for Canada in the year 1884, but seven years afterwards he admitted that his position had been formed in a moment of weakness and that the matter had better go no further. There was a commission appointed to sit and get information to enlighten us, but he could not, he would not, make up his mind as to what he would do.

Well, this was three years [ago and] we have not yet received the result of that commission. Three years have elapsed but the result has not yet been made known. It took six months to appoint three commissioners, and then it took three commissioners two years to collect evidence to draw a report which may never appear. I don't know how long it will take to publish and print this report. I doubt if we will have it at all. I think the Minister of Finance practised a trick somewhat like a famous charlatan. Speaking to a crowd he said that he could take a donkey and teach it to write. "Bring me a donkey," he said. "The most donkey of all donkeys and I warrant that in ten years I will teach him how to read and write and make him a professor." "Done," said the King of the country; "but, mind you, if at the end of ten years the donkey does not read and write, off goes your head." "Accepted," said the charlatan, but one of his friends told him that he was sure to lose his head at the end of ten years. "Don't you fear," he replied. "At the end of ten years either myself or the King or the donkey will be dead." (Laughter)

Seeing that after three years we have not had the report, may I venture to say that Mr. [George] Foster, when he issued that commission, said to himself, "Before this commission has reported, prohibition or the Government will be dead." Prohibition is not dead, at least not in Manitoba, if I am to judge by the last election. (Applause) Prohibition is not dead but the Government is very sick. (Applause)

If our Minister of Finance has moments of weakness, he also has moments of frankness. Last session he told us that his object in putting taxes upon the people was not the replenishing of the treasure, but the favouring of special industries. What is the meaning of all that? It sounds well, but what does it mean? It means simply that if there are in Canada certain industries which cannot live by themselves, they will be made to live at the expense of the rest of the community. Are you of the opinion that it is well for the country that certain industries, no matter what their character, should be fed at the expense of the rest of the community? Do you believe that the community will be enriched by taxing itself to favour special industries? And do you, workingmen, believe that you will be rich if every day you have to pay part of your earnings to help somebody else in Eastern Canada? Taxation is an evil, but it is the price to be paid for civilized government. I do not tell you that we must have no taxes; but, I do say that the Government has no right to take a cent from you or me except for the necessities of the revenue. (Applause) And if the Government take from you any portion of your earnings, whether the portion is large or small, to give to somebody else, that Government is as much a robber towards you as the highwayman who puts a pistol to your forehead and says, "Your purse, or your life."

Is not what I have said the truth? Yet the other is the doctrine of the Government. Mr. Foster says he places taxation upon the people not to raise revenue, but to favour special industries. I denounce any such policy. Protection cannot be defended on any fair principle. What has protection done for your own Manitoba? It is a young giant manacled. The limits of Manitoba are bound to the ground, but if they were set free, and the shackles removed, it would go forward with leaps and bounds to a period of unprecedented prosperity. (Applause)

Protection was imposed upon the peoples of Canada by an appeal to all the selfishness that can be found in the human heart. The farmers were told that by protection the price of wheat would be increased. In 1878 wheat was about one dollar a bushel. Well that was not enough for the farmers; they wanted to have more. I don't blame them for that. Immediately after the National Policy went into force there was an increase in the price of wheat. I remember that a certain gentleman who was a member of the House of Commons said: "I am going to vote for the Government which has increased the price of wheat from one dollar to $1.40 a bushel." I would not blame that gentleman if the Government had been the cause of the increase in the price, but if the Government then increased the price of wheat, I ask what is the Government doing at the present time when the price of wheat has fallen below fifty cents a bushel? The Government are not doing their duty if they pretend that the National Policy increases the price of wheat.

Protection has developed millionaires in this country. It has developed combines in this country, but it has been at the expense of the great consuming masses of the population. When William the Conqueror invaded England, he divided his dominions with his followers. The people of England have been toiling ever since for their masters. The Government here are creating sugar lords and cotton barons for whom the people struggle and work every day of their lives.

Why should I denounce protection? It stands condemned in the House of its friends. In July 1893 there was such an outcry against protection from all points of Canada that the Government felt compelled to take the question up and they promised to hold our investigation and see how they could reduce taxation. They went out interviewing the people in the east and west. The Ministers went about meeting the business men in secret and the farmers in the open. You had here last year two of these Ministers, Mr. Foster, the Minister of Finance, and Mr. Angers, the Minister of Agriculture.

They came to you not to investigate, but to tell the farmers of Manitoba that if they were not as prosperous as they might have been it was their own fault. "Why don't you go into mixed farming," asked the Minister of Agriculture. That was the remedy that Mr. Angers prescribed. The Ministers came back thinking that they had taught the farmers of Manitoba how to farm. The Government had to come down with some measure of reform.

I am a fair opponent and I always endeavour to give some measure of credit to the Government when they are deserving of it. On one occasion last session, I gave them credit for a good intention. Would to God I could have given them credit for a good action. In conscience, I cannot go farther. They went little short of a good intention, but they fell back when it came to a good action. Not that you should be surprised at that. The Government are guided by the example of the United States. You remember in 1877 Sir John Macdonald, Sir Charles Tupper and the leaders of the Conservative Party told us that we [the Mackenzie government] should borrow a leaf out of the book of the United States, that if they would not give us reciprocity of trade, we would give them reciprocity of tariffs. That is to say, that if they were fools we would be fools too. The Americans were protectionists at the time and we became protectionists too. They gave us reciprocity of tariffs. The Americans had a tariff of forty to forty-five per cent and the

Government taxed our people to the extent of thirty-five per cent.

Today they have a system of taxation in the United States which is not altogether to be envied, and in Manitoba today there is a somewhat similar taxation. A session has just been closed in the United States in which much work of its kind has been done. There is in that country a system of protection whereby the Ministers have been looking after the interests of combines and I am sorry to say that what is taking place in the United States today is taking place in Canada.

This same cause has produced the same results in Canada as have taken place in America. When our Canadian Government came down with a measure in which, I am bound to say, there was a modicum of relief, there also came down to Ottawa from the north, east, south and west, a procession of gentlemen representing combines and monopolies. These gentlemen were armed with a dagger, which they held to the throat of the Government at Ottawa and caused them to go back.

As a result of this action you have now before you a most humiliating spectacle – the Government advancing forward, then receding, then advancing again and once more receding. This course of things took place for the space of about three months and when we come to sum up the results of their actions, with the exception of a reduction on agricultural implements and lumber, it would be impossible to find any reform given last session by the Canadian Government.

Can you expect anything else? Can you expect reform from those who do not believe in reform? Can you expect a reduction of taxation from those who have always told you that taxation makes a country prosperous? No, Sir. It would be impossible to expect the leopard to change its spots or not to use its teeth, or those instruments with which nature has endowed it. If, gentlemen, you wish reform you must not ask it at the hands of Conservatives. The Tories are a party who do not believe in reform and this reform is the policy which the Liberals have never ceased to proclaim – a policy of freedom in trade. (Applause)

And now, I will ask you, what is the policy of the Liberal Party? At the expense of great labour and trouble in the past we have obtained religious and civil freedom. This has not been obtained, as I have just said, without a hard struggle. I refer to freedom of trade such as exists in England, freedom of trade as it is practised in Great Britain, freedom of trade as it was in vogue at the time of Cobden and Bright.[110] Sir Robert Peel[111] at one time was a protectionist, but, finding that he was in the wrong, altered his views and went over to the other side and by the policy of such gentlemen as these England has been made rich and placed in the honourable position which she holds amongst the nations at present day. This is the policy we have to adopt; we cannot have it at the present time, I am sorry to say, but we can advance towards it and I can tell you that as soon as we shall have a Liberal administration at Ottawa, and I think we shall have one before very long, although it is not for me to say when – there can be a very radical alteration of affairs looked for.

As I have just told you, I do not know when we shall have this Liberal Administration at Ottawa, but this we may be sure of, that when we have the elections it seems to me that the people of Manitoba will not be slow in condemning the present Government's policy, which is fraught with so much injury to the country. We shall give you freer trade and although it will be a hard fight, we shall not give one inch or retrace one step until we shall have reached the goal, and that goal is the same policy of free trade as exists in England today. (Applause)

In the meantime, as long as we must put up with the condition of affairs as they exist at present, we must content ourselves with obtaining our revenue from customs and similar sources. When the

Liberal Party comes into power we shall examine very closely as to which is the best way to raise the amount necessary for carrying on the affairs of Government. We shall, I say, examine the proper objects upon which to levy taxation. We shall make it as easy as possible upon those things which have to be used by the common people to get this money, which will be lost if we take off some of the present taxation, and to make up the deficit which will arise. It will be necessary to get an addition from some other sources. This will be attempted to be done in this manner: In the first place, there will be a difference made in the present tax imposed upon raw materials which is to be used for manufacturing articles.

Since I have been in Winnipeg, only some six or seven hours, at least fifty persons have asked me what my policy is in general, but, as Manitoba has a greater interest in freight rates than some people who live in other parts of the country, these people have asked me in particular what is my policy with regard to freight rates. This I am well aware is a question in which the people of Manitoba have a very great interest. With regard to this question, I must admit that it is a most important one and it is also one which I had heard of before coming to this part of Canada. I heard of it so recently as the last session of Parliament. The Government has promised to give us some more information upon this important subject.

At the present time, the Canadian Pacific Railway have been given certain privileges on this question of freight rates. The law distinctly lays down and declares that the Government have no right to interfere with the freight rates until the Canadian Pacific Company shall have received some ten per cent of the money invested in the undertaking. If that is the situation at the present time, it is surely not the fault of the Liberal Party, for, if you will bear in mind the action taken by the Honourable Edward Blake, there would be no such questions needed to be asked of me as were put to me this morning.

Mr. Blake in 1881 informed the public exactly what would be the position of affairs today; and in very clear language and in terms which could not by any possibility be misconstrued stated what would be the condition of affairs at the present time. He stated then that there would be exorbitant rates, and today you all know what rates are being charged. At the time of which I am speaking, Sir Charles Tupper, who was the spokesman of the Canadian Government, made some observation on this same subject. Sir Charles Tupper said in 1881 that "the people of Manitoba will have a competing [line] to the Hudson Bay."

These were the remarks of Sir Charles Tupper in 1881 and his remarks were believed by the people of Manitoba. That was thirteen years ago, and it is a well-known fact that the present Government in power at Ottawa are always unable to make up their minds, but they are also not in favour of a railway to Hudson Bay. They do not care to take the trouble to make any investigations as to the character of the Hudson Bay navigation.

This is the state of things. Well, I can say this for the Liberal Party, it is our duty to make an investigation of these resources, but there is a remedy at hand for the exorbitant freight rates, and that, I have already indicated, is freedom of trade. Let trade, especially with the neighbouring great republic, flow freely from north to south, and from south to north and I tell you, you will be able to have a reduction of the freights of which you complain at the present time. Some will tell you this is a very remote remedy. I have the proof in hand.

By the last revision of the tariff you have been favoured to a small extent by a reduction on lumber. Well, this reduction of duty on lumber has already compelled a reduction of freight on the C.P.R. (Applause) I have it from a lumber merchant at the Lake of the Woods whom I met yesterday that since the change in the last spring which reduced the duties on lumber, the freight rates have been reduced twenty-five per cent. I give you this as an example that, if you favour a policy of freedom of trade, you will not only develop the Northwest, you will bring people amongst you, you will make the country a cheap one to live in and freight rates will have to be decreased gradually as trade is increased. Since I have been here I have received two or three letters asking my opinion on various matters, but before I proceed, let me call attention to a matter to which Mr. Mulock has already referred.

I charge the Dominion Government with corruption such as has made Canada a shame over every civilized nation. Corruption may creep into any political organization; no part can be blamed for corrupt men being among them unless instead of purging itself from them it systematically encourages them. We heard recently that a Minister had told us all offenders would be brought to justice and punished whether high or low, rich or poor; but how many of these offenders have been brought to justice? I could tell of five or six who might have been arraigned; I could tell you of two, Thomas McGreevy and Nicholas Connolly,[112] who were punished because the administration of justice was in the hands, not of Sir John Thompson, but of Sir Oliver Mowat. They were found guilty and condemned to twelve months' imprisonment, but scarcely had they been two months in prison when the Government gave them their liberty on the pretense that their health was suffering. (Laughter) Well, I am not surprised, but is a prison a hospital for the cure of invalids? It is with shame I proclaim that such pretense was given, but I pass over that. It is a small matter, after all.

I charge again that there is systematic corruption in the Railway Department and in the Public Works Department. Some will say these words are too strong and cannot be substantiated with evidence. In the construction of the Quebec and Victoria docks the estimate was exceeded by $700,000. In the Curran Bridge, the appropriation was exceeded by $260,000; in the Cornwall Canal, after $125,000 had been spent upon that work, the work was cancelled and another contract given and the canal placed elsewhere; therefore the sum of $125,000 was completely lost. In the Little Rapids lock, the appropriation was for works which cost $40,000; they are not yet completed and they have cost the country $295,000. Here is a discrepancy of over $250,000. In the Tay Canal, the appropriation was $300,000, but now over $900,000 has been spent and there is $100,000 still pending.

The St. Charles branch, a small branch railway extending from Pointe Lévis opposite Quebec, fifteen miles, was estimated to cost $200,000; it has now cost over a million dollars. Then there was the dam at Yamaska which was built to make the river navigable. It was completed at a cost of $200,000. Within two months afterwards a freshet burst it open, but the Government never dared to repair the breach, because it was found that thousands of acres of farmers' lands would be flooded. In every instance the appropriation has been exceeded two, three or four hundred per cent.

The Province of Ontario has just lost a man, Christopher Finlay Fraser,[113] who was for twenty years Minister of Public Works for Ontario. He built public works every year, and, last of all, that great building in which he died, but he never allowed the expenditure to exceed the appropriation. Could we not have a saving at Ottawa? It is an honest Minister which makes a competent engineer. Sir, when we have a Liberal Administration at Ottawa, we shall not have such a system as that. We shall not have these errors which have been occurring because the Minister will then say to the engineer, "My Government wants the plan of a bridge, or the plan of a clock or building; prepare plans, but, mind, if the contract which is given is not filled exactly as it is wanted, or one cent more has to be paid, off goes your head at once."

It is such men as Oliver Mowat and Alexander Mackenzie who make competent engineers. Even the race of the Mowats and the

Mackenzies is not yet extinct. From such men today in the ranks of the Liberal Party can be produced such Ministers of Railways and such Ministers of Public Works that there would be no disgrace upon the brow of any Canadian.

As I told you a moment ago, I have received letters asking me to give my views upon certain matters. I have been asked to give my opinion upon prohibition for Manitoba. This is a question upon which I have not hesitation to speak, because last year at Ottawa, as Mr. Mulock said, we dealt with that question. Then it was given much consideration. The Liberal convention dealt with it, and they pronounced upon it, and their pronouncement upon it is this which I am here to speak about.

It was due to Sir Oliver Mowat in the Province of Ontario and Mr. Greenway[114] in the Province of Manitoba, that a plebiscite was taken to discover the opinions of the people of this country with regard to the question of prohibition, and I have only this to say here, that we will stand by the wishes of those by whom we are placed in power, and we will act according to the will of the people whose desires will be carried out, even if it were to throw out of power forever the Liberal Party. (Loud and continuous applause) Sir, I do not desire to make any political capital out of this question. I am simply stating what is the pledge of the Liberal Party and by that pledge we will stand or fall. . . .

Now, there is another question, a delicate question, on which my opinion has been asked. I am sorry that I did not bring with me the letter which I received upon that question. I thought I had it in my pocket, but I find I have forgotten it. I am sorry for this. I received a letter, not signed by anybody, written in type and, therefore, I am unable to trace whence it came, but I am as sure that it was written by a Tory as that I am a Christian. (Laughter)

Tories have a peculiar way of doing things, whether they are from the Province of Manitoba or of Quebec. It is the same thing everywhere and it is to us like making political capital at the expense of the passions. The Tories of my Province are called *Bleus*, the Tories of the Province of Manitoba are called by the good old name of Tories. Well, the Tories of the Province of Quebec asked me to give my views on the Manitoba school question and as soon as I came here a letter was handed to me asking me to express my views upon the Manitoba school question.

Sir, I do not need to be reminded of that subject. (Laughter) I would not be worthy of the name of man if I were not able to speak my own mind to my countrymen. Whether I speak in the Province of Ontario, the Province of Quebec, or the Province of Manitoba, I am a Canadian. (Loud applause) I believe in the principles of the Liberal Party and by these principles I will abide. In Winnipeg, I will speak upon that question also; but, sir, can we say as much of the Canadian Government which is at Ottawa today?

The Legislature of Manitoba passed an act. . . . The Catholic minority refused to abide by that act and they appealed to the Government at Ottawa [which] dilly-dallied with that question, they gave promises on every side, but except those they never gave anything to anybody. Well, sir, I believe it is the duty of every man to express his opinion as a man upon these subjects. In a country like our own where there are men of different religions, it is impossible to speak [a] language which would please everybody. It is impossible, if you speak your honest mind, the honest opinion of your heart, to please everybody, but I believe it is possible to use language which will appeal to the honest opinion of every man.

Instead of appealing to passions and prejudice, you must appeal to those great principles of liberty which have made the Liberal Party the party of reform of progress and of freedom.

It is upon this principle that I stand. (Cheers) I am a firm believer in Provincial rights. (Renewed cheers) In the Dominion House of Commons, I have stood up for the authority of the provinces.

When I took up the petition of my fellow-religionists of Manitoba, complaining of the legislation of the Government of Manitoba, I asked myself, "What is the complaint?" I took the petition of the late Archbishop Taché, a man who, I believe, was revered in this Province by friend or foe. I took up the petition of the Archbishop and those who signed it with him, and the complaint which was made was that the Government of Manitoba – I speak here in the presence of the members of the Government – had adopted legislation which, instead of imposing Public Schools upon the minority, imposed upon them the Protestant schools, and that they were bound to send their children to Protestant schools.

On the other hand, the Government of Manitoba denied the statement *in toto*. They did not admit that the legislation was to have the effect of sending Roman Catholic children to Protestant schools. I said to the Government, here is a simple question of fact. You have to determine whether the statements are true or not; but, instead of doing that, they went on appealing to the courts and evading the question. I did more. I said then, I say it here now – if the complaint of the Catholics were true, that Catholic children had been forced to attend Protestant schools; if that were true it would be such an outrage upon the rights of conscience that no community would permit it.

I said upon the floor of the House of Commons – "Prove to me that the complaint of the Roman Catholic minority is true, that their rights are outraged to this extent, that, instead of sending their children to schools where there is not religious teaching, they are forced to send their children to schools where there is religious teaching, and I will be prepared to go before the people of Manitoba and tell them that such legislation should not stand."

I have nothing else to say in Winnipeg that I have [not] said on the floor of Parliament, in Quebec and elsewhere. You have heard that question discussed again and again by the Prime Minister in papers of state, and I defy any man, friend or foe, Liberal or Conservative, to find a single expression of opinion on the part of the Prime Minister.

It is not by such cowardice as this that we can expect to build up a great nation on this continent. On this question, as upon every other question, I would spurn to appeal to the feelings of any race, to the passions of my own creed or race. On the present occasion, let me say that the one aim that I have is to unite all races on the continent into a Canadian nation to develop this Confederation upon the lines that once impelled Sir John Macdonald and George Brown to cease a life-long struggle and unite for the common good.

These are the views which I hold and the way in which I think my fellow countrymen should be treated. I dare hardly look at the disastrous effects which the policy of selfishness and cowardice of the Government at Ottawa has already produced in Canada. This policy of selfishness and cowardice has almost dismembered Confederation, and where it is to end it is very difficult at present to say. The effects of such a policy are not confined to one particular locality, but I have seen them in the north, east, south and west, and now, when I come to Manitoba I have not the slightest difficulty in being convinced of the fact that the people of Manitoba are at last awakening from the long lethargy in which they have been for some time past.

Those who take an impartial view of the actions of the Liberal Party must, if they will be honest in their discriminations, admit that those holding these views have been actuated by honest intentions and firm decision. Our work has been done in the cause of freedom, justice, fair play to all and favour to none.

If we will but stand true to these principles it seems to me that the day will not be far distant when these fertile plains shall be teeming with population: with millions of people, happy, contented and progressive. These are the last words which I have to tell you, and, in conclusion, let me tell you just one other word. I have been told in the Province of Ontario that I was not just now on my wedding tour. "Yes," I said to those people, "I have come to woo your fair Province, but in matters political, I am going to be a Mormon, and I am also going to woo the fertile Province of Manitoba, and the western Provinces of the continent."

(The Honourable Gentleman resumed his seat amidst loud applause and cheering.)

By David Asper

I received my invitation to comment on this speech whilst ensconced at my summer residence at Lake of the Woods near the former town of Rat Portage (now Kenora) in northwestern Ontario.

The reason I begin with this is because, coincidentally, Wilfrid Laurier was also here about 121 years ago, on September 1, 1894, as he made his way west toward Winnipeg by rail. Like modern-day tourists visiting Kenora, he even took in a cruise on the lake, among other things that he did with the locals.

So, in Laurier's honour and as an homage to history, I went out in my boat on the lake and read this speech, wondering where Laurier's cruise might have taken him.

I'm always intrigued by these trivialities because, unlike today, whoever was driving Laurier's boat didn't have GPS, so they had to really know where they were going on this complex lake, and if the boat broke down they wouldn't have had a cellphone to call a boat repair person – as I could do!

Reflecting on the speech reminds us that history can often illustrate how far we've come as a society and give reason for celebration about all our accomplishments. But it can also reveal great visions unfulfilled and connect the past with the present in a sort of sad way.

In this brief commentary I'll try to highlight what I mean, because some of the themes articulated by Laurier are as relevant today as they were back then.

The context of the speech is important. In September 1894, Wilfrid Laurier was in full campaign mode in the run up to the federal election that would be held in 1896.

After the death of Sir John A. Macdonald in 1891, the Conservatives were in disarray and wound up churning through four leaders in five years. Laurier sensed this was the Liberals' opportunity to wrest government away from the Tories. This speech in Winnipeg was part of a national tour designed to build Liberal support in the west.

Laurier was greeted by very large crowds, both at the railway station when he arrived in Winnipeg, and then especially later on at his formal speech, where thousands attended and many had to be turned away. The speech was interrupted several times by loud cheers.

Its over-arching theme is free trade and prosperity for Manitoba. After complimenting the locals for the progress made and the "pluck of the early pioneers of this city and province," Laurier goes on to attack the Tories by asking this question: "Is it not a fact that after thirty years of the life of this province the goal which you had set for yourself has not yet been attained?"

This was his message bridge into the failure of immigration policy to grow the population of the west, protectionist customs, tariff and other taxes, uncompetitive freight rates, and the failure to develop the port of Churchill. Laurier declared that the solution lay with freer north/south trade, and it's on this point where the past intersects with present-day Manitoba.

While the port of Churchill was eventually developed and a rail line built there, Manitoba is still grappling in many ways with the issues advanced by Laurier over a century before, in spite of the fact that free trade deals with the United States and other countries around the world have been accomplished.

We are still wondering if Churchill is viable, especially with a longer shipping season due to climate change. We still have to deal with the capacity of the rail line to Churchill and its problematic rail bed construction. We are building a massive inland port called CentrePort, along with expensive road upgrades along Highway 75, which runs to the United States. We have a brand new airport with enhanced cargo capacity.

It's clear that we want to have the infrastructure to facilitate a much larger degree of north–south and east–west trade. But are the expectations being met? Has free trade brought all the benefits that Laurier thought would enrich Manitoba?

To put it another way, if a modern-day politician were to give a version of the same speech Laurier gave in 1894, the question is whether it would resonate, and I suggest the answer is Yes.

There are a couple of other things to note about Laurier's speech.

First is the Manitoba Schools question, which I submit Laurier mostly dodges, partly because it was so divisive along religious lines, as well as because the Liberals were very much in favour of respecting provincial rights, and education was within provincial jurisdiction under the British North America Act. He refers to it as a "delicate" question and in the larger political context that's quite an understatement.

Secondly, Laurier condemns the federal government for corruption and cites several examples from the Railway and Public Works departments.

While the Schools question was ultimately resolved, can we say that its underlying connection to race and religion is that far removed from some of the issues confronting modern society in this regard? Has the issue of Catholic versus Protestant schools been replaced with other forms of racial and ethnic tension, such as our relationship with indigenous people?

Similarly, has there ever been a Government without some kind of public works spending controversy?

For me the lesson from this speech is to remember that we have to keep whatever occupies us about politics today in historical context. It's a strong reminder that news isn't necessarily new.

David Asper is a Winnipeg-based lawyer, educator, businessperson, and philanthropist.

THE SUNNY WAY

MORRISBURG, ONTARIO
OCTOBER 8, 1895[115]

I am not here to solve this [Manitoba schools] question, because it is not in my province to solve it, but I understand that the ministerial press of this country and of this province [Ontario] has been very anxious to know what was the policy of Mr. Laurier with regard to it. I would not be worthy of the position I occupy and of the trust that has been placed in me by my colleagues of the House of Commons if I were afraid to speak on this question.

I intend to do so though I am sure I shall not satisfy the ministerial press. I do not hope to, but I hope to satisfy, as far as I can, every sensible man. I hasten to plunge at once into that question, because it is to be faced with courage by every man that has on his own conscience the duty of doing well by the country in which we live.

I have been accused by the Conservative press of having expressed no opinion on this question. I expressed an opinion more than once upon this question, but I have not yet expressed the opinion which the ministerial press would like me to express. I am not responsible for that question, but I do not want to shirk it; I want to give you my views, but remember that war has to be waged in a certain way. When the Duke of Wellington was in Portugal, as those of you will remember who have read that part of the history of England, he withdrew at one time within the Lines of Torres Vedras,[116] and there for months he remained, watching the movements of the enemy. The French at the time were commanded by Marshal Masséna,[117] and Masséna said: "I want that man to come down from his lines: let him come down into the plain and I will thrash him, but I cannot assail him within the lines." Gentlemen, I am within the lines of Torres Vedras. I will get out of them when it suits me and not before.

There is a way of discussing that question. Time and time again I have laid down my views before the Government, and I do not hesitate to tell you what my views are. I have to speak the same words here as I have spoken everywhere else. I have the same sentiments whether I speak in one language or the other. I would not be worthy of the position I occupy today if I did not, as far as I could, educate the Liberal Party to the views which I think are the sound views upon that question.

There is a question to be settled. There is an appeal of the minority in Manitoba to the Governor-in-Council, which has to be heard and determined upon. We have a very peculiar constitution as you know. Section 93 of the British North America Act provides that whenever a minority in any province where a system of separate schools has been established is not satisfied and thinks itself aggrieved by the legislation of that province, that minority has an appeal to the federal executive.

As you know, it has been decided by the Judicial Committee of the [British] Privy Council that in this matter the minority has a grievance and has the right of appeal. What are we to do here? That is the question. The minority has the right to appeal. This is conceded and granted.

I say this and I submit it to your knowledge. If the minority has an appeal, you must not conclude, as some men conclude, that this appeal is to be denied in every case; but if the minority has an appeal it is the duty of the Government to investigate the subject and to ascertain what the facts are in order to see whether or not a case has been made out for federal interference.

The Government, instead of investigating the subject, proceeded to render – what shall I call it? – an Order in Council they called it, commanding Manitoba in most violent language to do a certain thing, to restore the schools or they would see the consequences. Manitoba answered as I suppose every man approached as the Government of Manitoba was approached, would answer; Manitoba answered it by saying, "We will not be coerced." I ask you now, would it not have been more fair, more just, more equitable, more statesmanlike, at once to investigate the subject, and to bring the parties together to hear them, to have the facts brought out so as to see whether a case had been made out for interference or not?

That is the position I take in the province of Ontario. I have never wavered from that position. Two years ago, when the question first came before the House, I said to the Government, which desired to consult the courts to ascertain whether it had the power to intervene: "You have the power to intervene; it is written in the constitution. The only question is a question of facts. Make an investigation; it is the first thing to be done." That is the position I have taken in the Province of Quebec. That is the position I take in the Province of Ontario. I have never wavered from that position. I venture to say that the question cannot be settled until there has been such an investigation, to see what are the rights and pretensions of the case. But what are you to investigate? There are many things to investigate. You will have to see what is the position of affairs, what is the relative strength of the population, how the groups of population are constituted and how far the pretensions of the minority can be met without encroaching upon the rights of the majority.

I am glad to find that a man who carries weight in this province by his character and ability, Principal [George Monro] Grant [of Queen's University], after going to the province of Manitoba and looking into the thing for himself, has come to the conclusion that first of all the Government is bound to investigate that subject.

Why, sir, there is a way and a way of doing things. I am asked, "What would you have done if you had the responsibility?" That is the way I would have acted, but instead of that you know how the Government have proceeded. They have proceeded in a way which, instead of solving the question, has made it far more difficult to solve than ever.

If they had proceeded in the way I have indicated there is reason to believe by this time, perhaps before this time, they would have accomplished something; but having done it in the way they have, you see the position in which they are. That position is that there is an entanglement out of which they do not know how they are to extricate themselves, and do not know, perhaps, what they are going to do at the next session of Parliament, which is to be summoned to deal with that question.

According to the fable, once upon a time the Wind and the Sun saw a traveller upon the highway, and the Wind said to the Sun, "I will make you a wager that I will go to that traveller who has a comfortable coat upon his shoulders and I will compel him to take if off." "Very well," said the Sun, "Try your hand at it, and when you have done I will try my hand at it also." So the Wind proceeded to blow and to rage and to blow, but the more he raged, the more he blew, the more the traveller stuck to his coat. After the Wind had exhausted all its force and blown down and rooted up trees from the ground, the traveller still had his coat upon his shoulders just as close as before.

"Now," said the Sun, "I will try my hand; you have exhausted your power, let me try." So the Sun commenced to smile upon the earth and sent down his sweetest rays, and by and by, as everything was blooming, as the birds were singing, the traveller commenced to open his coat, and as the Sun continued to send down his gentle warmth, the traveller presently wiped his brow and then took off his coat altogether.

Well, sir, the Government are very windy. They have blown and raged and threatened, but the more they have threatened and raged and blown the more that man Greenway has stuck to his coat. If the Government has anything better than this to offer, let them do so and they will receive my heartiest support.

If it were in my power, and if I had the responsibility, I would try the sunny way. I would approach this man Greenway with the sunny ways of patriotism, asking him to be generous to the minority, in order that we may have peace amongst all the creeds and races which it has pleased God to bring upon this corner of our common country.

Do you not believe there is more to be gained by appealing to the heart and soul of men rather than by trying to compel them to do a thing? If you have a difference with one of your neighbours, and if he comes to you and says, "You must do this," in a moment you will say, "No, I will not do it." Your manhood will rise against it. But if you go and appeal to your neighbour and say, "We have a difference, and must settle it," he will say, "I will meet you half way."

But the Government of Canada, instead of appealing to Mr. Greenway in this way, have threatened to coerce Mr. Greenway, and the people of Manitoba have declared: "No, we will stand no coercion." This is not the way to settle the question. I have stated to the Government again and again the first thing they must do is to investigate the question. I stand upon this ground today, and I have done so in all the provinces in which I have discussed this question, and tomorrow you will hear the Conservative press say: "Mr. Laurier has spoken about this question again, and he has said nothing."

I am prepared for that. I cannot hope to satisfy them. But, while I cannot satisfy them, I hope, at all events, I can satisfy the honest people, the thinking people of Canada, that this is the only way in which you can give justice upon that question. If there is any other method whereby the Government can give justice upon that question, why let us have it by all means, and for my part I shall be ready to give them a fair hearing and consideration, but so long as they continue to do as they have been doing in their press and to say that I do not discharge my duty upon this question, I discharge my duty as an Opposition leader, but I am not bound to frame a policy for the Government, it is not to me that the petitions of the minority have been addressed. I have not been charged by the constitution with the duty of looking into this case.

The only thing I can do is to point out the means by which the end can be attained, if there is any better means than that let the Government adopt such means and they will be welcome to it. But if it does not, it will not do for the Government to be acting as they have been acting upon this question, and for their organs to say in the province of Ontario: "There shall be no interference," and for their organs in the province of Quebec to say: "There shall be interference." It must be the same thing whether in Quebec or in the province of Ontario, on this question, as on all other questions.

I have held to the language which I do here today. You have heard in the ministerial press that in the province of Quebec I use different words to those I speak in the province of Ontario. I am quite willing to stand here responsible for my acts. Let a speech of mine be quoted that has been delivered anywhere: let it be quoted entirely and I will be responsible for it. But when a speech of mine that has occupied one hour in delivery is condensed into six lines, I refuse to be bound by such a report as that.

The last time I spoke on this question was at St. Anne de la Perade and I will give you the words, because they were reported verbatim, not in any paper supporting me, but in the *Evenement* and this is what I said: While the Government has done nothing, all the party organs throughout all the provinces have demanded what was my policy. It does not belong to me to settle this question, but I shall not wait until the responsibility is put upon my shoulders to outline what I believe to be the true way.

Two years ago when the question first came before the House, I said to the Government which desired to consult the courts to ascertain whether it had the power to intervene, "You have the power to intervene. It is written in the constitution. The only question is a question of facts. Make an investigation: it is the first thing to be done." But they said: "Why an investigation; are the facts not clear?" I simply replied: "These facts are clear to you and to all those who believe in a system of separate schools, but remember there are those who do not think as we do on this question and they are the majority. I know that when I say that the first thing to be done in this question is to have an investigation. I do not, perhaps, express an idea that will be very popular I this province, but I hold to the same language in all provinces. Remember that there are differences of opinion, and profound differences on this question, and that to solve it we must enlarge our horizon and place ourselves on a basis that all who are Canadians, without a distinction of race or creed, may accept."

This is the language I spoke in the province of Quebec; this is the language I repeated in the province of Ontario. This is a question which should not be approached from any standpoint of creed or race, but I appeal to all my countrymen, whatever may be their race or creed, to place themselves beyond these narrow inclinations, to stand up as Canadians to do justice to whoever justice may be due. Gentlemen, that is the policy which I advocate to you at present, and I say again, I would be beneath contempt if I dared approach this question, as every other question has to be approached, that is to say from the standpoint of a Canadian nationality before all other nationalities, and placing our common country before any other considerations that may animate us.

We are here a population of different races and creeds. We never can be a people unless we are able to stand up in any corner of this Canada of ours and repeat upon that corner what has to be said everywhere else. That is the ground upon which I arraign the policy of the Government. A policy – I make a mistake in using the word, for they have no policy – they never had a policy. That is the ground upon which I arraign their conduct. Their conduct is to appeal to the sentiments of one race in one province and to the sentiments of another race in another province.

Do you think when I spoke a few weeks ago in the parish of Ste. Anne de la Perade in the language I have just quoted to you, do you think that it would not have been an easy matter for me to have made myself very popular by saying that there must be interference in the same manner that the ministerial organs and speakers are saying every day? I could have made an appeal to the passion, to the prejudices of my fellow countrymen. I despise such conduct. I could appeal here to passion and prejudice because there are passions and prejudices in every human heart.

I am here to speak my mind, to try to lay down the principles upon which this great country is to be governed and, whether my words are popular or not, I have to stand by them because I believe in my heart and conscience it is the only way in which Canada can be governed, not only on this question, but on all other questions as well. The Liberal Party, in whose favour I am now speaking, has a record not only in this province and country, but in England as well, of fighting for the minority wherever minorities are oppressed, but there are laws for minorities as well as for majorities, and here we have not to appeal to the sympathy or to sentiment, but to apply the constitution such as it is.

In applying the constitution the remedy will be found and in no other way. Of course, there may be hostility to face and prejudices to overcome, but I trust that if you appeal to the best sentiments of the people everywhere, whether in Quebec, Manitoba or Ontario, you will find the solution of that question, and you will find it in no other way but that. That is the statement I have to make at this moment. Again, I say I know very well what will happen. Tomorrow you will read in the *Mail and Empire* that I have said nothing. The day after tomorrow you will read in the *Evenement* and the *Courrier du Canada* that I have betrayed my countrymen. Tomorrow and the day after tomorrow you will read again that Mr. Laurier is shifting upon this question. Shifting upon this question! What plainer language can be spoken than I have just uttered?

I tell the Government to do this and appoint a commission, and I will support you. Can I say anything more than that? Is that not as plain as it could be. Still that is not satisfactory to the Government. I will tell you what would be satisfactory. If I would say: I will support Sir Mackenzie Bowell. They would be pleased with a statement like that. I will support Sir Mackenzie Bowell when he is in the right. I will fight him when he is in the wrong, and, unfortunately, I will have to fight him more than support him. I know that.

The Conservative press today is very anxious to have my views upon the question, but I remember very well, and you remember also, that the Government is not very anxious to have my opinion as a rule. When they gerrymandered Canada in 1882 they did not consult any of the Liberals. When they passed the Franchise Act they did not consult any of the Liberals, and even last session when they brought in their legislation they never consulted us, but upon this question they want to consult me and to have my views. Here they have them. Let them act upon them and we will be in accord; but more than that I will not do. I will not say that I will support the policy of Sir Mackenzie Bowell until I know what that policy is, and then when we have it in black and white it will be time for me to speak upon it. Let the ministerial press abuse me all they can: I stand within the lines of Torres Vedras and I will not come out until I choose my time.

It may be that my position is not satisfactory to the Government or the supporters of the Government. I cannot help that. I am sorry it is so. I am an opponent of the Government. I have not much confidence in them, but after all if they gave me the satisfaction, for once, of supporting them, I would be only too happy to do so, but it is a pleasure, as you know, which has not very often been given to the Opposition, and I do not expect it on this question any more than upon any other question they have had to deal with.

By Dr. Thomas S. Axworthy

Justin Trudeau began his victory night address on October 19, 2015, by invoking Wilfrid Laurier, that most iconic of Liberals: "Sunny ways, my friends, sunny ways," he said. "This is what positive politics can do." Sunny ways certainly defined Laurier's approach to politics, and it defined Trudeau's 2015 campaign – positive, optimistic, and conciliatory. Both Laurier in 1895 and Justin Trudeau in 2015 condemned the divisiveness and fear mongering of their times and appealed to the better angels of our nature. "Sunny ways" became the leitmotif of Wilfrid Laurier's career; time will tell if it similarly endures in Justin Trudeau's.

In 1895, Canada faced a crisis that was tearing it apart. In the wake of the execution of Louis Riel in 1885, French–English tensions ran high and Orange Lodge agitators like Conservative MP Dalton McCarthy fanned the flames higher by introducing a bill in January 1890 calling for the abolition of French-language guarantees in the Northwest Territories Act of 1875 and provocatively stating in the preamble to the bill that "in the interest of national unity in the Dominion . . . there should be community of language among the people of Canada." McCarthy's bill was defeated, but he gained an important ally when the Liberal government of Thomas Greenway

*in Manitoba moved in the 1890 session to abolish the constitutionally guar-
anteed rights to the official use of French and to religiously denominated, or
"separate," schools. The Manitoba Schools question bedevilled Canadian
politics for the next several years by unleashing the passions of anti-French
and anti–Roman Catholic bigotry.*

*On October 8, 1895, Laurier addressed the issue. He told an audience
in Morrisburg, Ontario:*

> *Intolerance and bigotry never had, have not, and never will have
> any part in the platform of the Liberal Party. If it were in my power,
> I would try the sunny way. I would approach this man Greenway
> with the sunny way of patriotism, asking him to be just and to be
> fair, asking him to be generous to the minority, in order that we may
> have peace among all the creeds and races which it has pleased God
> to bring upon this corner of our common country. Do you not believe
> that there is more to be gained by appealing to the heart and soul
> of men rather than to compel them to do a thing?*

*In the 1896 election, Laurier stuck to his theme of "the sunny way,"
advocating co-operation with the provinces and conciliation among the races.
He settled the Manitoba schools question, more or less, with a compromise:
agreeing to the secularization of the public school system, as the province had
demanded, but with the provision of religious instruction at the end of the
school day. He never wavered from this mission of reconciliation, and French–
English amity became the hallmark not only of his administration but of the
Liberal Party that he, more than any other individual, created.*

MANITOBA SCHOOLS

HOUSE OF COMMONS, OTTAWA, ONTARIO
MARCH 3, 1896

Mr. Speaker, if in a debate of such moment it were not out of place for me to make a personal reference to myself, a reference, however, which may perhaps be justified, not so much on account of the feelings which may not unnaturally be attributed to me, being of the race and of the creed of which I am, but still more in consideration of the great responsibility which has been placed on my shoulders by the too kind regard of the friends by whom I am surrounded here, I would say that, in the course of my parliamentary career, during which it has been my duty on more than one occasion to take part in the discussion of those dangerous questions which too often have come before the Parliament of Canada, never did I rise, sir, with a greater sense of security; never did I feel so strong in the consciousness of right, as I do now, at this anxious moment; when, in the name of the constitution so outrageously misinterpreted by the Government, in the name of peace and harmony in this land; when in the name of the minority which this bill seeks or pretends to help, in the name of this young nation on which so many hopes are centred, I rise to ask this Parliament not to proceed any further with this bill. . . .

There was at the head of the Government of Nova Scotia at that time a gentleman [Sir Charles Tupper] who today has been brought back from England to force this measure upon the people of Canada. Instead of applying himself to persuading his own fellow countrymen of the grandeur of this Act of Confederation, he forced the project down the throats of the people of Nova Scotia by the brute force of a mechanical majority in a moribund Parliament.

[Tupper's action had left a bitterness] which never will entirely disappear until it is buried in the grave of the last man of that generation. [And what of the agitations which had marked the years since, the dispute with Ontario over the Streams Bill, the dispute with Manitoba over the railway charters, the dispute with Quebec over the Jesuits' Estates law? Had not one and all of these dangerous strains been caused by attempts] to abridge the independence of the provincial legislature?

[The powers of control over the provinces which the constitution assigned to the Dominion were of doubtful wisdom, probably never to be applied without friction and discontent. But the remedy of federal interference is there; it must be applied, but so applied as to avoid irritation. It is not to be applied mechanically, it must be applied intelligently] only after full and ample inquiry into the facts of the case, after all means of conciliation have been exhausted, and only as a last resort. [In this case, when the Roman Catholic minority urged its grievances, the federal government should have made inquiry, should have searched out the facts, should have gone to Manitoba, not to the courts. It is said inquiry, negotiation, would be of no avail. Yet the Government of Manitoba had expressed its willingness, once the grievances were investigated, the wrongs proved, itself to give the minority redress. The province had never been approached in the proper way. The federal government had bungled the case from first to last.]

There are men in this House who are against separate schools, but who would have no objection to the re-establishment of separate schools in Manitoba, provided they were re-established by the province of Manitoba itself. There are men in this House who are not in favour of separate schools, but who think very strongly that it would not be advisable to interfere with the legislation of Manitoba at all until all means of conciliation had been exhausted. Sir, in face of this perilous position, I maintain today, and I submit it to the consideration of gentlemen on both sides, that the policy of the Opposition, affirmed since many years, reiterated on more than one occasion, is the only policy which can successfully deal with this question, the only policy which can remedy the grievance of the minority, while at the same time not violently assaulting the right of the majority and thereby perhaps creating a greater wrong. This was the policy which, for my part, I adopted and developed the very first time the question came before this House, and upon this policy today I stand once more. . . .

Sir, I cannot forget at this moment that the policy which I have advocated and maintained all along has not been favourably received in all quarters. Not many weeks ago I was told from high quarters in the Church to which I belong that unless I supported the school bill which was then being prepared by the Government and which we now have before us, I would incur the hostility of a great and powerful body. Sir, this is too grave a phase of this question for me to pass over in silence. I have only this to say: even though I have threats held over me, coming, as I am told, from high dignitaries in the Church to which I belong, no word of bitterness shall ever pass my lips as against that Church. I respect it and I love it. Sir, I am not of that school which has long been dominant in France and other countries of continental Europe, which refuses ecclesiastics the right of a voice in public affairs. No, I am a Liberal of the English school. I believe in that school which has all along claimed that it is the privilege of all subjects, whether high or low, whether rich or poor, whether ecclesiastics or laymen, to participate in the administration of public affairs, to discuss, to influence, to persuade, to convince – but which has always denied even to the highest the right to dictate even to the lowest.

I am here representing not Roman Catholics alone but Protestants as well, and I must give an account of my stewardship to all classes. Here am I, a Roman Catholic of French extraction, entrusted by the confidence of the men who sit around me with great and important duties under our constitutional system of government. I am here the acknowledged leader of a great party, composed of Roman Catholics and Protestants as well, as Protestants must be in the majority in every party in Canada. Am I to be told, I, occupying such a position, that I am to be dictated the course I am to take in this House, by reasons that can appeal to the consciences of my fellow Catholic Members, but which do not appeal as well to the consciences of my Protestant colleagues? No. So long as I have a seat in this House, so long as I occupy the position I do now, whenever it shall become my duty to take a stand upon any question whatever, that stand I will take not upon grounds of Roman Catholicism, not upon grounds of Protestantism, but upon grounds which can appeal to the conscience of all men, irrespective of their particular faith, upon grounds which can be occupied by all men who love justice, freedom and toleration.

So far as this bill is concerned, I have given you my views. I know, I acknowledge, that there is in this Government the power to interfere, there is in this Parliament the power to interfere; but that power should not be exercised until all the facts bearing upon the case have been investigated and all means of conciliation exhausted. Holding these opinions, I move that the bill be not now read the second time but that it be read the second time this day six months.

By Patrice Dutil

Laurier must have thought he had been placed on earth precisely for this moment when he rose in the House of Commons in early March 1896 to deliver this speech. He knew the governing Conservatives were on the ropes. Sir John's party had been in power since the fall of 1878 and had struggled through three of Macdonald's successors: John Abbott (1891–1892), Sir John Thompson (1892–1894), and Sir Mackenzie Bowell (from 1894) in less than five years.

Rudderless under Bowell, the party was deeply divided over the Manitoba Schools question. Two months before, on January 4, 1896, seven cabinet ministers had resigned from Bowell's administration, demanding that Charles Tupper, now seventy-four years old, return from his post as Canada's high commissioner to the Court of St. James and assume the prime ministership. Dr. Charles Tupper, one of the fathers of Confederation and an ardent Nova Scotia politician despite his absence from the country for over a decade, was elected to the House of Commons as the member for Cape Breton in a by-election on February 4, 1896. Tupper was practically the prime minister; it was a foregone conclusion that he would be named at any day.

Laurier had Tupper in his sights when delivering this speech, knowing that the Government leader in the House of Commons (Bowell was still prime minister, sitting in the Senate) had not yet found his footing. Tupper was a deeply experienced prime minister, having served under Macdonald in many different demanding ministries, such as public works and finance), but on the implications of western expansion, he was outplayed by Laurier.

For Tupper, the policy on French schools in Manitoba was clear-cut and rooted in what Macdonald had accomplished. For him, the Manitoba Act of 1870 had given French Catholics in Manitoba the right to separate, state-funded French-language Catholic schools and the Government of Manitoba had to honour the agreement.

For Tupper, the problem was the division inside his own party. Many of his colleagues supported the Manitoba Schools Act, which removed state funding to French-Catholic schools. Championed by the likes of Dalton

McCarthy, an anti-French, anti-Catholic, independent MP, the act had been challenged in all the courts. It had even been upheld by the Judicial Committee of the Privy Council in Great Britain, which was still the highest court of appeal for Canada. (While Canada did have a Supreme Court, it was not yet considered the final locus of appeal.)

True to his principles, Tupper wasted no time in presenting a bill in the House of Commons that would disallow Manitoba's legislation. The bill went through first reading. On March 3 began the debate on the second reading.

Laurier, sensing that the government was dying, could not give it an opportunity to shine. The March 3 speech – Laurier's first volley in a filibuster that would last an excruciating six weeks – was a master stroke. It started with what is surely the longest run-on sentence ever uttered in the House of Commons. No doubt the transcribers had trouble capturing the interruptions and catcalls that broke Laurier's cadence. Laurier was careful not to laud the legislation but instead focused on the Conservative government's ongoing wars with the provinces.

He projected his party's policy in terms of his very own personality. Much of the speech is given to describing himself as a bridge between cultures and religions. The implication was that the Liberal policy would be to remove conflict. There had to be compromise. To twist a phrase that would come later in Canadian politics, his would be a policy of federal intervention where necessary, but not necessarily one of intervention. His approach would be to seek a resolution but to do so without "irritation." "It is not to be applied mechanically, it must be applied intelligently," he announced, "after all means of conciliation have been exhausted, and only as a last resort." Deep down, of course, Laurier was in full agreement with the Conservative stance, but thought of it as a last resort. He would be able to negotiate a deal with the Manitoba government. His move was pure tactic: a motion that debate be suspended for six months. He was gambling that a Liberal victory in the upcoming election would give him the opportunity to deploy his "sunny ways" and win an acceptable agreement with the Manitoba Government. It was, after all, a Liberal one.

Bowell asked that Parliament be dissolved on April 24, 1896, two days before its five-year constitutional mandate was to expire. The bill never passed. A week later, Tupper was sworn in as the sixth prime minister and faced the electorate as the leader of his party. Laurier campaigned with two strategies. In Quebec, he promised to bring a final resolve to the Manitoba Schools question. In English Canada, his emphasis was on reassuring the electorate that he would continue the National Policy and that he had renounced the free policy platforms he had campaigned on in 1891. The Conservatives won the national vote, but the Liberals won far more seats. Tupper reluctantly gave up the reins of power.

Patrice Dutil is professor in the Department of Politics and Public Administration at Ryerson University. His publications on Laurier include *Canada, 1911: The Decisive Election that Shaped the Country* (2011, co-written with David MacKenzie) and *Devil's Advocate: Godfroy Langlois and the Politics of Liberal Progressivism in Laurier's Quebec* (1994). He is president of the Champlain Society.

PART III:

PRIME MINISTER

1896–1911

We now join Laurier as he reaches the summit, becoming Canada's first French-Canadian prime minister. Canadians reward him with a string of four consecutive election victories. But this section ends with Laurier on the hustings, fighting – and losing – on the issue of free trade with the United States.

Many of the addresses assembled here are delivered by Laurier in the House of Commons, where he pays tribute to fallen leaders such as Sir Oliver Mowat, William Gladstone, and Queen Victoria. On the floor of the House he is also presented with a portrait of himself from admirers, and responds graciously. John Willison, writing so near to these events, notes how Laurier's rhetoric soars on these occasions:

"In all of his speeches which do not touch [upon] strictly controversial issues, there is the even poise and the deep-searching spirit of the historian, and a serenity and sanity which reveal qualities that rarely find expression in the narrow field of partisan controversy," he writes. "It is understood that Sir Wilfrid Laurier at one time designed to write a history of Canada . . . but was deterred by political duties and particularly by his acceptance of the leadership of the Liberal Party. . . . Many of his speeches reveal the true historical insight and a profound conception of the underlying motives and the currents of the conspicuous events of the age in which he has lived."[118]

Readers will find further evidence of the accuracy of Willison's views in other addresses presented in this section. A lecture about the British and American constitutions Laurier delivers before a women's group in 1909 is another example.

Laurier on the world stage is also showcased in this section. In 1897 he delivers a famous Dominion Day address in London,

England, in triumph after taking Queen Victoria's Diamond Jubilee celebrations by storm on his inaugural foreign visit as prime minister. He also addresses an American audience in Chicago with the U.S. president sitting prominently in the audience. Later, he returns home from a European tour and is greeted by thousands of Ottawa residents who, whatever their partisan views, listen with pride as he describes the world capitals he has just visited on their behalf.

But the years of his premiership are not all about lofty ideas, Canadian progress, and idealism. Laurier, after all, leads a political party and government in the political trenches. We see Laurier the partisan helping Ontario's provincial Liberals in a campaign and witness a seasoned prime minister, in 1907, swiftly confront a ministerial scandal involving that potent (and volatile) mixture of sex and alcohol.

Although we glow at Laurier's promise from the stage at Massey Hall (and other venues) that the twentieth century will be Canada's moment, we also cringe, from today's vantage point, as he discusses – a man of his times – such issues as Chinese immigration to Canadian shores.

The Canadian West figures prominently in this section. Laurier's government grants provincial status to Alberta and Saskatchewan in 1905. Five years later, readers follow Laurier, starting in Thunder Bay, Ontario, as he travels across the West and is greeted by thousands wherever the train stops.

Then comes the 1911 campaign – and the end of the Laurier Years.

FIRST MAJOR PARLIAMENTARY
ADDRESS AS PRIME MINISTER

HOUSE OF COMMONS, OTTAWA, ONTARIO

AUGUST 24, 1896

Mr. Speaker, I have assuredly no fault to find with the speech to
which we have had the pleasure of listening, nor is it my intention
to offer any criticism upon it. It was a moderate speech, and if we
remember the source from which it came [Sir Charles Tupper], I
think it was a very moderate speech, indeed. True, Sir, there was
throughout it, from the fist to the last syllable, a tone of disappointment and bitterness; but with this I find no fault, and indulge in
no criticism. I waive it in deference to the feelings of a man who,
having abandoned a high and honourable position [high commissioner to the United Kingdom] in the service of the country for the
more noble and higher ambition of restoring the wrecked fortunes
of his party, and having failed in the task, has not yet recovered from
the surprise and the shock, that, like Caesar, he came and saw, but
unlike Caesar, he did not conquer.

It is manifest from the tone of the speech of the Honourable
Gentleman that he has not rightly apprehended the full significance
of the verdict which was pronounced by the people of the country
on twenty-third June last. It is quite evident from the speech

delivered that the Honourable Gentleman up to this day does not know what are the causes which have produced that upheaval, that earthquake which shook the whole of Canada, from the island of Vancouver to Prince Edward Island on twenty-third June last – an earthquake which was very similar to some earthquakes which we read about in the olden times, and in which the sinners were buried alive, and the just were spared and saved.

Now, Mr. Speaker, the Honourable Gentleman told us in the opening part of his address, that the Liberal Party had not obtained a majority on any of the issues submitted to the people of this country. I fail to understand what was the object of the argument of the Honourable Gentleman. He says we have not obtained a majority on any of the issues which were submitted to the people of the country. Well, Sir, I care not to go very minutely into that argument, but I look at the result only, and whatever may be the cause the result is: there is the Honourable Gentleman in Opposition, and here are we at the head of the Government of Canada.

The Honourable Gentleman stated more. He said that although his party were in the minority in this House, yet that they had obtained at the polls, no less than nineteen thousand votes more than the party which is victorious. Again I refuse to go very minutely into those calculations of the Honourable Gentleman, but all I have to say is that if the victorious polled a minority of the votes in the country, what has become of the Gerrymander Acts of [the] Honourable Gentlemen opposite? They certainly were never intended for that purpose, and if that be their result I am sure we shall have the support of my Honourable Friend when we repeal these Acts, as repeal them we shall. Nor do I consider that my Honourable Friend was any more happy in his reference to the Honourable Gentleman who moved the Address, when he said that although the Honourable Gentleman . . . had a seat in this House he had a minority of the votes in his constituency.

True there were three candidates in the field, one Liberal and two Conservatives. There were two different kinds of Conservatives, however, in the constituency of Vancouver, as in many other constituencies in this country. There were Conservatives who were Ministerialists and who were prepared to swallow everything in connection with the Ministerial policy, but there were also Conservatives, who though remaining Conservatives, and yielding nothing of the conviction of their lives, were, however, no longer ready to follow the Government of the Honourable Gentleman. That is the reason why my Honourable Friend . . . is here. But, Sir, if the Honourable Gentleman [Sir Charles Tupper] does not know yet what are the causes which have brought on this change of Government, I may tell him. There are three causes. The Honourable Gentleman and his party were defeated because their fiscal policy, which by a strange misnomer has been termed the National Policy, had not fulfilled the expectations of the people, and although that policy had not fulfilled the expectations of the people, still the Honourable Gentleman adhered to it.

The Honourable Gentleman and his party have been defeated because the administration of public affairs under his Government had been extravagant and corrupt. The Honourable Gentlemen and his party have been defeated because upon a grave and important question – a question which for its solution required great tenderness and care of treatment – instead of appealing to the honest intelligence of the people, instead of appealing to the convictions and the consciences of the people, the hon. gentleman and his party appealed to sectional prejudices and to religious feelings.

He was defeated, because by his policy on this question he created amongst the better classes of his party a distrust, which rent his party into factions which are now irreconcilable. Sir, these are the reasons why the Honourable Gentleman did not succeed. And in view of the tactics which were adopted by the Honourable Gentleman and his party to succeed, in view of the methods which were resorted to by them, I say: blessed and thrice blessed is the day when these tactics were defeated, when these methods were rebuked, and when these appeals to sectional feelings were trampled underfoot by the people to whom they were addressed.

I am doing no injustice to my Honourable Friend when I say, that his speech today was rather a doleful and mournful one. But there was a single ray of sunshine in it. There was a ray of sunshine in it when he came to speak of my hon. friends, the mover and seconder of the Address. He paid them just and well-deserved compliments, which I am happy to re-echo. . . .

But the Honourable Gentleman devoted by far the greater and most important part of his speech to the Manitoba school question, and the whole tendency of his argument today was to try and put us in contradiction with ourselves. He said that we had one policy here and another there. I take issue with him upon that. The Honourable Gentleman wants to know what is the policy of the Government upon this question. If I were to extend to him the same treatment which was meted to us when on the other side, I would ask what is the policy of the Opposition.

Now, we heard during the last session from the lips of the Honourable Gentleman, not once or twice but a dozen times, a declaration which is very different from what we have heard from him today. We heard from him then the declaration that in this matter the sovereignty of Parliament was abridged, that Parliament was not a free agent, but was forced to lay violent hands upon the school legislation of Manitoba and restore the Roman Catholic separate schools. Nay more, we heard also the Honourable Gentleman state, in deep and solemn tones, that he was ready to die, if his death were necessary, to procure of the minority the justice in which they were entitled. . . .

All I can say at the present time is that I have every reason to hope, every reason to believe, that when again this Parliament assembles, this question will have been settled satisfactorily to all parties concerned. Sir, when I say that this question will have been settled satisfactorily to all let me make on exception. I know full well that any settlement we can make, however just, however fair, however meritorious it may be, it is condemned in advance by those extreme men who are ready to exact their pound of flesh even though they are cutting it out of the very heart of their country, those men who, whether they belong to one section of the Conservatives or the other are today sharpening their knives, in order to obtain from the bleeding corpse of their country, not justice but the satisfaction of revenge.

These men I do not expect ever to satisfy. But I expect we shall be able to satisfy all reasonable men, all right-minded men, all those who, whatever may be their views upon this question, are prepared for the sake of peace, harmony and good-fellowship, to make some sacrifice upon the altar of their common country even of opinion and preference. And I hope that when we appeal to the sense of fair play, of justice and generosity in behalf of a united Canada, it will meet with a clear and unmistakable response from all classes. But I should despair of the future of my country, not merely as to the settlement of this question but as to the settlement of every other question which may come up if the tactics followed by the hon. gentleman opposite and his friends were to prevail in this country, if those who blow hot and cold, who today are vociferously clamouring against the policy which they supported no later than the month of June, were to prevail.

Sir, the Honourable Gentleman dealt a few moments ago with a subject which I was not surprised that he should tackle, because it is one which I am sure must have caused him some uneasiness and even pain as a Canadian for some time, because he cannot but regret, I hope, at all events, that he does regret the language which he made use of on former occasions. The Honourable Gentleman has at last taken some issue with me because I reproached him that upon that question he had made an appeal to feelings of race and religious prejudice. Well, Sir, I accept the challenge and I repeated today in his presence the charge which I proferred against him throughout the provinces visited during the late election.

Here in the great assizes of the nation, before the assembled representatives of the people, I arraign the Honourable Gentleman and his friends for that in the late election they did their utmost to arouse the religious prejudices not only of the people of Quebec but those of the Protestant and English-speaking provinces as well.

Let us join issue at once. The Honourable Gentleman quoted the speech he delivered at Winnipeg. Let me quote it again. . . .

"To my Conservative friends who have turned their backs upon me I want to make another appeal, and it is this: I want to know where is the man with any brains in his head, where is the man who has any capacity for exercising intelligent reasoning capacity, who would justify himself, or would justify himself to his country, if he oppressed a feeble minority, and that for the purpose of bringing into power a Roman Catholic French Premier, who declares he will do more."

A Roman Catholic French Premier. The Honourable Gentleman was speaking in the City of Winnipeg, to an English-speaking audience. He was addressing his friends, as he said – his English-speaking friends in Winnipeg in the Province of Manitoba where the great bulk of the people are opposed to intervention in this matter. If he wanted to make a point against me by saying I had promised to do more than his Bill provided, why, in the name of common sense, was he so particular to tell them that if they turned him out of power they would bring into office a "French Canadian Roman Catholic Premier"? There was innuendo in that. He disclaims having had any intention of appealing to sectional or race or religious prejudice.

A few days afterwards the Honourable Gentleman was at Port Arthur and this is the language he made use of there:

"I am speaking now not to Liberals – it is no use speaking to them – but to Conservatives, and ask can you vote to turn out the present Government and put in a French Roman Catholic Premier."

If that was not an appeal to race and religion, what is the use of language? But the Honourable Gentleman went to the Province of Quebec. Does the Honourable Gentleman pretend that he used in the Province of Quebec the same language that he used in Winnipeg or Port Arthur? Here I have the speech he made in Montreal, at Sohmer Park, before a French-speaking audience. I quote from the report of the *Montreal Gazette*:

"I am prepared to say that what I said at Winnipeg was this":

Now mark the words. The Honourable Gentleman was explaining to a French Canadian and Roman Catholic audience what he stated at Winnipeg, which language I have just quoted.

"I made an appeal to the Liberal Conservative electors who were under the impression that the Dominion Government was forcing separate schools upon the Province of Manitoba. I said, 'Is there a man of intelligence here who does not see that the Government are only carrying out the judgment of the Judicial Committee of the Queen's Privy Council, a judgment which declares that the privileges which belonged to the Roman Catholic minority have been taken away, and that it is the duty of the Parliament of Canada to restore those privileges?' I took the ground that every Liberal Conservative was in honour bound to stand by his party in endeavouring to restore the privileges of which a feeble Roman Catholic minority had been robbed, instead of striking down that party for the purpose of bringing into power a French Roman

Catholic Premier who himself had declared that he had opposed the Bill because –"

He promised more? No, but because, "it was too weak to accomplish its object."

Here is the language of the Honourable Gentleman in Winnipeg. Speaking to English Protestants his language is: Are you going to turn us out and bring into power a French Roman Catholic who promises that he will do more? But in Quebec he says: Are you going to turn us out of power and put into office a French Canadian Roman Catholic Premier who declares the Bill is too weak, and that he will bring in a stronger Bill?

There is the language of the Honourable Gentleman – an appeal to prejudice on both occasions, an appeal to the French Canadians because I had opposed this Bill on the ground that it was too weak; an appeal to the Protestant and English-speaking electors of Manitoba because I had opposed the Bill on the ground that I desired to bring in a stronger one. Sir, on each occasion the Honourable Gentleman was doing his very best in order to arouse local prejudices in each province. . . .

Sir, this is the time and the day to clear up that issue. This is the time and the day. I insist upon it. Let us deal with this question now. . . .

No person has a right to speak of French domination, or English domination, or Scotch domination or German domination. We stand on British Canadian citizenship. What matters it, Sir, whether the majority supporting the Government come from one province or another if the policy of the Government rests upon the broad principles of truth, justice and honour? What matters it whether the majority comes from one province or another if the arguments we used in one province were those we used in all provinces?

Sir, the men who today occupy these benches are fully conscious that upon this and upon other matters they have before them difficult and anxious questions to deal with and to settle, not by appealing to one class, not by appealing to one section; but upon all questions and on all occasions, by appealing to all classes, and to all sections, with the view and with the end, with the supreme view and with the supreme end of making Canada a country, not a country only, but one country as well.

By Arthur Milnes

It is easy to forget how even in triumph in 1896 Laurier still faced questions about whether he was truly ready to lead his party and the country as prime minister. In their study of Laurier (and Sir Robert Borden), professors Patrice Dutil and David MacKenzie turn to Oscar Douglas Skelton to assist us in setting the scene as Laurier rose to his feet in the Commons for the first time as prime minister.

"There were many who doubted," Skelton wrote in 1922, "even after his nine years of party leadership, whether he would be more than the titular head of the government. They did not think it possible that a man so courteous could show himself firm when firmness was called for. Could a leader who had made his fame by his oratory develop the qualities needed to control a ministry and to guide a distracted country through difficult days?"[119]

The critics Skelton referred to were ignoring some of the evidence Laurier had already presented to the contrary, one of which was his speech of August 24, 1896. This address makes clear that the Commons and country had a new prime minister at the helm, one who was confident, clear, and ready to govern.

Rhetoric aside, Laurier had also already assembled a group to govern with him that would be christened the cabinet of "all the talents" before history.[120] Showing supreme confidence, Laurier had elected to invite not one but three sitting provincial premiers to enter his cabinet. Perhaps more importantly is the fact all three – Sir Oliver Mowat of Ontario, William Fielding of Nova Scotia, and Andrew Blair of New Brunswick – agreed to become the new prime minister's juniors.

That historic summer, another of Laurier's minister's, Joseph-Israël Tarte, wrote to a friend suggesting that his chief's critics would soon be surprised. "These people do not understand Laurier; he has a governing mind; he wants to do things; he has plans. He will walk the great way of life with anyone of good intention who will join him."[121]

And so the Laurier Years began. There would be many.

DOMINION DAY BANQUET

HOTEL CECIL, LONDON, ENGLAND

JULY 1, 1897[122]

. . . . The celebration . . . today derives additional charms and pleasure from the fact that it takes place upon the soil of the old motherland. (Cheers) Yet, if I may be permitted to speak my own feelings,
I would say, without any hesitation, that never, perhaps, was my
own native land, Canada, dearer to me than it is at this moment.
(Cheers) I might, perhaps, be permitted to repeat the words once
made use of by Daniel O'Connell on the occasion of a banquet
being given him in the city of Edinburgh. When speaking of the
relations of the three countries, he said: "Yes, I love England, I love
Scotland, but – why should I not say it? The first place in my heart
is Ireland."

I may say in the same way, I love England, I love Scotland, I
love Ireland, but may I be permitted to say today that the first place
in my heart is Canada, my native land. (Loud cheers)

We Canadians love Canada, our native land, or our land of
adoption, and we are proud of her. We love her not only because it
is the land of our home – there would be no merit in that; even the
Eskimo loves his ice-bound hut – we love her for her many beauties
and attractions. We love her for her majestic rivers, we love her for

her lakes, equal to the seas, we love her for her boundless prairies, for her virgin forests, for her lofty mountains, for her fertile plains; we love her for her beautiful climate – warm in summer, cold in winter, but dry at all times. (Laughter and cheers)

We love her even for her snows. Rudyard Kipling has called Canada "the land of snows – Our lady of the snows." Someone objected to it; I do not. The snows of Canada are one of the charms of Canada which England cannot boast of; and we love her for her snows, though, as everyone knows, in summertime her skies are as blue as the skies of Italy.

We are proud of her and of her history – (cheers) – her history as romantic and touching as fiction. It is no exaggeration, it is only the sober truth, to say that the history of Canada cannot be excelled by the history of England, or even by the history of France.

From the day after that famous battle in which Wolfe died thanking God as his eyes closed on the victory of his army, and when Montcalm was carried away from the field conscious that he would not survive the first defeat of his hitherto ever-victorious army. It is sober truth – it is no exaggeration – to say that the history of Canada exceeds, perhaps, in interest, in construction, the history of any country, from the time she became a colony of England all through the long struggle maintained by the new subjects of England for constitutional government up to the present day, when the principle of freedom has been extended to Canada, and has resulted in the magnificent spectacle which we now give to the world of united races previously enemies. (Loud cheers)

You have truly said that Canada is now a nation. Her population is now five million of souls and she has, as you have stated, readily available fertile lands which can give home, food, and shelter to at least one hundred million of men.

It might be an independent nation, but Canada does not seek to become an independent nation, because Canada today practically is an independent nation. (Cheers) Were we severed from England we could not have more power and more freedom than we have at the present time –(cheers) – and all thinking men with us here come to the conclusion – that there is as much freedom, more power, more wealth, and more happiness in union than in separation. (Cheers)

We are giving thus a fresh example, as you stated a moment ago, to our sister colonies, and if the example we have given is followed elsewhere, if a confederation takes place in Australia, if another confederation takes place in South Africa by and bye, in a few years the earth will have been settled by a series of independent nations, which, however, will recognize the suzerainty of England; and it seems to me that in this fact alone there will be security for the peace of the world at large. (Cheers)

We in Canada may perhaps do something more. You have stated that we share the continent of North America with a great nation of kindred race, but with which the relations of England have not always been of the most satisfactory character. Since I have been in England, within the last few days, it seems to me that I have found evidences not a few that there is perhaps in the minds of public men in England, and not only in the minds of public men, but in the minds of the people at large, some apprehension of the latter sentiment on the part of the American nation not altogether friendly to her Motherland.

I would say without any hesitation at all that the sentiment which prevails among the American nation is a sentiment of affection and of reverence, though unfortunately there still remain many causes of friction between the two nations. The memories of the unfortunate state of things which prevailed under the old regime and which led to the War of Independence have not altogether been forgotten. The rancour created by the war is still living in the minds of the American people.

This might have been cast away, but unfortunately, as we know in our own generation, there was a civil war in America – a civil war waged, I know in the minds of all men today, for as noble a cause as ever excited men to fight – for the abolition of slavery; yet it is a matter of history, strange as it may seem to us in these days, that at that period the sympathies of the civilized world were not inclined on the side of the cause of freedom. If I may be permitted to speak my own mind – and I do so because what I state here I have often stated in my own country, and I do not know how to flatter – I have always said in Canada that the attitude maintained by England and by Canada was neither worthy of England or Canada at that time. . . .

But if there were a spirit of friction, rancour and enmity at work at that time, let me say at once that those enmities have been to a large extent removed by the conduct of the Queen of England herself. (Cheers) In the worst days of the war, when the opinion was prevalent in the United States of America that the English people were not as friendly to them as they ought to be, the opinion was also prevalent that the heart of the Queen of England was engaged on the side of liberty. . . .

At the close of the war, when the hand of the assassin struck down the great and wise man [Abraham Lincoln] who had carried his nation safely through the awful crisis, the Queen herself, then in the first years of her own bereavement, sent a letter of condolence and sympathy to the wife of the martyred president. That letter from a widow to a widow appealed to the American heart. It brought tears to the eyes of strong men, it caused tears to stain the farrowed faces of many veterans. Sir, this letter of the Queen did more to erase the battement that had been caused by the attitude of the British people than anything else could possibly have done. (Cheers)

There is more. At that time we did not know, as we now do, the history of diplomacy on this matter, but we know now, thanks to the researches which have been made, that on a previous occasion of the unfortunate Trent Affair,[123] when the sacred soil of England – because her ships are part of her soil – had been invaded by Americans to abstract forcibly from the soil of England men who were guests of England – when the dignity of England forced them to claim back those prisoners, we know that the hand of Her Majesty herself corrected the dispatch of her Foreign Minister and erased every offensive word from it, and left it in such a state that it was possible for the American nation to surrender without any surrender of dignity.

Now, these causes have worked and have had their effect. I am sorry to say that there are still too many causes of friction remaining between Great Britain and the United States. When I say that the people and the Government of England were not blameless, yet for all the troubles which have arisen since the Civil War the blame, in my estimation, rests not with England, but with the United States. Let me hope, however, that better feelings will prevail. Nay, they are prevailing even at this moment.

I am sure, of which we have been witnesses during the Jubilee Week, the most impressive by far was the service at St. Paul's Cathedral, when the Sovereign of England, the dignitaries of England, the people of England with uncovered heads appealed to God and thanked him for the blessing of this reign. This was a scene of great moment, yet there is another scene going on every Sunday upon the decks of the great ships which ply between England and the United States.

There every week you see passengers – American citizens, British subjects – pray to God together for her Majesty the Queen of England and for his Excellency the President of the United States. (Cheers) Let us hope these prayers shall not be in vain, but hope that the gods of war shall never spread their wings between England and the United States. (Loud cheers) But if ever they come to that, let me say here that the feeling of my own people in the colony of Canada would stand true by the flag which protects her and her liberty. (Cheers)

For these considerations – nay, for every consideration – let me tell you that, for my part, I have the greatest hope and confidence in the future of the young nation to which I belong. I trust that as she did in the past she will ever do – that she will never play a weaker part, that she will on every occasion boldly strike out in the ever-advancing cause of freedom, of progress, and of civilization.

(Cheers) What more shall I say? You have spoken of me in terms altogether too kind. Let me say that when the time comes for myself that my eyes must close for ever to the light of this world, if I can on my death bed say that through my effort racial feuds have disappeared from the land of Canada, that through my effort a step forward has been made towards uniting this great Empire, I shall die happy in the belief that my life shall not have been lived in vain.

(Loud cheers, the entire audience rising and waving handkerchiefs.)

By the Right Honourable Tony Blair

As prime minister of the United Kingdom in 2001, I had the rare honour of addressing the Parliament of Canada. The speech came almost sixty years after Churchill had addressed parliamentarians in Ottawa, and a decade before David Cameron did. We all had different politics and different issues to deal with at the time, but one thing has remained constant: the strength of Britain and Canada's relationship.

The enduring nature of this alliance is something Sir Wilfrid Laurier foresaw in an 1897 address in London. Canada's first French-Canadian prime minister – a special hero to my friend Jean Chrétien – believed that Canada would serve as a linchpin between the North American and European nations. This it has done – and continues to do – with the skill Laurier predicted.

Since the year of Queen Victoria's Diamond Jubilee much has of course changed for our countries. The nation Laurier did so much to craft has now successfully incorporated two great European civilizations. But beyond being bilingual Canada has also been enriched by the contributions of other cultures from around the world, as well as its indigenous peoples.

As a committed Atlanticist, I am confident Laurier would celebrate that modern Canada is so close in values to Europe. Because the trans-Atlantic relationship is – and should always be – fundamental to the security and prosperity of our nations. This is particularly important today, as more political and economic power shifts East, while we face a new battle to replace those of twentieth-century Islamist extremism.

This is why our countries' alliance, founded on historical connection, culture, language, and tradition, but also on belief, shared values, and a common outlook is not only crucial, but should always be renewed and strengthened. And so just as Laurier deepened our bonds and worked to unite Canada and the U.K., so should we. This is not just about mutual interest or our prosperity, but also about the pursuit of global values. They are values that have endured throughout history. They are the ones Laurier believed our relationship should be founded on. And they are the ones that we should fight for today.

The Right Honourable Tony Blair served as prime minister of the United Kingdom from 1997 to 2007. He is the founder and patron of the Tony Blair Faith Foundation www.tonyblairfaithfoundation.org and Africa Governance Initiative www.africagovernance.org.

By Gordon Campbell

On July 1, 1897, Sir Wilfrid Laurier was in London as part of the celebration of Queen Victoria's Diamond Jubilee. He had just been conferred the order of Knight Grand Cross in the Most Distinguished Order of

St. Michael and St. George on June 21, ten days earlier. As prime minister of the Dominion of Canada he was an honoured guest at Queen Victoria's Diamond Jubilee, which established Her Majesty as the Mother of the Empire upon which "the sun never sets."

While Laurier embraces England, Scotland and Ireland, he makes clear from the outset that "first place in my heart is Canada, my native land."

Although the style and pattern of his words would not be repeated today, the substance and spirit still resonate. Canada's geography and the beauty of the land still inspire awe in the United Kingdom. Still today the British mind stretches to imagine a country with six time zones and thousands of kilometres wide and deep. Canadians equally still need to understand that the entire U.K. represents just 2 per cent of Canada's land mass. The vastness of space continues to shape our view of the world.

Laurier is equally proud of the social unity of Canada in spite of the stress of history, culture, and region. It was the celebration of the opportunities that Canada represented to the world – cemented at Queen Victoria's Diamond Jubilee – that led in part to the successive waves of immigration that fuelled Canada's prospects, as Laurier saw them, for the twentieth century.

He is a proud advocate and bridge builder. Laurier is clear that to him the attitude of "England and by Canada" toward the American civil war and the abolition of slavery wasn't worthy of nations who share our principles. You could hear the same arguments made by Canada's representatives in today's London as they sit at the Board of Governors of the Commonwealth. How in today's world do we stand for the principles to which we give lip service when the power of the status quo and the conventional look away from injustice? Principles such as the rule of law, parliamentary democracy, human rights, and religious freedom must be the clear principles upon which we stand.

Laurier searches for common ground and common interests. Laurier is the great Canadian optimist. For him the twentieth century would belong to Canada, and Canada would "on every occasion strike out in the ever-advancing cause of freedom, of progress and of civilization." Today Canada's voice is a strong and free advocate for the elimination of forced and early childhood marriage, for human rights, for democratic reform, for the rule of law, and for religious freedom.

Canada still strives to reach the goals so strongly expressed by Sir Wilfrid Laurier 118 years ago in London at Queen Victoria's Diamond Jubilee.

A former premier of British Columbia, Gordon Campbell served as Canada's high commissioner to the United Kingdom from 2011 to 2016.

TRIBUTE TO GLADSTONE

HOUSE OF COMMONS, OTTAWA, ONTARIO
MAY 26, 1898

England has lost the most illustrious of her sons; but the loss is not England's alone, nor is it confined to the great Empire which acknowledges England's suzerainty, nor even to the proud race which can claim kinship with the people of England. The loss is the loss of mankind.

Mr. Gladstone gave his whole life to his country; but the work which he did for his country was conceived and carried out on principles of such high elevation, for purposes so noble and aims so lofty, that not his country alone, but the whole of mankind, benefited by his work. It is no exaggeration to say that he has raised the standard of civilization, and the world today is undoubtedly better for both the precept and the example of his life. His death is mourned not only by England, the land of his birth, not only by Scotland, the land of his ancestors, not only by Ireland, for which he did so much, and attempted to do so much more; but also by the people of the two Sicilys, for whose outraged rights he once aroused the conscience of Europe, by the people of the Ionian Islands, whose independence he secured, by the people of Bulgaria and the Danubian provinces, in whose cause he enlisted the sympathy of his own native country.

Indeed, since the days of Napoleon, no man has lived whose name has travelled so far and so wide over the surface of the earth; no man has lived whose name alone so deeply moved the hearts of so many millions of men. Whereas Napoleon impressed his tremendous personality upon peoples far and near by the strange fascination which the genius of war has always exercised over the imagination of men in all lands and in all ages, the name of Gladstone has come to be, in the minds of all civilized nations, the living incarnation of right against might – the champion, the dauntless, tireless champion of the oppressed against the oppressor.

It is, I believe, equally true to say that his was the most marvellous mental organization which the world has seen since Napoleon – certainly the most compact, the most active and the most universal. This last half century in which we live has produced many able and strong men who, in different walks of life, have attracted the attention of the world at large; but of the men who have illustrated this age, it seems to me that in the eyes of posterity four will outlive and outshine all others – Cavour,[124] Lincoln, Bismarck and Gladstone. If we look simply at the magnitude of the results obtained, compared with the exiguity of the resources at command – if we remember that out of the small kingdom of Sardinia grew United Italy, we must come to the conclusion that Count Cavour was undoubtedly a statesman of marvellous skill and prescience.

Abraham Lincoln, unknown to fame when he was elected to the presidency, exhibited a power for the government of men which has scarcely been surpassed in any age. He saved the American union, he enfranchised the black race, and for the task he had to perform he was endowed in some respects almost miraculously. No man ever displayed a greater insight into the motives, the complex motives, which shape the public opinion of a free country, and he possessed almost to the degree of an instinct, the supreme quality in a statesman of taking the right decision, taking it at the right moment, and expressing it in language of incomparable felicity.

Prince Bismarck was the embodiment of resolute common sense, unflinching determination, relentless strength, moving onward to his ends and crushing everything in his way as unconcernedly as fate itself.

Mr. Gladstone undoubtedly exceeded every one of these men. . . . He had the aptitude for business, the financial ability which Lincoln never exhibited. He had the lofty impulses, the generous inspirations which Prince Bismarck always discarded, even if he did not treat them with scorn. He was at once an orator, a statesman, a poet, and a man of business. As an orator he stands certainly in the very front rank of orators of his country or any country, of his age or any age.

I remember when Louis Blanc[125] was in England, in the days of the Second Empire, he used to write to the press of Paris, and in one of his letters to *"Le Temps"* he stated that Mr. Gladstone would undoubtedly have been the foremost orator of England if it were not for the existence of Mr. Bright. It may be admitted, and I think it is admitted generally, that on some occasions Mr. Bright reached heights of grandeur and pathos which even Mr. Gladstone did not attain. But Mr. Gladstone had an ability, a vigour, a fluency which no man in his age or any age ever rivalled or even approached. That is not all. To his marvellous mental powers he added no less marvellous physical gifts. He had the eye of a god, the voice of a silver bell; and the very fire of his eye, the very music of his voice, swept the hearts of men even before they had been dazzled by the torrents of his eloquence.

As a statesman, it was the good fortune of Mr. Gladstone that his career was not associated with war. The reforms which he effected, the triumphs which he achieved, were not won by the supreme arbitrament of the sword. The reforms which he effected and the triumphs which he achieved were the result of his power of persuasion over his fellow men. The reforms which he achieved in many ways amounted to a revolution. They changed, in many particulars, the face of the realm. After Sir Robert Peel had adopted the great principle which eventually carried England from protection to free trade, it was Mr. Gladstone who created the financial system which has been admitted ever since by all students of finance as the secret of Great Britain's commercial success. He enforced the extension of the suffrage to the masses of the nation and practically thereby made the Government of monarchical England as democratic as that of any republic.

He disestablished the Irish Church; he introduced reform into the land tenure, and brought hope into the breasts of those tillers of the soil in Ireland who had for so many generations laboured in despair. And all this he did, not by force or violence, but simply by the power of his eloquence and the strength of his personality. Great, however, as were the acts of the man – after all he was of the human flesh, and for him, as for everybody else, there were trivial and low duties to be performed, it is no exaggeration to say that even in those low and trivial duties he was great. He ennobled the common realities of life.

His was above all things a religious mind – essentially religious in the highest sense of the term. And the religious sentiment which dominated his public life and his speeches, that same sentiment, according to the testimony of those who knew him best, also permeated all his actions from the highest to the humblest. He was a man of strong and pure affections, of long and lasting friendship, and to describe the beauty of his domestic life no words of praise can be adequate. It was simply ideally beautiful, and in the later years of his life as touching as it was beautiful.

May I be permitted, without any impropriety, to recall that it was my privilege to experience and to appreciate that courtesy, made up of dignity and grace, which was famous all over the world, but of which no one could have an appropriate opinion unless he had been the recipient of it. In a character so complex and diversified, one may be asked what was the dominant feature, what was the supreme quality, the one characteristic which marked the nature of the man. Was it his incomparable genius for finance? Was it his splendid oratorical powers? Was it his marvellous fecundity of mind?

In my estimation, it was not any one of those qualities. Great as they were, there was one still more marked, and if I have to give my own impression, I would say that the one trait which was dominant in his nature, which marked the man more distinctively than any other, was his intense humanity, his paramount sense of right, his abhorrence of injustice, wrong and oppression, wherever to be found or in whatever shape they might show themselves. Injustice, wrong, oppression, acted upon him, as it were, mechanically, and aroused every fibre of his being, and from that moment, to the repairing of the injustice, the undoing of the wrong, and the destruction of the oppression, he gave his mind, his heart, his soul, his whole life, with an energy, with an intensity, with a vigour paralleled in no man unless it be the first Napoleon.

There are many evidences of this in his life. When he was travelling in southern Italy, as a tourist, for pleasure and for the benefit of the health of his family, he became aware of the abominable system which was there prevailing under the name of constitutional government. He left everything aside, even the object which had brought him to Italy, and applied himself to investigate and to collect evidence, and then denounced the abominable system in a trumpet blast of such power that it shook to its very foundation the throne of King Ferdinand and sent it tottering to its fall.

Again, when he was sent as High Commissioner to the Ionian Islands, the Hellenic population separated from the rest of Greece, separated from the kingdom to which they were adjacent and towards which all their aspirations were raised, struck his generous soul with such force that he became practically their advocate and secured their independence.

Again, when he had withdrawn from public life, and when, in the language of theirs, under somewhat similar circumstances, he had returned to "ses chères études" [his dear studies], the atrocities perpetrated by the Turks on the people of Bulgaria brought him back to public life with a vehemence, an impetuosity, and a torrent of fierce indignation that swept everything before it.[126]

If this be, as I think it is, the one distinctive feature of his character, it seems to explain away what are called the inconsistencies of his life. Inconsistencies there were none in his life. He had been brought up in the most unbending school of Toryism. He became the most active Reformer of our own times. But whilst he became the leader of the Liberal Party and an active Reformer, it is only due to him to say that in his complex mind there was a vast space for what is known as Conservatism. His mind was not only liberal but conservative as well, and he clung to the affections of his youth until, in questions of practical moment, he found them clashing with that sense of right and abhorrence of injustice of which I have spoken.

But the moment he found his conservative affections clash with what he thought right and just, he did not hesitate to abandon his former convictions and go the whole length of the reforms demanded. Thus, he was always devotedly, filially, lovingly attached to the Church of England. He loved it, as he often declared. He adhered to it as an establishment in England, but the very reasons and arguments which, in his mind, justified the establishment of the Church in England, compelled him to a different course as far as that church was concerned in Ireland. In England the church was the church of the majority, of almost the unanimity of the nation. In Ireland it was the church of the minority, and therefore he did not hesitate. His course was clear; he removed the one church and maintained the other.

So it was with Home Rule; but coming to this subject of Home Rule, though there may be much to say, perhaps this is neither the occasion nor the place to say it. England is today in tears, but fortunate is the nation which has produced such a man. His years are over, but his work is not closed; his work is still going on. The example which he gave to the world shall live forever, and the seed which he has sown with such a copious hand shall still germinate and bear fruit under the full light of heaven.

By Bruce Yaccato

Though Laurier was born just four years after the trauma of Britain's brutal quashing of the 1837 Rebellion, by the time the underwhelming new MP arrived in Ottawa in 1872, he proclaimed himself to be a British Liberal. The reverence with which he held the creed's greatest practitioner, William Ewart Gladstone, burned bright as ever when Prime Minister Laurier rose in his place to eulogize his hero in 1898.

Laurier was a fervent and faithful disciple of Gladstonian Liberalism even when it came to suffering electoral defeat twice on one its central tenets, that of free trade. The two men shared fiscal prudence, a disdain for foreign entanglements in the name of Empire, and intolerance for injustice. They were also among the best, if not the best, prime ministers their respective countries enjoyed. The luminous praise of the mentored almost deifies his mentor, attributing to him "the eye of a God." No mean orator himself, Laurier places Gladstone "in the front rank of orators in his or any country in his age or any other." The "marvellous fecundity of his mind" and "unrivalled genius for business" made him, in Laurier's view, "undoubtedly" the greatest man of his time, over even Lincoln and Bismarck. Some may question Laurier's qualifications for the judging of business genius, as he was not known for his grasp of economic policy. It was once said that "the only figures Laurier understands are figures of speech."

Despite the reverence and similarities in substance, it is interesting to note how different were the styles in which they conducted their politics and lives.

Laurier had immense personal charm, his famous "sunny ways" would lead author Lucy Maud Montgomery to observe that, for a time, he was "little lower than the angels." His mentor, however, was more feared and revered than loved. His wife once chided him, "It's a good thing you're such a great man, otherwise you'd be such a bore!"

The two men met only once, at Hawarden Castle, Gladstone's Welsh estate, in 1897. Laurier had just moved into the Prime Minister's Office the year before, while his host would be in his grave the next. Though it would seem like an aspiring fresco painter meeting Michelangelo after the Sistine Chapel opened, the event is little written about, possibly because the two were polar opposites in personality. Gladstone was like the bull in the proverbial china shop; Laurier was more like the china. It could be said that Sir Wilfrid was a somewhat delicate figure despite his height, perhaps even a fastidious neat freak. Gladstone was a horse who revelled in strenuous walks and hikes, and especially in deforesting all before him with his incessant chopping down of trees. Even Laurier's reference to their meeting seems curt and slightly chilly, especially in contrast to the soaring praise in the rest of his remarks. "I had the privilege to experience and appreciate [his] courtesy of dignity and grace. . . ."

Whatever their fleeting personal relationship, their lives and careers shared equally striking parallels. They would both execute a complete 180 degree turn from their youthful beliefs. Laurier vehemently opposed Confederation and then went on to govern the country for fifteen years. Gladstone began as a High Tory. In fact, they both exhibited strong undercurrents of conservatism, which Laurier references prominently in his speech as one of "the inconsistencies of his [Gladstone's] life." Laurier disliked almost every innovation of the twentieth century. He certainly was no fan of universal suffrage. The only thing he hated more than the invention of the car was the invention of the telephone.

That being said, they were both at their finest when fighting what they perceived as injustice. They would both risk taking on intractable issues of minorities and religion, Laurier with Riel and the Manitoba Schools question,

Gladstone with the Irish Church and Home Rule. They would both be singed by war, Laurier by the Boer War, Gladstone by the fall of Khartoum. They both won four elections, Laurier consecutively, Gladstone periodically after total implosions. Both are considered among the greatest in their respective countries' history, yet both were, in baseball terms, barely over .500.

There was also an interesting symmetry in the political heroes Laurier chose in life. Edward Blake may not be much remembered today, but in the late nineteenth century he was a towering figure in the Liberal Party – though Sir John A. Macdonald played him like a cheap violin at election time. It was said he "wished neither to lead nor be led" and reluctantly stayed on, urged by his devoted follower, Wilfrid Laurier, who compared him to his illustrious Westminster counterpart. Blake could not resign, Laurier told him, because "like Gladstone events will come around to you." When Blake finally foisted the leadership on his lieutenant, he escaped to London to become a Liberal MP under Gladstone himself.

While the eulogy enumerates and extolls Gladstone's exceptional abilities, there are two qualities that, for Laurier, set him high above other renowned leaders. He was "the dauntless, tireless champion of the oppressed against the oppressors" and he "raised the standard of civilization" without resorting to the force of arms. The palpable abject sense of loss in a way foreshadows the same sense conveyed by Canadians in their final tribute to their beloved Sir Wilfrid, the still deeply moving picture of him, alone, lying in state in the House of Commons, all other seats removed, as if acknowledging as he did with Gladstone the unworthiness of all who mourn him.

Bruce Yaccato is a journalist, author, and award-winning documentary filmmaker. He wrote and directed *Sir Wilfrid Laurier and the Romance of Canada* for the History Channel in 1998.

CANADA, ENGLAND,
THE UNITED STATES

CHICAGO, ILLINOIS
OCTOBER 9, 1899[127]

I very fully and very cordially appreciate the very kind feelings which have just now been uttered by the toastmaster in terms so eloquent, and which you gentlemen have accepted and received in so sympathetic a manner. Let me say at once, in the name of my fellow Canadians who are here with me, and also, I may say, in the name of the Canadian people, that these feelings we will at all times reciprocate; reciprocate, not only in words evanescent, but in actual living deeds.

I take it to be an evidence of the good relation which, in your estimation, gentlemen, ought to prevail between two such countries as the United States and Canada, that you have notified us, your next-door neighbours, in this day of rejoicing, to take our share with you of your joy. We shall bring back to our own country the most pleasant remembrance of the day.

We have seen many things here today very much to be admired; the imposing ceremonies of the morning, the fine pageant, the grand procession, the orderly and good-natured crowds – all these are things to be admired and, to some extent, to be wondered at.

But the one thing of all most to be admired, most to be remembered, is the very inspiration of this festival.

It is quite characteristic of the city of Chicago. As a rule, nations and cities celebrate the day of their foundation or some great victory or some national triumph; in all cases, some event which, when it occurred, was a cause of universal joy and rejoicing. Not so, however, of the City of Chicago. In this, as in everything else, she does not tread in beaten paths; the day which she celebrates is not the day of her foundation, when hunters and fur traders unconsciously laid down the beginnings of what were to develop into a gigantic city; neither does she celebrate some great action in which American history abounds; nor even does she commemorate a deed selected from the life of some of the great men whom the State has given to the nation, though Illinois can claim the proud privilege of having given to the nation one as great as Washington himself.

The day which she celebrates is the day of her direst calamity, the day when she was swept out of existence by fire.[128] This, I say, is very characteristic of Chicago, because if history recalls her destruction, it also recalls her resurrection. It recalls the energy, the courage, the faith, the enthusiasm with which her citizens met and faced and conquered an appalling calamity.

For my part, well do I remember the awful day, for, as you well know, its horrors were reverberated far beyond the limits of your country, but of all the things which – I was then a young man – I most remember, of all the acts of courage and heroism which were brought forward by the occasion, the one thing which at the same time struck me the most was the appeal issued by the business men of Chicago on the smoking ruins of their city.

They appealed to their fellow citizens. They appealed not for alms, not for charity of any kind, but in most noble language they appealed to their fellow citizens, especially to those who had business connections in Chicago and whose enterprise and energy had conferred honour on the American name, to sustain them in their business in that hour of their trial.

Mark the language. The only thing that they asked was to be sustained in their business, and if sustained in their business they were ready to face and meet the awful calamity which had befallen their city. Well, Sir, in my estimation, in my judgment, at least, that was courage of the very highest order. Whenever you meet courage, you are sure to meet justice and generosity. Courage, justice, and generosity always go together, and therefore it is with some degree of satisfaction that I approach the toast to which I have been called to respond.

Because I must say that I feel that though the relations between Canada and the United States are good, though they are brotherly, though they are satisfactory, in my judgment they are not as good, as brotherly, as satisfactory as they ought to be.

We are of the same stock. We spring from the same races on one side of the line as on the other. We speak the same language. We have the same literature, and for more than a thousand years we have had a common history.

Let me recall to you the lines which, in the darkest days of the Civil War, the Puritan poet of America issued to England:

Oh, Englishmen! Oh, Englishmen!
In hope and creed,
In blood and tongue, are brothers,
We all are heirs of Runnymede.[129]

Brothers we are, in the language of your own poet. May I not say that while our relations are not always as brotherly as they should have been, may I not ask, Mr. President, on the part of Canada and on the part of the United States, if we are sometimes too prone to stand by the full conceptions of our rights, and exact all our rights to the last pound of flesh? May I not ask if there have not been too often between us petty quarrels, which happily do not wound the heart of the nation?

Sir, I am proud to say in the presence of the Chief Executive of the United States that it is the belief of the Canadian Government that we should make a supreme effort to better our relations and make the Government of President McKinley and the present Government of Canada, with the assent of Great Britain, so to work together as to remove all causes of dissension between us.

Shall I speak my mind? (Cries of "Yes!") We met a stumbling block in the question of the Alaskan frontier. Well, let me say here and now the commission would not settle that question, and referred it to their particular governments, and they are now dealing with it. May I be permitted to say here and now that we do not desire one inch of your land?

But if I state, however, that we want to hold our own land, will not that be an American sentiment, I want to know? However, though that would be a British sentiment or Canadian, I am here to say, above all, my fellow countrymen, that we do not want to stand upon the extreme limits of our rights. We are ready to give and to take. We can afford to be just; we can afford to be generous, because we are strong. We have a population of seventy-seven millions. I beg pardon, I am mistaken, it is the reverse of that. But pardon my mistake; although it is the reverse, I am sure the sentiment is the same.

But though we may have many little bickerings of that kind, I speak my whole mind, and I believe I speak the mind of all you gentlemen when I say that, after all, when we go down to the bottom of our hearts we will find that there is between us a true, genuine affection.

There are no two nations today on the face of the globe so united as Great Britain and the United States of America. The

Secretary of State told us some few months ago that there was no treaty of alliance between Great Britain and the United States of America. It is very true there is between the United States of America and Great Britain today no treaty of alliance which the pen can write and which the pen can unmake, but there is between Great Britain and the United States of America a unity of blood which is thicker than water, and I appeal to recent history when I say that whenever one nation has to face an emergency – a greater emergency than usual – forthwith the sympathies of the other nation go to her sister.

Sir, an incident took place in the month of June last which showed to me at all events conclusively that there is between us a very deep and sincere affection. I may be pardoned if I recall that instance, because I have to speak of myself.

In the month of June last I spoke on the floor of the House of Commons of Canada on the question of Alaska, and I enunciated the very obvious truism that international problems can be settled in one of two ways only: either by arbitration or war. And although I proceeded to say immediately that war between Great Britain and the United States would be criminal and would not be thought of for a moment, still the very word "war" created quite an excitement in this country.

With that causeless excitement, though I was indirectly the cause of it, I do not at this moment find any fault, because it convinced me, to an absolute certainty, that between your country and my country the relations have reached a degree of dignity and respect and affection that even the word "war" is never to be mentioned in a British Assembly or in an American Assembly. The word is not to be pronounced, not even to be predicated. It is not to be pronounced at all. The very idea is abhorrent to us.

There was a civil war in the last century. There was a civil war between England and her American colonies, and their relations were severed. If they were severed, American citizens, as you know they were, through no fault of your fathers, the fault was altogether the fault of the British Government of that day. If the British Government of that day had treated the American colonies as the British Government for the last twenty or fifty years has treated its colonies; if Great Britain had given you then the same degree of liberty which it gives to Canada, my country; if it had given you, as it has given us, legislative independence absolute, the result would have been different – the course of victory, the course of history, would have been different.

But what has been done cannot be undone. You cannot expect that the union which has been severed shall ever be restored; but can we not expect, can we not hope that if the unity cannot be restored under the law, at least there can be a union of hearts? Can we not hope that the banners of England and the banners of the United States shall never, never again meet in conflict, except in those conflicts provided by the arts of peace, such as we see today in the harbour of New York, in the contest between the "Shamrock" and the "Columbia" for the supremacy of naval architecture and naval prowess?

Can we not hope that if ever the banners of England and the banners of the United States are again to meet on the battlefield, they shall meet entwined together in the defence of the oppressed, for the enfranchisement of the downtrodden, and for the advancement of liberty, progress, and civilization? . . . .

By David Jacobson

On October 9, 1899, United States president William McKinley and Canadian prime minister Wilfrid Laurier addressed a crowd gathered at the Auditorium Theater in Chicago to commemorate Chicago Day on the twenty-eighth anniversary of the Great Chicago Fire. The prime minister delivered remarks which are as meaningful in 2016 as they were in 1899.

He evidenced an instinctive understanding of what it means to be a Chicagoan. He recognized that the day Chicago celebrates is not the day she was founded, not the day some great action took place, not the deed of some great citizen. Instead:

"The day [Chicago] celebrates is the day of her direst calamity, the day when she was swept out of existence by fire. This, I say, is very characteristic of Chicago, because if history recalls her destruction, it also recalls her resurrection. It recalls the energy, the courage, the faith, the enthusiasm with which her citizens met and faced and conquered an appalling calamity."

Today, 145 years after the fire and 117 years after Prime Minister Laurier spoke, his words still capture the essence of what this city I call home is all about.

The flag of Chicago that flies outside my office window has four stars to mark the city's four great events; one of those stars is for the Chicago Fire.

Our world-famous technology incubator is not named after a great Chicago inventor or entrepreneur – though we have many. It is named "1871" to commemorate, in Laurier's words, "the resurrection . . . the courage, the faith, the enthusiasm" of Chicago's people.

I belong to a club of Chicago business leaders named simply "1871." Laurier – in his brief encounter with this great city – understood us so well. And his understanding endures.

But the prime minister understood so much more. He understood the nature of the relationship between Canada and the United States. And again, his understanding is as relevant in the twenty-first century as it was in the nineteenth.

After recognizing that the relations between Canada and the United States were "brotherly," he continued:

"Our relations are not always as brotherly as they should [be]. May I not ask, Mr. President, on the part of Canada and on the part of the United States, if we are sometimes too prone to stand by the full conceptions of our rights, and exact all our rights to the last pound of flesh? May I not ask if there have not been too often between us petty quarrels, which happily do not wound the heart of the nation?"

Those words could just as easily be said by a Canadian prime minister or an American president today. Indeed, in a far less eloquent way, I said them myself several times when I was the United States ambassador to Canada. I regularly asked audiences if they thought there might be another pair of neighbouring countries anywhere in the world who wouldn't trade their problems for ours. No one, on either side of the border, ever volunteered an answer.

Prime Minister Laurier understood that the nature of the relationship between our two great countries is brotherly. That we ought to avoid petty quarrels. We ought not seek the last pound of flesh. Then – and only then – will our relations be "as brotherly as they should be."

Truer words were never spoken.

David Jacobson, vice chairman BMO Financial Group in Chicago, served as United States ambassador to Canada from 2009 to 2013.

TRIBUTE TO QUEEN VICTORIA

HOUSE OF COMMONS, OTTAWA, ONTARIO

FEBRUARY 8, 1901

We have met under the shadow of a death which has caused more universal mourning than has ever been recorded in the pages of history. In these words there is no exaggeration; they are the literal truth. There is mourning in the United Kingdom, in the Colonies, and in the many islands and continents which form the great empire over which extend the sovereignty of Queen Victoria. There is mourning deep, sincere, heartfelt in the mansions of the great, and of the rich, and in the cottages of the poor and lowly; for to all her subjects, whether high or low, whether rich or poor, the Queen, in her long reign, had become an object of almost sacred veneration.

There is sincere and unaffected regret in all of the nations of Europe, for all the nations of Europe had learned to appreciate, to admire, and to envy the many qualities of Queen Victoria, those many public and domestic virtues which were the pride of her subjects.

There is genuine grief in the neighbouring nation of seventy-five million inhabitants, the kinsmen of her own people, by whom at all times and under all circumstances her name was held in high reverence, and where, in the darkest days of the Civil War, when the relations of the two countries were strained almost to the point of snapping, the poet Whittier well expressed the feeling of his countrymen when he exclaimed:

"We bowed the heart, if not the knee,
"To England's Queen, God bless her."[130]

There is wailing and lamentation among the savage and barbarian peoples of her vast empire, in the wigwams of our own Indian tribes, in the huts of the coloured races of Africa and of India, to whom she was at all times the Great Mother, the living impersonation of majesty and benevolence. Aye, and there is mourning also, genuine and unaffected, in the farmhouses of South Africa, which have been lately and still are devastated by war, for it is a fact that above the clang of arms, above the many angers engendered by the war, the name of Queen Victoria was always held in high respect, even by those who are fighting her troops, as a symbol of justice, and perhaps her kind hand was much relied upon when the supreme hour of reconciliation should come.

What is greatness? We are accustomed to call great those exceptional beings upon whom heaven has bestowed some of its choicest gifts, which astonish and dazzle the world by the splendour of faculties, phenomenally developed, even when these faculties are much marred by defects and weaknesses which make them nugatory of the good.

But this is not, in my estimation at least, the highest conception of greatness. The equipoise of a well-balanced mind, the equilibrium of faculties well and evenly ordered, the luminous insight of a calm judgment, are gifts which are as rarely found in one human being as the possession of the more dazzling tho' less solid qualities. And when these high qualities are found in a ruler of men, combined with purity of soul, kindness of heart, generosity of disposition, elevation of purpose, and devotion to duty, this is what seems to me to be the highest conception of greatness, greatness which will be abundantly productive of happiness and glory to the people under such a sovereign. If I mistake not, such was the character of Queen Victoria, and such were the results of her rule. It has been our privilege to live under her reign, and it must be admitted that her reign was of the grandest in history, rivalling in length and more than rivalling in glory the long reign of Louis XIV, and, more than the reign of Louis XIV, likely, to project its lustre into future ages.

Undoubtedly we may find in history instances where death has caused perhaps more passionate outbursts of grief, but it is impossible to find instances where death has caused so universal, so sincere, so heartfelt an expression of sorrow. In the presence of these many evidences of grief which come not only from her own dominions, but from all parts of the globe; in the presence of so many tokens of admiration, where it is not possible to find a single discordant note; in the presence of the immeasurable void caused by the death of Queen Victoria, it is not too much to say that the grave has just closed upon one of the great characters of history.

If we cast our glance back over the sixty-four years into which was encompassed the reign of Queen Victoria, we stand astonished, however familiar we may be with the facts, at the development of civilization which has taken place during that period. We stand astonished at the advance of culture, of wealth, of legislation, of education, of literature, of the arts and sciences, of locomotion by land and by sea, and of almost every department of human activity.

The age of Queen Victoria must be held to be on a par with the most famous within the memory of man. Of course, of the many facts and occurrences which have contributed to make the reign of Queen Victoria what it was, to give it the splendour which has created such an impression upon her own country, and which has shed such a luminous trail all over the world, many took place apart and away from her influence. Many events took place in relation to which the most partial panegyrists would, no doubt, have to say, that they were simply the happy circumstance of the time in which she lived.

Science, for instance, might have obtained the same degree of development under another monarch. It is also possible that literature might have flourished under another monarch, but I believe that the contention can be advanced, and advanced truly, that the literature of the Victorian age to a large extent reflected the influence of the queen. To the eternal glory of the literature of the reign of Queen Victoria be it said, that it was pure and absolutely free from the grossness which disgraced it in former ages, and which still unhappily is the shame of the literature of other countries. Happy indeed is the country whose literature is of such a character that it can be the intellectual food of the family circle; that it can be placed by the mother in the hands of her daughter with abundant assurance that while the mind is improved the heart is not polluted. Such is the literature of the Victorian age. For this blessing, in my judgment, no small credit is due to the example and influence of our departed Queen. It is a fact well known in history that in England as in other countries, the influence of the sovereign was always reflected upon the literature of the reign. In former ages, when the court was impure, the literature of the nation was impure, but in the age of Queen Victoria, where the life of the court was pure, the literature of the age was pure also. If it be true that there is a real connection between the high moral standard of the court of the sovereign and the literature of the age, then I can say without hesitation that Queen Victoria has conferred, not only upon her own people, but upon mankind at large, a gift for which we can never have sufficient appreciation.

Queen Victoria was the first of all sovereigns who was absolutely impersonal – impersonal politically, I mean. Whether the question at issue was the abolition of the Corn Laws, or the war in the Crimea, or the extension of the suffrage, or the disestablishment of the Irish Church, or Home Rule in Ireland, the Queen never gave any information of what her views were upon any of these great political issues. Her subjects never knew what were her personal views, tho views she had, because she was a woman of strong intellect, and we know that she followed public events with great eagerness. We can presume, indeed we know, that whenever a new policy was presented to her by her Prime Minister she discussed that policy with him, and sometimes approved or sometimes, perhaps, dissented.

But that is not all. The most remarkable event in the reign of Queen Victoria – an event which took place in silence and unobserved – the most remarkable event in the reign of the late Queen was the marvellous progress in colonial development, development which, based upon local autonomy, ended in colonial expansion.

What has been the cause of that marvellous change? The cause is primarily the personality of Queen Victoria. Of course the visible and chief cause of all is the bold policy inaugurated many years ago of introducing parliamentary constitutional government, and allowing the colonies to govern themselves. But, sir, it is manifest that self-government could never have been truly effective in Canada had it not been that there was a wise sovereign reigning in England, who had herself given the fullest measure of constitutional government to her own people. If the people of England had not been ruled by a wise Queen; if they had not themselves possessed parliamentary government in the truest sense of the term; if the British Parliament had been as it had been under former kings in open contention with the sovereign, then it is quite manifest that Canada could not have enjoyed the development of constitutional government which she enjoys today. It is quite manifest that if the people of England had not possessed constitutional government in the fullest degree at home, they could not have given it to the colonies; and thus the action of the Queen in giving constitutional government to England has strengthened the Throne, not only in England, but in the Colonies as well.

At the close of the Civil War, when the union of the United States had been confirmed, when slavery had been abolished, when rebellion had been put down, the civilized world was shocked to hear of the foul assassination of the wise and good man who had carried his country through that ordeal. Then the good heart and sound judgment of the queen were again manifested. She sent a letter to the widow of the martyred president – not as the Queen of Great Britain to the widow of the president of the United States, but she sent a letter of sympathy from a widow to a widow, herself being then in the first years of her own bereavement. That action on her part made a very deep impression upon the minds of the American people; it touched not only the heart of the widowed wife, but the heart of the widowed nation; it stirred the souls of strong men; it caused tears to course down the cheeks of veterans who had courted death during the previous four years on a thousand battlefields.

I do not say that it brought about reconciliation, but it made reconciliation possible. It was the first rift in the clouds; and today, in the time of England's mourning, the American people flock to their churches, pouring their blessings upon the memory of Britain's queen. I do not hope, I do not believe it possible, that the two countries which were severed in the eighteenth century, can ever be again united politically; but perhaps it is not too much to hope that the friendship thus inaugurated by the hand of the Queen may continue to grow until the two nations are united again, not by legal bonds, but by ties of affection as strong, perhaps, as if sanctioned by all the majesty of the laws of the two countries; and if such an event were ever to take place, the credit of it would be due to the wise and noble woman who thus would have proved herself to be one of the greatest of statesmen simply by following the instincts of her heart.

Sir, in a life in which there is so much to be admired, perhaps the one thing most to be admired is that naturalness, that simplicity in the character of the Queen which showed itself in such actions as I have just described. From the first day of her reign to the last, she conquered and kept the affections of her people, simply because under all circumstances, and on all occasions, whether important or trivial, she did the one thing that ought to be done, and did it in the way most natural and simple.

She is now no more – no more? Nay, I boldly say she lives – lives in the hearts of her subjects; lives in the pages of history. And as the ages revolve, as her pure profile stands more marked against the horizon of time, the verdict of posterity will ratify the judgment of those who were her subjects. She ennobled mankind; she exalted royalty; the world is better for her life.

Sir, the Queen is no more; let us with one heart say, Long live the King!

By Dr. Christopher McCreery

The death of Queen Victoria in the early days of 1901 brought a formal end to the era that would come to carry her name. The demise of the sovereign took place at a time when Canada's autonomy was growing, largely through the efforts of the country's prime minister, Sir Wilfrid Laurier, this amidst the backdrop of a young nation very much attached to the Crown and the British Empire. While the South African War of 1899–1902 exposed some of the fissures in Canadian society, admiration for the Queen Empress was pervasive and entrenched.

Victoria was the only sovereign that most Canadians, including Laurier himself, knew. Born four years after Victoria ascended the throne, Laurier would come to know her through several encounters, most notably the 1897

Diamond Jubilee. This pan-imperial celebration saw Laurier feted as one of the great exemplars of the progressive and multifaceted face of the British Empire. Leader of the largest self-governing Dominion, yet a francophone and Roman Catholic, the prime minister exemplified the success and power of the British imperial ideal of the period.

Mother of Confederation, the woman credited with choosing Ottawa as the Dominion capital, and after whom more streets and geographical points are named than any other, died in the early evening of January 22, at Osborne House on the Isle of Wight. The identity of the British Empire was as much personified in her as it was in the Union Jack and the pink tincture that coloured a quarter of the earth's surface on all maps. The generational stamp of Victoria continued to cast its shadow well into the 1950s, and the legacy of the period can still be found in all manner of institutions, public buildings, and state programs.

For the young country, it was the first occasion on which a prime minister could reflect on the death of a reigning sovereign, thereby encapsulating the feeling of the nation in a moment of mourning. By the time Laurier rose in the House of Commons, the central block of Parliament was draped in mourning crepe, the Canada Gazette, newspapers, postage stamps, and letterhead were all edged in black, and the nation joined in that curious business that was mourning in the Victorian era.

Laurier's admiration of Victoria was rooted in his deep belief in the British parliamentary system and the position of the Crown. For him, one of the late Queen's cardinal achievements had been to become a modern constitutional monarch: one who reigned, but did not rule. Her Majesty's judicious approach allowed for the "fullest measure of constitutional government to her own people," and in that, Canada had achieved an unsurpassed degree of self-government and autonomy. His enthusiasm for all things British was not universal, and one only has to consider Laurier's attitude towards peerages and knighthoods, although he did accept the latter during the Queen's Diamond Jubilee in 1897. From this ambivalence we can discern Laurier's egalitarian streak, and his discomfort with the rigid class distinctions and snobbery often associated with such accolades that were so often used as tools of patronage – both in Britain and in Canada.

Laurier's tribute to Victoria was as much to the Queen as it was to her era; one that in his estimation had brought about great advances in Western civilization. Culture, literature, legislation, education, the arts and sciences had all been greatly enhanced and the social condition of millions around the globe had been remarkably improved.

The largest Dominion, and a pioneer in so many aspects of British imperial development, Canada's achievement of full independence remained a distant and still controversial topic – one that Laurier judiciously navigated throughout his career. The mantra, "One Fleet, One Flag, One Throne," embraced in English Canada, held less resonance amongst French-Canadians, and the public discourse around Canada's involvement in the South African War brought these divisions to the surface. Nevertheless, even the most ardent critics of Canada's participation in the imperial adventures of the period, Henri Bourassa, was careful to limit his criticism to British and Canadian policy, and not Victoria or the institution she headed.

Much of the Canadian identity of the period – the sense of place and pride in the world, and the feeling of greatness and prosperity – were intertwined with being part of the Empire. Laurier's oration touched upon these elements, and while the sense of loss was reflected, it was not a sorrow-filled eulogy; rather, it revealed the sense of collective accomplishment of what had been achieved in Canada and Britain, throughout the late Queen's long reign.

Laurier's protégé, and the man who would succeed him as leader of the Liberal Party, William Lyon Mackenzie King, recorded in his diary the sentiment expressed in newspapers from coast to coast.

My thought as the thought of most men & women in all parts of the British Empire has been anxiously turned towards the bedside of the dying Queen. . . . It is wonderful the way in which the Queen has won her way into all our hearts. . . . We have all loved her, we will all ever be proud of having lived while she was Queen.[131]

It was the first time since the death of Macdonald that the country came together with a profound sense of loss — albeit one accompanied by a feeling of confidence in the future. It was one of those signal moments in the life of the nation that historians have used as a transitional point, and one that those who lived through the event would forever remember.

Dr. Christopher McCreery, MVO, holds a doctorate in Canadian political history from Queen's University and is the author of more than a dozen books. He is private secretary to the lieutenant governor of Nova Scotia and serves on the board of trustees of the Canadian War Museum.

LAURIER RECEIVES
HIS PORTRAIT

HOUSE OF COMMONS, OTTAWA, ONTARIO
MAY 15, 1902[132]

W.S. Calvert, MP Liberal Party whip:[133]
We your friends and admirers of the Liberal Party beg to present
you with an oil portrait of yourself as a token of the high esteem
and regard in which we hold you. Others have performed a like
duty but we desire that this souvenir shall specially be our contribution as well as expressing our loyalty to you as a man and our devotion to the cause you so conspicuously lead. We are attached to you
personally as well as proud of you as our leader. Your life's work has
been given up to fostering accord and harmony among all classes of
the people regardless of creed or origin, and your success in the
great and noble task will live to your honour and glory as a grand
example for Canadian statesmen for all time.

Your leadership when in Opposition or as Premier has won our
unstinted fealty. You have cemented in both positions the great
Liberal Party of which you are the noblest chief. As you look at this
memento, remember that at back of it is our ungrudging attachment and that you can rely on our devotion and at all times feel sure
of its continuance.

You are again to visit our new King,[134] as you visited his illustrious mother. We have no fear but Canada now, as then, will be represented in you with greater glory to our Dominion than it would by any other Canadian. All faithful Liberals and true Canadians are with you in all your efforts to enhance our common heritage and secure for it greater recognition. Whether the donors accompany you or not they will all be with you in spirit and will applaud your actions. We will enthusiastically welcome you back to continue your great work of building up a united Canada, free from prejudice, loyal in sentiment and prosperous in all that makes a country glorious.

We pray that Providence extend to Lady Laurier and yourself the blessings of a long and happy life of which this great international visit which you are about to undertake shall be one of the most brilliant and pleasant episodes and that you both will return to your native shores to enjoy the love and esteem of the Canadian people for many long years to come.

Laurier's response:

It is with a very sincere heart indeed that both in my own name and in the name of my wife, I accept from the unknown friends – unknown in the sense that their names are not known to me at this moment – this memento which is the work of a great Canadian artist. It is a gift which would be most acceptable to me under all circumstances. Under existing circumstances, it is doubly precious. It is precious in that this is the work of a great Canadian artist. The name of Mr. [John Colin] Forbes is well known throughout Canada and throughout the Motherland and is somewhat also in the land to our south.[135]

It is with a sense of regret that we must acknowledge that although Mr. Forbes is Canadian, he has taken his abode in another land. He has done so I am sure not from any choice of his own. Had the choice remained with him he would have stayed in Canada and brought up his family in the land of his birth. Unfortunately Canada, which is still a young country, has not afforded to artists all the help it might have given in the past. I trust that in the future Canadian artists and talents will receive more encouragement from the Canadian people than they have received hitherto. For my part, it is with some regret, I acknowledge that perhaps the Government might have done more than it has for the encouragement of native, artistic talent.

There is a scheme which long have I had in my mind to encourage Canadian artists. Perhaps if we were to propose something in the near future, to have these walls adorned by paintings reporting Canadian history and commemorating the names of Canadian artists, such a proposition would meet with universal favour. (Cheers) I venture to hope that the Government brings forward such a proposition, and my friend Mr. Borden,[136] for whose presence I am especially grateful, will find it possible to second such a motion.

Some two hundred years ago, the Government of the French monarchy instituted a way of encouraging native talent by establishing a *"grand prix de Rome"* under which prizes are given to the best students in painting, sculpture, architecture and music. They are sent to Rome for four years, there to study the art to which they are especially to devote themselves. Perhaps this would be too ambitious a scheme for young Canadians to undertake. But if we were to do something of the kind I think the Canadian people would respond generously. .

With regard to the sentiments which you have expressed in this address, I have only one fault to find. That is, they are already too flattering to me. It is now fourteen years since I assumed the position of Leader of the Liberal Party and I have endeavoured since that time to the best of my ability [to perform] the duties then entrusted to me. Of course we all know that in matters of this kind we cannot all feel alike. On this side of the House we hold one set of views and on the other side they look at matters from a different standpoint. Nevertheless we differ only in means. We do not differ in purpose either on one side or the other. What we aim at is the prosperity and the glory of our country and the great empire to which we belong.

In the discharge of my duties it has been my lot, of course, to have to differ from those to whom I was opposed. Nevertheless I have endeavoured to carry on the warfare, at all events so far as I was concerned, by methods directly inspired by those of the British Parliament – that is to say [by] treating opponents not as enemies, but as friends. In this matter I sometimes have perhaps transgressed, although I am not conscious of having done so. If I have done so I hope the example will not be followed by anyone. On the contrary, I take this occasion, since we are all here on the floor of Parliament, to extend to my fellow citizens who occupy the seats that were long held by gentlemen on this side, the cordial hand of fellowship and hope that notwithstanding all our differences we shall always behave as patriotic Canadians. (Cheers)

You were kind enough to allude to the part which I have endeavoured to play insofar as I am a Canadian to promote harmony and peace amongst us. This is indeed a very congenial task, and there should be no other one in the Parliament or throughout the broad Dominion. We cannot unmake the history of the past. We have a future we should look [towards] rather than to the history of the past. As to the history of the future, I hope it will continue to be what it is today, that is prosperity, cordiality, good fellowship and goodwill amongst those whose privilege it is to be inhabitants of this good land of Canada.

You were kind enough to refer to my previous visit to the Motherland. I am conscious that in this I shall have thrust upon me perhaps more than ever a severe task and a very important one. I can't hope to perform that task to the satisfaction of all. I cannot hope to be free from mistakes. But you can rest assured that I shall endeavour to discharge the duties which are imposed on me not simply as the leader of the Liberal Party, but in a matter that befits the Premier of Canada, that is to say, [to] speak for Canada as a whole.

Please accept my own thanks and the thanks of my wife for this souvenir. It shall occupy a prominent place in my house. I am sorry indeed to say I have no children to leave it to. I wish it were otherwise, but I must accept fate as it is. Someday I hope it will be in a national museum, not with a view of remembering me to posterity, but for the glory of Mr. Forbes, the artist who painted it.[137] Once more accept my sincere thanks and my sorrow that I cannot find expressions adequate to convey to you as I wish in the fullness of my heart. (Cheers)

[Mr. Borden said this was one occasion when the Opposition had no amendment.]

By Catherine Clark, Caroline Mulroney Lapham, and Elizabeth Turner

Reading Sir Wilfrid Laurier's gracious speech on the day his friends presented him with his portrait on Parliament Hill brings back fond memories for us and our families.

Starting in 2000, our fathers – the Right Hon. Joe Clark, the Right Hon. Brian Mulroney and the Right Hon. John Turner – have seen their own portraits unveiled in special ceremonies, organized by the Speaker of the House of Commons, on Parliament Hill. We are very proud that these portraits form part of the Prime Ministers' Portrait Gallery in Centre Block and are seen by upwards of four hundred thousand Canadians each year.

These ceremonies were important events for our families. All of us remember with pride the privilege of watching our fathers' public service recognized, in non-partisan fashion, by the leaders of the day.

It was therefore a pleasure to see from Sir Wilfrid Laurier's address that the non-partisan nature of these events, as represented by Laurier's generous comments about his opponents in the House, and returned to him by Robert L. Borden on that special day in 1902, is of long standing.

In reading Sir Wilfrid's address, it is also gratifying to see that he took special time – like our own fathers did – to celebrate and honour the portrait artist with whom he worked. The unveiling of the portraits, after all, represents the culmination of months and months of work by the artists and others in arranging these paintings.

Finally, we were happy to see that tribute was paid to Lady Laurier the day her husband was celebrated. We can attest that, as did Maureen McTeer, Mila Mulroney, and Geills Turner following in her footsteps decades later, Lady Laurier also served Canada with pride, honour, and grace.

Catherine Clark is a nationally respected broadcaster, public speaker, emcee, and writer, and now also serves as president of Catherine Clark Communications Inc. Through her work in television and radio, she interviews influential Canadians to reveal the personal, human side of public life.

Caroline Mulroney Lapham is a graduate of Harvard College and the NYU School of Law, and is vice-president at BloombergSen, an investment fund based in Toronto. She is also a co-founder of the Shoebox Project for Shelters, a charity that delivers holiday gifts to women in shelters and in need across Canada.

Elizabeth Turner is a lawyer licensed to practise in Ontario and New York. She lives with her two daughters in New York City, where she is executive director of Advocates for Justice, a non-profit organization providing pro bono legal representation to lower income individuals.

CIVIC WELCOME UPON
HIS RETURN TO OTTAWA

CITY HALL, OTTAWA, ONTARIO
OCTOBER 18, 1902[138]

Circumstances brought me to be a resident of Ottawa; choice will keep me a resident of Ottawa. I am proud of receiving this demonstration, the character of which I cannot misconstrue: I am proud of receiving it as it comes to me spontaneously from my fellow citizens, irrespective of creed, race or party.

On this occasion I will forget that I am a politician, will forget that I am a member of a party, and rather will remember that there are only Canadians here. Let me say still more, as I have said elsewhere: I come back more of a Canadian than I was four months ago when I left you. (Cheers) I come back as a citizen of the capital of the Dominion, as a citizen of Ottawa.

A moment ago I said that I was to forget that I was a politician at this present time, but it has been my fortune to be the Prime Minister of the Dominion. (Cheers) This is the circumstance which brought me to take up my residence here. I may say that I do not anticipate any change in the near future. (Cheers) But, Mr. Mayor, you and I are politicians and we do not always say or think alike, and perhaps it is just possible that in the near or distant future, there may be a change, and as you have been kind enough to wish me a long life, then it will be my pleasure to remain here a private citizen and do my part in assisting in the additional task and work of beautifying the city. . . .

[*Sir Wilfrid then said that he had just visited several of the great cities of Europe but believed that no city had been as blessed by nature as Ottawa was. He added that nothing equalled the beautiful architecture and the site at Ottawa's Parliament Hill.*]

There are cities where the public buildings equal our own, but there are none which surpass our own, and certainly no site is equal to the hill on which our buildings repose. That block with which I am not unfamiliar cannot be surpassed in London, Paris or Rome, or any of the capitals of Europe. There are several matters upon which we may differ, but there is one on which we can all agree and that is that we should work harmoniously together to make Ottawa one of the finest cities in the Dominion, which nature certainly intended it to be. It will be my pleasure to do my little part in that direction. (Cheers)

By Andrew Cohen

Sir Wilfrid Laurier spent forty-five of his seventy-seven years in the Parliament of Canada as a private member, leader of the Liberal Party, and prime minister. His four-and-a-half decades in the House of Commons is a record in our history.

As great as his ardour for politics was his affection for Ottawa. It was a brimming fondness for a city from a striver who arrived in the capital in 1874 as a newly elected parliamentarian. He liked Ottawa so much that he later declared that he would never leave. He never did.

Many of his successors remained in Ottawa – Robert Borden, Lester Pearson, Joe Clark, and Jean Chrétien among them – after they left politics. But none felt as warmly about Ottawa as Laurier. He had been to London, Paris, Rome, and to Washington, which he thought Ottawa should emulate.

He saw those cities and their legislatures, their monuments, museums, and memorials, and believed that that is what a capital should be.

It is not in the job description of prime ministers to champion the national capital — or even to like the national capital — but it matters when they do. Mackenzie King, our longest-serving prime minister, fostered the ambitious architecture of Confederation Boulevard; he approached urban planner Jacques Gréber, in Paris in 1936, to act as consultant on the beautification of Ottawa, which later produced an ambitious blueprint for the city. Louis St. Laurent saw 24 Sussex Drive become the official residence of the prime minister. Lester B. Pearson created the National Arts Centre as part of Canada's centenary. Pierre Trudeau began construction of the National Gallery of Canada and the Museum of Civilization; Brian Mulroney finished them. Laurier, for his part, talked often of the "beautification" of the capital, vowing to make it one of the finest cities in Canada, worthy of the country he famously predicted would own the twentieth century.

He cared how Ottawa looked. In 1907, for example, he was disappointed that the promised new downtown railway station and hotel (for which his Government had allocated parkland) was not yet under construction. He vowed that it would be "my first duty" to see it built. In 1912, Union Station was opened on Wellington Street, facing a grand hotel on the other side. It was called the Château Laurier.

No prime minister talks about Ottawa as Laurier did. Jean Chrétien, who wanted to be an architect, proposed a sweeping boulevard on Metcalfe Street. Later he suggested converting the stately National Research Council laboratories on Sussex Drive into the Prime Minister's Office and official residence. That did not happen, but his government built the Canadian War Museum and announced plans to create the Canadian History Centre (in the now-abandoned Union Station) and the Portrait Gallery of Canada (in the empty U.S. Embassy on Wellington Street, across from Parliament).

For the last dozen years or so, though, official Ottawa has been in genteel decline. Paul Martin and Stephen Harper cancelled plans for Chrétien's museums. The Conservatives found money for renovating the Museum of

Nature and the Museum of Civilization, yes, but neither Martin nor Harper supported new national institutions or projects of any significance.

Were Laurier here today, he would recognize the brooding Parliament Hill, overlooking the mighty Ottawa River. It was a sight that dazzled Jan Morris, the travel writer, who thought it showed the power of nature. Laurier would like its restoration – an endless task – and some of the statues on the Hill. He would thrill to Ottawa's growth, and would appreciate the cross-town street named after him, where his home is preserved as a historic site in Sandy Hill. He would find himself well accommodated in the Château, the finest hostelry in town.

But for a country of thirty-six million souls, more than four times its population on Laurier's death, he might wonder about Ottawa. In 2016, does it look like the capital of the world's second-largest country, one of its great economies, and a successful multicultural society? Have we built great institutions and monuments for Canadians to visit and admire? Does it feel like a repository of hope and a reflection of dreams?

Pleasant, polite, and tidy as Ottawa is, he would probably think not.

Beyond the parliamentary precinct, the city is shabby. Federal buildings are resolutely bland. Sparks Street, where D'Arcy McGee was shot outside his boarding house in 1868, is a pedestrian mall with few pedestrians. Bank Street, which runs north to the Hill, is sleepy. Rideau Street, which moves east from Wellington, is home to tattoo parlours, seedy fast-food shops, and empty storefronts: a varicose vein. The Byward Market has no covered market building in a cold climate.

The city centre echoes with empty federal buildings, from the former U.S. Embassy to the old Union Station, now the Government Conference Centre. Along Sussex Drive, Laurier would find the embassies of France and Britain and the United States, but, mysteriously, also those of Saudi Arabia and Kuwait, hardly old allies of Canada. The former War Museum sits empty ten years after it was given to the Aga Khan to become the "Global Centre for Pluralism." The "Canada and the World Pavilion" nearby is also empty.

The National Arts Centre looks like a Stalinist detention centre (though its brutalist exterior is to be refaced by 2017). The Lester B. Pearson Building is a castellated, ochre redoubt. As for 24 Sussex, it is falling apart, desperate for ten million dollars in repairs that no prime minister has been willing to spend – until now, under Justin Trudeau.

As for monuments, the Conservatives have created a few. The biggest, though, will sit on the grounds of the Supreme Court of Canada. It is to honour the "Victims of Communism." Ottawa's mayor has called it "a blight" and city council has condemned it. Critics have gone to court to stop it.

Dreams? Hopes? Ottawa has no new museum of science and technology, showcasing our achievements, as do other countries. (The one we have is forty-five years old and sits in a former bakery along an ugly commercial boulevard, far from downtown, where it is now being foolishly restored.) We have no portrait gallery, displaying our founders and great men and women. We have no new national library and archives, like the National Archives in Washington, to display our founding documents.

Washington festoons itself with new monuments, memorials, and museums. London bans cars from the city centre and offers free admission to its remarkable public museums. Berlin spends hundreds of millions of euros reuniting and recapturing its rich cultural heritage on Museum Island.

Ottawa, little Ottawa, has ambition no more. Sir Wilfrid promised to die here, and in 1919 he did. His successors have been either indifferent or hostile toward the capital. In 2016, it is a diminished, forlorn place, awaiting a prime minister who loves it as much as he did.

Andrew Cohen is an award-winning journalist who writes a syndicated column for Postmedia News. The author of seven books, many of them best-sellers, he is a professor of journalism and international affairs at Carleton University and the founding president of the Historica-Dominion Institute (Historica Canada).

CHINESE AND JAPANESE IMMIGRATION

HOUSE OF COMMONS, OTTAWA, ONTARIO

MARCH 27, 1903

The House is aware that in the province of British Columbia there exists a very strong feeling against Asiatic immigration. This feeling is confined exclusively in Canada to the province of British Columbia, and, as we are told, does not extend to other provinces of the Dominion, for the reason there is no Asiatic immigration which is settled outside the province of British Columbia.

As far back as twenty-five or thirty years ago this feeling which exists in British Columbia commenced to manifest itself. In this regard the Province of British Columbia is not at all isolated from other portions of the work in which Asiatic or Mongolian immigration has settled. In California, in Australia, in fact wherever the two races, Caucasian and Mongolian, have come into contact, the same feeling has manifested itself.

After giving it full consideration, everyone who has looked into the matter must come to the conclusion that this antagonism is based upon ethnical consideration, the difference between the two races. It seems impossible to reconcile them, and the conclusion of all who have considered the matter seems to be that the amalgamation of the two is neither possible nor desirable. There are so many differences of character that it is supposed to be impossible to overcome them.

At all events, in the Province of British Columbia, this feeling is very strong. In 1885, the Government of Sir John Macdonald introduced a measure to impose a capitation tax of $50 on Chinese immigration coming into the Dominion. It was supposed that this tax would be sufficient to prevent, for the time being, the increase of this immigration; and for some years, it has had that effect. But, of late years, the immigration has increased very rapidly, and a new agitation arose in the province, and representations were made to the Government that there should be an increase in the capitation tax. In 1900 we doubled the capitation tax, making it $100. It was represented to us at that time by the members of British Columbia, whether they sat on this side of the House or the other, that the resolution then introduced would be inadequate to effect the purpose in view, which was to check the immigration of Asiatic labourers into the country.

We were aware that there was a good deal to be said in favour of the contention which was urged upon us. At all events we proceeded with our legislation and we then organized a commission to investigate the subject and report. The commission made its report. That report has been in the hands of Honourable Members of this House for eighteen months and I presume that by this time it has become familiar to all of us. The commissioners, who seem to have done their work very thoroughly, came to the conclusion that this kind of immigration ought to be prohibited and that, if it was not absolutely prohibited, the tax should be increased to such a figure as to restrict the immigration to very narrow limits. . . .

I must say that I entertain no hope in the present condition of China of having such a treaty [as with Japan, which prohibits immigration of its citizens to Canada]; therefore we have taken the course of asking Parliament to increase at once the capitation tax from $100 to $500 as here recommended.

Now, with regard to Japanese immigration, the same prejudice, I am sorry to say, exists in British Columbia concerning the Japanese as the Chinese. I say I am sorry for it, because for my part I make a distinction between Japan and China. Japan is one of the rising nations of the present day. It has shown itself to be very progressive. It does not seem to me at all doubtful that within a short period Japan will have placed itself in the forefront among the civilized nations of the earth. But whatever may be my feelings in this matter, it is a matter of record, for there can be no dispute that in British Columbia the feelings towards the Japanese are exactly the same as towards the Chinese.

The Japanese is not looked upon as a desirable immigrant. But as I said a moment ago, though I am prejudiced in favour of the Japanese, I must confess that there is little probability that it will be possible to assimilate the Japanese immigrant to the standard of Canadian civilization. The ethnical differences are also of such a character as to make it very doubtful whether assimilation of the two races could ever take place. But the problem has been solved so far as British Columbia is concerned by the Japanese Government themselves, who have undertaken not only to restrict but absolutely to prohibit Japanese immigration to Canada. The report of the commissioners upon this point is also pertinent. Some two or three years ago the Japanese Government issued an order . . . to prohibit within certain limits, immigration from Japan into Canada. . . .

Of course if the Japanese Government had refused to take any action and had allowed the subjects of that empire to flood the British Columbia labour market, we would have been probably induced to reconsider our own views. . . . We intend to have trade between Japan and Canada. We intend to bring about a development of the relations which exist between that progressive people and our own people. We have steamers plying today between this country and the Orient, steamers which are subsidized by this Government. We have at present in Japan exhibition commissioners who are trying to promote trade between Canada and Japan. Under such circumstances I ask my Honourable Friend [Robert Borden] whether it is not good policy to try and promote friendly relations between Canada and Japan. The conditions would have been very much different if the Japanese Government had not undertaken to act in a friendly manner towards the Government of Canada. The Japanese Government went out of their way to prohibit their own people coming to Canada. They did this as a friendly act towards Canada. They wanted to preserve the good relations that existed between us.

Under these circumstances was it not good Canadian policy, from consideration of Canadian interest, to take such action as was calculated to promote the best interests of Canada and not to irritate people who wanted to have friendly relations with us? What was the cause of irritation between us and Japan? It was that there were Japanese subjects coming to Canada who were settling in British Columbia and working in competition with our own workingmen where their presence is not welcome. They have undertaken to remove that cause of irritation by preventing their own people from coming into competition with our workingmen, and under such circumstances, it seems to me that the action of the British Columbia Legislature [in trying to also prevent immigration from Japan by their own laws] was, to say the least, ill-advised, that it was not calculated to promote the best interests of Canada, or those friendly relations that ought to obtain between two neighbouring nations, such as Canada and Japan are, because, after all, we are neighbouring nations.

For this reason we represented to the legislature of British Columbia that if they were to restrict their action to Chinese immigration, that if they were to except Japanese immigration from their legislation, we would not interfere, leaving them to exercise their own will in regard to Chinese immigration. It did seem to me that it was an ill-advised action to still persist in giving a slap in the face to the Imperial Government of Japan by including Japanese labourers in their legislation.

By the Honourable Christy Clark

Like the country it reflects and helps shape, Canadian political history has a lot to be proud of – and, unfortunately, episodes that make us cringe.

For generations of Canadians, Sir Wilfrid Laurier is someone to admire, a man of vision who understood not only what Canada was, but what it could become. As farsighted as he was, however, his vision was also hindered by racial prejudices we have thankfully left behind.

Laurier's speech on Chinese and Japanese Immigration shocks the modern reader. Today, Canada's and British Columbia's ancestral and increasing business links with Asia are one of our greatest competitive advantages. One hundred and three years ago, we had not yet learned that diversity is a source of strength.

Canada did not financially penalize immigrants from anywhere in the world – except East Asia. Those proud immigrants must have been aware they were being singled out because of their ethnicity. In the hopes of building a better life, thousands paid anyway – maybe not for their own sakes, but for their children and grandchildren.

They did not, as we know today, capitulate.

Those able to pay made some of the biggest contributions of all, literally connecting British Columbia with the rest of the country – all too often at the cost of their lives. For every mile of track between Vancouver and Calgary, one Chinese worker died. It's unsettling to remember that most of them had to pay for the privilege.

Sadly, things would get worse before they got better. After making approximately eighty-two thousand Chinese immigrants pay, in 1923 the head tax was replaced by the Chinese Immigration Act, which attempted to end all Chinese immigration. It remained in effect for twenty-four years.

We can't undo the past. The best we can do is make sure future generations never forget the mistakes that were made and never make them again. In B.C., we made a formal apology in the legislature in May 2014, and are working with B.C.'s Chinese community to update our school curriculum and increase public awareness.

You can't hide from history. Confronting the past can be profoundly uncomfortable, but only by acknowledging it, and apologizing for historical errors, can we hope to build a better future.

Christy Clark is premier of British Columbia.

ON THE DEATH OF
SIR OLIVER MOWAT

HOUSE OF COMMONS, OTTAWA, ONTARIO
APRIL 20, 1903

Mr. Speaker: Before we proceed further with the business of the House, it is my painful duty to inform it officially of the death of the Lieutenant-Governor of the Province of Ontario. Although Sir Oliver Mowat never was a member of this House, he was for some time a respected member of another branch of the legislature and for more than forty years he occupied in the national life of this country a position of such prominence that the House would be remiss to a proper sense of its own dignity if it failed in some great way to record its appreciation of the great loss the country has sustained.

This loss will be all the more keenly felt because Sir Oliver Mowat was one of the last of the few survivors of that generation of exceptionally strong men who, after the Union of Upper and Lower Canada in 1840, contributed to revolutionize, peaceably but thoroughly, the relation which had previously existed between the colonies and the parent state, and to shape our destiny and institutions to the form and condition which we now enjoy. In that remarkable galaxy of men which included Brown, Macdonald, Cartier, Dorion, Mackenzie, Holton, Galt and McGee, Sir Oliver

Mowat was one of the most remarkable, and to him belongs the undisputed distinction of having given more continuous years of service to the state than any other man in our history.

If we examine his career, we realize what gigantic strides have been made in the comparatively short period of a single life, from those old days when the provinces of British North America were a few small and scattered Crown colonies to the present statues of Canada, a nation. His life embraces the whole space that has elapsed from those old days when the rights, the opinions, the sentiments and the feelings of the people were haughtily scorned and tramped upon by an audacious oligarchy, to those happier days of our own time, when questions arising from the conflict of opinions and sentiments inseparable from human affairs, are settled by the regular and normal action of constitutional government.

He was a mere youth when the abuses of the former regime culminated in the rebellion of 1837, and one of his last officials acts was to help to obtain without violence, legitimate, honourable and fair concessions to the just claims of the minority in the province of Manitoba.

During the whole of that space of time, Sir Oliver Mowat took an active and ever-growing part in the contests, agitations and struggles which eventually brought about Confederation. His was a remarkably successful career. It can be said of him, as was said of the Duke of Wellington, that he scarcely ever had a reverse and never lost a battle. Whatever he understood, to whatever tasks he applied himself, he easily came to the front rank.

After having completed his classical studies, he chose the bar as his profession and rapidly rose to the greatest eminence as a lawyer. He entered politics in a time of violent perturbation and at once took a prominent part as a debater in an assembly composed of men as capable of adorning any assembly in the world, and of such ability as to be equal to any emergency. Then he was appointed to the bench, where he was distinguished by all the qualities of an able and learned judge. After a time he re-entered politics and became the premier of his native province, a position which he maintained for twenty-four years in the face of stirring Opposition, and only abandoned at my invitation to enter the Dominion Government in order to give us the benefit of his advice, experience and ability in the settlement of very important and irritating questions.

During these twenty-four years that he was premier of the Province of Ontario, every man must agree that he gave to that province a government which can be cited as a model for all governments, a government which was honest, progressive, courageous and tolerant.

If there was one thing in particular which marked his career at this time of life, I think it could be found in the policy which he always maintained of giving a broad, generous and tolerant treatment to the minorities of that province. In this he performed a great service not only to the Province of Ontario, but to the whole people of the Dominion of Canada.

Still, if I were called on to say what in my estimation is the one characteristic which will chiefly mark the career of Sir Oliver Mowat when it comes to be reviewed by the historian of the future, it seems to me that the one special feature of his character and career, which will stand out in bolder relief than any other, is that of all the men who contributed to shape our institutions and bring them to the degree of excellence they have now reached, he perhaps performed the largest share. I do not believe that statement can be successfully disputed; there is abundant authority to justify it. True it is that he did not take as active part in the preparatory work which eventually culminated in Confederation as some of the other men with whom he was associated, for after the principle had been confirmed by the Quebec Conference in 1864 he withdrew from the political arena to become a judge, and for some years was removed from political contests.

George Brown is given the credit of having, by his powerful agitation, forced the issue of Confederation; Sir John A. Macdonald has the merit of having brought Confederation into active operation; but to Sir Oliver Mowat belongs the credit of having given it its ultimate character as a federal compact. Shortly after Confederation had been launched, and while its fundamental principle was still on trial, while its orientation was still uncertain, while it was doubtful if the union of the provinces would be in a legislative union though federative in name, he gave up the quiet and dignity of repose of a judicial life to become the leading champion of the federative principle.

At that time Sir John Macdonald was the most commanding personality of our national life; perhaps it may be said that he was then in the zenith of his fame and power; and for twenty years his most successful opponent was Sir Oliver Mowat. For twenty years Sir John Macdonald, as the head of the Government of Canada, and Sir Oliver Mowat, as the head of the Government of the Province of Ontario, were engaged in a contest which, whether it was on one point or another, always centred around the federative principle of the constitution. . . . It is a well-known fact that Sir John Macdonald was not at heart a federationist; he was a legislative unionist. It is a matter of history that if Sir John Macdonald had had his own way at the conference of 1864 at Quebec the union of the provinces, instead of being federative would have been legislative. It is also a matter of history that after he had become the leader of the new Government after Confederation, his constant efforts were directed towards centralization. It is equally a matter of history that on every occasion it was part of his policy to claim for the federal administration powers which under the compact of union seemed fairly to belong to the provinces.

On the other hand, Sir Oliver Mowat was a very pronounced federalist, and Sir John Macdonald found, on every occasion, the premier of Ontario before him determined and resolved to uphold and maintain the federalist principle of the constitution. It is a matter of history that in all those contests, Sir Oliver Mowat invariably came out successful. The interpretation he gave to our constitution was invariably maintained by the courts, and he is certainly entitled to be pronounced the most correct interpreter of our constitution that Canada has yet produced.

Of course, on these questions men differ and opinions are not identical. There are men who believe the views held by the late Sir John Macdonald were the most correct views. There are others who believe the views held by Sir Oliver Mowat more accurately interpret our constitution. But whatever may be the opinion we entertain, whether we agree with Sir John Macdonald or with Sir Oliver Mowat, we must admit that as between the two great men who did so much for Canada, at all the events the merit of constitutional ability in the interpretation of the constitution seems to belong rather to the gentleman whose loss we so deeply deplore.

There was, however, another point upon which Sir Oliver Mowat and Sir John Macdonald were in perfect agreement. Much as they differed on the question of the interpretation of the constitution and other questions, they were both extremely devoted in their attachment to the land of their ancestors. On every occasion it was their motto to be true to the British connection. Sir Oliver Mowat was ever true to the province of which he was the premier, true to the Dominion of which he was one of the architects, and true to the British Empire of which we form a part.

It is no doubt the wish of every one of us to do what we can to show our respects to his memory.

By Dalton McGuinty

Wilfrid Laurier is remembered as an eloquent speaker, but his flair with words was used in the service of the one achievement in politics that makes all progress possible: he won elections. He was the only prime minister (including Sir John A. Macdonald himself) to win four elections in a row, he had the longest unbroken tenure as prime minister, and he was the longest serving MP in history, at forty-five years. His success at the ballot box, supported by his gifts as a speaker, was the means by which he acted on unshakeable ideals.

So, it is not surprising that, in addition to a shared party affiliation, he saw a kindred spirit in Oliver Mowat. As Laurier points out, Sir Oliver Mowat, in forty years of public life, "contributed to revolutionize, peaceably but thoroughly, the relation which had previously existed between the colonies and the parent state, and to shape our destinies and institutions to the form and condition which we now enjoy."

I served as premier of Ontario with the benefit of strong institutions and a relatively clear delineation of federal and provincial powers. It is hard to imagine the career trajectory of a politician, such as Mowat, who began public life under an old regime of colonial rule and oligarchs, and who left public life having built the foundations of a new nation that would grow to protect the rights and interests of all.

As premier, Oliver Mowat fought to establish provincial rights, not merely for the exercise of power, but to ensure that Ontario's strengths could be maximized for the benefit of a stronger Canada. One of those strengths was a flourishing francophone community, which, with its rights protected, contributed to our culture and economy in all the years since, and continues to do so today. That lesson – that respecting our differences makes us all better off – continues to guide our province.

In reading the words of Laurier in honouring Mowat, we are reminded that Canada, and Ontario, were built on compromise. What the politicians of Laurier's and Mowat's era taught us is that there is strength in compromise. Compromise builds nations and provinces that last. In Canada, we have successfully reconciled the interests of two founding nations, separated church and state, protected the rights of minorities, and built a federation with the flexibility to meet new challenges – through compromise.

Many peoples of the world are bound by a founding myth. In Canada, our national character was an active choice. Leaders like Laurier and Mowat were among those who chose to build a tolerant, diverse nation. It is up to every generation of Ontarians and Canadians to not only honour this legacy but to actively choose to build on it.

Dalton McGuinty was Ontario's twenty-fourth premier.

CANADA'S CENTURY

MASSEY HALL, TORONTO, ONTARIO
OCTOBER 14, 1904[139]

Yet once more it is my privilege to appear before an audience of my fellow citizens of this the banner city of the banner province of the Dominion. (Applause) It is always a pleasure for me to come to the City of Toronto, for in the past years, more than once, I have experienced your kindness towards me and every time in past years it has been my privilege to come before you, you have tendered me such a reception as . . . can be excelled nowhere except in Toronto itself. In this city, however, it is possible for you to excel yourselves. . . .

I do not claim credit for the prosperity which this country has witnessed, that as a result of the policy followed by this Government the name of Canada has gained a prominence it had not eight years ago. (Applause) I assert that the name of Canada during these eight years has travelled far and wide, and whether a man must be a friend or foe he knows that he must admit that there are today in Europe thousands and thousands of men who had never heard the name of Canada eight years ago and who today, every day, turn their eyes towards this new star which has appeared in the western sky. (Applause) . . . .

We are just at the beginning of the twentieth century. It is the year 1904. We are a nation of six million people already; we expect soon to be twenty-five, yes forty millions. There are men living in this audience, men over there (points to the young people in the gallery), the hope of the country (applause) who before they die, if they live to old age, will see this country with at least sixty millions of people. (Renewed applause)

Under such circumstances are we not to provide for the future, or shall we be content to grow up in the gutter and not take steps towards our higher destiny? It is often the mistake of nations that they do not apprehend fully the necessities of the situation. They fail in boldness. That is not and never shall be the case with the Government which I represent before you today. (Applause) We shall not, whatever our errors are otherwise, we shall not err for want of boldness. (Renewed applause) . . . .

I tell you nothing but what you know when I tell you that the nineteenth century has been the century of American development. The past one hundred years has been filled with the pages of her history. Let me tell you, my fellow countrymen, that all the signs point this way, that the twentieth century shall be the century of Canada and Canadian development. (Cheers) For the next seventy years, nay for the next one hundred years, Canada shall be the star towards which all men who love progress and freedom shall come.

Men of Toronto, I have no right to speak to you; I am simply a Canadian like yourselves, coming from another province, but trying my best to unite our common people. (Applause) Men of Toronto I ask you – and this is the prayer I want to convey to you – I simply ask you to forever sink the petty differences which have divided you in the past and unite with us and take your share of the grand future which lies before us. (Cheers) I give that prayer to you.

But if there is one class to which above all others I would convey the appeal it is not you older men, you middle-aged men, but to the young boys in the gallery, the hope of the country. (Cheers) To those, sir, who have life before them, let my prayer be this: Remember from this day forth never to look simply at the horizon, as it may be limited by the limits of the province, but look abroad all over the continent, wherever the British flag floats, and let your motto be Canada first, Canada last, Canada always. (Applause lasting several minutes)

By Anthony Wilson-Smith

There is something distinctly Canadian about the fact that the author of a famously bold prediction about his country's future was originally opposed to its creation. "All the signs point this way," Sir Wilfrid Laurier told an adoring crowd at Toronto's Massey Hall in October, 1904: "the twentieth century shall be the century of Canada and Canadian development." It was a claim he made more than once that year, and when he said those words, Laurier was in his sixties, frail in health but sure in his views, a political icon who had eight years of experience as prime minister, and a life filled with achievements, frustrations, turnabouts, and more than a few triumphs. He was a long way in every way from the young man who, four decades earlier, had been a political radical who once called Confederation "the tomb of the French race and the ruin of Lower Canada [Quebec]."

In many ways, Laurier mirrored the evolution of the country he served as its first-ever francophone prime minister. He overcame the shared suspicion between the country's two founding linguistic groups, as he came to believe each was stronger together than apart. He realized that for Canada to flourish, it would need newcomers from other countries and cultures, so he encouraged immigration (although he blotted his copybook in 1911 by supporting efforts to suppress immigration to Canada by black people). He preserved Canada's independence by resisting efforts to draw it closer into the sphere of a powerful friend (Great Britain). And he deftly played off the interests of Britain and the United States against each other in order to be friends with both — without becoming more beholden to either. He was one of Canada's first proponents of free trade with the United States – although in that he was too far ahead of his time – which led to his 1911 electoral defeat.

An eloquent speaker open to compromise but sure of his views, the paradox of Laurier was that he professed little interest in political leadership. "I know I have not the aptitude for it," he said when he was chosen leader in 1887. "And I have a sad apprehension that it must end in disaster." In fact, he had similarly taken his time getting into elected politics, and even longer in deciding to temper his relatively radical early views as well as his initial dismay at the prospect of a large, unified Canada.

But by the time Laurier got up in front of his Massey Hall audience that night, he was sure in his convictions, and forward-looking in his views. Far from looking back, he looked ahead, focusing on all the strengths he foresaw for Canada in future. In fact he aimed many of his remarks specifically – and unusually – at the twenty-somethings in the crowd, rather than older voters. He told them he expected that in their lifetimes, they would see the country's population rise from its then total of six million people to "at least sixty millions." At a time when many people were instinctively suspicious of outsiders – at least those who were not British – he forecast that "Canada shall be the star towards which all men who love progress and freedom shall come." Along with Clifford Sifton, he had already implemented steps in favour of immigration that led to the West becoming one of the economic engines of Canada's growth.

Laurier's buoyancy that night is particularly striking, measured against the challenges and hardships that still lay ahead. His party was almost destroyed in the 1911 federal election, when his opponents turned his support of free trade against him and accused him of plotting the destruction of Canada. From there, now in his seventies, he worked desperately to rebuild the Liberals even as the country plunged into the First World War. In 1917, he ran – and lost – again, and died two years later.

But even as Laurier's final years belied the hope and cheer he expressed in 1904, a longer-term look shows he was far more right than not. Throughout the twentieth century, Canada's two major language groups continued – for the most part – to get along. Immigration became a cornerstone of the country's growth. Canada increasingly asserted its independence from Britain and, of course, finally achieved Laurier's free trade objective with the United States. His Liberal Party, which appeared on the edge of collapse near the end of his life, rebounded to dominate Canadian politics for much of the century. And his beloved Canada, while it never attained the level of achievement he forecast, continued to grow and prosper, becoming the destination point of dreams for millions of people around the globe. In his goals and ambitions, Canada was a country always looking beyond itself, seeking to continually improve. Much like Sir Wilfrid Laurier – the man who did so much to set it on that track.

Anthony Wilson-Smith, a former journalist and long-time political observer, is president and CEO of Historica Canada.

HELPING PROVINCIAL COUSINS

OTTAWA, ONTARIO

JANUARY 20, 1905[140]

It is as a resident of Ottawa that I have the pleasure of appearing before you tonight. When I came to the city of Ottawa some eight years ago I did not think that Ottawa would become so dear to me as it is today. But it has become the city of my heart after the good old city of Quebec, where I spent my younger days. As a citizen of Ottawa I am an elector of Ontario and as an elector of Ontario I have a duty to perform and therefore I come here to give my voice for Hon. G.W. Ross.[141] I have nothing against the Conservative candidates . . . who are respectable gentlemen. But our two candidates . . . are two excellent men and they are better men for they are Liberals. (Laughter)

I can see no reason why the Ross Government would not receive your full support. The same tactics are being pursued in their election by the Conservatives as in all others. There is nothing new about this campaign. I claim to be acquainted with the conditions in Canada since Confederation and the tactics have always been the same. Whoever [was] the leader of the Liberal Party was subject to a campaign of vituperation and abuse.

Sir Oliver Mowat, one of the cleanest and best politicians

Canada ever saw and who is revered today, was vilified, slandered and abused as Mr. Ross is today.

We hear it said: "If Mr. Ross were only as good as Sir Oliver Mowat was." Mr. Ross has given as good government as Sir Oliver Mowat. The cry was raised during the regime of Sir Oliver Mowat that "Mowat must go," and the same cry is being raised today that "Ross must go." The people of Ontario will, I am sure, pay no more heed to the cry now than they did then.

As good a man as ever breathed God's air was Alexander Mackenzie. He is represented now as "watching the Treasury against friend and foe," by the Conservative press. But what treatment did he receive from the Opposition then? He was vilified, abused and traduced.

He was as pure as a dove, but was represented as a corruptionist. This shows that there is as much in the one way as in the other. Knowing Mr. Ross as I do for more than thirty years, I know him to be a true, honest and upright man. But there are some men who follow him who are a blight upon the Liberal Party, but if I rely upon anyone to reform that party it is Mr. Ross. It is not the fault of Mr. Ross if some of his followers are guilty of ballot switching, ballot stuffing, etc. But he would be in fault if he countenanced it and did not attempt to prevent it. But we can trust him to do this, as he can do and has done it.

Although I am not a Scotchman as Mr. Ross is, yet are we both Canadians and as such are both working for the welfare and interests of the country. I rely upon Mr. Ross's Scotch blood to make him a Scotch reformer.

I heard my friends . . . champion the cause of the ladies. I am neither a young man nor a bachelor, but I do not need anyone to speak for me in this matter: I speak for myself. [Some Ontario Liberals] want the ladies to have the suffrage extended to them. I don't care, as far as Quebec is concerned, whether they have it or not, for I find the ladies do not vote by rule. (Laughter)

[Ottawa's provincial Liberal candidates who support women's suffrage] are sure to be elected. I do not profess to know much about Ontario politics, but I have seen no reason why the Liberal Party in Ontario should be defeated.

By Jane Taber

Little has changed in politics since Liberal prime minister Wilfrid Laurier delivered a speech in Ottawa on January 20, 1905 to support his provincial cousin, Ontario Liberal leader George William Ross, who was attempting to win a third term as premier.

To attract a few laughs, Laurier mocked women getting involved in politics, and he defended his political ally from scandal. Sadly, Laurier could have delivered that speech today, and no one would have blinked an eye.

It's discouraging.

There is nothing new, either, about politicians of the same stripe helping out their federal or provincial counterparts as Laurier did in Ottawa that January day. It's never clear, however, if that kind of political support helps or hinders.

For example, in the 2008 and 2011 federal elections, former Liberal prime minister Jean Chrétien, who had won three majority governments, stumped for his successors, Stéphane Dion and Michael Ignatieff.

They both lost their bids.

In 2015, Ontario premier Kathleen Wynne helped out federal Liberal Justin Trudeau, appearing with him at a major rally in Toronto during the election campaign. She was returning a favour. In the 2014 provincial election, Mr. Trudeau lent his star power to her, appearing at a rally in Ottawa. His strategists credit his appearance to the fact that she won all five Ottawa ridings on election day – and went on to form a majority government.

This brings us to women in politics. Kathleen Wynne is an oddity – there are still too few women in high political office in Canada. In his speech, Laurier joked about women, politics and their vote: "[Some Ontario Liberals] want the ladies to have the suffrage extended to them.

I don't care . . . whether they have it or not, for I find the ladies do not vote by rule."

Laughter followed his comments.

Although women have had the vote for decades, they continue to be diminished in the political world, having to work twice as hard as men to achieve higher office. Never has there been, for example, a female federal finance minister. When women raise their voices in the House of Commons to emphasize a point, they are characterized as shrill and aggressive. Male politicians are never described that way.

In 2013, a B.C. communications consultant launched a blog to highlight the sexist and inappropriate comments made on social media about female politicians: "Someone please punch this woman in the face," was one of the comments the consultant published on her blog – and it was mild compared to ones that she couldn't print.

It's discouraging.

Canada ranks fiftieth of nearly two hundred countries on the Inter-Parliamentary Union's "List of Women in National Parliaments." It is behind Suriname and the United Kingdom, for example.

And then there are the political scandals, which never seem to go away. In his speech, Laurier described Ross as a "true, honest and upright man." At the time, Ross's government was hit by a number of scandals, including one involving vote-buying.

Laurier explained away the controversy, saying it was not Ross's fault if "some of his followers are guilty of ballot switching, ballot stuffing, etc."

"But he would [be] in fault if he countenances it and did not attempt to prevent it," said Laurier. "But we can trust him to do this, as he can do and has done it."

In 2014 and 2015, the Conservative government in Ottawa was rocked by a scandal involving charges of fraudulent spending by some senators, including Tory senator Mike Duffy.

Mr. Harper gave a similar explanation as did Laurier about Ross for acting swiftly once he discovered there was wrongdoing. Mr. Harper repeatedly *said that when he found out that Mr. Duffy had not repaid the money he owed to Canadian taxpayers, and that instead his chief of staff Nigel Wright had made the payment, "I took the appropriate action against people who were involved in that."*

By the way, G.W. Ross lost the election.

Veteran political observer Jane Taber is the *Globe and Mail*'s Queen's Park columnist.

TWO NEW PROVINCES:
ALBERTA AND SASKATCHEWAN

HOUSE OF COMMONS, OTTAWA, ONTARIO

FEBRUARY 21, 1905

It has been observed on the floor of this House, as well as outside of this House, that as the nineteenth century had been the century of the United States, so the twentieth century would be the century of Canada. This opinion has not been deemed extravagant. On this continent and across the waters, it has been accepted as the statement of a truth, beyond controversy.

The wonderful development of the United States during the space of scarcely more than one hundred years may well be an incitement to our efforts and our ambition. Yet to the emulation of such an example there may well be some exception taken; for if it be true that settlement of the western portion of the American union has been marked by almost phenomenal rapidity, it is also true that every other consideration seems to have been sacrificed to this one consideration of rapid growth.

Little attention was given, up to the last few years, to the materials which were introduced into the republic; little regard was paid among the new settlers to the observances of the law; and it is not a slander upon our neighbours – for, indeed, the fact is admitted in their current literature – that frontier civilization was with them a by-word for lawlessness.

We have proceeded upon different methods. We have been satisfied with slower progress. Our institutions in our own Northwest have been developed by gradual stages, so as to ensure at all times among these new communities law and order, and the restraints and safeguards of the highest civilization.

The time has arrived when we are all agreed, I believe, nay, I feel sure, upon both sides of the House, that another step, and the last, can now be taken to complete the passage of the Northwest Territories from what was once necessary tutelage, into the fullness of the rights which, under our constitution, appertain to provinces.

I may remind the House, though the fact is well known to everybody, that when Confederation was established in the year 1867, the Canada of that day was not at all what is the Canada of the present day. The Canada of that day did not extend beyond the western limits of Ontario. On the other side of the continent, on the shores of the Pacific Ocean, there was a British colony, British Columbia, absolutely isolated; and between British Columbia on one side and Ontario on the other side there was a vast expanse of territory, the fairest portion perhaps of the continent, which was under British sovereignty, but in which British sovereignty had always been dormant. . . .

I need not tell you, Sir, the fact is well known and present to the memory of all, that it was the intention of the Fathers of Confederation not to limit it to the comparatively narrow bounds in which it was included in 1867, but to extend it eastward and westward between the two oceans. I need hardly tell you, Sir, the fact is known to all and well remembered by everyone, that provision was made in the instrument of Confederation itself, for the admission of British Columbia, Prince Edward Island, and even Newfoundland, and especially for these territories which at least have come in today as part of the Canadian family. . . .

When we came to consider the problem before us it became very soon apparent to me, at all events, that there were four subjects which dominated all the others; that the others were of comparatively minor importance, but that there were four which I was sure the Parliament of Canada and the Government of Canada and the Canadian people at large might be expected to take a deep interest in.

The first was: How many provinces should be admitted into the Confederation coming from the Northwest Territories – one, or two or more? The next question was: In whom should be vested ownership of the public lands? The third question was: What should be the financial terms granted these new provinces? And the fourth, and not the least important by any means, was the question of the school system that should be introduced – not introduced because it was introduced long ago, but should be continued in the Territories. . . .

A question which has given some difficulty to the members of the committee, who had the preparation of this Bill, has been the selection of the capitals of the respective provinces. As the capital of the Province of Saskatchewan, the difficulty is easily solved; it will be, as it is at present, Regina. But as to the capital of Alberta, the selection was not so easy. There were three claimants for it – Calgary, Red Deer and Edmonton, each of which had a good claim. We have decided that we would not make any final selection, leaving the final selection to the province itself. In the meantime, if you look at the map, you will see that Edmonton seems to be the most central point, and therefore we propose to make Edmonton the capital for the present. Beyond this, I have only to say that it is the intention to have this Bill come into force on July 1 next.

The point being settled as to the number of provinces to be admitted into Confederation, the next question is that regarding the public lands. In whom should the ownership be vested? Should they belong to the provinces or to the Dominion?

A strong plea was presented to us on behalf of the provinces. It was represented that as a matter of law and equity, the public lands in these two provinces should belong to their governments. This plea was no doubt suggested by the fact that at the time of Confederation, all the parties to the original contract, that is to say, the provinces of Nova Scotia, New Brunswick, Ontario and Quebec, each retained her own lands; and when at a later day the province of British Columbia was admitted to the Dominion, she also retained her lands.

But, Sir, the cases are not at all parallel. When the provinces which I have named came into Confederation, they were already sovereignties. I use that term, because barring their dependence as colonies, they were sovereignties in the sense of having the management of their own affairs. Each had a department of government called the Crown Land Department, which was entrusted with the power of dealing with those lands, either for revenue or for settlement.

But the case of these new provinces is not at all similar. They never had the ownership of the lands. Those lands were bought by the Dominion Government, and have been administered by the Dominion Government. Therefore I say the two cases are not in any way parallel; they are indeed absolutely different. When the provinces which I have named came into Confederation they retained the ownership of their lands; but when the two new provinces come into the Dominion, it cannot be said that they can retain the ownership of their lands, as they never had the ownership.

Therefore, the proposition that in equity and justice these lands belong to the provinces is not tenable. But for my part I would not care, in a question of this importance, to rest the case on a mere abstract proposition. We must view it from the grounds of policy; and from the highest grounds of policy, I think it is advisable that the ownership of these lands should continue to be vested in the Dominion Government.

We have precedents for this. This is a case in which we can go
to the United States for precedents. They are in a situation very
much as we are regarding the ownership of lands and the establish-
ments of new states. Whenever a new state has been created in the
American Union, the federal government has always retained the
ownership and management of the public lands. And when we take
the records of our own country, we know that when Manitoba was
brought into the Dominion, that province was not given ownership
of her lands, but it remained in the Dominion Government.

True it is that Manitoba made several efforts to acquire the
ownership of the lands within her boundaries. She applied more
than once to the successive governments of the Dominion, but
her application was always met in the same way. It was always met
by the statement that it was impossible to grant her request. The
matter was finally closed in 1884 when the Government of Sir
John Macdonald, which had been approached on the subject, gave
very forcibly and clearly the reason why the prayer of that province
could not be answered.

I may be allowed to quote to the House the language used by
the Government of Sir John Macdonald on the occasion. It will be
found in an Order in Council of the thirtieth of May 1884:

"The success of the undertaking of the Dominion government
in and for the Northwest depends largely upon the settlement of the
lands. Combined with a great expenditure in organizing and maintaining an immigration service abroad and at home, Parliament
pledged its face to the world that a large portion of those lands
should be set apart for free homesteads to all coming settlers, and
another portion to be held in trust for the education of their children. No transfer could, therefore, be made, without exacting from
the province the most ample securities that this pledged policy shall
be maintained; hence in so far as the free lands extend there would
be no monetary advantage to the province, whilst a transfer would

most assuredly seriously embarrass all the costly immigration operations which the Dominion government is making mainly in behalf of Manitoba and the Territories." . . .

These reasons, strong and forcible as they were in 1884, are even stronger and more forcible in 1905, because the current of immigration is now flowing into these Territories in an unprecedented volume, and we are therefore compelled to say to the new provinces that we must continue the policy of retaining the ownership and control of the lands in our own hands. . . .

I now come to the question of education, and this question is perhaps under existing circumstances the most important of all that we have to deal with. There are evidences, not a few coming to us from all directions, that the old passions which such a subject had always aroused are not, unfortunately, buried; indeed, already, before the policy of the Government has been known, before the subject is fairly before the people, the Government has been warned as to its duty in this matter, and not only warned but threatened as well.

The Government has been warned, threatened from both sides of this question, from those who believe in separate schools and from those who oppose separate schools. These violent appeals are not a surprise to me, at all events, nor do I believe they are a surprise to anybody. We have known by the experience of the past, within the short life of this Confederation, that public opinion is always inflammable whenever questions arise which ever so remotely touch upon the religious convictions of the people.

It behooves us therefore all the more at this solemn moment to approach this subject with care, with calmness and deliberation and with the purpose of dealing with it not only in accordance with the inherent principles of abstract justice, but in accordance with the spirit – the Canadian spirit of tolerance and charity of which Confederation is the essence and of which in practice it ought to be the expression and the embodiment.

Before I proceed further, before I pass the threshold of this question, I put at once this inquiry to the House: What are separate schools? What is the meaning of the term? Whence does it come, what was its origins and what was its object? Perhaps somebody will say: What is the use of discussing such a question? The term separate schools ought to be familiar to everyone.

Sir, if anyone were to make such an observation and to interpose such an objection, I would tell him that never was objection taken with less ground. Mankind is ever the same. New problems and new complications will always arise, but new problems and complications, when they do arise, always revolve within the same well beaten circle of man's passions, man's prejudices and man's selfishness. History therefore should be a safe guide, and it is generally by appealing to the past, by investigating the problems with which our fathers had to deal, that we may find the solutions of the complications that face us.

If we look back to the history of our own country, if we find what is the origin of the separate schools, perhaps history may be the pillar of cloud by day and the pillar of fire by night to show us the way and give us the light. . . .

Sir, Mr. [George] Brown told his friends that he did not believe in separate schools; but there were fellow citizens of his in Ontario and in Quebec who believed in separate schools, and, in order to remove their objections and to win their co-operation in the scheme which was the great work of his life, he agreed to make the sacrifice of his own convictions. In order to achieve the great object he had at heart, he agreed to fasten upon his own province a system in which he did not believe, but in which others did believe. Sir, for more than twenty years Mr. Brown has been in his grave; but his memory is not dead. And if his teachings and his spirit be still alive, it is surely in the hearts of that staunch yeomanry of Ontario who gave him such constant support during the years of his political struggles.

They followed him devotedly in his crusade against separate schools. They followed him even more devotedly when he asked them to accept separate schools, to sacrifice their own opinions, and his own, upon the altar of the new country which it was his ambition to establish on this portion of the North American continent.

If it were my privilege that my poor words might reach that staunch yeomanry of Ontario, I would remind them that the work of Confederation is not yet finished; I would tell them that we are now engaged in advancing it; and I would ask them whether we are now to reverse our course, or whether we are not to continue to work it out to completion on the lines laid down by the great leader himself. . . .

When I compare [Canada and the United States], when I observe the social condition of civil society in each of them and when I observe in this country of ours, a total absence of lynchings and an almost total absence of divorce and murders, for my part, I thank heaven that we are living in a country where the young children of the land are taught Christian morals and Christian dogma.

Either the American system is right or the Canadian system is wrong. For my part I say this and I say it without hesitation. Time will show that we are in the right and in this instance as in many others, I have an abiding faith in the institutions of my own country.

By Alison Redford

I remember turning on a CBC broadcast about eight years ago and listening to a researcher on population and economic growth talking about how exciting it would be if we lived in a country with 100 million people. He talked about the economic potential, how our cities would change, that we would be able to develop a research agenda and secondary industries as well as second- and third-generation economies, so that we were not reliant mostly on exporting our natural resources and manufacturing for export to the United States and Asia.

I was excited and was looking forward to the calls from across the country, but before the phone lines were opened up, a fierce discussion started with the host on why it was not a good idea – it would change Canada too much – our world would look different – things might happen that were different from what we had seen before, or had so far anticipated in the future.

In the past ten years in Canada we have seen that discussion about how to deal with change, and whether we should change, play out again and again.

In 1905, Prime Minister Laurier's perspective on Canada's past and prospects for the next one hundred years put so many of our present-day discussions in focus.

Canadians will always have to make choices about our political leadership, and for many people there is a variety of qualities that can influence their decision. Canadians weigh their personal beliefs with their life experiences and their family circumstances, as well as personal worries and challenges. In response, politicians will always try to identify with what Canadians care about – the test of leadership is to move beyond the immediate to inspire us to think about our future and the tremendous opportunities before us as Canadians: Sir Wilfrid Laurier achieved that.

We will all think of people who inspired us to think ahead and to be excited about the future, and thus it is likely that in tumultuous times, one of the hallmarks of great leadership is helping people to understand and accept, perhaps even embrace, change. Change in our lives, in our world, in our families, and in our communities.

In 1905, Canada was starting to consider itself a fully developed country and, although only thirty-eight years old, we had begun to build a shared history, consisting of experience, values, and achievements, including a growing population, new provinces, a strong economy, and national institutions such as the Canadian Pacific Railway, which joined us from coast to coast.

Even in 1905, Laurier recognized that Canada was evolving, that we were only beginning to reach our potential, and that the twentieth century could belong to Canada. He identified that we were a growing success because we had made choices that meant that we understood that "The Canada of that day [thirty-eight years prior to Confederation in 1867] is not at all the Canada of the present day [1905]." If that was the case in 1905, it is most certainly the case for Canada in 2016.

Laurier's greatest strength of leadership, speaking that day before the House of Commons in announcing the creation of my own province, Alberta, is not only in asking Canadians to remember the past and the history that had made us, but also to understand the need for Canadians to change so that we would continue to grow: by welcoming new people, creating new provinces, and respecting our institutions and our traditions. The combination of recognizing our success and understanding that ongoing success must embrace the uncertainty of the future.

Great leadership in Canada in the twenty-first century must ask the same of us today. While great leadership still must honour our traditions and beliefs, so aptly referred to by Prime Minister Laurier, "It behooves us therefore all the more at this solemn moment to approach this subject with care, with calmness and deliberation and with the purpose of dealing with it not only in accordance with the inherent principles of abstract justice, but in accordance with the spirit – the Canadian spirit of tolerance and charity for which Confederation is the essence and of which in practice it ought to be the expression and the embodiment."

We can be greater Canadians and build a stronger country by understanding who we are and remembering what has made us strong, while also accepting that change is difficult and understanding what change involves. Of course, change can mean many things to many people, but fundamentally it involves embracing differences, accepting immigration as key to our success and long-term growth, and knowing that new ideas and new people in our community can enrich our own humanity, while not being afraid to say that.

So how has change been represented in Canada? While we will all have a hallmark issue that represented change in our country, depending on our perspective and our age, as well as the prevailing social issues, some of them include women getting the vote, the Charter of Rights and Freedoms, Canada–U.S. free trade, bilingualism and multiculturalism, changing our *flag, the continuing expansion of First Nations consultation, Quebec refer-enda, and removing barriers to the* LGBTQ *community. These changes, difficult at the time, are now by and large accepted as the norm by Canadians and demonstrate our capacity to change and our ability to continue to evolve as a society.*

Laurier was astute in observing that "New problems and new complica-tions will always arise, but new problems and complications, when they do arise, always revolve within the same well beaten circle of man's passions, man's prejudices and man's selfishness. History therefore should be a safe guide and it is generally by appealing to the past, by investigating the prob-lems with which our fathers had to deal, that we may find the solutions of the complications that face us."

It would be folly to suggest that any leader in 1905 could have antici-pated how much change would come to our country during the following century, or that he would agree with all of them, just as today it is not pos-sible to predict how Canada and the world will change in the future. However, if we rely on our strengths and have confidence in our destiny, we will con-tinue not only to succeed, but to succeed as a compassionate, diverse, and whole society.

Alison Redford was Alberta's fourteenth premier.

INAUGURATING THE
PROVINCE OF ALBERTA

EDMONTON, ALBERTA
SEPTEMBER 1, 1905[142]

I have an advantage over His Excellency, the Governor General,[143] who visits this City of Edmonton for the first time: I come here for the second time. It is many years since I was here before, so many years that probably you have forgotten it, but I have not. It is just eleven years this month of September. It was in 1894, when it was a privilege for the first time to visit this immense portion of our common country, which extends from the western shore of the Lake of the Woods to the Rocky Mountains, which was known as Rupert's Land and the Northwest Territories, and which today is springing into existence to take its rank and stand in the Confederation of Canada as the two provinces of Alberta and Saskatchewan.

Eleven years have passed and if someone had told me at that time that my next visit to the City of Edmonton would be in connection with the auspicious event which has brought me here today, His Excellency the Governor General and this throng not only from the province but from the neighbouring province of Saskatchewan, from Manitoba, and from the provinces of the east, and I am proud also to say from our neighbour to the south, the

American Republic, I am sure if this had been prophesied then, I could not have believed it.

Eleven years have passed and as had been hinted a moment ago by the new Lieutenant Governor of Alberta,[144] many and many changes have taken place. In 1894 expectations which you indulged in of rapid development for this new territory had not been realized. The sun shone, the rain fell, the soil responded generously to the efforts of the farmer, but markets were far, the means of access were few, the profits of the farmer were scanty and small. Agriculture, upon which all wealth is derived, was sorely depressed, and it being depressed, everything suffered in consequence.

The City of Winnipeg, the pioneer city, after making a splendid start, had reached the rank of a provincial town and seemed to have reached its further possibility. The five cities which now adorn the new provinces, Regina, Moose Jaw, Calgary, Edmonton, and Prince Albert, were nothing but struggling villages. You know as well as I do that at that time Regina had nothing royal but its name; Moose Jaw was not far removed from the primitive condition which its name implied; Calgary had made a splendid start but stood still.

Of Edmonton what shall I say? I am sure I will not offend the pride of any citizen when I say I could count upon the fingers of my two hands all the buildings, public and private, which then constituted your town, now the capital of Alberta. But now everything is changed. Gigantic strides are made on all sides over these new provinces.

Only eight years ago I had the honour of representing in Parliament the third largest city in Canada, the old City of Quebec; but now, I am sorry to say I have taken a back seat and that honour now belongs to the City of Winnipeg. But in the name of the people of Quebec let me say I am not jealous, and I may also say that the two largest cities of Canada, Toronto and Montreal, if they are going to keep their supremacy had better look out – or to use a western phrase, they had better hustle right away.

Nor is this all. Sir, if I look about me in the vast sea of upturned faces I see the determination of a young and vigorous people: I see the calm resolution, the courage, the enthusiasm to face all difficulties, to settle all the problems which may confront this new province. And, if it be true everywhere, it must be more true here in this bracing atmosphere of the prairie that "hope springs eternal in the human breast."

Now, gentlemen, what is the cause of this change? Well, sir, if I were addressing a political audience perhaps I might find many causes for this change. Perhaps also there might be gentlemen on this board platform who cannot agree with me upon these reasons, but this is not a day of political controversy, this is a day of national rejoicing. This is a city where today we only remember one thing – that we are Canadians and British subjects. Therefore, ladies and gentlemen, I will abstain from going into the causes. But, sir, whether we agree or whether we disagree, there is one thing which we all admit; that the prosperity of this new province, past, present, or future, is undoubtedly connected with the question of transportation, with railway facilities. Well, sir, I will not go further, because perhaps I might trespass upon the ground from which I wish to abstain.

But, gentlemen, in order to bring out this new province to the standard which we expect it to attain, it is necessary that we should have the hearty co-operation of all the people, of all the citizens of Alberta. We must have the co-operation of the old settlers, of the pioneers, the old pioneers chiefly from the province of Ontario who came here when the last was a desert and made the desert to smile. We must also have the co-operation of the new citizens who come from all parts of the world, to give to Canada, and to Alberta, the benefit of their individuality, of their energy and their enterprise, and since it happens that I have the honour of occupying the position of fist servant of the Crown of this country, let me say on behalf of the Crown and with the concurrence of His Excellency, that to these new fellow countrymen, to these new subjects of the King, I offer the most cordial welcome. I welcome those of our kith and kin from the old land. I welcome those from the older portions of Europe. I welcome those who come from the neighbouring, the kindred Republic on the other side of the line.

Let me say to one and all, above all those newly our fellow countrymen, that the Dominion of Canada is in one respect like the Kingdom of Heaven: those who come at the eleventh hour will receive the same treatment as those who have been in the field for a long time.

We want to share with them our lands, our laws, our civilization. Let them be British subjects, let them take their share in the life of this country, whether it be municipal, provincial or national. Let them be electors as well as citizens. We do not want nor wish that any individual should forget the land of his origin. Let them look to the past, but let them still more look to the future. Let them look to the land of their ancestors, but let them look also to the land of their children. Let them become Canadians, British subjects and give their heart, their soul, their energy and all their power to Canada, to its institutions, to its King, who like his illustrious mother, is a model constitutional sovereign.

By the Right Honourable Joe Clark

Three themes of Laurier's Edmonton address, welcoming Alberta to province-hood, reveal how well Laurier understood the differences of Canada, and how prescient he was about the distinct challenges that this then newest province would encounter:

He called for "co-operation of the old settlers . . . the pioneers [and] the new citizens, who come from all parts of the world," and affirmed that "those who come at the eleventh hour will receive the same treatment as those who have been [here] for a long time."

He evoked the future: "We do not want nor wish that any individual should forget the land of his origin . . . but let them still more look to the future . . . to the land of their children."

And he spoke of the challenge of connecting across the great physical distance of Canada: ". . . we all admit that the prosperity of this new province, past, present or future is undoubtedly connected with the question of transportation."

That speech, in 1905, was smack in the middle of Canada's greatest immigration wave, from 1895 through 1914, which ended with the First World War. In 1913 alone, immigration increased Canada's population by nearly 5 per cent: the country's total population was just over seven million people, and there were more than four hundred thousand immigrants from continental Europe.

Only some 40 per cent of that group came from the so-called mother countries of the United Kingdom and France. In the West, in particular, large numbers of those newcomers were German, Ukrainian, Scandinavian, and other Europeans, sometimes settling singly, often settling in communities, where their culture was a bond as they built their new home. That had two consequences.

First, because the population base of the prairies broadened earlier in our history, literally in our formative years, we have been diverse longer, not simply in terms of the historic relation among our "founding" peoples – indigenous, English, and French – but in our general attitude toward newcomers, people not like us.

Second, the prairie society grew up more egalitarian. Compared to older parts of Canada, nobody but the Aboriginal people has been there very long. There are pioneer families, but no "old families" in the sense of descendants of the Family Compact or the Château Clique. There is little sense of aristocracy. Alberta and the other Prairie Provinces are more populist places.

In 1932, my mother's first teaching position, as the Great Depression cut in to the Canadian prairies, was in Warspite, Alberta, northeast of Edmonton, where a large proportion of the community had come from

Ukraine. Many of the parents spoke limited English and had scant prospects of moving beyond the land they had homesteaded.

But they had come to Canada for their children, for their future. And the parents knew their children would need more to succeed than just a place to sleep and a crop on the prairie; education was the key to their futures. In a full and rich teaching life, my mother never again encountered a community of parents so determined to have their children learn – because learning would open the future, and the future is why their parents came.

Transportation is seen narrowly as moving goods and services and people, and getting from here to there. But it is also about a much broader sense of connection. When distance mattered more, during most of my growing up, Alberta felt itself a long way from power, distant from "the centre." The idea of being in the hinterland took root. Even after the discovery of oil transformed our wealth and our material prospects, Alberta considered itself an outlier – and often acted that way.

Distance is psychological as much as physical, and both Laurier and his far-sighted predecessor, Sir John A. Macdonald, recognized that. Both of them shared a mastery of their own time, a century and more ago, but are revered statesmen now because they sensed – and they prepared for – what this young country could become.

The Right Honourable Joe Clark was Canada's sixteenth prime minister.

RESPONSE TO SCANDAL

HOUSE OF COMMONS, OTTAWA, ONTARIO
APRIL 2, 1907

Mr. Speaker: Before the Orders of the Day are called I have a communication to make to the House. For some time my Honourable Friend and colleague, the Minister of Railways of Canada (Hon. H.R. Emmerson of New Brunswick), has been subjected to insinuations and rumours of a most injurious character – rumours and insinuations hitherto impalpable and intangible, but which now at last have taken the form of a very injurious newspaper article.[145]

This article I have no doubt is familiar to the members of the House. My friend the Minister of Railways and Canals absolutely denies the truth of the allegations set forth in the article, and, in order to better vindicate his character, has tendered his resignation and it has been accepted. The correspondence which has taken place between my friend and myself is as follows:

"Dear Sir Wilfrid: You and I, and indeed the whole country, have been aware that the attention of Parliament has been interrupted by certain innuendoes against members of the cabinet. More gossip is difficult to meet: but when the medium of the press has been sought to name me as one of your colleagues, in a slander, false on its face, I have directed that proceedings be taken against certain newspapers for the purpose of vindicating myself not only against the direct charge, but against the insinuation involved therein. I am conscious that I am in a position to be exonerated in the eyes of the country and yourself.

My object in taking these proceedings is to vindicate my character, aside from all political considerations. It is expected that you will leave here Thursday for England in the interests not only of Canada but of the Empire, and I would be very sorry to prove to be in any way an obstacle to that departure. Of necessity the decision of the courts will not be in time to make you feel free. Feeling as I do that it would be unfair to you, to my colleagues and to the party generally, that I should be under such an imputation while occupying a place in your cabinet, I have therefore to ask you to accept my resignation as Minister of Railways and Canals."

Laurier: To this communication I sent to Mr. Emmerson the following reply:

"I have come to the conclusion that the course which you take is, under existing circumstances, in the public interest. You owe it to yourself, to your colleagues and friends, to clear your character of the charges levelled against it. You could well ignore mere insinuations, but direct and specific charges you do well to face as soon as uttered. I will place your resignation in the hands of His Excellency."

By Jacques Poitras

What defines a regional power broker? When Laurier rose in the House of Commons in April 1907 to announce Henry Emmerson's resignation, he offered the standard rationale that the New Brunswick MP was leaving cabinet "in order to better vindicate his character."

Character aside, Emmerson's legacy as a regional power broker was already secure. The previous year, in the wake of a destructive fire, Emmerson had persuaded Laurier to rebuild and expand the CN repair shops in Moncton, the economic engine of the city and his constituency.[146] *Emmerson was determined to block suggestions that they be rebuilt in Halifax or Rivière-du-Loup.*

This is how Maritimers see their federal cabinet representatives. Cynically, they are purveyors of Ottawa's largesse; more generously, they are champions who bring home "a fair share" of federal spending – "character" be damned.

What defines character? Emmerson's drinking problem was well known and had caused Laurier to hesitate before naming him minister of railways and canals in 1904. It was the Fredericton Gleaner, *in which an Opposition Conservative MP owned a stake, that identified Emmerson three years later as having been tossed out of a Montreal hotel along with two women on account of what were called "immoral considerations."*[147] *Five days later came his resignation. He sued the newspaper for libel, but the case fell apart in court. The allegations would never be discredited.*

And what defines a career? The local obituaries published after his death in 1914 made no mention of his fall from grace. Such references would have been contrary to the public mood: "the ten-thousand-plus people who lined the streets for his funeral procession [in a city of just eleven thousand people] is evidence of the impact he had," according to his great-great-grandson Steve Scott.[148] *No doubt his saving of the* CN *shops explains this turnout, the prominent place given to his grave in Elmwood Cemetery, and the street that bears his name near the former shops site.*

But there was more to Emmerson than patronage and scandal: he was also a modernizer. In 1891, after failing to win a seat in the provincial legislature, he was appointed to its unelected upper chamber, the Legislative Council, where he oversaw passage of a bill to abolish the body, more than a century before today's Senate abolition debates.

And he was an early champion of female suffrage, a counterpoint to his downfall for "immoral considerations." In April 1889, as a provincial member, he supported a bill to give widows and single women with property the right to vote. To deny them, he said, was "a relic of barbaric prejudice."[149] *The bill was defeated, but a decade later, as premier of New Brunswick, Emmerson tried again.*

He lost that vote, too (women in New Brunswick gained the franchise only in 1919), but the episode adds another nuance to this almost-forgotten figure. "A radical of a pronounced type," the Toronto Globe *said when he died, "he held views far in advance of his contemporaries."*[150]

This fuller picture of the man emerges not through the yellow journalism of his foes, the imperfect nature of contemporary obituaries, or, indeed, the tropes uttered by his friend and ally Wilfrid Laurier. It could only come into focus after history finally caught up with Henry Emmerson.

Jacques Poitras is the provincial affairs reporter for CBC News in New Brunswick and the author of four books, including *Irving vs. Irving: Canada's Feuding Billionaires and the Stories They Won't Tell* (2014).

THE BRITISH AND AMERICAN
CONSTITUTIONS: A LECTURE

WOMEN'S CANADIAN CLUB OF
MONTREAL, MONTREAL, QUEBEC
OCTOBER 27, 1909[151]

. . . . My object . . . in appearing here is to lay before you in as concise a manner as the subject will permit, the principles which characterize, which differentiate, and which, at the same time, are common to both the British and the American Constitutions. It would be a very trite and oft repeated observation were I to remark at the outset that the British Constitution is not a written instrument. No! It is not to be found anywhere in book form; it never was congealed in frigid and rigid sentences spread on paper or parchment: it is a living thing, always growing, always susceptible of improvement, always adaptable to the ever-varying changing needs of the nation, but so strong and so enduring that during the last century, the whole of the Continent of Europe convulsed by Revolutions, while Constitutions and Dynasties went crashing and tumbling down, the atmosphere of England was as calm and reposeful as the flight of the eagle on a clear summer sky. The only book in which any record is to be found of the British Constitution is the *History of England*. In that history from the first to the last page you will find the evolution of the principles which were first controverted but finally accepted, and which, one by one, have brought the British Constitution to what it is today: the most noble code of political wisdom that ever was devised by man for the government of man.

But I should observe at the outset that all the countries which, at the present moment, constitute the fairest portions of Europe are fragments of the once great Roman Empire. Italy, France, England, the Iberian Peninsula, the noble Valley of the Rhine, the beautiful Valley of the Rhône; all these countries were at one time under the domain of Imperial Rome. The day came when the mighty fabric tumbled to pieces as much by the weight of its concentration as by the efforts of Northern Barbarians, and for several centuries the condition of Europe was chaos. From this confusion arose, not the Europe of the present time, but feudal Europe, to be again followed by the Europe as we have known it during the last few centuries. When the Northern tribes burst the frontiers of the Roman Empire, the rich provinces which composed it were cut up and divided amongst the invaders. These new territorial divisions became the possessions of the most successful soldiers and at the head was the most renowned soldier of all. He was the King, but his powers as such were rather vague and undefined; he was more a military Chief than a Civil Ruler. His office, if office it were, was not hereditary but elective; he was simply the first among his equals. He was elected by his own companions and the position to which he was elected he held for life unless he was displaced by a more successful rival, and the powers which he executed for the guidance of the community were subject to the advice of a Council selected from the tribe.

Then the same thing took place among all the countries of Europe. Whenever in any place there arose a strong ruler to dominate and over-awe his companions, he rudely set aside the election of a successor and divided his estates and realm, or the community such as it was, amongst his children. That was the course of Charlemagne; that was the course of William the Conqueror. This division, or cutting up of states, which, under a strong ruler, might have reached a high state of unity and strength was, of course, a source of weakness. A new modification took place and finally the crown was placed on the head of the Sovereign's eldest son. This was the origin of hereditary monarchy in Europe.

Then in every country except England the same thing took place. The King discarded all checks upon his authority. He became absolute. His will was the law, and his word executed the law. This took place everywhere, as I have said, except in England. Listen to the language of the King of France, Louis the XIV, written for the guidance of the young prince who was to be his successor:

"France is a monarchal state in the full acceptation of the term. The King represents the whole nation, and each person represents only an individual towards the King. Consequently, all power, all authority are in the hands of the King, and there can be none other in the Kingdom than that which he himself sets up. The nation is not a separate entity in France; it is wholly in the person of the King."

This language was accepted by the people of that age, much as it may shock our ideas as British subjects. Such was the rule in France; such was the rule in every country in Europe, England alone excepted. It must not be supposed, however that the Kings of England were different and better than any of the sovereigns of the rest of Europe; they were human, and very human. The Norman Kings, the Plantagenets, the Tudors, the Stuarts, were all as fond of arbitrary powers as the other sovereigns who ruled in Europe, but here was the difference. In Europe, the assumption of despotic authority by the King may have been more or less resisted at first, but in the course of time it grew and at last was tamely submitted to; but in England, at all times and by all classes, all attempts at unbridled authority by the King were met by determined, unflinching and unconquerable resistance.

In all the tribes which invaded the Roman Empire, the Angles in Great Britain, the Franks in Gaul, the Goths in Spain, and the Lombards in Italy, then there was very little Government, but there was some rude system of representation to transact the business of the community. In every country in Europe, save England, their system of representation was gradually done away with, was set aside by the ruler; but in England, the first crude system of representation grew and developed in power and in influence, until it became the Parliament; the Parliament of England; the pride of all British subjects in all parts of the world, and alike the envy and the aim of all friends of freedom, law and order, all the world over.

It was by this nascent Parliament that the ambition of Kings was checked, and this was done through the principle which was asserted almost with the origin of the monarchy in England, that in the realm of England, the King has no power to levy taxation upon his subjects, except by the consent of his subjects. This was a bold principle in the middle ages when the doctrine was prevalent of the ever-growing omnipotence of the King, of the anointed of the Lord, as the phrase was then current. That principle bred in the people of England strength of character and a spirit of freedom which was not then to be found in any other race.

It was, as I have said, the nascent Parliament of England which checked the powers of the King, and I am bound to say that the sovereigns of those days cast a covetous eye upon the prerogatives of the other monarchs of Europe who could tax their subjects at their own sweet will, and to their hearts' content. That principle was the cause of a long struggle between the Kings and the Parliament, which lasted, with various fortunes, until the days of Charles the First, when Parliament asserted it, not only by resolutions, not only by speeches, but when they embodied it in a statute to which the King ungraciously assented, and from which he vainly sought to escape. The principle was established in the Statute of 1641, and asserted that it was: "The ancient right of the subjects of this Kingdom, that no subsidy, custom, impost, or any charge whatsoever ought or may be laid or imposed upon any merchandise exported or imported by subjects, denizens or aliens without common consent in Parliament."

And this is the first cardinal principle of the British Constitution, that the King has no power in taxation except by the common consent of Parliament. You may ask me what, in those early days, was the composition of Parliament? It was exactly as it is today, composed of hereditary Peers and the Elected Commoners. There was no difference, save that in those early days the Lords and the Commons sat together. There was only one House. How the House was afterwards divided into two Houses, one the House of Lords and the other the House of Commons, is a matter of history, which I need not dilate upon; suffice to say that for the five hundred years which have elapsed since the days of Edward the Third, the legislative power of England has resided in the King, the Lords, and the Commons, the three estates of the Realm. In other words, no law can be passed in England, except by the consent of the three entities composing the Parliament; the King, the Lords and the Commons. There is perfect equality. They have as much power, the one as the other, excepting in matters of finance, where it has long been recognized; at all events, the Commons have long claimed that they have the initiative power, and that the Lords have no right whatever to change or to amend their measures, but must reject or approve them, just as they are, and they can go no further.

This is the second principle of the British Constitution: that the legislative power resides, not in the King, as was the case in ancient France and in many countries of Europe, but in the three estates of the Realm, the King, the Lords and the Commons. Now with regard to the Executive power in every civilized nation, it is vested in the Chief Magistrate, and, in England, the Chief Magistrate is the King; but under the present system the exercise of the executive power is subject to a condition which is absolutely unique, which was never found in any nation until it was adopted in England, and that is that the King, in the exercise of his Executive power, is subject to the will and the control of Parliament. Even the most despotic King must have Ministers. He cannot do everything himself in connection with any of the great departments of State, but he appoints Ministers who carry on the business and advise the sovereign or president, as the case may be. It would be natural, the King having appointed his Ministers, that his Ministers should be responsible to him. So it was for many centuries and ages in Great Britain; but when the long contest which took place between the British Parliament and the King, over the legislative power, had been closed, Parliament advanced a step further.

It was found, by the course of events, that if the Ministers of the King were not in close sympathy with the majority in Parliament, they could easily baffle the will of Parliament, as expressed in the Law, and, therefore, Parliament advanced the doctrine that the King must be served by Ministers who were in sympathy with the elected representatives of the people, and responsible to them. This principle was not adopted in a day. It was strongly resisted by the Crown. In fact, it was only in the early years of our late Sovereign, of that great, good and wise woman, Queen Victoria, that the principle was at last fully admitted, recognized and acted upon. This principle was as distasteful to the Georges as the other principle of taxation by the consent of the people had been distasteful to the Plantagenets, to the Tudors and to the Stuarts; but today it is fully recognized. The moment a Ministry has ceased to command the majority in Parliament, they must make way for other men, and even then the Sovereign is not free to select anybody he pleases to take their place; he must choose men who are in sympathy with the parliamentary majority. This, Ladies and Gentlemen, is the third great cardinal principle of the British Constitution.

I have named you three; first, no taxation except by the consent of Parliament, no legislation except by the consent of the three estates of the Realm, no Executive Authority except with the consent of Parliament. Now, I am bound to say, in truth and in justice to History, that the merit of first checking the ambition of the Sovereign, the merit of first planting the seed of constitutional government does not belong to the class which we today call "the people" but it belongs to the Barons, to the Lords, to the aristocracy of Britain. Under the feudal regime in every country in Christendom, the great land proprietors were almost as strong and powerful as the King himself. In France, Hugues Capet, who was the first King of the French after the fall of the Carlovingian Dynasty, once said to a subject who had taken the title of Count: "Who made thee Count?" The insolent rejoinder was: "Who made thee King?" In England, during the reign of Edward the First, the King desired the Earl of Norfolk to take part in an expedition to Gascony, and the latter peremptorily refused. The King, in a fit of petulant passion, exclaimed "By God, Sir Earl, you will go or hang." The cool answer was: "By God, Sir King, I shall neither go nor hang." The spirit of resistance was the same in France as in England, but it perished in the first whereas in the latter country it remained a flame which never was extinguished and permeated the whole body. All honour, I say, to the aristocrat of England. History does not record a class which has done better service for the State, and which can boast of more illustrious fame. Happy England, if the nobles of the twentieth century, faithful to the traditions of the past, in the new principles which come up under new conditions, will stand, as [did] their forefathers, in the vanguard of freedom and reform.

By the side of the Lords arose the Commons. The Commons at first were recruited from the landed gentry and the town burgesses. It remained so for many centuries. In 1832, there was a Bill of Reform followed by several similar measures in quick succession, which extended the franchise until now, in Great Britain, the right to vote is given to every respectable wage earner, and that country has come to the day of Democracy. Happy England, if her Democracy remembers that moderation in triumph is the keynote to stability and progress, and that what has made England what she is today, is not Revolution, but Evolution and Reform.

The British Constitution is the result of a process of Evolution; the application of a few leading principles, supplemented by maxims, rules and precedents, too long to enumerate, which have grown with the ages, determined one at a time, and all tending towards one single object: the Government of the people by the people themselves. How true are the words of Tennyson, in my estimation the most English of all the English poets since the days of Shakespeare, when he thus summarized the blessings of England's free institutions:

You ask me, why, tho' ill at ease,
Within this region I subsist,
Whose spirits falter in the mist,
And languish for the purple seas.

It is the land that freemen till,
That sober-suited Freedom chose,
The land, where girt with friends or foes
A man may speak the thing he will;

A land of settled government,
A land of just and old renown,

Where Freedom slowly broadens down
From precedent to precedent:

Where faction seldom gathers head,
But by degrees to fullness wrought,
The strength of some diffusive thought
Hath time and space to work and spread.[152]

No better definition of the British System has ever been written than is contained in these beautiful lines. During the last century, the great American Statesman, Daniel Webster,[153] was a visitor in the old City of Quebec. At that time there was a detachment of the English Army doing garrison duty in that Gibraltar of the American Continent. One evening the ears of Webster were saluted by the tattooing of the English troops, and a thought crossed his mind which shortly afterwards, in a speech delivered in Congress he expressed in these words. Speaking of England he said it was:

"A power, to which, for purposes of foreign conquest and subjugation, Rome, in the height of her glory, is not to be compared; a power which has dotted over the surface of the whole globe with her possessions and military posts whose morning drum-beat, following the sun and keeping company with the hours, circles the earth with one continuous and unbroken strain of the martial airs of England."

This beautiful language graphically expresses the power which has been reached by the small Island whose modest beginning has just been explained. If today Webster were to speak upon the same subject, if he could gaze upon what we today see with our own eyes, and were to descant upon the same subject, with what images could he describe the power of England. He could speak of her, not as encircling the globe with her garrisons, but as the centre of a group of daughter nations who have found in the adoption and application to themselves of the British Constitution, not only a charter of liberty, but a closer bond of union with the Motherland.

Proud as we may be as British Subjects of these achievements of a country to which we belong, there is another respect in which, it seems to me, the British Subjects can derive still greater pride. The British Constitution in another way encircles the globe. It has been carried over the globe not only by British hands, but by friends and lovers of Liberty. During the last century, all the nations of the continent of Europe have been convulsed by Revolutions in the struggle of the people for liberty, and they found it at last in the application to themselves of the British Constitution. France, Italy Spain, Portugal, Germany, Austria, Hungary, Greece, Denmark, Norway, Sweden, all these countries have adopted in whole or in part, the British Constitution. All have adopted those two cardinal principles, "No taxation except by the consent of the people, and ministerial responsibility." Nor is that all. These great principles have crossed the farthest oceans, and by them the dormant civilization of the Orient has been quickened to life. Japan has adopted it, and by doing so it has jumped at one bound into the highest rank in peace and war, and even the Empire of Turkey itself, the decadent power, the sick man, as Lord Palmerston used to call it, is seeking and may find in the British Constitution, regeneration.

And there is one other that has also adopted the British Constitution and it is the most illustrious of all, that is the American Republic. . . .

Ladies and Gentlemen, you will ask me this: "Is there not a great advantage which the Americans have over us in the fact that theirs is a written and the British an unwritten Constitution?" For my part, I must say that I do not attach very great importance either to one form or the other. Whether it is a written Constitution or an unwritten one, after all it is the will of the people which must prevail and though the Americans have a written Constitution, their history shows that it is possible, without changing a word of that Constitution, to so vary the spirit of it as to effectively amend it.

That is the case in regard to the election of Presidents by an enactment of the Constitution as it was originally framed and supplemented by the twelfth amendment: the President is elected by what is called the Electoral College. Well you would suppose it was the intention of the Constitution that these electors, selected for that purpose, great and eminent men should proceed to the election of a President. Nothing of the kind. They have that task assigned to them but they are not free agents, they simply have to record the will of the people as it is expressed at the polls. You are all familiar with the manner in which a Presidential election is carried on in these modern days. We had such an election not very long ago, and you heard the people shouting for Taft or for Bryan.[154] On election day we were all looking to see who was elected; was it Taft or was it Bryan? The modem method of selection is this: A Convention of each of the parties, the Republican Convention or the Democratic, selects Taft or Bryan, but the electors do not vote for Taft or Bryan, they vote for Mr. So-and-So and Mr. So-and-So, men whom they do not know and have never seen, but who have been carefully selected by the machine.

The original Constitution, as contemplated by the Fathers, has been completely set aside and instead of having an election by the Electoral College, we have in reality an election by the popular vote, so that there is not much difference whether the Constitution is written or not. It can be changed tacitly.

Now, you will ask me, what conclusion is to be drawn from these comparisons? I will answer that question by saying that barring the fact that the American Union is a Federative Union, there is no possible doubt in my mind that the British Constitution is far superior to the American. But the differences are not very material after all, because the cardinal principle is that the will of the people is the supreme arbiter in one as in the other. It does not follow that public opinion is always in the right, it is very often in the wrong; but the course of history has shown us that both in Great Britain and the United States, under free institutions, truth and justice may be for some time ignored and even impeded but in the end it will prevail. Under those free institutions the triumph of truth and justice is generally of slow growth; it is not [as] sudden as the conversion of Saul on the road from Jerusalem to Damascus. But, I claim that under these free institutions principles have been evolved from time to time which, though at first resisted, have at last been accepted as emanations from truth eternal.

I might give you another illustration of what I assert; that in the long run under free institutions truth and justice, however thwarted, will at last triumph, in the manner in which slavery in the United States has been dealt with. Today, looking at the past, one can hardly conceive that slavery was not always regarded with horror as the curse of mankind, but forty years ago, when I was a law student in the City of Montreal, the existence of slavery was a very acute question in the American Union. When the thirteen colonies separated from Great Britain slavery, which was concentrated in the southernmost states of the Union, was legal. Six of the original thirteen states of the American Union were slave owners. George Washington, one of the greatest men of history and a man of unblemished character, was a slave owner, [Thomas] Jefferson, who wrote the Declaration of Independence, and who penned the sentence that all men are equal, was a slave owner, and many of the Fathers of the American Union were slave owners. It is the plain truth of history that amongst these men there was no sympathy for slavery; they were all averse to it, and if they could have had their own way, they would have extirpated it from the Constitution; but public opinion would not allow it.

When the Fathers of the American Constitution met at Philadelphia to frame an Act of Union, if they had attempted to strike out slavery from the Constitution, union would not have taken place; the Southern States would not have come into it. So the Fathers closed their eyes upon the question of slavery. They expected, however, that public opinion would move and would extinguish it, and they placed their hopes in the Article in the Constitution which declares:

"The migration or importation of such persons as any of the States now existing shall think proper to admit, shall not be prohibited by the Congress prior to the year one thousand, eight hundred and eight."

The word "slavery" or "slave" was not inserted. They would not pollute such a noble instrument with such words as "slavery" or "slave," but it was slavery which they meant under the word "migration." They expected that, in the course of time, public opinion would move, and they were right in that opinion. Public opinion did move, but it moved in different directions; in the northern States the sentiment grew fierce against the curse and the shame of such an institution. In the South, on the contrary, the impression grew in favour of slavery, from the supposition that African labour was a necessity of the climatic condition in the South, a semi-tropical country. So the two currents went on and on and on, the passion growing fiercer and fiercer, and for fifty years the best men of the United States concentrated all their efforts in devising compromise after compromise to keep the numerical balance between Free States and Slave States.

In 1854, a new party was organized, the Republican Party, chiefly and only, I might say, to deal with slavery. Their programme was a very moderate one; it did not propose to extinguish slavery; it did not propose to interfere with this domestic institution of the South, as it was called, but to prevent the extension of slavery beyond its then existing limits. They put candidates in the field in 1856, but so strong was the public feeling, that its moderate programme was defeated. They put another candidate in the field in 1860 and then they won, but simply because it was a three-cornered fight; Abraham Lincoln, the Republican candidate, had not the majority of the popular vote, but simply of the Electoral College. Abraham Lincoln is one of the greatest men in history. . . . I look upon him as one of the greatest men of history. He had an intuitive and instructive discernment in political problems and, with all, he had a most tender heart, and the most humane soul.

When he was a young man he had gone down the Mississippi as far as New Orleans on a business errand and he had seen with his eyes something of the cruelty, shame and degradation of slavery, and it is said that he remarked to a friend, "If ever I have an opportunity, I shall hit slavery hard." He was elected President of the United States, he was installed in office, and you might have thought he could have hit slavery hard; but he could not do it because public opinion would not permit him to do it. The Civil War broke out; it was to go on for four long years; the Northern States were invaded by the Southern armies, and even then Abraham Lincoln could not carry out his own instinct. He had to submit to contumely, and to insults, and to taunts from ardent abolitionists, but he stood the infliction and did not move until he thought the time had come.

I may, perhaps, upon this point read you a letter which he addressed to Horace,[155] an able, passionate, petulant man, who clamorously called for the immediate enfranchisement it of the slaves.

"I have just read yours of the nineteenth, addressed to myself through the *New York Tribune*. If there be in it any statements or assumptions of fact, which I may know to be erroneous, I do not, now and here, controvert them. If there be in it any inferences which I may believe to be falsely drawn I do not, now . . . argue against them. If there be perceptible in it an impatient and dictatorial tone,

I waive it in deference to an old friend, whose heart I have always supposed to be right. As to the policy I seem to be pursuing, as you say, I have not meant to leave anyone in doubt. I would save the Union. I would save it the shortest way under the Constitution. The sooner the national authority can be restored the sooner the Union will be the Union as it was. If there be those who would not save the Union unless they could at the same time save slavery, I do not agree with them. My paramount object in this struggle is to save the Union and is not either to save or destroy slavery. If I could save the Union without freeing any slave, I would do it, and if I could save it by freeing all the slaves, I would do it; and if I could save it by freeing some and leaving others alone, I would also do that. What I do about slavery and the coloured race I do because I believe it would help to save the Union. I shall do less whenever I believe that whatever I am doing hurts the cause, and I shall do more whenever I shall believe doing more will help the cause. I shall try to correct errors when shown to be errors and I shall adopt new views so fast as they shall appear to be true views. I have here stated my purpose according to my view of official duty, and I intend no modification of my oft-expressed personal wish that all men everywhere could be free."

I have quoted you this letter because it shows that in a democracy such as ours, American as well as British, public opinion has always to be scanned and measured, and that it is possible while respecting it to lead it. Mark the way in which Abraham Lincoln at that time places the question before the country. He says it is not a conflict to save or to destroy slavery, but that it is a conflict for the Union and upon that ground he appealed to the nation, and his appeal was responded to; but, had he asked the nation to fight to abolish slavery, his appeal would have remained unheeded. Yet, at the very time that Lincoln was penning that letter, he had in his desk a proclamation already prepared for the abolition of slavery; he was biding his time, and two months later, when he thought the moment had come, he issued his proclamation. It was simply a war measure, not applicable all over the Union, but only in the insurgent States.

As the war proceeded public opinion at last commenced to move, and then moved rapidly. At first the Northern people, who were averse to slavery, out of the respect they had for the views of their fellow countrymen in the South, had refused to interfere with it; but, when they found their country invaded, the Union jeopardized, then they were prepared to go to the bottom and to deal with slavery, and Abraham Lincoln, the keenest judge of the fluctuation of public opinion that ever lived, saw the time was ripe. He advised the Republican Convention, which met in 1864, to adopt a plank in favour of the total abolition of slavery. His advice was accepted, the plank was adopted, and in November following the principle was ratified by the people, and, in the following March, 1865, the curse and the shame of slavery was forever blotted out from the fair name of the American Republic.

Now, Ladies and Gentlemen, it may be interesting if I give you the judgment which was passed by Lincoln himself upon slavery, its origin, its course and the responsibilities of the American people for the same. I will, therefore, if you will permit me, read you the Second Inaugural Address of Abraham Lincoln, delivered by him on the fourth of March, 1865, a few weeks before his assassination, and to me it is one of the most extraordinary papers that was ever written. I think you will agree that in it there is a tone which has been observed by one of Lincoln's historians that is not far from the dignity of the ancient prophets:

"At this second appearing to take the oath of the Presidential office there is less occasion for an extended address than there was at the first. Then a statement somewhat in detail of a course to be pursued seemed fitting and proper. Now, at the expiration of four years, during which public declarations have been constantly called forth on every point and phase of the great contest which still absorbs the attention and engrosses the energies of the nation, little that is new could be presented. The progress of our arms, upon which all else chiefly depends, is as well known to the public as to myself, and it is, I trust, reasonably satisfactory and encouraging to all. With high hope for the future, no prediction in regard to it is ventured.

On the occasion corresponding to this four years ago all thoughts were anxiously directed to an impending civil war. All dreaded it, all sought to avert it. While the inaugural address was being delivered from this place, devoted altogether to *saving* the Union without war, insurgent agents were in the city seeking to *destroy* it without war – seeking to dissolve the Union and divide effects by negotiation. Both parties deprecated war, but one of them would *make* war rather than let the nation survive, and the other would *accept* war rather than let it perish, and the war came.

One-eighth of the whole population were coloured slaves, not distributed generally over the Union, but localized in the southern part of it. These slaves constituted a peculiar and powerful interest. All knew that this interest was somehow the cause of the war. To strengthen, perpetuate, and extend this interest was the object for which the insurgents would rend the Union even by war, while the Government claimed no right to do more than to restrict the territorial enlargement of it. Neither party expected for the war the magnitude or the duration which it has already attained. Neither anticipated that the cause of the conflict might cease with or even before the conflict itself should cease. Each looked for an easier triumph, and a result less fundamental and astounding. Both read the same Bible and pray to the same God, and each invokes His aid against the other.

It may seem strange that any men should dare to ask a just God's assistance in wringing their bread from the sweat of other men's faces, but let us judge not, that we be not judged. The prayers of both could not be answered. That of neither has been answered fully. The Almighty has His own purposes. 'Woe unto the world because of offences; for it must needs be that offences come, but woe to that man by whom the offence cometh.' If we shall suppose that American slavery is one of those offences which, in the providence of God, must needs come, but which, having continued through His appointed time, He now wills to remove, and that He gives to both North and South this terrible war as the woe due to those by whom the offence came, shall we discern therein any departure from those divine attributes which the believers in a living God always ascribe to Him? Fondly do we hope, fervently do we pray, that this mighty scourge of war may speedily pass away. Yet, if God wills that it continue until all the wealth piled by the bondsman's two hundred and fifty years of unrequited toil shall be sunk, and until every drop of blood drawn with the lash shall be paid by another drawn with the sword, as was said three thousand years ago, so still it must be said 'the judgments of the Lord are true and righteous altogether.'

With malice toward none, with charity for all, with firmness in the right as God gives us to see the right, let us strive on to finish the work we are in, to bind up the nation's wounds, to care for him who shall have borne the battle and for his widow and his orphan, to do all which may achieve and cherish a just and lasting peace among ourselves and with all nations."

I do not know how you regard it, but it seems to me that these last words sound the loftiest note that could be struck in politics.

Now, Ladies and Gentlemen, I have just one more word to say and I will conclude. This is a world of evolution. Principles are eternal, but their application eternally varies. I have shown you the Roman Empire, followed by feudal Europe and then by Monarchical Europe, and now we have entered into a new era, the era of Democracy. We cannot hope that Democracy will be free from those errors, faults and vices which are the lot of human nature, but it seems to me that there are in Democracies certain vices such as corruption, envy and jealousy, against which we must always guard. It also seems to me that we have every reason to expect that Democratic Institutions, which mean the emancipation of long suffering masses, will be more and more impregnated with those generous impulses to which the martyred President gave unequalled expression. Indeed, the force of democratic institutions has been well illustrated in the marvellous manner in which the American Republic emerged from the Civil War.

Not a drop of blood was shed by the Civil Power, not a man was put upon trial for his participation in the rebellion; malice there was to none; charity there was for all, and the result is that today, notwithstanding the terrible cleavage caused by that Civil War which raged for four years, the most stupendous evil struggle that ever tore the bosom of any Nation, all traces of the conflict have disappeared and the Nation is united as it never was before.

This, Ladies and Gentlemen, is a great and most glorious triumph, but I think that we, British subjects, can lay claim and can show a still more phenomenal triumph. It is only ten years ago this month that on the field of South Africa, Dutch and British met in mortal combat. It was not, as in the American Civil War, a conflict of men of the same kin and kind in which the possibility of reconciliation was made more easy on account of the same blood flowing in the veins of the combatants, and where hands were impelled to join by the thousand memories of a common history.

No, on the field of South Africa, conflict was between men of alien races, embittered by the stinging recollection of recent humiliations inflicted on each other. But such was the faith of those who believe in the British Constitution that, if I may be permitted to speak of myself, during a debate which took place in the House when the war was raging, I ventured to make this prediction, speaking of the Dutch population: ". . . that if they have lost their independence they have not lost their freedom. There is but one future for South Africa, and that is a confederation on the pattern of the Canadian confederation in which Cape Colony and Natal, and the Orange Free State, and the Transvaal, and Rhodesia, shall be united together under the British flag, and under the sovereignty of England. And when they have the British flag over South Africa, they shall have that which has been found everywhere, during the last sixty years, under the British flag: liberty for all; equality for all; justice and rights for English and Dutch alike."

When I thus spoke, I uttered the feelings of my heart: I behaved, I felt, I knew that the British Constitution would justify my words, that truth and justice would prevail and that right would be done. But, I did not expect that the problem would be solved so soon as it has been solved. Only seven years have elapsed since the close of the war, and yet, already at this present moment that I am speaking to you, Dutch and Briton, burying and burying deep, the bitter memories of the past, have joined hands, together, to bring forth under the Southern Cross, a new nation, a new star, to be added to the constellation of nations which compose the British Empire.

Ladies and Gentlemen, and this is my last word, this is the last, the most consummate triumph of the British Constitution.

By the Right Honourable Kim Campbell[156]

Among Canadian prime ministers there has been no greater student of history than Sir Wilfrid Laurier. As we see from this 1909 address in Montreal, he was particularly conversant with British and American history. Having lived for many years in the United States, I was particularly attracted by Laurier's discussion of Abraham Lincoln – also a hero of mine – in this speech.

Laurier – who himself knew U.S. presidents William McKinley, Teddy Roosevelt (whose daughter sometimes holidayed privately in Canada with Sir Wilfrid and Lady Laurier)[157] and William Howard Taft – held a life-long admiration for Lincoln. He was well schooled in Lincoln's speeches and read as many biographies of the fallen president as he could.

While this might come as a surprise to many Canadians today, Laurier stood in contrast to large swaths of official Canadian and wider public opinion with his support for the Northern cause during the U.S. Civil War. This was coupled with his unwavering respect for its leader.

During a later address Laurier explained the roots of his long-held views.

"I have never denied that I was an admirer of the American Republic," he said during the 1911 free trade campaign. "Perhaps this was due to the fact that when eleven-years-old I read an American book, a French translation of Uncle Tom's Cabin. It appeared serially in a Montreal magazine."[158]

As a Montreal student during the U.S. Civil War, Laurier was well aware of the role colonial officials and public opinion played in allowing Confederate raiders to launch their attack on St. Albans, a small community in northern Vermont, from there in 1864. This was the most northern land-based military action of the entire war and was to cast a long shadow over Canadian–American relations for many years to come.

Following the Civil War, leading Confederates like former president Jefferson Davis were greeted as heroes in Canada during their visits here. Davis, in fact, even spoke to an enthusiastic audience of Canadians on July 1, 1867, the very day Canada came into being, so to speak.

An early biographer of Laurier, Professor O.D. Skelton of Queen's University, focused on the prism through which Sir Wilfrid viewed Lincoln.

"He [Laurier] had escaped being carried away by the enthusiasm for the South which marked official circles and the larger cities in Canada during the Civil War, when Southern refugees swarmed in Montreal, and plotted border raids," Skelton wrote. "He had pierced below caricature and calumny to the rugged strength of the Union leader, and held in highest honour his homespun wit, his shrewd judgement, his magnanimous patience. More than one shelf of his library was set apart for Lincolniana."[159]

Laurier, who spent a lifetime of public service seeking reconciliation and partnership between French and English Canadians, also greatly admired Lincoln's political skills. In his studies of Lincoln he found a master at the art of both the interpretation and the leading of public opinion.

"No man ever displayed a greater insight into the motives, the complex motives, which shape the public opinion of a free country," Sir Wilfrid once told the House of Commons in describing Lincoln. "He possessed almost to the degree of an instinct, the supreme quality in a statesman of taking the right decision, taking it at the right moment, and expressing it in language of incomparable felicity,"[160]

There are many lessons both Canadians and Americans can learn from studying Lincoln and Laurier in our own time. Both were politicians who appealed to the "better angels" of their respective electorates, rejecting the politics of division. While proud and fierce partisans for sure, they would both reject much of the negativity that is a feature in North American politics today.

In the area of Canadian–American relations Laurier left history a prediction that has been fulfilled. "It has been the goal of my life that between these two races there should be peace and no emulation but the friendly rivalry of commerce and science," he said. "By this we shall give a fine example to the world, as noble a future to one nation as to the other."[161]

We are right to continue to celebrate Lincoln and Laurier today.

The Right Honourable Kim Campbell was Canada's nineteenth prime minister. She also served as Canada's consul general in Los Angeles and taught for many years at the John F. Kennedy School of Government's Center for Public Leadership at Harvard University. She now serves as the founding principal of the Peter Lougheed Leadership College at the University of Alberta.

LAURIER RESPONDS
TO CIVIC ADDRESS

THUNDER BAY AND FORT WILLIAM, ONTARIO

JUNE 10, 1910[162]

[Arena at Fort William, Ontario]

. . . . You have been kind enough to tell me that the efforts I have
made on behalf of Canada have not been barren of success. Let me
tell you that for whatever success I may have had during my political
career, and especially since it has been my privilege to be at the head
of the Government, I claim not personal merit. It has been the result
of the fact that through a happy circumstance I have led a crew,
which was better than the captain himself. Whatever success has
attended my effort, I give altogether to those with whom it has been
my good fortune to be associated. . . .

You may ask me what is the object which brings me here at the
present moment. We are on a journey which will take me over the
four western provinces, Manitoba, Saskatchewan, Alberta and
British Columbia. We shall go over prairies and mountains; from
the water of Lake Superior to the water of the Pacific Ocean. The
object is a very plain and simple one. I give it not only to my friends
but to my foes also, so as to remove all other doubts which may still
linger in their minds. The object of this trip is that we, I and my

colleagues, should become better acquainted with this new and rapidly progressing western country. It is to visit and to see with our own eyes these new communities, cities, towns and villages which are springing up in every direction, almost as by magic.

It is to extend a hand of welcome to those new citizens who come to us from other lands to make our country their country; to become Canadians and to make Canada a country ever to be proud of it. It is to ascertain what are the wants and requirements of these new communities and what may be the duties devolving upon us with the responsibility of government. This is our object, nothing more and nothing less, and it is an object which I believe is part of the duty which I above others owe to my fellow countrymen and to the country which has entrusted myself and my colleagues with their confidence. . . .

You people here have a high opinion of your two cities, but important as you think they are, I am sure you do not conceive what they will be, great as the trade of the west is already producing 100 million bushels of wheat . . . it is the fringe of what it will be. Last year the first crop of the west was 100 million bushels. Within a very few years the wheat production of the west will reach one billion bushels. The wheat must come here. Nature had intended that this immense basin should be the great artery to carry the trade of the west to the outside world, and the trade of the outside world to the west.

Under these circumstances what is our duty? The duty of the government is to prepare to carry the immense trade. We are doing this at the present time but we have a good deal more to do in the future. Such things as these are material to this part of Canada, and also material to the whole of Canada, because what is good for one part is good for the whole. It is not enough, however, to look after our trade. We must also look after the defence of that trade. (Applause)

The doctrine of defence is as old as man himself, and we in Canada are bound to protect ourselves. We have a militia of which we are all proud, and it would no doubt give a good account of itself if unfortunately it should be called upon to do so. It was intended from the first days of Confederation we should have a naval militia, and we are now determined to have one.

We passed a resolution to that effect in March 1909. We declared in the House of Commons by a unanimous vote that the time had come. . . . Responsible Government in 1841 led to union, and our navy will lead us to closer union with the Motherland. (Cheers) I charge the Opposition with not understanding their country. They apparently do not understand the age in which we live. It is with colonies as it is with individuals. They grow into manhood.

We want to have our own laws, our own constitution, our own militia, our own navy. Call it a tin-pot navy if you will. That navy is ours, small as it is, and may the time never come when we shall be forced to make it larger. But if the time ever comes, which God forbid, when the old land is in the face of danger, I tell you our brawn and hearts will be arrayed by her side against any enemy that may come. . . .

We want our own navy, but while we want our own navy the King of England will be the King of our navy. (Cheers) The Canadian Parliament is a Parliament of the King of England. He is our sovereign. We lost a few months ago our late sovereign – one of the best and wisest men that ever was on the Throne of England or on the throne of any nation. (Cheers) He has gone to his fathers with a prouder title than ever was bestowed since there were kings – Edward the Peacemaker. (Applause)

Well, sir, I speak with some knowledge and some authority, and I can say that the King of today is a worthy son of his sire. (Cheers) Like his father, I think, he will say: "I have striven to do my duty." (Cheers) And my last words to you are simply these, that in this age, in this Canada, we say, as in the days of old, "The King is dead. Long live the King." (Loud cheers and continued applause)

[Thunder Bay, Ontario]

. . . . I am delighted above all things to know that this address represents not the sentiments of one party, but the sentiments of all parties. It is our privilege to live under the British constitution, and we may say without exaggeration that it has been proved by the test of time that the British constitution is the most perfect that has yet been invented by man for the government of men. (Cheers)

The carrying out of that constitution rests upon party organization. We belong to various parties. Of course there is one party good, and one which is not so good. (Laughter) As to the one which is not so good, I will not express an opinion upon this occasion. I have an opinion, of course, but just now I will keep it to myself. However, I am sure of one thing, and that is that whatever may be the difference of opinion, we all have one end in common, and that is the welfare of our country. (Cheers) . . . .

Why only this morning I was told in Fort William that Fort William was the key to the situation, and I have no doubt that when I get to Winnipeg on Tuesday, they will say the same about Winnipeg. In my opinion the key of the situation is not Fort William or Port Arthur; it is both. (Cheers) Although I have only been here a short time, I am impressed with the magnitude of the future which is before you. I see before me, not Port Arthur or Fort William, but one great city covering the western shore of Lake Superior, a city which will be one in intent and purpose, as it ought to be. (Cheers) If I am to live as long as you tell me I should – I have no objections, but I know quite well I shall not – I shall see here one city and one harbour.

So far as the Government is concerned, I can only say, it is like the Kingdom of Heaven, it will help those who help themselves.

Speaking for the Government, I can say, we will help you, and for every step you make, we will make two. For every dollar you spend, we will spend two. (Applause)

I am here on a great enterprise and I am so grateful that in this, the first step I make, I am received, not as if I am the Prime Minister of Canada, but as a fellow Canadian. (Cheers)

By Derek H. Burney

When I grew up in the 1940s and '50s in what was Fort William, now part of Thunder Bay, Sir Wilfrid Laurier was not a household name. C.D. Howe, the all-powerful, Liberal cabinet minister at the time, definitely was. He represented the neighbouring constituency of Port Arthur and, on the rare occasion when he did come to town, it became a school holiday – in Port Arthur only. We were envious.

I became much more aware of Laurier later in life as I found myself in the 1980s at the epicentre of the great free trade debate and the election of 1988, in many ways the sequel to 1911. I distinctly remember Flora MacDonald bringing to cabinet samples of the Conservative cartoons that had been used to attack Laurier's initiative in 1911. They prompted some laughs but fortunately did not revive much opposition. (That came later in the campaign from many of Laurier's Liberal descendants.)

Laurier was a true visionary and not just on the issue of free trade, or "reciprocity" as it was then known. When he visited the twin cities of the Canadian Lakehead (Fort William and Port Arthur) in June 1910, he stated, "I am impressed with the magnitude of the future which is before you. I see before me, not Port Arthur or Fort William, but one great city covering the western shore of Lake Superior, a city which will be one in intent and purpose, as it ought to be. If I am to live as long as you tell me I should . . . I shall see here one city and one harbour." Laurier's vision came through, albeit not in his lifetime, but more than fifty years later as the two cities amalgamated to become Thunder Bay.

Laurier was confident that my hometown would become "the great artery to carry the trade of the west [primarily wheat] to the outside world, and the trade of the outside world to the west." And this was long before the St. Lawrence Seaway helped make that a reality.

Laurier was also prescient about our history. Speaking in Simcoe during the lively 1911 election campaign, he acknowledged that Sir John Macdonald had actually been "the Moses of the policy of reciprocity and, like Moses, he was not destined to see the Promised Land." Macdonald had indeed tried to negotiate reciprocity with the Americans, but in the immediate wake of their brutal civil war, his overtures evoked little interest. Nonetheless, he genuinely regarded his National Policy as the second best or fallback option at the time for Canada's economic growth.

Laurier, too, missed the Promised Land of Free Trade. Ironically, it was another Conservative, Brian Mulroney, who ultimately fulfilled the vision that Laurier and Macdonald had initiated and shared. In a way, their vision on trade came around full circle politically.

All three Canadian leaders were no doubt mindful of the epitaph on the Peace Tower: "Where there is no vision, the people perish." They acted and made common cause on a vision that has proven to be vital to our economic growth and to the strength of our national fabric.

Derek H. Burney, chancellor of Lakehead University and senior strategic advisor at Norton Rose Fulbright Canada, was chief of staff to Prime Minister Brian Mulroney and later Canada's ambassador to the United States.

AT THE UNIVERSITY
OF SASKATCHEWAN

SASKATOON, SASKATCHEWAN
JULY 29, 1910[163]

I find great pleasure in being able to take part in so important a ceremony as this. A great honour has been done me. Education is truly patriotism, for it is the best heritage which a people can have given [to] them. I was certainly impressed last night when I read the inscription on one of the arches with which you have decorated your city. "Saskatoon affords a complete education from the kindergarten to the University."

When a child has gone through the four stages of kindergarten, primary school, high school, and university, he is well equipped for the battle of life. Canada cannot afford to be behind the other races of the world; she is young, but she has already universities which are distinguished and of high rank in the world. There is no doubt that this university will in time be one of the world's greatest.

The Agricultural College is one of the important buildings of the university. Agriculture is not only a work of the hands, but a work of brain. It is an art, and I hope that this study will take a foremost rank in the curriculum. It is the finest of all studies and sciences. The necessity of that is very great, for agriculture, which is the chief occupation in this province, is the most ancient of occupations and sciences; and when farmers realize that by education they can obtain two, three, or four times what their fathers obtained, they will be enthusiastic in the study of agriculture.

The parent who can give a good education to his boy gives the best heritage, better than gold or diamonds. But it will not be the lot of all to be university graduates. If a man has not an education he need not be discouraged. In this country a man can get things for himself; there are no grades here; all are equal. The university has an advantage, but the man without education need not be confined to the second rung. In this democratic country under the British Constitution, it is possible to attain the highest position without schooling. As an instance of that there is John Bright, who rose to be the first statesman of his time. In France also there have been many examples of self-made men. In science we have such men as Stevenson,[164] who have acquired their knowledge entirely through their own efforts.

But if these men had had the privilege of education, what labour could have been saved, what energy, consumed in acquiring a training, could have been given to the service of mankind. Let all who can, come to this university. Let the father send his son, if need be, by personal sacrifice, but without such an opportunity one does not need to be discouraged. It has been a proud privilege to me to lay this stone. I could not have had a more agreeable task.

Let a university arise here which may be a worthy disciple of Oxford, Cambridge, and other universities which have done so much for mankind.

By the Honourable Roy Romanow

When Prime Minister Wilfrid Laurier declared that "Canada shall fill the twentieth century," he envisioned a country united in purpose and determination. Seeded within the core of this vision was the birth of new provinces and stunning transformations of a society still young and uncertain of its identity and values. In the years since, the Canadian state has woven itself together from the Spartan strands of an often undiscovered countryside into the beautiful quilt of a good and compassionate state.

For Saskatchewan, the truth of this remarkable vision was first borne out in the deep fields of prairie grasses, being tilled for the first time by waves of immigrant farmers. A new province was emerging during a time of intemperate fates and a rush of technological and social change. This growing community demanded its citizens set aside the differences that divided them – whether it was language, religion, or culture – and learn to live together and build together.

A cornerstone of the great project called Saskatchewan was a university – the highest of ambitions – where, as Prime Minister Laurier described so eloquently, "The parent who can give a good education . . . gives the best heritage, better than gold or diamonds."

The heritage that is the result of the hard work and the perpetual contributions of generations of Saskatchewan people is a strong province and a more united Canada. Since Saskatchewan's entrance into Confederation, its citizens have punched above their weight in building their own province and their country. In science, researchers have developed new crop varieties and pioneered achievements in nuclear medicine and the Cobalt-60 radiation therapy. Public servants and leaders have launched ground-breaking campaigns to enact public Medicare and Canada's first human rights legislation. Businesses have created innovative new products and industrial processes that have seen once inaccessible resources brought to markets around the world. Farmers have grown, for over a century, food that has fed millions. Great Saskatchewan artists have demonstrated the province's ability to inspire emotion and imagination.

Building a vibrant community has not come without sacrifices, as every Canadian knows. Saskatchewan is marked by the hard history of the Great Depression and the losses of its brave citizens in the two world wars and in those conflicts around the world that continue to persist. Its citizens have struggled through lean years in the wheat and natural resource economy more than once. But Saskatchewan's shared values of compassion and perseverance have helped it transcend the seemingly insurmountable and stay on the path of the good state.

Now, as Saskatchewan advances further into the twenty-first century, it is challenged to build on its strengths and ameliorate its weaknesses. Perhaps most important is the need for First Nations peoples to achieve their full potential and more completely contribute their many unique qualities to all of Canada's society. A renewed dream is that the foundations of under-standing and education work to include the First Nations communities that have so often been excluded in the past. When elders say that "Education is our buffalo," they mirror the words of Laurier: "the best heritage, better than gold." In this spirit, it is assured that Saskatchewan's strength as a home to innovation, advanced education, resourcefulness, and opportunity can only grow and contribute to a better Canada.

The future is as bright today for the land of living skies as it was when Laurier laid a cornerstone and declared, "I could not have had a more agree-able task."

The Honourable Roy Romanow, senior policy fellow at the College of Arts and Sciences at the University of Saskatchewan, was his province's twelfth premier.

THE GATEWAY OF CANADA

VANCOUVER, BRITISH COLUMBIA
AUGUST 16, 1910[165]

Response to civic welcome:

After five weeks of continuous travel we have at last reached the great City of Vancouver, of which we have constantly heard so much. As has been said in these addresses you have presented to me, we have seen many evidences of prosperity as we have moved westward, but I think my friends will agree with that the "bag" goes to Vancouver. (Laughter and cheers)

I had heard much of this city as we progressed westward and I was prepared to believe some of it, but I thought I would be justified in making some little allowance for the exaggeration of stories which comes out of the West. I find I was mistaken. (Cheers)

I say now to those eastern croakers (laughter) – those doubting Thomases – (renewed laughter) – that if they want to see the truth of the tales of the great progress of which we have heard so much they must come out here and see for themselves. I must, as a good Canadian, rejoice for the progress which this city has made.

Coming west on the train . . . I was fortunate in escaping from a serious accident. Now that was because I was born under a lucky star. And I wish to assure you that if the country has prospered under my regime it has not been due to efforts of mine, but to the fact I was born under a lucky star. (Laughter)

I said that your city showed evidence of a great progression. But I noticed . . . that you finished progressing and you want a little more protection. (Laughter) I have just left a section of the West in which they all appear to want free trade! (Laughter) You want a little more protection and on the prairies they want a little freer trade! I'll have to refer this matter to the Minister of Finance and I have no doubt that in due time he will evolve a scheme that will satisfy your desire for a little more protection and the prairies a little more free trade, that should be satisfactory to both sides.

★ ★ ★

Luncheon at Dominion Hall:

. . . . In many ways we have to acknowledge the superiority of the West over the eastern part of the Dominion. There is nothing like this city there. I can detect a tremendous difference now in your city since I was here nine years ago. Then I thought very much like the general who was informed by Napoleon Bonaparte, when he questioned the practicability of a certain order, that there was no such word as impossible in the language. I have derived the same impression here from the great change that has been wrought.

And yet, I understand you are in need of assistance; at least I gather so from the address that has been presented to me [from the mayor]. In what can I assist you? I saw one great evidence of the work of the Dominion government that has made me feel proud: the Post Office. It is a worthy monument to this great city of Vancouver. But there is a lot to do yet in the way of improving this city, and I am sure that the people themselves are seeing us as a very worthy example. It is apparent that Vancouver is destined to be the Gateway of Canada, and at present this city is one of the greatest in the Dominion.

After my return to Ontario in 1894 when I visited Vancouver and British Columbia, I remarked to one of my friends that although Ontario had been hitherto regarded as the banner province of Canada, she would have to look to the laurels or British Columbia would be so thought of in the near future. (Cheers)

With your wealth of forests, mineral resources of every description, it is almost impossible to fully determine the full extent of which they exist and I shall not be at all surprised if in years to come the magnificent mountains are utilized in the same manner as those of Switzerland have been, and the thousands of valleys devoted to agriculture.

I am an enthusiastic admirer of the great western country, and I have only one regret in this connection – that I did not come out here myself years ago. (Loud and prolonged applause)

I judge from the expressions that have greeted me on every hand that you have no fault to find with me, but you must not attribute any of the great prosperity that has attended this country during the past year to my efforts. I have only been following the example set by the Premiers who have preceded me. (Applause)

(At the conclusion of the address, a scene of the wildest enthusiasm reigned: men jumped upon chairs in their excitement, the salvoes of applause and vociferous cheers marked the Premier's triumphant departure.)

By David Mitchell

His previous visit to British Columbia had been nine years earlier, which might in part explain the combination of curiosity and enthusiasm that greeted Prime Minister Laurier in the summer of 1910.

B.C. had been a Canadian province for less than two generations. Still a developing frontier, Vancouver was confidently emerging as the new province's metropolis, but still being rebuilt on the ashes of the great fire that had demolished the city less than a quarter of a century before. Even so, the bustling young city, surrounded by an extraordinary wealth of natural resources, was bursting with potential. And Laurier was no doubt sincere when he suggested that eastern Canadians "must come out here and see for themselves."

When the silver-haired, silver-tongued prime minister expressed his regret "that I did not come out here myself years ago," he was giving voice to a sentiment that would be often heard over the next century from easterners visiting Canada's westernmost province.

At the time of this visit, Wilfrid Laurier was at the peak of his popularity and nearing the end of his lengthy tenure as prime minister. He was received by large crowds and spoke passionately about British Columbia's future role in Canadian Confederation. The transcontinental rail line connecting Vancouver to the rest of the country had been completed only in 1886. The process of becoming linked both physically and emotionally to Canada was still in its early stages for most British Columbians. In fact, federal party labels such as "Liberal" or "Conservative" had only recently been introduced in B.C. politics.

Nevertheless, Laurier's presence and his prophesies stirred a nascent sense of patriotism among the diverse, largely non-partisan gatherings he addressed. He ruminated about "the superiority of the West" and openly speculated that "Vancouver is destined to be the Gateway of Canada and at present this city is one of the greatest in the Dominion." Perhaps it's little wonder that Wilfrid Laurier was received so warmly. Not only were prime ministerial visits a rarity at the time, but there was also a special fascination with Laurier, whose celebrity as an eloquent francophone political leader preceded him, creating great expectations throughout his western Canadian tour. He rarely disappointed the eager crowds that turned out to hear him speak.

Another noteworthy quality that drew people to Laurier was his irrepressible optimism and positive attitude. This had become part of his political trademark. Indeed, when he was first elected as prime minister, Laurier had neutralized the difficult Manitoba Schools question by appealing to "the *sunny way" rather than forcing a province to abide by the wishes of Ottawa. Now, during his trip to the west coast, British Columbians were anxious to embrace the prime minister's hopefulness. And, in fact, more than a century later, when a new Liberal leader, Justin Trudeau, won Canada's prime ministership, his election-night victory speech explicitly invoked Sir Wilfrid Laurier's "sunny ways."*

The aura of optimism so palpable during Laurier's 1910 Vancouver visit has clearly stood the test of time.

David Mitchell is an author and historian who has served as a member of the British Columbia legislature and as vice-president of three Canadian universities: Queen's, the University of Ottawa, and Simon Fraser University. He is currently the Chief External Relations Officer at Bow Valley College in Calgary.

THE ENTHUSIASM OF THE WEST

MEDICINE HAT, ALBERTA
SEPTEMBER 3, 1910[166]

I left home a Canadian to the core. I return ten times more Canadian.
I have imbibed the air, spirit and enthusiasm of the West. I am a
true Westerner henceforth; nay, I should say Canadian, for we must
in future aim to know West and East only in emulation of doing
more for Canada, our common country.

So I am going home now. I have learned a great deal in the past
two months. I have learned to know my country. On July 7, I set
my face toward the setting sun. On September 2, I am setting my
face toward the rising sun. Yet, whether rising or setting the same
sun (shines) all over Canada. . . .

During my tour I have met multitudes of new Canadians. Thousands of them were settlers from the United States. I asked them
whether they were satisfied with their conditions under our institutions here and without exception the reply was "Yes! And proud to
become Canadians." Experiences of this nature have given me intense
satisfaction. The Republic is learning that monarchical institutions
in Canada are not less democratic than those in the south. The King
of England is subject to the law just the same as the President of the
United States and without possessing so many autocratic powers.

We are all working together to build up Canada as a nation. We are not following in a beaten path but by choosing our own course and hewing out our own road. Our experience has no parallel in any part or age of the world. History tells us of countries which have reached the status of nationhood by severing their connection with the parent seat. We have the secret of becoming a nation without breaking off with the Motherland. We are proud of our nation. . . . [We support] all that conduces to the glory, welfare, prosperity and happiness of the Canada of our birth and the Canada of our adoption.

By the Honourable Rachel Notley

After hockey, curling, and our reverence for the great outdoors, asking what it means to be Canadian is perhaps our most Canadian of pastimes. Reflecting on Sir Wilfrid Laurier's speech I was struck by the similarities between how he answered the question of what it means to be Canadian, just five short years after Alberta's birth, and how I would answer it today.

Sir Wilfrid's statement that "we must in future aim to know West and East only in emulation of doing more for Canada, our common country" still animates us today. Like him, I have met thousands of newcomers who are so proud to be Canadians and Albertans. This dualism is an essential trait of all Canadians — each of us is as devoted to our home province as we are to our neighbours who share our common country. And in that dual identity Canada finds its strength.

And for good reason: from East to West, we are a country of stark and beautiful difference. Rugged coast lines become Rocky Mountains giving way to foothills and vast prairie stretching to the bedrock of the Canadian Shield. We are a nation of languages, religion, and culture spanning five continents, a nation of newcomers and indigenous peoples. It is through these differences that we improve the whole of our nation.

Just as Fort McMurray benefits from the great numbers of Maritimers whose labour allows the oil sands to succeed, so does Banff benefit from the many young Québécois who come to work and explore in the Rocky Mountains each summer and share their culture with us. When fires threaten our vast forests, trained people from our neighbouring provinces and territories come to assist, just as we would for them. When farmers and ranchers in Alberta suffer from drought you can count on a news story about farmers in another province donating hay to help them through the winter. And our urban centres are made more diverse and creative by resourceful, young, highly educated people from across the country (and beyond) who are joining with the best in Alberta to incubate new ideas. It is the vitality of these relationships between our provinces, our First Nations, and their people across this vast country that will determine the prosperity of Canada in the future.

It is the recognition of our common mission to provide a fairer, more just, and more prosperous Canada that allows our provinces to find strength where there is difference and achieve together far more than each could individually. This recognition of strength in our diversity is at the heart of federalism and has strengthened Confederation, bringing Canada together across the longest continuous border in the world. And it is this common mission that will allow Alberta to overcome our greatest challenges: delivering our natural resources to the world, increasing the prosperity of all families, and showing true responsibility to our environment and our fellow citizens, so that the Alberta and the Canada our children inherit is as abundant, pristine, and prosperous as that which we live in today.

On September 3, 1910, Sir Wilfrid said "we are all working together to build up Canada as a nation." His statement is as true today as it was then.

The Honourable Rachel Notley is premier of Alberta.

THE FIGHT FOR FREE TRADE I

ST. EUSTACE, QUEBEC (AFTERNOON MEETING)
AUGUST 22, 1911[167]

I am a party man but I address not only my own party, but all parties in Canada. I respect the sincerity of others as I hope they respect mine. Many people thought that when I was elected in 1896 the end of industrial activity had come, but this was not so. Suppose the farmer had $200 worth of produce to send to the United States, on this he would have to pay about $50 duty. Wouldn't it be just as well to let him keep that in his pocket? That is what reciprocity meant. Mr. Bourassa,[168] who today said he did not know if he was for or against the agreement, said in 1902 that New England was the natural market for Quebec. Tell me, do you want that market?

Mr. Monk carried the trumpet on which Bourassa played.[169] But when I see the name of Mr. Sifton and Mr. Bourassa stuck together I am simply revenged for the attacks on me. If there is one man Mr. Bourassa hates, one man he has insulted, it is Mr. Sifton. Now they are exchanging the kiss of peace and singing the chorus "we must overthrow Laurier. . . ."

I am a champion of no race or tongue. It is said I have been dazzled by honours. More honour has come to me than I expected or wanted, but the King of England can give me no greater honour than to be Prime Minister of Canada and when I cease to be that, I shall become a simple Canadian citizen. I am a Canadian and this is all my policy and that policy will prevail.

THE FIGHT FOR FREE TRADE II: THE "SALAD" SPEECH

AHUNTSIC, QUEBEC (EVENING MEETING)
AUGUST 22, 1911[170]

Reciprocity has been the policy of every public man in Canada for fifty years. . . . It is time the farmers of Canada have their turn. . . . I could scarcely believe my ears when I heard Mr. Borden oppose this agreement, nor my eyes when I read Mr. Bourassa's declaration that he was neither for it nor against it. I don't know where Mr. Monk stands. The more I see of him the less I understand him. But when I see Mr. Borden, Mr. Sifton and Mr. Bourassa united against me, I say to myself, "What a salad."

I suppose Mr. Sifton furnishes the oil for it, and I am sure Mr. Bourassa supplies the vinegar, while poor Mr. Borden has to eat it. The Conservative Party has fallen just as it reached the gates of paradise. What was the tempter that caused it to fail? Was it the Canadian manufacturer? I have been told so, but I do not believe it. It was the English jingoes and the Canadian jingoes, the castors in Quebec and Ontario jingoes, the men who say that the different parts of the Empire should trade only within the Empire.

Our policy is grander. We believe that we should trade with the Empire, but also with all the world. We have given a special preference to Great Britain, we have negotiated an agreement with France, and now we come to you with one with the United States.

What about the Navy? Men of Laval [riding], we will not leave our defence to anybody but ourselves, that is our policy, a virile policy, a proud policy, a policy worthy of Canada. We have the rights of a nation: shall we not have its responsibilities? We have those rights and we demand the privilege of defending ourselves. Appeals have been made to passion, and to the basest passion of all, that of fear. Only one word in conclusion that I may close the mouth of some calumniator who may come to you saying that the naval service has been obligatory. That is not a fantasy. It is not even a calumny; it is purely and simply a lie.

I have been attacked as an imperialist and as an anti-imperialist. I am neither. I am just a Canadian, a Canadian first, last, and all the time.

By Arthur Milnes

Free trade with the United States.

For decades after Laurier's defeat in 1911, the concept was considered the third rail in Canadian politics: touch it and you (politically) die. Even the wily and effective Mackenzie King, who himself was defeated in his riding in 1911 while serving in Laurier's cabinet, would later shy away from attempting to conclude such an agreement with our American neighbours.

This changed in the 1980s with the rise to power of Progressive Conservative leader Brian Mulroney. He dared touch the third rail that had defeated Laurier, and Canada and the U.S. concluded the Free Trade Agreement, later expanded into NAFTA.

But those, particularly in English Canada, who lived through the 1988 Free Trade election will never forget it. Passions were inflamed and arguments over the agreement took place in workplaces, classrooms, and around dinner tables.

That is why a study of Laurier's defeat in 1911 is so important for Canadians of our own time. Laurier, as we see from these two 1911 campaign speeches, was attacked on all sides. Unlike in 1988, when Quebec public opinion was generally in favour of the FTA, *this wasn't the case for Laurier. Throw in the naval issue and the stage was set for an incredible election campaign in 1911.*

It began, however, with Laurier feeling great confidence in both the deal his government had reached with the U.S. administration of William Howard Taft – whose summer home was in Quebec – and in his own abilities. This despite Laurier's having been in power for fifteen years.

"Henry of Navarre at the battle of Ivry said: 'Follow my white plume and you will find it always in the forefront of honour,'" Laurier told a Montreal audience during the summer of 1911. "Like Henry IV, *I say to you young men, Follow my white plume – the white hairs of sixty-nine years – and you will, I believe I can say without boasting, find it always in the forefront of honour."*[171]

Yet despite these pleas, Laurier went down to defeat that fall. These two speeches capture the forces aligned against the seventh prime minister in 1911. In many ways they remind us of the challenge Wilfrid Laurier faced throughout his career: being viewed by some as too English for the French and too French for the English.

The perfect Canadian prime minister, perhaps.

PART IV:

THE OLD CHIEFTAIN

1911–1919

Though the Old Chieftain was defeated at the polls, Canadians did not lose their affection and respect for Sir Wilfrid Laurier. And though a new prime minister, Sir Robert Borden, has replaced him, the owners of Ottawa's new showcase hotel don't feel the need to rename the Château Laurier that stands next to a Parliament Hill now ruled by Conservatives.

In the Commons, Laurier's oratory again soars at great national moments, such as when the House pays tribute to Sir Charles Tupper on his death, or when MPs meet at the Victoria Museum, their temporary home while Centre Block still smoulders after the parliamentary fire. (It is there that they will face the nearly impossible task of paying worthy homage to Laurier upon his death in 1919.)

As a politician, however, Laurier in many ways seems to relish being relieved of power. He presents new policies (such as those he introduces during one of his addresses in Hamilton), reviews before Liberals the reasons for their loss, and ably tangles with future threats to his party during Commons debates that feature future prime ministers Arthur Meighen and R.B. Bennett. Included here is what is believed to be Laurier's final public address, delivered before – not surprisingly – the Eastern Ontario Liberal Association. He would die a month later.

During this closing period of his life, the "Old Chieftain" of Canadian politics, as he had become (much in the manner of Macdonald before him), shares advice and words of wisdom with tomorrow's Canadian leaders. In London, Ontario, for example, he tells young people, in phrases he's used throughout his career, that "faith is better than doubt" and "love is better than hate."

As he gives that advice to young Canadians assembled before him, the world is being tested as never before: the First World War rages. Thousands of Canadians have died in the bloody trenches of Europe, and back home Canada's unity – the great cause of Laurier's life – is threatened.

Many of his own supporters desert him in the 1917 campaign, as both English and French withdraw to the safety of their tribal camps. While it is not a speech, Laurier's 1917 "Election Manifesto" is included here, as is the Commons address where he confronts in person those Liberals who wouldn't follow his white plume that year. One can only imagine the atmosphere that day, when those Liberals who had turned their backs on him were forced to listen to their former leader.

Those days are long forgotten, however, when in August 1927 the Prince of Wales, Liberal prime minister Mackenzie King, and Conservative prime minister Stanley Baldwin of the United Kingdom, joined by thousands, dedicate Laurier's statue on Parliament Hill. An older man, Sir Robert Borden, one who, like Laurier, also knew the frightful costs of war, pays on that day perhaps the greatest tribute of all.

From our own era, two other Canadians, who also know about power and the costs of holding the premiership, the Right Honourable Jean Chrétien and the Right Honourable Stephen J. Harper – one French and the other English – look back with respect on their predecessor. The first is Liberal, the second Conservative. One suspects that Sir Wilfrid Laurier would approve of them closing his book.

EXCHANGE WITH A FUTURE PRIME MINISTER: R.B. BENNETT[172] AND SIR WILFRID

HOUSE OF COMMONS, OTTAWA, ONTARIO
NOVEMBER 20, 1911

Bennett [making his maiden address to the House]: While I mention the name of the Right Honourable Gentleman, may I be permitted to tender to him my sincere congratulations upon his having attained another anniversary of his natal day [Laurier turned seventy on this day], with the expression of the hope that he may be long spared faithfully and illustriously to serve the state in the position which he at present occupies [as Leader of the Opposition].

Laurier [later in the day]: Mr. Speaker, the House has listened with more than ordinary interest to the two addresses in support of the motion now in your hands. We can congratulate ourselves upon the fact that we welcome to our ranks two members, young in years and of eminent ability, ability which might accomplish a great deal for this country if the hope could be entertained that these young men would direct their ability in the proper direction — a hope, however, which judging not from the manner but from the matter of their speeches, I fear I must not be too sanguine of.

The Honourable Member for Calgary (Mr. Bennett) was preceded to this House by a high reputation for fluent oratory, and the speech with which he has favoured us has not only sustained but enhanced that reputation. I think I can with perfect appositeness compare his speech on the present occasion – judging from its easy and copious flow of sentences – with the crystal waters of the Bow River rushing down from the summit of the Rocky Mountains towards that young and enterprising city which he has the honour to represent in this House.

Nor is my Honourable Friend the member for Dorchester (Mr. Sévigny) new to political life.[173] I am unaware that he has ever served in any legislative body as has the member for Calgary, but my Honourable Friend (Mr. Sévigny) is well known to us in the Province of Quebec as amongst the most brilliant and ardent orators of the Nationalist party. . . .

My Honourable Friend, as did the member for Calgary, was kind enough to offer me his congratulations upon the fact that this is my seventieth birthday. I tender to both gentlemen my sincere thanks, and I thank Honourable Members on both sides, and especially Honourable Gentlemen on the opposite side of the House, for the kind manner in which they received these compliments. The Honourable Member for Calgary was profuse in his good wishes towards me, and he concluded by hoping that for a long time I shall occupy the position which I now do, meaning of course that for a long time to come I should remain Leader of the Opposition discharging the difficult task of watching and criticizing the acts of the Government.

I must say in all candour to my Honourable Friends, that judging from the manner in which the present Government has commenced its career I feel that task will be too great for my advancing years.

By Lawrence Martin

By taking a position in favour of a reciprocity agreement with the United States in 1911, Wilfrid Laurier paved the way, unwittingly of course, for the entry into federal politics of a future prime minister.

R.B. Bennett, a member of the Alberta provincial legislature, was an ardent British Empire loyalist. He saw Canada's future as an independent nation embedded in the Commonwealth. He favoured a preferential trade system with Britain and was a lifelong foe of continentalism. Laurier's free trade plan convinced him to come to Ottawa.

Laurier and Bennett clashed in terms of their vision of Canada. But they were alike with respect to their fertile minds and their way with words. The latter is a quality we don't value so much today: rich vocabularies, poetic rhythms, rapier wit, a capacity to weave together memorable passages without the use of notes.

Their first exchanges in the Commons were noteworthy. At the time of Bennett's maiden address, November 20, 1911, Laurier had just become leader of the Opposition after fifteen years as prime minister. Defeat for a prime minister back then did not mean he was expected to step down as leader. At the ripe age of seventy, Laurier was well contented to continue to serve his country as Opposition leader and his Liberal Party was prepared to let him do so. It was a sign of the abiding respect party members had for him. Mackenzie King would experience setbacks in the elections of 1925 and 1930 and was still wanted as leader.

It being Laurier's seventieth birthday, Bennett congratulated him with the wish – in the form of a clever dig – that he continue to serve the country illustriously but in the position he currently occupied.

Laurier noted the capacities of the new member from Calgary and added that if properly directed they could be of benefit to the country. But judging from Bennett's initial offerings in Ottawa, it was a hope "I must not be too sanguine of."

Instead of the sledgehammer political rhetoric of today, Laurier employed subtlety and also imagery. In praising Bennett, the latter was on display:

"I think I can with perfect appositeness compare his speech on the present occasion — judging from his easy and copious flow of sentences — with the crystal waters of the Bow River rushing down from the summit of the Rocky Mountains toward that young and enterprising city which he has the honour to represent in this House."

Bennett could do the same. On the glories of Canada he would often hold forth. He described the country as *"a land endowed by heaven with incalculable wealth. A people free and brave and strong with the strength that comes from the mountains and the prairies, the rivers and the sea. A shrine this Canada — which holds inviolate those laws of truth and justice and equality."*

A difference between the two men was that Bennett could also be biting with his language and hostile to others. He couldn't match the sophistication of Sir Wilfrid Laurier. Few could. Laurier, however, unlike Bennett, never had to face the Great Depression of the 1930s. Had he done so, he would have been sorely tested. But it is likely he would have found a way to be comforting to Canadians in times so trying.

Lawrence Martin is a public affairs columnist for the *Globe and Mail*. He is the author of numerous books, including a two-volume biography of Jean Chrétien and a seminal study in the field of Canadian–American relations, *The Presidents and the Prime Ministers* (1982).

IN THE SHADOW OF DEFEAT

MONTREAL REFORM CLUB,
WINDSOR HOTEL, MONTREAL, QUEBEC
MAY 29, 1912[174]

. . . . You have referred, sir, a moment ago to the fact that we meet under the shadow of defeat, and perhaps had I been as wise as I might have been, and had I followed my own inclinations, on the morrow of the 21st of September, I should have gone back into private life, and handed over the reins to some younger and abler hands. But, sir, I am the servant of the people. And, since it was the wish of those with whom I was associated that I should retain the trust which had been placed in my hands, I repeat, I am the servant of the people.

It matters not to me whatever is the post assigned to me, I am ready to serve as captain of the forces, or to serve as a private in the ranks, and whatever position I am called to fill I shall in the future, as I have done in the past, give to it the best of my heart, of my life, and of my ability.

I might repeat in the words of the Canadian poet:

My orders are to fight;
Then if I bleed, or fail,

Or strongly win, what matters it?
God only doth prevail.
The servant craveth naught
Except to serve with might.
I was not told to win or lose,
My orders are to fight.[175]

And fight I will: and fight you will, and so shall we all, in the sense in which fighting is meant, under our British constitution. Fight we will with malice towards none, with charity for all, with firmness in the right, as God gives us to see the right. I borrow these words from that great and wise man, Abraham Lincoln,[176] and I would wish that to be now and forever the motto of the Liberal Party. . . .

I feel today undaunted. I have asked our friends in the late contest to follow my white plume. I may, perhaps, on the present occasion, renew the same request, to follow my white plume, and I can tell them I shall never show the white feather[177]. . . .

This brings me naturally to a review of the contest that we had some eight months ago. We appealed to the country upon the question of Reciprocity. It was not, however, the question of Reciprocity which was uppermost in the discussion that took place, in this Province at all events. There were other issues brought up which ought not perhaps to have been brought up, but which were brought up just the same, and if defeated we were not defeated on the main issue before the country, so far at all events, as this province was concerned, and I might say so far as the Province of Ontario was concerned. We were defeated by a combination of the most heterogeneous elements which could combine together for destruction, but which could never hold up together for construction.

We had against us the Conservative Party led by Mr. Borden. That was natural. They were our natural antagonists. In addition to that we had against us the dissentient Conservatives led by Mr. Monk. We had against us the Nationalists, led by Mr. Bourassa. . . .

Perhaps it would not be altogether inconsistent or out of place to review here what was the attitude of the different parties on the main question which was in issue before the Canadian people at the time. As I told you a moment ago, we had our natural antagonists, the Conservative Opposition. But, if the Conservative Opposition were our natural antagonists they never were our natural antagonists upon the question of Reciprocity, because they had been just as much in favour of Reciprocity as we had been. Indeed, it had been part of their programme and platform for forty years and more.

In the year 1854, when Lord Elgin went to Washington to negotiate a Treaty of Reciprocity, a treaty which was, I might say, the same as our own agreement with the United States, he was then representing the Liberal Government of Sir Francis Hincks, but when a year after, that Treaty was ratified by the legislature of the day, in the old Colonial Legislature of Canada, as Canada existed at that time, it was not the Government of Sir Francis Hincks which asked for the ratification of the treaty, but it was the Coalition Government of Sir Allan MacNab, in which [the young] Sir John A. Macdonald was a prominent Member.[178]

Later on, after the treaty had been repealed, in 1866, and when Sir John A. Macdonald was at the helm of affairs, he sent delegation after delegation to Washington to obtain a renewal of it. In 1877, when Sir John A. Macdonald introduced the famous resolution which was the origin of the National Policy, in principle as well as in idea, the object was to obtain a renewal of the treaty of Reciprocity.

Two years afterwards, Sir John having come into office, when the National Policy was put upon the statute book, you remember that one of the features of the National Policy as then introduced was a permanent offer of Reciprocity with the United States in regard to natural products.

In 1891, Sir John A. Macdonald again endeavoured to have a renewal of the treaty of 1851, and in 1892 Sir John Thompson and Mr. Foster, our own George Eulas Foster, went to Washington again and again in order to obtain a renewal of the Treaty of Reciprocity.

But, what is perhaps more significant is this: In the year 1909, when we asked the Canadian Parliament to ratify our commercial treaty with France, the Conservative Party very reluctantly agreed to that ratification, and one of the reasons given, at that time, was the possibility that we might thereby injure a successful negotiation of a treaty with the United States. Well, sir, it is not surprising that when my friend, Mr. Fielding, in the month of January, 1911, laid before Parliament the agreement which he had just concluded with the American Government for an exchange of natural products between the two countries, it is not to be wondered at, that many Members on the Conservative side rose in their places and cheered this agreement, and it is not surprising that some of the other Members on the Conservative side had to be held down by their coat tails in order to prevent them from similarly acclaiming it.

It is an open secret, so open that everyone in Ottawa knows it, that at the caucuses of the Conservative Party, which were held to ascertain whether or not the convention would be accepted, there was a great searching of hearts before their minds were at last made up to oppose the agreement. When it was ascertained that Mr. Sifton and some of the Members of the Liberal Party in the City of Toronto were opposed to the agreement, then from that date the Conservative Party made up their minds to oppose it, and they turned just as complete a somersault as ever was turned in Barnum's circus.

Now, sir, that was the attitude of the regular Conservative Party, headed by Mr. Borden. What was the attitude of the dissentient Conservative Party, headed by Mr. Monk? There would perhaps be no need of referring to it here. You gentlemen of the Province of

Quebec know that in the last election, and in the campaign which preceded it, the question of Reciprocity was not very much discussed by the dissentient Conservatives, headed by Mr. Monk. I followed the discussion very closely, and they had not much to say in regard to it. What concerned them especially was the naval question and the Manitoba School question.

The Manitoba School question, as we supposed, had been settled fifteen years ago, in so far as the Federal Government was concerned at all events. We were told by these gentlemen that the question was not settled at all, that the Laurier–Greenway settlement was no settlement, and that if they [the Conservative Party] were returned to power, then there would be a real settlement of the question.

On the naval question you also heard their pledges to the people. Let the Laurier Government be defeated, and the naval law will be wiped off the statute books as soon as Parliament assembles.

That was the attitude of the dissentient Conservatives, led by Mr. Monk.

Now, what was the attitude of the Nationalist Party, led by Mr. Bourassa? As far as the Nationalist Party and the Quebec Conservative Party are concerned, for my part I never saw any difference between them. The policy of one was the policy of the other.

What was the attitude of the jingoes of Toronto? The naval policy was not satisfactory to them, but not for the reason given by the Nationalists. The latter opposed the very idea of a navy. The jingoes wanted a navy and a contribution to the Imperial navy.

As a consequence we had all these forces, from all points of the horizon coming upon us. They created a maelstrom under which we succumbed. Well, sir, for my part let me tell you once more that I have never regretted the result personally. I certainly regret it for the country, and we have reason to regret it. However, there is no cloud which may not have a silver lining, and in view of the events which have taken place since our defeat on the twenty-first of September, I do not know that there may not even be cause for some rejoicing.

What is the compensation? The reason and the compensation is that if we have suffered defeat the consequence of our defeat has been to unmask the Nationalist and the Quebec Conservatives, and show them as they really are.

Let me ask you a question. What is the difference between a Quebec Conservative and a Quebec Nationalist? I ask the question because, so far as I am concerned, I do not know of any difference at all. If you scratch a Nationalist you are sure to find a Quebec Conservative, and if you scratch a Quebec Conservative you are sure to find a Nationalist. The only difference is that before the elections to capture the vote in the Province of Quebec, they are all Nationalists, but after the elections they are all Conservatives, to get the patronage of the Government.

Men there were who took the Nationalists and the Quebec Conservatives at their word before the last election, and who thought that they were what they represented themselves to be. They denounced Laurier, as you know, but they denounced Borden as well as Laurier. Laurier was bad, but Borden was no better. They had nothing at all to do with Borden and did not want to have anything to do with him until Borden had patronage to give, commissionerships, collectorships, even messengerships. Then they ceased to be Nationalists, and they were all Conservatives. They were tamed; so tamed as to go and eat out of his hand and lick his fingers.

Men there were who supposed that Conservatives and Nationalists were actuated by noble motives, by principles, by high ideals, who supposed that after the election they would be as firm as they were before. . . . Poor deluded men they were. They found their mistake when they saw their friends at work. They know now that the patriotism of the Nationalists and the patriotism of the Quebec

Conservatives does not spring from the heart, but from the stomach. When their stomachs are full their hearts cease to beat, and their tongues are mute.

That is the lesson which the last election has taught us, and I say that perhaps it was worth being defeated. The Quebec people now know that when men come before them and tell them that all questions which come before Parliament can be settled from the point of view of one Province, and one Province alone, irrespective of the views of the other Provinces, that these men are either charlatans or demagogues, if they are not both.

Eight months have elapsed since the last election, and, therefore, perhaps we are sufficiently removed from the heat and agitation of the contest to be able to review with calmness and impartial judgment the issue which was before the country at the time. Of course the main issue was the question of Reciprocity. Perhaps the time has come when we may look upon that question and see what it meant, and what was the value of the objections which were made against it, and what is the policy now to be followed. I say we are sufficiently removed from the heat and the agitation of the contest to be able to look at the question squarely as it is, without bias, and without prejudice.

I need not remind you that on the Conservative side froth and fury took the place of argument and reasoning. I need not tell you that Reciprocity was presented by our opponents as the first step to annexation. I need not tell you that the contest was represented as one between two flags, between the American flag and the British flag. I need not tell you that in all the Conservative papers of this city, and the other cities throughout the Dominion, there appeared every day dismal columns, under dismal headlines, out of which Conservative orators drew an endless torrent of tears and lamentations.

In so far as such tactics were pursued, for my part, I stand again today as I did at that time, and I say that all such appeals to passion and prejudice are unworthy of serious men. If it is still asserted that if we sell to the Americans wheat, cattle, apples, potatoes, fish, and lumber, we must as a necessary consequence sell them our allegiance, our nationality, our citizenship, our birthright, such an argument may scare Mr. Borden, Mr. Foster, or Mr. Monk, but it cannot scare me, nor do I believe it can scare any Canadian worthy of the name. . . .

When everything has been said against us, there remains to the credit of the Laurier Government that we have done more to create a Canadian sentiment in Canada than was ever done by any other Government. We have established Canada before the world. We have revealed Canada to itself. Nay, we did more; we were not satisfied with creating a Canadian sentiment. We fully recognized the necessity of obtaining larger markets for Canadian products, and we applied at once with a fair measure of success to obtain such markets.

You talk today of the home market. This is an expenditure of misspent energy. The home market is certainly the best of all. It is better than the English market; better than the American market; better than the French market; better than the German market, or any other market, but at the same time there is this fact to be recognized, that the Canadian market cannot absorb the whole of the natural products of Canada.

Let us take wheat as an instance. Last year the wheat crop fit for human food was about 130 million bushels. How much of that crop can Canada absorb? Canada cannot absorb more than sixty-five or seventy million bushels at the outside (fifty million for food and fifteen or twenty million bushels for seed). Our population is not more than seven million, and if the consumption per head of population is put as seven bushels of wheat, we find that we can only use about fifty million bushels for food and at the outside twenty million bushels for seed, or altogether not more than seventy million bushels. Now where would the other sixty million bushels go? You must find markets abroad.

We have the English market, the best of all next to the home market, but, if the English market is what it is today it is due to the Laurier Government and to the Fielding tariff of 1897. The British Preference has doubled our exports to Great Britain during the past fifteen years. The British preference has been a boon to Canada, a boon to England, and a boon to the British Empire, in every sense of the word. At the present time I am only speaking of it as a commercial proposition. It has done a great deal for this country in the way of advertising, and has forced the English people to take almost three times as much of our products as they did in 1896.

The same thing applies to the French market. We negotiated a treaty with France; not that there is much in the French market for us, but everything counts. The same thing may be said of the German market. Germany attempted to bully us, but strong as she was she could not succeed, and when she offered to reverse her policy and to open the gates on her side as on our side, we were ready to meet her.

The offer of the American people to trade with us was not accepted by our people, because of the very sentiment which we had created. The national spirit which we had evoked was aroused. It was strong and proud of its strength, and yet it would not and did not trust its strength. That is the only reproof which I have against the business men of Canada, that they feared American competition.

Analyze what took place last year and you will find that there is the secret of the rejection of Reciprocity. Oh! Ye of little faith! Oh! Ye Canadian business men, who refused to open wide the avenues of trade, I have more faith in you than you have in yourselves.

Will you tell me that Canadians are not the equals of Americans? Will you tell me that in a fair field we cannot compete with them and hold our own against them? Until you tell me that Canadians are not the equals of Americans, I refuse to believe that we made a mistake last year.

There was before us last year, and there is before us this year this same problem of larger markets. The agreement which we proposed last year would have largely solved that problem, but it was rejected by the Canadian people. I am a Constitutionalist, and therefore I have to accept the verdict. However, that problem is still there, just as it was last year. Not only is it still here, but it is more acute than it was last year.

The problem of larger markets is an important problem in the east, but it is more important in the west. Larger markets for the provinces east of Lake Superior are an advantage apparent to everybody, but in the provinces west of Lake Superior, in the prairie provinces, larger markets are an indispensable necessity. How shall I prove it? Let me appeal to your judgment and your experience. We have been pouring population into the Western Provinces. Every year thousands, and hundreds of thousands of acres of virgin soil are brought under cultivation. Last year the wheat crop fit for human food was about 130 million bushels. This year, if Providence blesses us at all, our wheat crop will be at least 200 million bushels. Where will the crop go?

You have had here in the City of Montreal within the last three months a gentleman who came to lecture before the Canadian Club on the conditions existing in the Prairie Provinces. I will give you his name, Mr. [R.B.] Bennett, Conservative Member for the City of Calgary. Mr. Bennett told you that unless the Northwest provinces had a larger outlet for their crops he would not answer for their allegiance. Did you hear that or did you not hear it?

If a statement of that kind had come from me, or from any of the men whom I see here associated with me, belonging to the Liberal Party, it would have been branded as treason. However, it came from a Conservative Member of Parliament, a strong

Imperialist. Coming from this source, his word could not be mistrusted. He told you plainly that he would not answer for the allegiance of the Northwest unless they were provided with larger outlets for their crops. He told you there was a possibility of secession. I do not believe it myself, but Mr. Bennett made the statement, not I.

There is something more than this. The problem of larger markets and of larger outlets was upon us last year. We wished to solve it in the way I have indicated, but the people would not have it so. This same problem was upon the new Government when they came into office, on the tenth of October last. At that time there was a crop which had just been threshed lying on the ground, waiting for transportation. The inclemency of the season threatened it with destruction; in fact destroyed some of it. There was a market almost at arms-length, but that market was closed by a high tariff and high freight rates. The Government was deluged with petitions. They did not know what to do. What do you suppose that Conservative Government did? That Government which had just been brought into office on the cry of "no intercourse at all with the United States. The trade must flow east and west, not north and south."

If, during the contest last year, I had come here and told you gentlemen of Montreal, if you defeat the Reciprocity agreement, which will open the American markets to the products of the northwest provinces, the new Government, the Conservative administration, will be forced to go to the United States and ask as an act of grace for the introduction of your products into the United States; if I said that to you, you would have told me that I was a humbug. There would have been a cry of indignation. Well, sir, the very thing which you would have denounced as humbug on my part, and which would have made you shudder, has been done by the present Government. . . .

There is, perhaps, another question to which I should draw your attention for a moment, simply for the novelty of the thing. I refer to the naval question. The novelty of the thing I say, for previous to the last election nothing else was talked of by the Conservative Party in this province; now they are as dumb as fish. It was not the trade question that was discussed before the people of the Province of Quebec during the campaign. It was the naval question.

Three years ago I was Prime Minister. We had the reins of government in our own hands. We brought before the House of Commons a resolution to the effect that Canada having reached the status she has reached – the status of a nation – should assume all the duties and all the responsibilities of a nation. Now, the duties and the responsibilities of a nation are to take care of its own defence by land and sea. That resolution was unanimously adopted in the House of Commons.

Mr. Borden spoke in favour of the resolution, and even suggested to me an amendment, which I accepted. Mr. Monk, the leader of the dissentient Conservatives in this province, did not speak in favour of it, but he told us he was in favour of it, and that he did vote for it. We did not perceive it at the time, but he told us later on that he voted for it by going to bed. That is one way of voting for a proposition, but we will not quarrel with him. If he chooses to manifest his support to a proposition by going to bed, well, all I have to say is every one to his own taste. That is not the way in which I would show my approval, but thank the Lord my views are different from Mr. Monk's views on this question, and on many others.

In any event, Mr. Borden was in favour of the resolution, and Mr. Monk was in favour of it. But, the following year, when we brought in a measure to put that resolution into execution, in the way we thought right as carrying out our duties as British subjects, and our rights as Canadians, why everyone was against it.

Mr. Borden was against it. Mr. Monk was against it, Mr. Borden and Mr. Monk agreed to destroy. They could not agree to construct. Mr. Monk was against it because we had gone too far, because we should not do anything at all. Mr. Borden was against it because we did not go far enough. Both of them agreed that the law we had put on the statute book should be repealed immediately.

Our Government was defeated, and everybody in this province expected that the law would be repealed. I expected it, in my innocence. I crave pardon from Heaven for giving them too much credit. I thought they would repeal the naval law, seeing that both sides had pledged themselves to its repeal. However, they did not do anything of the kind.

The session was called and day after day we expected a notice on the paper for the repeal of the naval law. Weeks passed, and months passed, but there was no sign of the repeal of the law. One day a young Member of the Conservative side of the House put a notice on the paper asking the Government whether it was their intention to repeal the naval law. The question was there for days, weeks, and months, and every time it was called the Prime Minister said "Stand." He was not prepared with an answer. As I told you, these men could destroy, but they cannot construct.

This young Member had been a real lion during the campaign, but before the House he was a gentle lamb. At last the question was approached and the news given out that after the session was over the Prime Minister and the Minister of Marine and Fisheries would go to England to consult the Admiralty. The session closed on the first day of April or thereabouts, and as the weeks passed, we expected an announcement that the Prime Minister and the Minister of Marine and Fisheries would go to England. About ten days ago there was a semi-official statement in the ministerial papers to the effect that Mr. Borden, Prime Minister, and the Minister of Marine and Fisheries were not going to England. Something passed during the interval because this morning we read that they are at last going. I wish them joy, and I hope they will do something.

You know what our policy is, and it was said some days ago by Mr. [Winston] Churchill, the First Lord of the Navy, that the policy would commend itself to the British people, as I believe it commends itself to the judgment of the Canadian people.

One thing I know and that is that the present Government cannot construct upon this question unless someone has to eat the leek, as happened last session upon the Manitoba School question. Upon all these questions, in a country like Canada, no one can attempt a solution from the point of view of one province alone. Upon such questions the provinces are not broad enough. You have to take in the whole of Canada, and the whole of the Canadian people. You must appeal to the best instincts of every man, irrespective of his creed, race. . . .

What has been our policy in the past, it is now and will ever remain our policy. We know by the teaching of history and by our own recent experience that questions and problems arise which have to be taken up by the men in office, whoever they may be. We know that the solution provided by a Government (although it may be the best under the circumstances) sometimes fails to command the appreciation of the people or nationality for whose benefit it is intended. History, and our own experience have taught us that it is no uncommon fate for reformers to suffer dire penalty for their courage and their foresight. When Mr. Gladstone undertook, by meeting the sentiments of the Irish people for local government, to settle the Irish problem, and to make Ireland a contented, happy, and proud Member of the United Kingdom and of the British Empire, he had to suffer, and did suffer the penalty of his courage and his foresight. He suffered the loss of friends, the loss of popularity, the loss of power, but he sowed deep in the ground, and he laid the foundation of eternal gratitude not only in the hearts of the Irish people, but in the hearts of the British subjects all over the world. He did not live to see the full fruition of his labour, but we are now witnesses of his labours coming to fruit.

We, too, in our humble way, and with our modest force, we have sown seed in the ground. We had to champion causes which were not immediately popular, such as the establishment of the Canadian navy. We have had to suffer the penalty of our courage and foresight. We have lost friends. We have lost power. We have lost popularity. So far as I am concerned, however, I tell you again that I regret nothing.

The seed will still germinate. Happier than Gladstone, it may be my lot to see it reach its full maturity; but that is not with me the supreme consideration. The supreme consideration I have given to you at the beginning, and I give it to you at the end: My orders are to fight.

By Arthur Milnes

There are great lessons for political parties today in studying Laurier in the aftermath of his party's defeat in the 1911 election.

Perhaps most striking in light of present-day practice in Canadian politics is the fact that despite his loss Sir Wilfrid remained his party's leader until his death in 1919. During this period he worked tirelessly to modernize Liberal organizational methods and structures. Like those in any long-term governing party, these had grown stale while he and his team occupied Canada's Treasury benches in the Commons: they needed a refit.

Today, in stark contrast, defeated leaders are usually eagerly tossed aside by parties to achieve a faster and simpler political victory at the earliest opportunity.

Another great leader who did not stand down and head off to retirement after a crushing defeat was Lester B. Pearson. While rightly considered today one of our greatest modern-era prime ministers, he also proved one of the finest Opposition leaders Canada has ever seen.

When defeated in 1958, when John Diefenbaker reduced his party to a small rump in the Commons, Pearson got to work. He attracted new and youthful candidates (the famous photograph of him welcoming three future prime ministers – Jean Chrétien, Pierre Trudeau, and John Turner – to cabinet is testament to his success in this area), reorganized the party by bringing in talent like Keith Davey and Walter Gordon, and fostered crucial policy discussions, such as the famous Kingston Conference held at Queen's University in 1960.

Studying the Opposition periods of Laurier, Pearson, and other leaders such as Robert L. Stanfield shows that important contributions can be made by parties in Opposition. It is also worth noting that after Laurier's death, leadership of the Liberal Party passed into the hands of William Lyon Mackenzie King. He then went on to serve as prime minister for approximately twenty-two years.

In turn, upon his retirement as prime minister in 1968, Lester Pearson saw the Liberal Party pass the baton to Pierre Trudeau, who then went on to serve as prime minister for almost the entire period between 1968 and 1984.

On the Conservative side, Robert Stanfield never became prime minister but fought three federal elections as leader. Along the way he attracted and encouraged the participation of young Tories, such as Joe Clark, Hugh Segal, Lowell Murray, and Brian Mulroney (to name only a few) in party affairs. They too would go on to leadership roles – two of them becoming prime minister – in the years after Stanfield stepped down.

So, in recalling Laurier's party address from 1912 and his continued service as leader of the Opposition for almost eight years after the 1911 election, one wonders if today's parties might better serve themselves and Canada if a leader's resignation after a defeat or two at the polls was something they reconsidered.

NEW POLICY FOR
CHANGING TIMES

FEDERATED LIBERAL CLUBS OF
ONTARIO BANQUET, HAMILTON, ONTARIO
NOVEMBER 26, 1913[179]

In this City of Hamilton, which today, as I understand, prides itself on a population of over one hundred thousand, go into the homes of the workingmen and mechanics, of the clerk in the dry good stores and the clerk in the warehouse, even the professional man and the clergyman, and the question which is discussed at this moment is not the price of Dreadnoughts; it is the problem of making ends meet as between expenditure and income. (Hear, hear)

It is true I might say something about reciprocity but I have no recriminations to make. The problem is before us. Let us bury the past and look to the future. There our duty lies. The situation requires action, prompt, unhesitating action. The policy I give you at this moment, the policy I believe every patriot in Canada ought now to support, and the policy I believe it to be the duty of the government to immediately inaugurate, is a policy of absolutely free food – food free from customs duty. (Prolonged cheering)

It will be said to me if you advocate that policy do you not advocate a revision of the tariff to that extent. Certainly I do. (Renewed cheering) But somebody will tell me that the tariff which is in force today is the Fielding tariff of 1897. So it is, but the Fielding tariff was made for the needs of that time, not for all eternity. It has been the policy of the Liberal Party at all times to stand so far as possible for stability in tariff, but when the needs of the people call for action, action must be taken. (Renewed cheers)

During the fifteen years that we were in office we had been very chary in making an alteration in the tariff. The reason is that when we place a tariff of customs duties we create an atmosphere in which our manufacturers and industries are developed, and if you were to cut out or remove that tariff all of a sudden the result would be very injurious. We proclaimed more than once during the fifteen years that we were in power that we would be prepared from time to time to revise the tariff, and whenever we found that it was pressing unduly upon any section of the community we would be prepared to remedy the condition accordingly. But I am glad to say that during those fifteen years there never came to us a demand for an alteration in the tariff. There were men who thought they could do better than we did. You have seen them work, and this is the result of their work.

A table of statistics lately compiled by the British Board of Trade . . . has stated that the cost of living had increased seven per cent in Great Britain during the last decade, and in Canada one per cent. Now just one point here.

And we have not reached the end of the high cost of living. The cost of living will be higher in two or three months than it is today. What is the cause? The recent reductions in the American tariff; milk, cream, swine, sheep . . . and many other articles have been placed upon the free list in the United States. Therefore these products are already rushing towards the United States. We know in the matter of cattle alone they are rushing carloads every day from all parts of Canada where there are cattle towards the American market.

But these articles I have named cannot come back free from the United States into Canada, and if no products of the same kind can come back from the United States into Canada the result is that all of the articles which are the staple food of the people are growing scarcer in Canada and the price increases, as that is a natural condition of things.

The situation requires prompt action and the policy which I give you, the policy which I think every patriotic Canadian ought to support at the present time, is that the duty of the government at Ottawa is to give us absolute free food of all kinds with no duty.

I call you to fight, you strong and virile young Liberals. (Cheers) I call you to fight with me, to fight the battle of public service, to fight the battle of your country and its citizenship. We will fight together. (Cheers) Never mind reverses if they come. Fight on. (Renewed cheers) Political life is often punctuated by big reverses. Keep on, on, on, meeting success without exultation, facing reverse without despondency.

Stand to your ideas. Stand fast, stand true. Fulfill the great duties that belong to British citizenship. Keep your idea before you like the cloud by day and the pillar of fire by night which guided the people of God from the tribulations of bondage to the Promised Land.

Let my last word be this: Let us all together, old and young, join hands, gird our loins, buckle on our armour, unfurl our standard and go forward together in service, in earnest, whole-hearted, unselfish service for Canada first, Canada last, and Canada forever.

By Steve Paikin

I was born and raised in Hamilton, Ontario, a proud city, but one which has yet to provide Canadians with a prime minister or premier. Having said that, we've had our share of political superstars.

From an early age, I can remember taking the bus downtown to see, in Gore Park, one of the handful of statues honouring our first prime minister,

Sir John A. Macdonald. I have no doubt that statue planted a seed in my head, stoking my curiosity about politics.

When I was a child, my mother (even though fiercely non-partisan) chaired a civic "welcoming committee" for the city on the occasion of Prime Minister Pierre Trudeau's visit. He would be in town to mark Hamilton's 125th anniversary. That was a big deal, and even though I didn't meet the PM, I did enjoy seeing the picture of Pierre and Margaret Trudeau, and Marnie Paikin.

As I got older, I did have many brushes with well-known political figures. Lincoln Alexander – Canada's first-ever black federal cabinet minister – was a family friend and someone for whom we had tremendous admiration.

In fact, Linc wasn't the only trailblazer from Hamilton. Even though it was before my time, I surely remember stories about the first woman ever appointed to the federal cabinet – Hamilton's Ellen Fairclough, in John Diefenbaker's 1957 government.

Twenty years after Dief broke that barrier, I had the honour of meeting him in Hamilton at a dinner in his honour. With beautiful penmanship, he signed a copy of the Bill of Rights that his Government passed in 1960, the same year of my birth. It hangs in my living room to this day.

Another political highlight of my years in Hamilton was a purchase my parents Marnie and Larry made from a charity auction. It was "Lunch with the Opposition Leader at Queen's Park" for my brother Jeff and me. The Liberal leader at the time was Stuart Smith, originally from Montreal but now representing Hamilton West. I still have fond memories of two teenaged Paikin boys breaking bread and talking politics in the legislative dining room with the leader of Her Majesty's Loyal Opposition. I still occasionally get together with Dr. Smith and forty years later we joke about that first meeting which was so memorable for me, and astonishingly he actually remembers it too!

Of course, I continue to see another Hamilton-based Opposition leader on regular occasions – Ontario NDP leader Andrea Horwath – although that's usually in our studios at TVO.

Thanks to my parents' (always non-partisan) involvement in politics, I met the legendary mayor, Victor Kennedy Copps, and then, as a journalist, did stories on his daughter Sheila, who eventually became deputy prime minister.

We knew Bob Bratina when he was the Hamilton Tiger-Cats play-by-play announcer and then watched him become mayor of The Ambitious City.

One of the most thrilling political leadership conventions I ever attended was in Hamilton's Copps Coliseum. In 1992, more than two thousand Liberals selected their first-ever woman leader, Lyn McLeod, on the fifth ballot, at one in the morning, by just nine votes over Murray Elston. I anchored the coverage of that event on CBC–TV, and it became another indelible memory of political experiences in the steel city.

The airport in Hamilton is named after John Munro, the Trudeau cabinet minister who had such an important impact on the city, yet finished his political career still trying to win just one more election and a chance to serve. I wrote a chapter about John in my first book and was grateful to spend so much time with a guy who was as tough as the city. He had to be, given all the challenges he faced in life.

Hamilton may not have provided the country with anyone as spectacular as Sir Wilfrid Laurier. But it has made its own modest contribution to, as Laurier so magnificently put it, Canada first, Canada last, Canada always.

Steve Paikin is the anchor of *The Agenda with Steve Paikin* on TVO. His seventh book, *Bill Davis: Nation-Builder and Not So Bland After All*, was published by Dundurn Press in October 2016.

SIZING UP A FUTURE PRIME MINISTER: LAURIER ON ARTHUR MEIGHEN

HOUSE OF COMMONS, OTTAWA, ONTARIO
JANUARY 19, 1914

The new feature that we have on the Treasury Benches, at long last, is a Solicitor General. It took a long time to fill that vacancy. The mantle remained suspended for something like two years, but at last it has fallen on the shoulders of my Honourable Friend (Mr. Meighen).[180] My compliments to the Solicitor General. I speak my mind frankly when I state that I believe he is well qualified for the position – well qualified from the legal point of view and still better qualified from the political point of view.

He has been in the House of Commons for some years. It has been my pleasure to observe him almost from the day he came here; and almost from his first appearance we have had evidences not a few that he is endowed with a very subtle mind, that he is a past master dialectician. But if I must speak my mind fully and give my Honourable Friend . . . all the credit to which he is entitled, I must say that while he is also a clever rhetorician, he is still cleverer a sophist. There are few men inside this House or outside it who can clothe fallacies and paradoxes with more fitting garments than can the Honourable Gentleman. When it comes to the task of making the worse appear the better reason, few men can do more than my Honourable Friend the new Solicitor General. . . . But the mystery to me is here: The qualifications of my Honourable Friend . . . were obvious; not only we but the public, everybody, knew them. Why, then, has it taken so long for my Right Honourable Friend the Prime Minister to discover them? I cannot imagine that my Right Honourable Friend with his acute mind did not see that which was obvious to everybody.

The mystery is why he should have allowed twelve months, twenty-four months, to elapse, without filling the portfolio which he has at last filled. Of course, the reason may have been that, while he was as well aware as others of the qualification of [Meighen], yet that Honourable Gentleman was not the only pebble on the beach. Looking before me now, I can see one, two, three, four, five, six –

Some Honourable Members: Oh, oh.

Laurier: Yes, six I can see, the friends of each of whom believed that he was entitled to occupy the position, and each one of whom believed that he was more entitled to it than his neighbour. How is it that they are left and [Meighen] chosen? That is where the subtle mind of my Honourable Friend . . . served him. That subtle mind taught him that something more than legal ability must play a part in the choice to be made. He was not satisfied to show only his ability as a member of this House; he showed his teeth also. And when the Prime Minister saw those sharp teeth bared and ready to sink into his quivering flesh, all hesitation was gone.

You will remember that towards the end of last session, the Bank Bill came back from the Senate, with some amendments. The Minister of Finance, who was in charge of the Bill, accepted the amendments, and explained them to the House. He said that they were trivial, nominal, and of no consequence; that although they were, perhaps, of some improvement by the measure, they affected in no way the principle of it. Thereupon there was a storm of indignation, or rather of pretended indignation, on the other side of the House. Some Honourable Gentlemen rose to protest, and the most valiant of these was [Meighen].

He attacked the amendments most violently; he said that they changed the whole tenor of the Bill; he shot at the Senate, which he could not reach, and over the head of the Government, whom he wished not to hurt. It was more than an attack; it was a warning.

The Right Honourable Gentleman remembered a page in the parliamentary history of England, upon which it is recorded that when Sir Robert Walpole was Prime Minister a young cavalry officer was elected to Parliament, and the moment he had spoken the Prime Minister said to his friend, "that warhorse must be muzzled." It is evident that when my Honourable Friend the Prime Minister heard [Meighen] he said to himself that the Honourable Gentleman would have to be muzzled. Unfortunately, as my Honourable Friend has chosen the great William Pitt, Earl of Chatham, as his model, and as the Minister of Finance has gone so far as to approve the action of the Senate, my Honourable Friend the new Solicitor General will have to use his best ability to approve also, whatever may be his own feelings.

By Michael A. Meighen

Some years ago, my close friend and colleague John Lynch-Staunton, then leader of the Opposition in the Senate and who has now, sadly, passed away, achieved something of great substance and importance. While it did not generate many headlines or clips on the television news, it is something for which Canadians — particularly those who work diligently to promote the study and understanding of our history — will be thanking him for decades to come.

I speak of course of Lynch-Staunton's work piloting the Sir John A. Macdonald Day and Sir Wilfrid Laurier Day Act through Parliament. This Act, approved in 2002, made the birthdays of our two greatest prime ministers (January 11 for Macdonald and November 20 for Laurier) special days of recognition on our calendar.

Some might ask why I, a lifelong and very proud Conservative, would encourage Canadians to honour Laurier, who, after all, was Canada's greatest Liberal prime minister. In this, I take my lead from my grandfather Arthur Meighen, an opponent of Laurier's who sat across from him in Parliament for many years.

At the time of Sir Wilfrid's death in 1919, my grandfather, a member of Sir Robert Borden's cabinet, took my aunt Lillian, then only nine years old, with him to the funeral visitation where he paid his respects to Lady Laurier and viewed Sir Wilfrid's body.

"You're too young to understand," he said to her, "but I want you to be able to say that you saw one of the finest men I have ever known."

Decades later, Arthur Meighen, in one of his final public addresses, delivered in Toronto in December 1957, also made sure he recognized his worthy foe from years before:

"There was never a man, not in my lifetime, from whom one could learn so much of the art of leadership as from Sir Wilfrid Laurier," he said. "One of the lamentations that I still indulge in is that I did not learn more from him."

What we can see, however, from Laurier's "welcome" to my grandfather in the Commons when Arthur Meighen became Solicitor General, is something sadly often missing from today's politics. I speak, of course, about mutual respect between political opponents. One can be tough in debate – as Laurier was on my grandfather on January 9, 1914 – when facing an opponent, but that does not mean that person is a personal enemy.

Outside of the cut and thrust of often fierce debates and disagreements in the House of Commons, Laurier and Arthur Meighen enjoyed cordial and respectful relations. Both Laurier and my grandfather cared deeply about

Canada and only differed in their approaches to improving the country's present and future.

Today, as we mark the 175th anniversary of Laurier's birth, I believe as strongly as my grandfather did that great figures from our history like Sir Wilfrid and Sir John A. should be celebrated and honoured, regardless of party.

Like John A., Laurier had that special touch and talent that makes nation-building possible. He was a visionary leader who built upon the foundations laid by Macdonald and who brought Canada into the twentieth century with success and a healthy confidence. In a country so divided in the early days – divided by race, religion, and geography – the guiding principle and mission of his life was the unity of our nation.

Some have said he was the perfect prime minister – too French sometimes for the English, and too English sometimes for the French. He challenged both main language groups in Canada, while simultaneously opening the door to the settlement of western Canada by immigrants from Eastern Europe.

Shortly before his death, Laurier addressed a group of youths in Ontario. His words are as inspiring today and we would do well to recall his advice well into the future:

"I shall remind you that already many problems rise before you: Problems of race division, problems of creed differences, problems of economic conflict, problems of national duty and national aspiration," Laurier said. "Let me tell you that for the solution of these problems you have a safe guide, an unfailing light if you remember that faith is better than doubt and love is better than hate. Let your aim and purpose, in good report or ill, in victory or defeat, be so to live, so to strive, so to serve as to do your part to raise even higher the standard of life and living."

As a nation, we don't do enough to honour, celebrate, and cherish our history. Great speeches like those of Laurier should be studied more often in our schools and on Parliament Hill.

Our national story needs to be retold, again and again, to each succeed-ing generation. With polls demonstrating that many Canadians have difficultly even recalling the name of our first prime minister, we must do better than we have.

Neither Laurier nor Macdonald (nor Arthur Meighen) were perfect men or leaders. But in the study of their lives and legacies we are reminded of the skill, vision, and courage it took to build what we have today: a nation that is the envy of the world.

Michael A. Meighen served in the Senate of Canada from 1990 to 2012 and is now chancellor of McGill University.

THE PARLIAMENTARY FIRE

HOUSE OF COMMONS (MEETING FOR THE FIRST TIME
AT THE VICTORIA MEMORIAL MUSEUM)
FEBRUARY 4, 1916

The old Parliament Building in which we sat yesterday, and which has been identified with the life of the Canadian people since Confederation, is a mass of ruins. Great though the material loss is to every Member of Parliament, to those of the present day and to those of an older generation still living, the loss of life is still more appalling. We had become attached to the scene and to everything which appertained to that building.

To the people of Ottawa especially it will be a sad loss because it was part of the life of the community, as it was the pride of every Canadian who came to Ottawa to see the British flag floating on the stately tower. The noble building will rise again with no loss of time and we will see it again at no distant date, in its pristine beauty.

But what can we say about the loss of life? We had yesterday in almost the full vigour of youth, Mr. [Bowan Brown] Law, the member for Yarmouth, whom we are not again likely to see in this life, and who a few hours before had given us his views on a very important question. Now we know his body is in that mass of ruins.

We had at the table an officer [René Laplante, assistant clerk of the House of Commons] who had been for very nearly twenty years a faithful servant of the House of Commons, a man whose courtesy, ability, activity and kindness every member had learned to appreciate. How he disappeared, we do not know, but unfortunately there is no hope that we will be able to see him again in life.

And what have we to say, Sir, of the loss of those two young ladies [Florence Bray and Mable Morin], young happy mothers, young happy wives, bright as the lark in the blue sky of the morning, full of life, full of contentment, and appreciating the benefit of their station visiting old friends in their present high station, and now no more?

I have nothing more to say except to endorse what has been said by my right hon. friend the Prime Minister that we should go on at once with the business of the country. When we look at the mass of ruin there on the hill, and when we know that it is the result of an accident, we are reminded of the ruins of Louvain, and of the ruins of Rheims, caused not by accident, but by the wickedness of a cruel foe. If there is anything which the present calamity should impress upon us, it is the desirability of going on with our work and doing everything to bring those cruel murderers to justice.

By Russell Mills

When the sun came up in Ottawa on Friday, February 4, 1916, Canada's capital was in shock. The historic Centre Block of the young nation's Parliament Buildings was a smoking pile of rubble.

A careless smoker in the Reading Room in the building's northwest corner had triggered a fire shortly before nine the previous evening. The fire spread rapidly and less than five hours later the Victoria Clock Tower fell in a blazing heap. Only the Parliamentary Library survived behind its metal doors. Seven people died in the fire, including a member of Parliament and the assistant clerk of the House of Commons.

Since Canada was at war, with sixty thousand troops already in the trenches in France and Belgium, rumours of sabotage swept the community. A fire caused by smoking seemed too simple an explanation for many.

In this climate of confusion and panic, Canada's leaders realized that their first priority was to ensure that the business of a nation at war continued uninterrupted.

The cabinet held a quick meeting in the Château Laurier and made a decision to move the House of Commons to the new Victoria Memorial Museum, which had been completed four years earlier as the home of the National Gallery and National Museum. (The building now houses the Museum of Nature.)

The day following the fire, while the ruins were still smoking, shocked members of Parliament gathered in the museum's auditorium for their first session outside the Centre Block.

Prime Minister Sir Robert Borden stood to speak first and focussed on the need for the government to continue at once with the business of the country. Sir Wilfrid Laurier, leader of the Liberal Party and the longest-serving parliamentarian, stood to respond.

The seventy-four-year-old Laurier's remarks were short and pointed. He supported Prime Minister Borden's determination to continue Canada's business and paid tribute to those who had lost their lives in the fire. He also tried to calm panic by describing the blaze as an accident, but cleverly linked the determination of Canadians to continue business as usual to the war effort in Europe.

In a little more than three years Laurier would be lying in state in the same museum as part of the largest funeral Ottawa had ever seen. He never sat in the new Centre Block's House of Commons, which would house its first session of Parliament in 1920, a year after Laurier's death. The new building, complete with the majestic Peace Tower, was finished in 1927.

In his brief remarks on that sombre February day, Laurier drew attention to what he described as the "sad loss" for the people of the capital because of the great pride they took in the Parliament Buildings as a symbol of Canada's sovereignty and democracy.

That sentiment has only strengthened in the century after 1916 as the National Capital Region has grown in importance along with Canada's role in the world. In recent years we have seen Canadians stand up to protest any use or activity that they believe would diminish their precious Parliamentary Precinct.

Sir Wilfrid would be pleased.

Russell Mills graduated from the University of Western Ontario. He spent more than thirty-five years in the newspaper industry and served as editor and publisher of the *Ottawa Citizen* and president of the Southam Newspaper Group. He is now chair of the National Capital Commission and president of the Michener Foundation, which supports public service journalism.

TRIBUTE TO
SIR CHARLES TUPPER

HOUSE OF COMMONS, OTTAWA, ONTARIO

FEBRUARY 7, 1916

Mr. Speaker, the House of Commons will honour itself, even more than it will honour the memory of Sir Charles Tupper, by testifying in the most solemn manner its appreciation of the many services and arduous labours of one who was in his time, and who must remain for all time upon its roll of honour, one of its most illustrious members, one who contributed in no small degree to making Canada what it is today.

Sir Charles Tupper was the last survivor of that galaxy of strong and able men whom the Canadian people delight to honour with the name of Fathers of Confederation. Amongst the able men, who in the fall of 1864, assembled in the City of Quebec with the object of finding a basis of union for the then disjointed provinces of British North America, and whose united efforts brought forth the Canadian Confederation, the name of Tupper stands eminent amongst the most eminent. Fifty years and more have passed since that date, and perhaps now, we are sufficiently removed from those stormy times to be able to frame a correct estimate of the part played by the statesmen of Canada in that intensely dramatic period of our history.

Undoubtedly to George Brown was due the first initiation of Confederation. He it was, who, by his strong and persevering agitation against the unwieldy union of Upper and Lower Canada, directed the destinies of Canada towards the Confederation of the older provinces of British North America. It seems to me to be equally true that it was Sir George Cartier who first put the idea into shape when he set upon it the seal of his essentially practical mind, and brought to it the support of the one province which was material to the idea, if the idea was ever to become a fact.

By his talent and ability, Galt[181] lent aid to the movement; still more did he do so by obtaining for it the influential adhesion of the strong minority in the province of Quebec, of which he was the illustrious representative. It was the good fortune of Tilley[182] to be able, almost from the first, to bring his province to support the idea with a minimum of division and difficulty.

Macdonald was the last to come into line. It is of record that for many years he objected to any change in then existing condition of things, and only a few days before the coalition of 1864 he had almost passionately antagonized the very idea of a federal union. But when he did adopt the principle he became at once the captain and the pilot. It was his master hand that took hold of the helm, met difficulties as they arose, arrived at solutions of unforeseen obstacles, and steadily and unerringly directed the course until port was reached.

And what was the part of Tupper? In his day, this question of Confederation antagonized friends and divided foes. Now that we may look upon it in the calm judgment of history, it must be admitted, I think, that Tupper brought to the cause more firm conviction and took more chances than did anyone else. It must be remembered that at that time Nova Scotia was completely against him, and that instead of using time and patience to win the province over to the idea of Confederation, he forced it into the union by the doubtful authority of a dying legislature.

The grandeur of the idea strongly appealed to his mind, and he would not let pass the opportunity which if missed might not occur again for many years. If he erred at all, he erred because he loved not wisely but too well. Indeed, in order to understand the action of Sir Charles Tupper at this important juncture in the history of our country, we must remember what was the chief characteristic of the man. In my judgment the chief characteristic of Tupper was courage; courage which no obstacle could down, which rushed to the assault, and which, if repulsed, came back to the combat again and again; courage which battered and hammered, perhaps not always judiciously, but always effectively; courage which never admitted defeat and which in the midst of overwhelming disaster ever maintained the proud carriage of unconquerable defiance.

This attribute of courage was the dominant feature of his whole public career, and perhaps never shone more prominently than in the manner in which he entered public life. It had not been his lot to be born to wealth or affluence. The son of a poor Baptist clergyman, he had succeeded by his own efforts in obtaining an education, and winning a diploma in the medical profession. He was a young practitioner, not known at all outside the precincts of his own town, and hardly known within them, when with splendid audacity he threw himself against one who was the darling of the people, the most potent influence in Nova Scotia, and perhaps the brightest impersonation of intellect that ever adorned the halls of a legislature in any part of what is now Canada.

Joseph Howe was then the member for Cumberland.[183] In the Province of Nova Scotia there is a tradition still extant, transmitted from father to son, and repeated at many firesides, that on one occasion, when Howe had addressed a meeting of his constituents and he brought his auditors to a pitch of enthusiasm even greater than that which his magnetic eloquence had ever before elicited, a young man rose from the audience to reply. It is stated that Howe was somewhat surprised and perhaps not a little amused but at once yielded assent with something like patronizing condescension.

If he was surprised at first, he had greater reason for surprise when he listened to the address of his hitherto unknown opponent. He found that in the speech of this young man there was meat and substance which moved the people and which gave cause for reflection and worry. The tradition further has it, that when Howe returned to Halifax he stated to his friends that he had met in Cumberland a young doctor who would be a tower of strength to the Conservatives and a thorn in the side of the Liberals.

The truth of his prediction was soon borne out, even at his own expense. At the elections which followed in 1855 young Tupper came forward against Howe in the county of Cumberland and wrested it from him. Howe at that time was at the zenith of his fame and it may certainly be said of his successful opponent that no one ever crossed the portals of any legislature through so wide an entrance.

Sir William Johnson was the leader of the Conservatives in Nova Scotia. He was a man of eminent ability, but being far advanced in years and in poor health, was only too glad to rely on the services of a young man of so much promise. From the day that young Tupper came to the fore in the legislature of Nova Scotia he became the guiding spirit of his party and the inspiration of all his followers. Almost from that day his life became associated with the life of Canada, because it was only a few years afterwards, when he had become premier of his province, that the movement for Confederation was suddenly started. In that movement for Confederation, with all the excitement that it produced, and with all the agitation to which it gave birth, he found a genial field for his great parliamentary ability.

I have said that courage was his chief characteristic; but it was not his only characteristic. His mind had been cast in a broad mould. Whatever question he had to deal with he never approached it from the narrow sphere of parochial limitation; on the contrary, he approached it always from the broadest conception it was susceptible of.

When I entered this House, more than forty years ago, these were the two things which particularly struck me in him. He was then in the prime of life and in the full maturity of his powers; he seemed to me the very incarnation of the parliamentary athlete, always strong, always ready to accept battle and to give battle. Though often my judgment was against him, in every case I could not say that he was animated by anything else than the broadest view of Canadian problems.

When Confederation had become an accomplished fact he rose to the front in the broader arena, just as he had taken the first rank in the legislature of his own province. From the day that he first entered the Chamber of the House of Commons, now unfortunately destroyed, his power was at once asserted and at once acknowledged by everybody.

He came into the Federal House under the most distressing circumstances, for at the elections of 1867, the first after Confederation, his whole province had gone against him; he alone had succeeded in retaining a seat. His conduct under these circumstances was worthy of all praise. He applied himself with untiring zeal and unselfishness to the task of binding the wounds of his province, and of reconciling the people to the new conditions. At first he met with but indifferent success; the feeling of resentment persistent only to be assuaged by the soothing hand of time. He had not the supreme gift of which Sir John A. Macdonald was pre-eminently the master: that of reconciling conflicting elements and, with the minimum of friction, of bringing them together as if they had always been one.

In this House his name must ever remain attached to two measures – measures very different in character, but each of which brought forth the particular qualities with which he was endowed; I refer to protection, and the Canadian Pacific Railway.

This is not the time nor the occasion to discuss protection as an economic principle, but I think everybody, friend or foe, must admit that the introduction of protection into Canada was, be it for weal or woe, due to Sir Charles Tupper. Sir John A. Macdonald, as in the case of Confederation, had at first been rather indifferent and doubtful; Sir Charles Tupper never had a doubt. He it was who first became its advocate in this House, and he it was who carried on the agitation in the country; and in my humble judgment, great as was the personality and prestige of Sir John A. Macdonald, the victory of 1878 was due more to Sir Charles Tupper than to anyone else. But it was not he, after all, who introduced the principle of protection as an actual measure. He had been the champion, but he was not its artisan in this House. That honour was reserved for Sir Leonard Tilley.

But if Sir Charles Tupper did not introduce the protective measure in this House, it was simply because he did not choose to do so. He might have had the portfolio of Finance, but he rather chose the portfolio of Public Works, which at that time included railways. With this portfolio he had the occasion to attach his name to another very great measure, the construction of the Canadian Pacific Railway.

All parties in this country had been in favour of a transcontinental railway, but no party had taken up the question with anything like serious earnestness until Sir Charles Tupper took it up with all the vigour of his nature. He organized the syndicate which built the railway. These terms were much criticized as extravagant and yet though we may yet criticize the terms granted the syndicate as extravagant – such was the immensity of the enterprise that it was more than once on the eve of collapse.

Nothing daunted the courage of Sir Charles Tupper. He never had any doubt of its ultimate success, and it was his good fortune to see all his predictions more than fulfilled. Sir Charles Tupper had reached the zenith of his fame and power in this House when suddenly he withdrew from parliamentary life to accept the High Commissionership in London. The reasons which induced him to that step never were given to the public. But whatever they might have been we who were his opponents thought that he had committed a great mistake. Undoubtedly his services in London were honourable and useful to the country, but in my opinion he was more fitted for parliamentary life, and his services to the country would have been still greater had he remained on the floor of this Parliament.

Though absent from Ottawa and in far-away London, his heart never deserted the field of his former activities, and whenever there was a battle to be fought he appeared on the scene, and with his characteristic vigour, was always in the thickest of the fray. Next to Sir John A. Macdonald, he was undoubtedly in his time the most powerful figure in the Conservative Party. Indeed, it has always been a mystery to me and to those who sat on this side of the House that Sir Charles Tupper was not sent for when the Old Chieftain died. He was sent for at last, but then it was too late. The battle was already lost, and notwithstanding the vigour and brilliancy with which he threw himself into the battle, he could not redeem the fortunes of his party.

The public life of Sir Charles Tupper ended with the elections of 1900, when he had reached the age of almost eighty years. His strong constitution had at last been shaken by a life of arduous labour, and he withdrew to a well-earned rest. But though he retired from public life and to the seclusion of his family circle, he continued from day to day to follow with passionate interest the fortunes of Canada. In that daily spectacle he had this great satisfaction, that the correctness of his estimate of the resources of this country, when they were still unknown and undeveloped, was abundantly justified.

When at last the end came his eyes closed upon a Canada whose population had doubled and more than doubled, whose national revenue had tripled and quadrupled, whose commerce had risen from a comparatively small figure to the billion dollar mark and more, whose products in agriculture and industry had reached figures that would have seemed fantastic in the first year of the Union – a Canada whose people were united even to the shedding of their blood in the defence and for the triumph of those principles of freedom and justice which the Fathers of Confederation had placed under the aegis of British institutions.

To say that the life of Sir Charles Tupper was without fault would be to say what cannot be said of any human life. But it must be said, and should ever be remembered, that but for the life of Sir Charles Tupper Canada would not be what it is today.

By the Honourable Lowell Murray

At seventy-four Sir Charles Tupper was the oldest person ever to become prime minister, his sixty-nine days in office the shortest in Canadian history, and his lifespan the longest at ninety-four years. These details were of little importance to Sir Wilfrid Laurier. His tribute was a brilliant, generous, and – with one significant omission – full appraisal of Tupper's forty-five-year public life and his crucial role in the most important political decisions in nineteenth-century Canada. Tupper had campaigned for union of the colonies when he was premier of Nova Scotia, years before John A. Macdonald's 1864 conversion to the idea; he was the first to advocate trade protectionism in the Commons; and the 1878 election victory of the Conservatives' "national policy" was primarily due to him. His name was attached to "another great measure," the Canadian Pacific Railway. There again, Tupper – according to Pierre Berton's The National Dream – *had to persuade a skeptical Macdonald of the need for a through line from Nipissing, Ontario, to the west coast.*

Laurier's references to Tupper's eminence as a parliamentarian reminds us of a long lost time when Parliament was at the centre of our national life and parliamentary skills a top requisite for success in politics. Tupper had left Ottawa in mid-career to become high commissioner to the U.K. A mistake, Laurier said – "He was more fitted for parliamentary life and would have done more for Canada had he remained on the floor of this Parliament." Among the abilities and achievements of more recent prime ministers, parliamentary skills would be unlikely to rate even a mention. Of course, more recent parliamentarians would be unlikely to round on their tormentors in the style of those days and Laurier draws a veil over Tupper's gift for invective. Tupper once described journalist Gordon Brown (son of George) as "drawing venom from the depths of his own black heart" and Donald Smith (whom he later embraced as leader of a syndicate financing the CPR) as "a mean treacherous coward."

Laurier said of Tupper that his chief characteristic was courage. He was explicitly referring to Tupper's persistence in fighting for Confederation when Nova Scotia "was completely against him," although twenty years earlier – in the 1896 debate on the Manitoba Schools bill – he savaged Tupper for having forced Confederation down Nova Scotia throats "by the brute force of a mechanical majority in a moribund Parliament."

Sir Wilfrid also said of Tupper that his mind was cast "in a broad mould," that he never approached a question narrowly but from the broadest possible conception. Could he have been thinking of the Manitoba Schools issue, which was central to the 1896 election that brought Laurier to fifteen years in the Prime Minister's Office and ended Tupper's brief tenure there? Curiously, Laurier's tribute to Tupper does not even mention that historic election. The campaign was described by Laurier's great admirer and biographer J.W. Dafoe as "on both sides lively, violent and unscrupulous. The Conservatives had two sets of arguments; and so had the Liberals." In Quebec, Liberals argued the inadequacy of the proposed remedial legislation and the need for negotiation; Conservatives campaigned as champions of the Catholic (mostly French) minority. Elsewhere in Canada they invoked respect for the British Privy Council ruling authorizing remedial legislation, while the Liberals defended provincial autonomy.

Still, there was no ambivalence in Tupper's speech introducing the bill for second-reading debate in the Commons. As told in O.D. Skelton's Life and Letters of Sir Wilfrid Laurier, *Tupper emphasized "the protection of minorities as the indispensable condition of Confederation, the foundation, therefore, of all Canada's later greatness." Almost identical words have been uttered by prime ministers at defining moments in our history down to our own time.*

Nova Scotia's Lowell Murray served in the Senate of Canada from 1979 until 2011 and was a leading member of Prime Minister Brian Mulroney's cabinet.

FAITH IS BETTER THAN DOUBT,
LOVE IS BETTER THAN HATE

LONDON, ONTARIO
OCTOBER 11, 1916[184]

Perhaps the occasion is not inappropriate that I should endeavour to set forth once again the traditions and hope and the ideals which have come to us from a long line of strong and patriotic men and which it has been my lot to endeavour to apply. Many questions have had to be solved during the last forty years and we have to apply their lesson to the conditions in which Canada and the Empire find themselves.

I need not tell you that we meet under the shadow of a terrible war which for the past two years has been desolating Europe and engrossing the attention of the civilized world. Neither would it be amiss if once more I recall that this is a war for civilization. If there be anyone in this audience, or elsewhere who may be of the opinion that this has been said too often that it might be left unsaid, I beg to dissent. It must be repeated and again, repeated so as to convince once more one and all in this country that the cause is worthy of every sacrifice. . . . (Cheers)

And so saying I abate not a jot of my lifelong profession, reiterated in the House of Commons and upon many a platform of the country, that I am a pacifist. I have always been against militarism and I see no reason why I should be on the contrary. I see many reasons why I should not change, but still stand true to the professions of my whole life. But it has been clear to all and the pacifists: to the Radicals of England; to the Labour Party of England; to the Radicals, nay to all classes in France: to the Radicals of Italy, that in face of the avowed intention of Germany to dominate the world, in face of their blatant assumptions and complacent belief in being the "superman"; in face of their brutal assertions that force and force alone was the only law – it was clear, I say, to all pacifists that nothing would avail but such a victory as would crush forever from the minds of their German authorities the belief in atrocious theories and monstrous doctrines. (Cheers)

Hence it was that when war broke out those of us who were entrusted with the confidence of the Liberals of our country had no intention in declaring that it was the duty of Canada to assist to the full extent of her power the mother country in her supreme task of maintaining civilization by resort to arms. In this conviction we acted together as members of the party and pledged to support all war measures. It was no time for more party strife. Yet, occasionally – yes, more than once – we were confronted by measures brought forward by the Government so vicious in principle, so grievous in effect, that we could not be true to those we represent and ourselves if we permitted them to pass without taking the position of irreducible objection. . . .

We expected and hoped that the Government would realize the new conditions created by the war and would set itself with earnestness and consideration to the great tasks before it. But in this we, and then the people of Canada, have been to a large extent disappointed. (Hear, Hear)

It became the bounden duty of the Government in view of the heavy calls for military expenditures and the serious sacrifices which confronted the people of Canada to reduce all civil expenditure and strike off every item that could be dispensed with without impairing the national service. Was this done? Alas no. The fact is expenditure has been growing and growing and growing – going on as merrily as in the piping times of peace. . . .

I do not question at all the sincerity of the charge of Sir George Foster. He was sincere at the time. I have no doubt but his confession was not accompanied with repentance and determination to do better. He wanted to do better. His confession resulted almost in these words: "Let us agree on this – both sides – that hereafter patronage shall be eliminated." (Laughter)

Hereafter – baneful word. This word "hereafter" – why not immediately? Why not unconditionally? Why wait until tomorrow. Tomorrow, and tomorrow and tomorrow (Laughter) "Tomorrow usurps in this petty pace from today, to the last syllable of recorded time."[185]

Tomorrow went by and with tomorrow went by also the suggestion and resolution of Sir George Foster never to return again until the last syllable of recorded time of this Government, the present Government of which he is an ornament, but not one of the masters. (Applause)

If his patronage had been eliminated from the Budget of this year, from the estimates of this year, it would have made an appreciable reduction. The patronage was there – patronage is an ubiquitous, omnipresent, omnivorous rover, devouring anything, everything in which there is any public money. It has a voracious insatiable appetite. Patronage is a plague, and if ever there was a time to be done with it, it is this calamitous time in which we are now living, in which everybody should be determined to have the biggest possible economy, the greatest possible reduction in the burden of the people. (Applause)

In the estimates of this year there is no less a sum than twenty-six million dollars appropriated to the Public Works Department presided over by the Hon. Robert Rogers,[186] whom I never knew to be a master or an example in economy. (Laughter, applause) Eight millions are appropriated to capital account eighteen million dollars, the largest amount is in public buildings, post offices, postal stations, armouries and drill halls in small towns and smaller villages for which there is no necessity now, and there may be no necessity hereafter.

In times of peace, when the revenues were affluent, this amount of expenditure might be justified, but in times of war what excuse can there be and what is the reason for these expenditures? The reason for these expenditures is the eternal question of patronage, and if these items are still to be found this year in the estimates it is because removing them would offend many influential patrons in one of these towns or villages who has a lot to sell for which he can find no purchaser, but who is put in good humour with the hope that someday a benevolent Government will relieve him of this unprofitable piece of property. Is this indictment too strong in this strenuous time in which we are living? The indictment is more than justified. Sir, we want to win this war. And we shall and will. (Cheers)

Let us look at the situation as it is. Very strenuous times are opening before us, and it becomes necessary that the strictest possible economy would be applied to the public service. Why these expenditures? When we challenged the Government do you know the answer they gave? It was that they had no intention of spending the money. If they had no special intention of spending it, why ask Parliament to vote for it? If the Government did not have the courage to deny their friends, then do you think they will find more courage now that they have the money voted? The Government are bound to give us not only the precept but the example of economy. (Hear, hear)

This is my chief grievance against them. But there are many questions I might speak of. I might speak of the administration of the Department of Militia, but I will not do so on the present occasion as I shall have time to speak of it elsewhere. In the meanwhile let me again repeat that we must win this war. We have made every possible sacrifice and we are ready to do more if need be. We have loaded ourselves. We have sent our boys to the front where they have fought on the battlefields of Europe and on the soil of France with the same bravery which characterized their ancestors. They have shown that the blood that flows through their veins is still the same as that which was poured upon the soil of France.

But if we are ready to do this I ask if it not be a crime against the common interest of our country and Empire that there should not be one dollar expended than is absolutely necessary for the carrying on of the civil business of the country? Yet while our men are fighting at the front there are amongst us men consuming the midnight oil and spending a lot of printers' ink in reconstituting the British Empire, but not along the old lines of British freedom, but upon the lines of German militarism! But it would be a sad day when we are engaged in a war the object of which is to save civilization if, as a result of this war, the victorious nations were to be saddled with militarism.

I ask you if anything has taken place in this war to lead any man to the conclusion that Britain has erred in her policy of antimilitarism or as maintaining her object the arts of peace, which have led her to where she is today? Is Britain in the wrong?

No sir, in the face of this there is no reason to believe that the policy of Britain in the past should be different from the policy in the future. There is an aphorism current that if you want peace you should prepare for war. I do not know the origins of the aphorism. But I assert that the experience of the world shows that the aphorism is apt to be fallacious. No, the experience of the world is that if you prepare for war, you will have war. Nothing better illustrates this than the policy of Prussian militarism.

Germany in this respect is only an enlarged Prussia. Prussia has dominated the German Empire and it is an admitted fact that Prussia impregnated Germany with that abominable lust of conquest which is now desolating the world. Prussia is the creature of the system of militarism. The first King of Prussia, Frederick William, invented the system. It has been extended again and again by his successors but it has not produced peace. On the contrary, more than one half of the wars which have desolated Europe in the last hundred and fifty years are due to Prussian militarism. . . .

Can you be surprised at this constant German aggression? No: if you educate men for war, if you prepare them for war and day after day teach them the doctrine of war then everyone from the Field Marshal to the humblest Corporal, during peace they sigh for the day when according to German conception, they will win glory and booty. In the first months of the present war we could hear the declarations of the German General Staff Officers and their exultation that in France they could fight for glory and in England there will be booty. The words may have been spoken or they may not have but they express the true spirit of the Prussian.

Even after the battle of Waterloo when Prussia and Britain were marching on Paris, the great Duke of Wellington maintained discipline in his army, but he wrote that the Prussians were simply thieves and robbers. (Cheers) Then when the old swashbuckler [Field Marshal Gebhard Leberecht von] Bluecher visited London and saw the rich city with its wealth piled up by British commerce, he, in true Prussian spirit, exclaimed: "What a city to sack!" (Laughter and cheers) This then is the spirit engendered by the system of militarism.

Against this history of Prussian arms and its organization and the glorification of war, let us look at a page of English history. The Kings of England, too, would have liked as the Kings of the European continent to have permanent armies, but the British people always looked upon permanent armies as an instrument of tyranny. They would not have them. The many devices of the Kings to get possession were baulked by Parliament. Today there is no law allowing a permanent army in Great Britain. . . . They have never had a standing army in the sense that European countries had them. The British conception supervened over all else, while the German conception led the people to look on war as a means to conquest and domination.

Between these two ideas there had to come a conflict and the conflict came. We are in it today. I ask you how shall it end. Sir, how it shall end is not now a question. Without haste, without undue exultation, with calm and confidence, with clenched fist and teeth, British subjects all over the world are determined that this conflict shall end in victory. (Loud cheers) But after victory comes the problem. That will be the question. What will follow? Shall we suppose that the old ideas, the old theories, which have made England and the British Empire what they are, shall it be supposed that the theories and the notions shall be thrown aside and a new military England and Empire be substituted for the old? Shall we have to say at the close of the war that old England is not the same?

For my part, British Liberal as I am – (cheers) – I do not know what the future may bring, but I have no hesitation in stating what my aspirations and hopes for British Liberalism may be. Let Britain remain true to the glorious past. (Cheers) Let her be in the future as she was in the past in the van of progress to that higher civilization which is now on trial, but which we hope to see, nay, are confident of seeing, emerge from the ordeal of blood and fire more glorious, more beneficent than ever. (Loud cheers)

I repeat, sir, this war has got to be fought to a finish. So it is that firmly, resolutely, we go on until victory is won. But then, let the better angels of our nature guide our course. There are many speculations now as to what should be our relations with Germany after the war. Sir, this is an idle question at the present time. It will depend on the extent of our victory. At all events if the victory be great or small, and I repeat that I think it ought to be great and thorough, it is not revenge that we are seeking. It is simple justice and freedom for the rest of Europe. (Cheers)

The German people are today under the ban of civilization on account of the atrocities which have been committed by the German army, on account of the innocent lives that are not sanctioned by war. For the victims of the *Lusitania*. For the babies killed by the Zeppelins. Yet for these atrocities the only persons to be held responsible are the German military authorities. And Germany will not only be answerable to history, but on the day of victory they will be charged before severe judges with the crimes they have committed not warranted by the law of war among the nations. But if the German authorities would be responsible it would be in the judgment of the British people whose motto has always been that of the old Roman *"Fortibus, debellure parcere victis, superbus"* which is to "fight the strong but to be merciful to the weak."[187]

Sir, I think we must hold the German authorities responsible. It would be unfair and unjust to hold all the German people to answer for such crimes. I believe, on the contrary, there is every reason to believe that when the new conditions will arise as must follow the war there will be an advance of democracy among the nations which compose the German Empire. There is every reason to believe that when the slaughter which has been going on for two years in Europe has come to an end the German people will realize that it is time the people, the common people as Abraham Lincoln used to say, who always in the end have to pay for the ambitious designs of despotism, should assert themselves. . . . There is every reason to believe that when the conflict is over the eyes of the German people will be opened and as a consequence despotism, feudalism, militarism shall be swept away by democracy, and democracy means peace, harmony, and good will amongst friends. (Applause)

And as for you my young friends, the Federation of Liberal Clubs, you who stand today on the threshold of life with a wide horizon open before you for a long career of usefulness to your native land, if you will permit me, after a long life, I shall remind you that already many problems rise before you: problems of race division, problems of creed difference, problems of economic conflict, problems of national duty and national aspiration. Let me tell you that for the solution of these problems you have a safe guide, an unfailing light if you remember that faith is better than doubt and love is better than hate. (Applause)

Banish doubt and hate from your life. Let your souls be ever open to the strong promptings of faith and the gentle influence of brotherly love. Be adamant against the haughty; be gentle and kind to the weak. Let your aim and your purpose in good report or in ill, in victory or in defeat, be so as to live, so to strive, so to serve as to do your part to raise the standard of life to higher and better spheres.

(Sir Wilfrid resumed his seat amid a tornado of cheering.)

By Edward Goldenberg

In the century since Sir Wilfrid Laurier graced Canada, he has been recognized as, if not the greatest, at least as one of the two or three greatest of our prime ministers.

Under his leadership during his fifteen-year tenure as prime minister, Sir Wilfrid's government transformed Canada from colony to nation. But his greatness derives not merely from the accomplishments of his government, such as the opening of the West, but rather from the values that guided him, the principles he upheld, and his courage in fighting for them no matter the currents of public opinion of the day. Those values — tolerance, respect, openness, generosity of spirit, optimism about the future even in the darkest times – have become part of the Canadian psyche, in no small part due to the example and the lasting influence of Sir Wilfrid Laurier.

One hundred years after his famous speech in London, Ontario, his words are as relevant to the circumstances of today as they were to the period in which Sir Wilfrid lived a century ago.

One hundred years ago, in the dark days of World War I, when the world recoiled at the atrocities being perpetrated by the German army and revenge was foremost in the minds of many, Sir Wilfrid was not courting political popularity when he proclaimed to his audience of Young Liberals in southwestern Ontario, "the only persons to be held responsible are the German military authorities. . . . It would be unfair and unjust to hold all the German people to answer for such crimes."

Fast forward one hundred years to a post–September 11 world where too often fear predominates over hope, intolerance over compassion, and anger over understanding. In this part of the twenty-first century, during a so-called war on terror, we too often see all Muslims tarred with the same brush because a few brutal terrorists profess to act in the name of Islam. The words of Sir Wilfrid in 1916 with respect to the German people are as relevant today, in our circumstances with respect to people of the Muslim faith, as they were then in the circumstances of his day.

Sir Wilfrid always projected a sense of optimism and hope; the test of leadership for him was the capacity to inspire citizens to believe that obstacles – no matter how difficult – could be overcome by holding true to values, not by sacrificing them in the name of expediency. He wanted Canadians to "let the better angels of our nature guide our course." After more than half a century in politics, where he had tasted defeat as often as or more often than victory, Laurier never gave in to bitterness or cynicism. Instead, while he looked back on his career and on the issues he had to confront, "problems of race division, problems of creed difference, problems of economic conflict, problems of national duty and national aspiration," he did so in order to draw lessons for the next generation and generations to come as to how to face them and overcome them.

Sir Wilfrid had brought together English and French; he had opened Canada to immigrants from many creeds and laid the foundation for the multicultural nature of the Canada of today; he had overcome economic downturns; and his aspirations for Canada soared to the point where he envisaged the twentieth century as belonging to Canada.

In today's world, there is sometimes an understandable tendency to look at our problems as unique and intractable compared to the problems of what some see as a much simpler time. Laurier never would have seen the problems he faced as simple; nor would he ever have seen the problems he faced as intractable. He faced them and overcame them in a way that is as valid today as it was a century ago.

"Let me tell you that for the solution of these problems you have a safe guide, an unfailing light if you remember that faith is better than doubt and love is better than hate. Banish doubt and hate from you. . . . Be adamant against the haughty, be gentle and kind to the weak. . . . Be so as to live, so to strive, so to serve as to do your part to raise the standard of life to higher and better spheres."

Sir Wilfrid Laurier's words on that long ago day in London were simple, their meaning profound, and their inspiration ageless; and they have made Canada an example for the world.

Edward Goldenberg had a long career in government and was senior policy advisor and later chief of staff to Prime Minister Jean Chrétien from 1993 to 2003. He is now a senior partner in the law firm of Bennett Jones, LLP.

1917 ELECTION MANIFESTO[188]

To the Canadian people: A consultation of the people at short and regular periods is the right of a free people. The constitution provides accordingly for a general election every five years. It is undeniable that there has existed a strong desire in the community to avoid an election during the war.

An impression prevails that had I accepted the invitation of the Prime Minister to join his Government, a new extension would have been possible. This impression is absolutely erroneous, the fact being that the invitation extended to me was coupled with the stipulation that the coalition government would pass a conscription measure, and then appeal to the country, thus making an election unavoidable.

The Government as recently reconstructed, the Union Government so-called, is now appealing to the country for support. Six Members of the Liberal Party, some of them close personal friends, have consented to become members of the administration, and the programme which they intend to follow has already been placed before the public, but in this programme, not one trace is to be found that the Liberal Members of the administration have succeeded in influencing their colleagues to the adoption of measures which they deemed essential not only to win the war, but for the welfare of the country at all times.

Most of the articles in the Government's manifesto are simply stale commonplaces extracted from the Conservative programme of 1911, forgotten after the election, resurrected for a new election. Such is the promise of economy of public expenditure, and such the promise of Civil Service Reform, two reforms which the Opposition would have been happy to support in the last Parliament, if the Government had afforded them the opportunity.

One particular item is deserving of attention. "A strong and progressive policy of immigration" is promised. This will be perhaps the most important question after the war. The burdens which are now being accumulated and which will have to be assumed and borne by the Canadian people can be faced if the enormous resources of the country are developed. But development demands a rapid increase in the population. Hence the necessity of a strong and progressive immigration policy. It is manifest that the promised strong and progressive policy has been seriously impaired by the breach of faith with naturalized Canadian citizens involved in the withdrawal of the political franchise from large numbers of these citizens. This must prove a serious blow to immigration, especially when the conduct of the Canadian Government is contrasted with the attitude of the United States, where no such indignity has been placed upon naturalized citizens.

An article of the programme of the Government speaks of the development of transportation facilities, but in vague though rather ambiguous terms. No mention is made of the acquisition of the Canadian Northern Railway; yet this subject was not exhausted by the legislation of last session, and it will be one of the most important duties of the next Parliament again to review it.

One feature of the act of last session is that the Government becomes the owner of the stock of the Company, of the nominal

value of sixty million dollars. There never was a dollar paid in that
stock. The experts employed by the Government to appraise the
value of the whole enterprise, men of acknowledged ability and
experience, themselves have reported that the stock of the Company
has no value whatever. Yet the Government have taken authority
to appoint a board of arbitrators to give a value to that property
without value.

The Opposition asked that the report of the arbitrators, whatever it might be, should be laid before Parliament for approval.
Though this motion was rejected, it is the right of the people to
declare that the case should not have been closed by the action of a
moribund Parliament, but that the whole matter should be reported
to, and adjudicated by the new Parliament.

It was natural to expect that the reconstructed Government
would give very serious attention to the economic situation of the
country, which is admittedly critical. There is no allusion to it
except the vague promise of effective measures to prevent excessive
profits, to prohibit hoardings and to prevent combination for the
increase of prices and thus reduce the high cost of living. The economic problems have to be grappled with at once, in no such vague
general terms, but in vigorous and concrete proposals.

The prices of all commodities have been steadily rising since
the beginning of the war. The daily provisioning of the family table
is from day to day becoming a more and more alarming problem
for all classes of wage-earners and for all people of small and of even
moderate income. It is no answer to say that this is the natural consequence of the war. When it is considered that the price of bread
and bacon, to speak only of these two commodities, is higher here
in Canada than in the United Kingdom, this of itself is proof sufficient that the prices here are inflated by methods which are in no
way connected with the war, unless the war is taken advantage of
for the very purpose of inflation. Indeed, the principal causes of

these ever soaring prices are none other than those described in the Government's manifesto as "excessive profits," "hoardings" and "combinations for the increase of prices." Since the Government knows where the evil is, what prevents the Government from striking the evil, and striking hard? The remedies are at hand, and I at once set down the policy.

No measure to reduce the cost of living can be effective until the tariff is reformed and its pressure removed from those commodities in which there are "excessive profits," "hoardings" and "combinations for the increase of prices." Of this obvious, fundamental reform there is not a word in the Government's manifesto. Indeed, Members of the present Government have announced that all questions of tariff legislation must be relegated till after the war.

Believing that increased food production is one of Canada's best contributions towards winning the war, I would propose if entrusted with the administration of the country to immediately relieve Agriculture from its disabilities in this regard.

Since the commencement of the war, the Government placed an increase of 7.5 per cent in our tariff on all commodities coming into Canada from outside Great Britain, and an increase of five per cent on the goods coming from Great Britain. I would immediately remove those two disabilities as respects commodities from all countries other than those with which we are at war. There is no doubt that under existing conditions, these increases in the tariff are a hindrance rather than a help to production in Canada, whilst it is certain, that in the final resort the consumer has to pay these extra taxes.

The increased duty on imports from Great Britain was an unfriendly and an unnecessary action on the part of Canada towards the mother country, at a time when British trade was staggering under the disadvantages incidental to the war. It continues to bear unfairly and unduly on existing trade and should be speedily removed.

In further mitigation of disadvantages to agricultural production, I would immediately remove the duties on agricultural implements and other essentials as demanded by the western farmers.

A general well-considered reform of the tariff for the purpose of helping Canadian production and relieving the Canadian consumers would also be an object of my administration.

In connection with the high cost of living, I would take drastic steps to bring under Government control any food producing factories so that food may be sold at a fixed price under the control of the Government, as has been done in Great Britain. To this end, arrangements should be made with the management of the food producing factories allowing for a fair interest on investment and fair and reasonable net profits, so that food may be obtainable by the ordinary consumer at the best possible prices. Should such arrangements not be possible, I would not hesitate to commandeer all food factories.

Nor is that all. The Government is invested with powers which they could and should have used to reduce the price of all commodities. These powers they have already exercised in the case of newsprint paper.

As far back as the month of February last an Order in Council was passed by which it was enacted that "with a view to ensure to publishers of Canadian newspapers, newsprint paper at reasonable prices" the Minister of Customs was "authorized and empowered to fix the quantity and price of newsprint in sheets and rolls to be furnished by the manufacturers to the publishers in Canada."

By virtue of this Order the Government have compelled manufacturers of print-paper, against the latter's protest, to supply publishers and newspapers at a price which they themselves fixed as reasonable. If they could thus reduce the price of paper to consumers of paper, why did they stay there? Why should the Government not also have reduced to the hundreds of thousands of anxious housewives and bread-winners the prices of all those commodities which make the ever increasing cost of living one of the most insistent and dangerous of all the problems that now confront us?

One of the most important contributions towards winning the war is to put a stop to profiteering for the benefit of its partisan followers. A first duty of my administration would be to secure to the country which pays for war supplies, the excess of exorbitant profits being realized by profiteers. Should it be necessary, I would not hesitate, in order to immediately stop profiteering, to take control of the factories which are engaged in the supply of war materials, as had been done in Great Britain, and run them on the principle of reasonable return on investment for the owners, and reasonable legitimate profit. I believe that one of the best methods of providing war supplies and saving the country from being exploited by profiteers would be to turn the Government shops which are suitable for such purposes to the production of war materials, ships, etc., for the benefit of the country. . . .

It cannot be said too often that this war could not have been avoided by the Allies, and that it is a contest for the very existence of civilization. Of this the entrance of the United States into the conflict is further proof, if indeed further proofs were needed. The American people long hoped that they would be spared that ordeal, but the ruthless violation by Germany of the most sacred canons of International Law left them no option; they had to join in the fight against a power which has become the common enemy of mankind.

At the very beginning, penetrated of the immensity of the struggle and of the necessity of bending all our efforts to the winning of the war, we, of the Opposition, gave to the Government every possible assistance. We assented to all their war measures, except when convinced that their measures would be detrimental rather than helpful.

This year the Government introduced a bill to make military service compulsory. With this policy I found it impossible to agree. If it be asked how this view is consistent with my often expressed determination to assist in winning the war, I answer without any hesitation that this sudden departure from the voluntary system was bound more to hinder than to help the war. It should be remembered that previous to the war, in all British countries conscription was unknown. It was the pride of the British peoples everywhere that compulsory military service, the bane of Continental Europe, had never been thought of in Great Britain, and that even the gigantic struggle against Napoleon had been fought on the purely voluntary system.

At the same time it must be pointed out that in Great Britain for some years before the war, in view of the immensity of war preparations amongst all the nations of the continent, the question of conscription was seriously and increasingly discussed in Parliament and in the press, so that at last when a measure to that effect was introduced by the government, it came as no surprise. It found the people prepared, and yet even then strong protests were heard from many classes of the community.

Very different was the introduction of Conscription in Canada. It came as a complete surprise. It never had been discussed in Parliament, and the voice of the press had been strong against it. In the month of July 1916 such an important paper as the Toronto *Globe* deprecated the very idea of Conscription. Here is what it said in a carefully reasoned editorial:

"The *Globe* in its editorial columns has consistently pointed out that in a country such as Canada conscription is an impossibility, and that no responsible statesman of either party capable of forming or leading a Canadian War Ministry would propose compulsory service. Nor has the *Globe* unduly criticised the failure of the Borden government to do more than it has done to assist voluntary recruiting. The criticism of the *Globe* and of Liberal papers have been exceedingly mild when compared with the vitriolic denunciations of the Toronto *Telegram*, the Winnipeg *Telegram*, the Montreal *Daily Mail* and other journals that have absolutely no sympathy with the Liberal Party."

And even as late as December 27, 1916, the *Globe* repeated its warnings against any effort "to force Canadians into the 'ranks'" and summed up public opinion thus: "Trades unionists are found opposing Conscription, and the leading opponents of every manifestation of democracy are favouring the system."

No less emphatic had been the language of the Government. At the beginning of the session of 1916, in answer to my enquiry whether the promise recently made by the Prime Minister of enlisting five hundred thousand men meant Conscription, he answered in these words:

"My Right Honourable Friend has alluded to Conscription, to the idea in this country or elsewhere that there may be Conscription in Canada. In speaking in the first two or three months of this war, I made it clear to the people of Canada that we did not propose Conscription. I repeat that announcement today with emphasis."

Equally emphatic and unqualified were my own declarations on the subject. Throughout the campaign of 1910 and 1911, I may recall that the Nationalist–Conservative alliance which opposed the naval policy meant conscription. Meeting these assertions I gave the public frequent assurance that under no circumstances would conscription follow the adoption of our policy. Again and again after the outbreak of the present war I insisted that conscription should not be introduced in Canada. Such was my position when the Government reversed its attitude and, without warning, introduced the Military Service Act.

To force such a drastic measure upon a people thus unprepared and against repeated assurances to the contrary, was neither wise nor prudent, nor effective. It may bring men to the ranks but it will not infuse into the whole body of the nation that spirit of enthusiasm and determination which is more than half the battle. It will create and intensify division where unity of purpose is essential.

I am only too well aware that the views which I here present have not met with universal acceptance, even in the party to which I belong, but even I hold that to coerce when persuasion has not been attempted, is not sound policy, and in this I appeal to the impartial judgment of all Canadians.

In combatting the policy of conscription, all that I asked was that a measure of such moment should not be enforced by Parliament without an appeal to the people. I supported a referendum for the reason that the referendum is the most advanced and the most modern method of consultation of the people, without the complication inseparable from a general election. A referendum had also been asked on this very question by organized labour. My request was denied.

I appeal with great confidence to the fair judgment of the country that the introduction at this juncture and in the manner above described was a grave error, if it is remembered that the supreme object should have been and still should be to bring all classes of the community in the task which we assumed.

A fundamental objection to the Government's policy of conscription is that it conscripts human life only, and that it does not attempt to conscript wealth, resources, or the service of any persons other than those who come within the age limit prescribed by the Military Service Act. This is manifestly unjust. The man who is prepared to volunteer his services and to risk his life in his country's defence is entitled to first consideration. Those dependent upon him, and who spare him from their midst are the next most deserving of the State's solicitude and care.

A policy which will accord first place to the soldier and the sailor in the concern of the State will, I believe, bring forth all the men necessary to fight its battles, without the need of recourse to conscription. If returned to power, I should adopt such a policy. . . .

The government have discarded that fundamental principle of the institution of a free people.

They have designedly altered the sanctity of the franchise, by choking discussion, by ruthlessly using the closure, they have deliberately manufactured a franchise with which they hope to win a victory at the polls; a passing victory for themselves, a permanent injury to the country.

This act, known as the War Times Election Act, is a blot upon every instinct of justice, honesty and fair play. It takes away the franchise from certain denominations whose members from ancient times in English history have been exempt from military service, and who in Great Britain never were, and are not now, denied their rights of citizenship.

It takes away the franchise from men whom we invited to this country, to whom we promised all the rights and privileges of our citizenship, who trusted in our promises and who became under our laws British subjects and Canadian citizens.

They are thus humiliated and treated with contempt under the pretense that, being born in enemy countries, in Germany and Austria, they might be biased in favour of their native country and against their adopted country. The assumption is false in theory and might easily be so demonstrated. It is sufficient to observe that it is also false in fact. . . .

It gives the franchise to some women and denies it to others. All those whose privilege it is to be amongst the soldiers will be voters. The right will be refused to all those not so privileged, though their hearts are as strong in the cause and though they have worked incessantly for it. . . .

The Act is vicious in principle, and is equally vicious in its enacting dispositions. We have in most of the provinces of the Dominion, a regular system of preparing the voters' lists, and against that system no complaint has been heard during the last twenty years. . . .

Should I be called upon to form a Government I would hope to include in it representatives of business, of labour and of agriculture, of the men whose sole object in dealing with the affairs of this country will be to devote the whole resources, wealth and energy of the country to the winning of the war.

It can only be done by honest agreement amongst all the different elements and interests of the country. I would hope to have a Government representative of the masses of the people, the common people whose guiding principle should be to defend them against organized privilege which has heretofore had far too much control over the Government of the country. In this election it is my desire that the common people should have the opportunity of expressing themselves in a free and untrammelled manner at the polls, so that their views may obtain in the new Parliament, and I trust that in every constituency candidates representative of this policy may be nominated so that the people can vote for them.

These considerations I now place before my fellow countrymen of all creeds and of all origins for their appreciation and judgment. I have deemed it my duty more than ever perhaps in the course of my long public life, to speak frankly and unequivocally upon the problems that now confront us. The obtaining of the retention of office is at all times only a secondary consideration. In this election the supreme end is to assist in the tremendous struggle in which we are engaged, to maintain the unity of the nation, to avoid the divisions and discords, which for many years kept in check, are now unfortunately again looming up dangerous and threatening, to resolutely face the economic situation with a view of avoiding and lessening privations and sufferings, which should not exist in a country so richly endowed by nature as our country.

Whatever may be the verdict at the polls, I will accept it, neither elated by victory, nor downhearted by defeat.

By Patrice Dutil

The 1917 manifesto bore all the imprints of Wilfrid Laurier: his last hopes, his sadness, and his quiet despair. This was his last campaign, and he knew it. It had a similar feel to the campaign that had led to his first defeat as leader of the Liberal Party in 1891. He sensed that the people were not with him. In 1891 he had campaigned, in part, on the bold idea of greater economic reciprocity with the United States. He had improved his party's record somewhat, but not much. This time he was again running against the government, but had no grand ideas to recommend.

Laurier turned seventy-six during the election campaign of November– December 1917. After a lifetime of argument and battles, he had had enough. There is a note of resignation in this statement, a "there you have it" that betrays a deep disappointment that his long career had not made a dint in the political culture of Canada. Could it be that his examples of fairness, of compromise, of "sunny ways" had no following? The campaigns of 1896, 1900, 1904, and 1908 seemed so distant now. As if Canada had become another country.

Much of the statement is boilerplate. Not surprisingly, it is sharply critical of the Union Government – a coalition of Conservatives and Liberals that had come together before the election to form a new administration. The Liberals who belonged to it were not "his" – they had distinguished themselves on the provincial scenes. Laurier painted this Union Government as nothing but a Conservative regime in new clothes.

The manifesto points to policy flaws, notably the nationalization of the Canadian National Railway, the cost of newsprint, the rate of inflation. One third of the manifesto is given to immigration issues, including the treatment of immigrants. The Liberals take aim at the withdrawal of the right

to vote for those who had immigrated from belligerent countries. It's all unfair
and wrong, the manifesto cries out.

Laurier reserves his greatest wrath for the imposition of conscription. The
entire policy is contrary to the Canadian way, he argues. He repeats candidly
that he is in favour of the war effort, as he has been from the beginning. But
the management of the war effort under Robert Borden has been deeply
flawed. In comparison with the British, the Borden/Union administration
has made countless errors that, on election day, should be fatal.

It was not all negative. The manifesto calls for new ways to bring relief to
the poor, the imposition of stricter price controls, and a repeal of tariff provisions
that, ironically, punished British industry in a time of unprecedented stress.

For Laurier, this did prove to be the last, bitter campaign. The results
of the December 17, 1917 election showed that this manifesto had not been
heard. The Liberals took slightly less than 40 per cent of the ballots, a drop
of almost eight points in comparison to the 1911 election. Only Quebec and
Prince Edward Island proved to be on his side. The West, which had always
been his electoral fire, was now cold to him. Ontario, which had turned
against him in 1911, shunned him even more. A dark curtain had fallen
on his brilliant career. Laurier died fourteen months later, in February 1919.

IN DEFEAT

ADDRESS IN REPLY TO THE SPEECH FROM THE THRONE
HOUSE OF COMMONS, OTTAWA, ONTARIO
MARCH 19, 1918

. . . . In the Address to which we listened yesterday there is no mention of a subject which does not require any legislation and in which
the public is much interested – that is to say, that since Parliament
prorogued in the month of September last there had been quite a
change in the Government. . . .

There is no new Government: we have the same Government
that has existed for the last six years. And so long as there is no
change in the Premiership it is a continuation of the same administration. There is the same control, the same principles and the
same everything in connection therewith. I emphasize that there is
the same control and the same principles. There is a change, I must
admit, in the complexion of the Government, and if I may say so it
is not only a change but an improvement.

As we look at the Government from this side of the House,
we cannot fail to notice that it is characterized by a healthier
complexion than it wore last session. There is not about it the
same pallor that existed then. Although I am not a follower of the
Government, I am glad to say that this present administration

displays a rosy red colour which is at all events pleasing to the eye.

Last summer the friends of the Government were much concerned as to its condition. Many of them, perhaps I should say all of them, believed that unless there was a copious draft of rich red blood injected into the system, things might go hard with them. This condition necessitated a surgical operation. Such operations have been very much resorted to of late, especially since the war began. Many have been the instances where healthy, strong men came forward and presented their bare arms to the surgeon in order to have a vein opened in the last desperate attempt to save a moribund life.

The records do show that the operation was successful. Indeed it so happened that in many instances the patient was so far gone that he could not be saved except by the sacrifice of another's blood, and sometimes the sacrifice was fatal even to the saviour who offered his blood for transfusion.

Let me say at once that to these Liberal members who joined the administration, I do not wish such a fate. With most of them it was my privilege for many years to be closely associated in intimate friendship. I know them too well not to realize that in what they did they were guided by wholly conscientious motives. Indeed we have the declaration of some of them that it was a sacrifice; indeed there is the written statement of others that they for a long time hesitated and resisted all advances.

Conscience is the supreme arbiter, and into the sanctity of conscience I will not enter. I respect the convictions of everybody, even of those with whom for the time being I may differ: but I may be pardoned if I say that so far as I am concerned I never could appreciate those many subtle disqualifications made in the effort to convince us that war necessitates and creates new standards of duty. There is no such thing as new standards of duty in war. Duty is on the concrete expression of eternal truth which never can vary, which remains the same in war as in peace. But war undoubtedly intensifies all duties and lifts them up to an altitude which of course is unknown in peace time. . . .

Sir, last session those who sat in the House were divided on the question of conscription. There were members of the Liberal Party who favoured conscription; others opposed it. Upon this point I as the recognized leader of the Opposition, did not interfere with the conscience of any man. Strong reasons were brought forward in support of each view, but there was no divergence of opinion on this side in regard to the outrageous measure known as the Wartime Elections Act. . . . Among members of the Opposition there was no divergence of opinion: they were unanimously opposed to it. Every feature of that law was an outrage, an odious violation of the very foundations of our system of democratic government. . . .

The Act was conceived in iniquity and was carried out in worse iniquity still. I say it, and I say it soberly in the presence of the new members of the House and of the old, that the Act by which the elections were carried was such that there was no fair play for the Opposition. With partisan enumerators, partisan returning officers, and partisan deputy returning officers, the true electorate of the country was diminished almost to the vanishing point. . . .

Now, what of the soldiers in Europe? I will refer to these soldiers in Europe, dealing with what has come to our notice in the press. I have in my hand a picture which was published in all the ministerial papers in the month of December 1917. It is a photograph of a polling booth for soldiers in London. The copy I have was taken from the *Toronto Star* of the nineteenth December, and under the cartoon I find the following:

"The picture shows Canadians at a London polling station on December second, and is from the first pictures to reach Toronto since the voting began on December first.

There is the recording officer. There is the voting soldier. There are the clerks; there are soldiers coming also to offer their votes, and on the wall is this placard: 'A vote against the Government is a vote for the Hun'."

We have seen that in Canada, sir, but not in the polls. We have seen it placarded in the streets of the city of Ottawa, that a vote against the Government is a vote for the Hun. We have seen more in the city of Ottawa. We have seen the statement made that a vote for Union is a vote for Christ. If the law can be thus openly, and even boastfully, violated in the polls in England, then we can have an idea of the opportunity which was left to the soldier to cast his vote untrammelled.

In the face of all these circumstances is it not evident to all classes of the community, to all impartial men – whether they are on the side of the Government or on the side of the Opposition, or whether they form part of that larger body, which associates with no party, and which is, perhaps, in the last resort, the grandeur of the nation – that the verdict recorded on the seventeenth of December for the Government is not a victory for democracy, but rather that it is a blow to the very foundation of the system of free institutions under which we live.

If democracy is to produce all that we hope and expect for it and from it, it must be apparent to everybody, it must be in the breast of every man that every consultation with the people ought to be carried out in such an open manner that every man must be satisfied that the vote recorded is an expression of the majority of the people. Not, sir, that the majority of the people is always right. Majorities are wrong sometimes, and so are minorities. But, after all, under our constitutional system, whether we sit on one side of the House or upon the other, what we want is that the Government of the country should be carried on by representatives of the people, according to the opinion of the people as it exists in the country.

Here are some of my friends on the side of the minority. It matters not whether we are on the right side or the left side of your chair, sir, what we want is that the voice of the people should be heard, and, even though we are in the minority, at all events that the people should rule. But, sir, in regard to the verdict which was recorded on the seventeenth December, and which I see represented before me today, however respectable the representatives may be, no amount of sophistry, no loud clanking of sonorous numbers can give it the character of certainty and respectability, which ought to be the commitment and the result of right done.

It is the misfortune of the Government and the misfortune of the country, but it is still more the misfortune of the Government that, by their own conduct, they have failed to obtain moral support with their majority; they have failed to obtained that support which is the one support a government should have, if the battle had been fought by fair and honest methods.

As to the members on this side of the House, we Liberals sitting here – what is left of us after these vicious practices – what is to be our attitude? Sir, so far as I am concerned, and so far as my friends about me are concerned, the answer is easy. Liberals, democrats and law-abiding citizens we come back from the fight. In number we are not as strong as we were, but we are stronger before the people, because we fought an honest fight according to our own rules.

What shall be our attitude? Sir, I have only this to say, that the lashes of the Government will in no way affect our conception of the duty which we owe to our country. We have our views upon the questions which are now before the Canadian people. We stood behind the Government in all of their war measures except one, and we will carry on the same policy: we will be behind them in all their war measures, with the same reservations. . . .

I have only to repeat once more that we on this side of the House stand exactly as we have at all times stood since the war began by this declaration: It is our fervent and solemn conviction that the fame which is now trembling in the balance of destiny is that of freedom and liberty itself. It is a sad thing that upon such an issue as this, when we are battling for the sacred cause of liberty and freedom, that I should have to arraign the Government for having itself sapped the foundations of the free institutions under which we live, a deed which has already produced its evil effects.

Men there are today who declare by voice and pen that all the militant powers are governed by the same selfish spirit. Against such an unfounded assertion I protest with all the force at my command and with all the energy I can put into my words. To say there is no difference between the belligerent – to put German on the same plane as France, as the United States, as Belgium, and as England – is simply to flout history. The rulers of Germany have shown that they will respect no law, neither of God, nor of nations, nor of men. . . .

But our first duty is to overcome the greater danger which threatens, and to that imperative duty we on this side of the House will give, with all our might, whatever it may be, and with our whole heart, we shall give it our undivided support.

By Thomas S. Harrison

Laurier's address in reply to the Speech from the Throne in 1918 was a watershed in Canadian political oratory.

In times of national stress, like those caused by the Great War, there is an undemocratic undercurrent that sometimes privileges the needs of the State over individual rights.[189] *Laurier's remarks underscored this tension, and highlighted many of the fractures caused by the Great War, but also presented an inviting appeal to aspirational Canadian values that resonates across the years.*

Like most Canadian prime ministers, both Borden and Laurier were members of the Bar. The association between lawyers and politics in Canada might suggest a strong commitment to such values as democratic rule of law.

To a great extent, these values were realized during Laurier's years in office.

During his long tenure as prime minister, Laurier oversaw the emergence of a diverse and growing democracy. The country opened its doors to literally millions of settlers who pioneered the northern prairie. This demographic surge led to the creation of two new Canadian provinces, Alberta and Saskatchewan, in 1905.

While perhaps less well known, Laurier's impact in other areas was also substantial. In the justice system, for example, he had curtailed the partisan judicial appointment practices, prevalent since Confederation, to enhance the rule of law throughout the country.[190] In many respects, the 1900s appeared destined, as Laurier proclaimed, to become "Canada's century."

However, the challenges of World War I stretched the young nation to the breaking point. Partisan election tactics employed by the Borden government in 1917, which Laurier later decried in his reply to the Speech from the Throne, were only the latest in a series of dismaying developments. Victory in the war, it seemed, required the sacrifice of cherished democratic principles.[191]

As noted by Arthur Lower, parliamentary governance in Canada was largely replaced at the time by executive order.[192] The strains of the war also prompted Borden's Government to pass the first War Measures Act,[193] which authorized the forced detention in labour camps of thousands who, only a few years before, had immigrated to start a new life in Canada.

The Act also mandated the registrations of tens of thousands, imposed strict censorship, and limited freedom of association.[194] The sense of national emergency even led the Government to the extraordinary measure of postponing the expected 1916 election, through constitutional amendment.[195]

Though Laurier had been defeated electorally, his words still carried tremendous power. Betrayed by members of his own Liberal Party, who had crossed the floor, Laurier remained both eloquent and gracious. His gentle but firm remonstrations reminded all Canadians that the fight, in war or politics, was not just about winning. It was also about upholding important principles, such as democracy and rule of law, on which the battle was based.

In this sense, Wilfrid Laurier's speech to Parliament in 1918 was a warning about the deep and undemocratic fractures caused by the war. But it was also a reminder of past dreams and future hopes, that Canadians and their leaders might yet work together to build a better Canada following the war.

Laurier's 1918 remarks also remind us that the past is often prologue to the present. Today, national security focuses not on a Great War, but on the threat of terrorism. Expanded Government powers to deal with this danger have alarmed many. In an echo of Laurier's earlier warning, some fear modern developments are similarly a threat to individual liberties. However, as in the past, such concerns are balanced against our aspirations as a country, and by those who, like Laurier, strive to keep Canada as a model of peace, stability, and democracy, for all the world.

Thomas S. Harrison is a lawyer, teaching fellow, and director of legal ethics and professionalism in the Faculty of Law, Queen's University, in Kingston, Ontario. He also holds a McCarthy-Tétrault Fellowship in legal ethics, which supports his current research into the relationship between an independent bench and Bar, and how both support access to justice in Canada.

ADDRESS TO THE EASTERN ONTARIO LIBERAL ASSOCIATION

OTTAWA, ONTARIO

JANUARY 14, 1919[196]

Resolution: That the Eastern Ontario Liberal Association take advantage of the opportunity afforded by this its first meeting, to place upon its records the unfaltering confidence of members in The Right Honourable Sir Wilfrid Laurier as the Leader of the Liberal Party of Canada, and to congratulate him upon the fact that, thanks to his moderation and wisdom, the ranks of Liberalism are rapidly reuniting, and that in the conflict that lies close at hand between the forces of progress and the advocates of class privilege and reaction, the Liberal Party, with strength renewed, will again lead the van in asserting the rights of Canadian Democracy.

Laurier's closing address:

. . . . We are entering upon a new era. We trust that the war which was lately devastating the world will not have to be fought again. But it is not enough that we have defeated the autocratic Government of Germany and that the ruins of that autocracy lie in the dust; it is not enough that . . . we have accomplished that which we had determined to accomplish, that is, to prevent the dismemberment of France and to restore to France her lost provinces; it is not enough that England is maintained in the proud position which she held before the war, [and] is raised today to an even prouder position than ever before, the great champion and defender of freedom and civilization; it is not enough even if we realise our great hope that all this shall be crowned by the forming of a League of Nations to prevent reoccurrence of war and to stand against any force that would bring war again.

And as to that, let me say that if conditions are not ripe for such a league of nations as we should like to see, yet we may joyfully believe that if there is today the beginning of a league of nations in the alliance which now exists between England, France, Italy, the United States and Japan, on the part of these nations, at least, I hope, a league will be formed at this Peace Conference under which it shall be provided that, so far as they are concerned, war shall not be permitted, so that if one country wishes to raise war against another the league will interfere to maintain peace. . . .

Sir, you have passed another resolution. I referred to it this afternoon. Let me speak of it once more. You spoke of myself and expressed your satisfaction with the leadership I have given to the Liberal Party. I am conscious that I have made many mistakes. I know also that occasions there have been when I had to disappoint some of my friends. But, Sir, if another had been in my place who knew this country as I know it, from end to end, and in all its component elements – and without boasting I state that perhaps I know it better than any other Canadian – then, even though he and I might have differed, I am sure that he would have realized that, acting as I did, my aim was to win the war – and that was my aim – and to promote the highest interests of Canada.

At the same time I realize . . . that it is still the privilege of every Liberal to have his own opinion, that in entering an association such as ours he does not rein in his conscience into the hands of another, but keeps it, to account of it to his Maker and to Him alone. I have had the confidence of the Liberal Party, I think, as much as any leader of a party ever had in this country. But there is not a man in the party who will say that I ever tried to influence his conscience. Upon every question that arose, I always told those who did me the honour to call me their leader that it was for each one to judge, and if his judgment should be contrary to mine, he would be my friend still, just as though our opinions were in accord. That is my policy still.

Some have differed with me in the past, in the recent past. But that difference was upon a transient question, and one that will not arise again, for has not Lloyd George pledged himself to "no conscription?" Then, I say, let the past be forgotten, and let us be all Liberals again, actuated only by conscience. If a man comes to me and tells me, "I was a Unionist at the last election," I will tell him, "I will not rebuke you for it; you have rebuked yourself. Give me your hand. We do not look to the past, but to the future; only in that direction is the horizon for us as Liberals."

I was placed at the head of the Liberal Party a great many years ago – so many that I had better not count them. I feel every day that I am getting riper and riper for Heaven. I would gladly resign the position which I owe to the confidence and friendship of the Liberals of Canada and leave the task to younger hands. But, so long as God gives me the health which I now enjoy – though I cannot say that it is as good as it was at one time, yet I believe has left in me a kick which I can use on occasion – I will remain and do my share. I will do my share in any position which is assigned to me by the party, whether it be that of general, captain or private in the ranks. Whatever my place may be I will do my duty cheerfully, happily. Nothing would be of greater satisfaction to me, now that I have begun to feel the weight of years, than, as I have said, to leave the task of leadership to a younger general. That satisfaction may be given me or it may not; but my duty still is to fight, and fight I will as long as God gives me health.

I regret that I am not some twenty years younger, and that I cannot carry on the fight with the same vigour I could have carried it on twenty years ago. Still our cause remains, and with the horizon broadening day by day, our ideals are higher and higher every day. So great is that cause and so high those ideals that no one has the right to falter, but everyone must do his bit according to his ability. And, looking to the future, my hope is that the day is not far distant when we shall hear again in the heavens the hopeful message brought years ago by the Angels: "Glory to God in the highest, and on earth peace and good will to all men."

A Last Roar from the Old Lion

By Dr. Thomas S. Axworthy

Political careers usually end in tears, to paraphrase the British politician Enoch Powell. So it proved with Laurier. He had fought all his life for a French–English partnership. He had fought all his life for a united Liberal Party as an instrument for that French–English partnership. His ideals shone and they endured. In his House of Commons office, Pierre Trudeau only had one picture in addition to that of his family – it was of Wilfrid Laurier.

But the devastation of World War I also reached Canada's shores, at least politically: the 1917 election was the most bitter in Canadian history following the introduction of conscription by the Conservative Government. Opposed to conscription, Laurier's Liberals won 73 per cent of the vote and sixty-two seats in Quebec, but in English-speaking Canada, especially Ontario, the Conservatives triumphed. Conscription split the Liberal Party, too: nine Liberals joined the Conservative cabinet and in 1917 voters had the odd option of voting for Liberal–Unionist supporters of the Borden government, or Laurier Liberals.

In his last speech, in January 1919, Laurier acknowledged that "we are entering upon a new era" and that "I feel every day that I am getting riper and riper for Heaven." (He died on February 17, 1919, with the words "C'est fini.") Yet at age seventy-seven, he continued to rally Liberals. He told the Eastern Ontario Liberal Association, "our cause remains and with the horizon broadening day by day, our ideals are higher and higher every day." In October 1916, he had spoken in a similar vein to the Young Liberals in London, Ontario, telling them that "faith is better than doubt, and love is better than hate." These words are a fitting memorial to a man who made reconciliation the cause of his life.

DEATH OF THE RIGHT HONOURABLE SIR WILFRID LAURIER, G.C.M.G.

HOUSE OF COMMONS, OTTAWA, ONTARIO
FEBRUARY 25, 1919

Hon. Sir Thomas White:[197] Mr. Speaker; I rise to refer to that sad occurrence, the sudden and lamented death of Right Honourable Sir Wilfrid Laurier which has cast a pall over the proceedings attending the opening of this session of Parliament, touched the hearts of all his fellow members, and created a profound and melancholy impression throughout the entire Canadian community. In years Sir Wilfrid Laurier had considerably exceeded the allotted span, yet such was the vigour of his mind, the animation of his appearance, the freshness of his interest in affairs, the charm and vivacity of his manner, and above all the great and conspicuous place which he had so long occupied in the minds and affections of his countrymen, that we had almost come to look upon him as immune from the vicissitudes of human infirmity, and, in a measure exempt from the conditions of our common mortality. For this reason the news of his departure has come with a sense of shock as well as of grief to all.

His death removes a most distinguished and commanding personality from the stage of Canadian public life. How considerable a part he played, we may realize when we reflect that he was actively engaged in national affairs at a period before many of us were born, that he was for almost half a century a legislative representative of the people, and for forty-five years a member of this House. He has been leader of the Liberal Party for more than thirty years, of which he was for fifteen years Prime Minister of Canada. During his long career he has been identified with all the great political controversies since the period of Confederation. His fame has carried far beyond the boundaries of Canada, and in Britain, France and the United States, as well as in other countries; the name of Sir Wilfrid Laurier has long been known, respected and admired as one of the outstanding statesmen of the age.

With such a career, with such titles to distinction, we of this House, who, next to his own immediate family and intimate personal circle, knew him best, may well upon this occasion, with profit to ourselves and in appreciation of him, examine as to the nature of the political principles to which he subscribed, his characteristics as a statesman, the personal qualities and attributes of the man himself, and the sources of the great power and influence which he exercised within and without the halls of Parliament. I am deeply conscious that there are many within sound of my voice who through longer association and acquaintance with him are much better qualified for this task than myself. Particularly do I wish that the head of the Government, the Prime Minister of Canada, the Right Honourable Sir Robert Borden, could be here to bear eloquent tribute to his great political opponent and warm personal friend.

It is not my intention to refer to the various controversies in which Sir Wilfrid Laurier during his long career was so actively engaged. Those controversies divided and some of them still divide the people and public men of this country. That is the natural and inevitable result of opposing views, opinions and convictions strongly and honourably held in a self-governing community such as ours. It is not my purpose to attempt to pass judgment upon the attitude of the dead leader towards these great questions. Even if it would be fitting and proper to do so, which it is not, we are too close to the events to make any contemporary opinion conclusive. The ultimate place and fame of Sir Wilfrid Laurier, will, like that of other statesmen, be determined by the impartial and impassionate judgment of history.

What were the foundations of this man's political creed, the principles which guided his political action? Without pretending to be exhaustive, two or three outstanding facts emerge. Firstly, the man was strongly attached and devoted to the ideals of freedom and liberty, personal, civil and religious. He believed in freedom of opinion, liberty in its expression – that is to say, free speech, freedom of conscience – that is to say, religious liberty. That these were his views may be gathered not only from his own speeches but from the names of those whom he most admired, Fox, Gladstone, Bright, Lincoln. These names were often on his lips and he had diligently studied their careers and utterances.

From this starting point of attachment to these ideals of liberty and freedom, to which I think most in this country and all in this House now subscribe, he was led to greatly admire the British political system and the security and guarantees for liberty which it embodies and affords. Owing to the influences surrounding him in that troubled period, Sir Wilfrid Laurier, then but a young man, appears not to have realized, at least in its fullness, the vision of Confederation. It is, however, to his great and lasting credit that once it was accomplished he accepted the new conditions with whole-heartedness, and in his subsequent career did much in collaboration with other political leaders to develop its structure, interpret its meaning and mould it to the purposes for which it was designed.

He became a strong Federationist, a great admirer, exponent and champion of the Confederation pact and no question interested him quite so much as one relating to or affecting the Constitution. He was a great constitutionalist, an ardent upholder of the principles of free government with all that it involves. As nearly all questions arising out of our constitution have long since been settled and acquiesced in by all political parties, it seemed to me at times that in his character of constitutionalist and in his continued interest in the Constitution he was the dignified and solitary survivor of that great group of statesmen, giants in their day, who after prolonged and fiery discussion and controversy laid broad and deep the constitutional foundation of Canada's national life. In this connection, and as again emphasizing the part played by Sir Wilfrid Laurier in Canadian affairs and the length of years spanned by his career, let us recall that he was minister in the Government of Alexander Mackenzie, served as lieutenant to Edward Blake, succeeded him as leader of the Liberal Party, and became the opponent of Sir John A. Macdonald, with whom he contended politically for many years.

Sir Wilfrid Laurier was an intense and ardent Canadian. He was a firm believer in Canada and its destiny, which he did much to mould. Particularly did he desire to harmonize the various nationalities of Canada with their conflicting ideals and aspirations. National unity he regarded as of paramount importance in a country of mixed races and diverse creeds such as Canada. He was regardful of the rights of minorities and a strong advocate of tolerance towards the opinions and convictions of others upon all questions, whether civil, racial or religious. He was a believer in democracy, but there was always in him a moderating and restraining influence, a pragmatical respect for experience and for the past which disinclined him to sudden or violent change and exercised a steadying influence in the determination of his policies.

For the British constitution and for the autonomy, freedom and security which it affords to all within the range of its beneficent sway, he had the greatest regard and admiration. In my last conversation with him he spoke in terms of highest eulogy of British administration in Egypt and said that he would have no fear for the mandatory system proposed at the Peace Conference if it would be carried out in accordance with the British mode of government in protectorates.

I am glad that he lived to see the end of the war and the triumph of the Allies – particularly Britain and France.

Coming now to the man himself and the sources of his personal power we find less difficulty in reaching conclusions. He was endowed by nature with a singularly graceful, picturesque and commanding personality, a stately bearing, a most gracious manner and rare charm of disposition. He had high intellectual culture and much personal kindliness of heart. The combination made him a great gentleman, whose distinction and individuality wrought an indelible impression upon all with whom he was brought in contact. While conciliatory and always a believer in persuasion rather than in compulsion, he had a firm will and strong tenacity of his settled views, opinions and policies. This gave him strength which always of itself attracts. He had in marked degree that mystic quality, that innate attribute called personal magnetism or personality, which is really the totality of excellence, physical, mental and moral, in its fortunate possessor.

His power of command over men was great. He was a natural leader because of his ascendancy in the realm of intellect and of will. When all we can say has been said, there still remains an indefinable, elusive and baffling something which we cannot express, but which gave him an amazing power in attracting and retaining the affection and devotion of his followers and adherents. It was this which caused him to be likened in the minds of many to Sir John A. Macdonald, who had the same notable faculty in supreme degree.

A further and great source of his power lay in his extraordinary gifts as an orator. As a speaker either in the House or on the public platform he took the highest rank. His oratorical achievements were greatly promoted and enforced by his individual characteristics and qualities, for it is an undoubted fact that much of the success of speech depends upon personality.

His style was simple, direct, lucid. It had been modelled upon the best examples of English prose, and had been fashioned and moulded by his study of the classics, which is the best school for literary form. Some of his speeches in this House were notable illustrations of the supreme art of the orator. Those upon the death of Sir John A. Macdonald, the Right Honourable Mr. Gladstone and Her Majesty Queen Victoria are among the finest in the history of panegyrical literature.

In the House, where he was a most assiduous attendant and an eager listener, he was always courteous and considerate of the views of opponents and was by them all personally liked and respected.

Such, in most imperfect outline, was Sir Wilfrid Laurier and the principles and ideals for which he stood. He was idolized among the French Canadian portion of our population as their great exemplar and representative on the floor of Parliament and as Prime Minister of Canada for so long a period. They were naturally and justly proud of his high intellectual qualities and the force and strength of his character, his political sagacity and his success as a statesman. But apart from those of his own race he had devoted followers and admirers without number throughout the other provinces of Canada. His private life was simple and blameless, and he leaves behind him a career unsullied by self-seeking or love of gain. To state that he had defects, that he made mistakes at times, is only to say that he was human and what he himself would be the first to admit and acknowledge.

We mourn his loss. We feel that a great gap has been created in this House, that a powerful link with the past has been snapped and broken beyond repair. The spirit of the age has altered since the days when Sir Wilfrid Laurier was in his political prime. Times change and men change with them – in appearance, manner, methods, characteristics.

We desire to express our most heartfelt sympathy to that most worthy helpmate, the light of whose life has gone out in the loss of him who was for more than fifty years of happy wedded life her constant comrade as well as husband, counsellor and protector. We pray that she may be granted strength to bear the heavy bereavement which has come upon her.

As for our dead friend and fellow member, he has joined the great majority, the unnumbered shadowy hosts of the dead. We shall see his face and hear his voice in these halls no more. He has left these scenes and these voices, and it will be indeed long before we shall look upon his like again.

His life was gentle, and the elements so mixed in him that nature might stand up and say to all the world: This was a man.

Mr. D.D. McKenzie (North Cape Breton):[198] Mr. Speaker, the task that falls to my lot on this occasion is a very serious one and one that I fully realize my personal inability to fulfill as it ought to be fulfilled and discharged. Speaking for the moment on behalf of the gentlemen who sit on this side of the House, and speaking, as I believe, for the late Right Honourable Sir Wilfrid Laurier's personal friends and admirers throughout this Canada of ours, I wish in the first place, if I may be permitted, most sincerely to thank the Acting Prime Minister of Canada [Sir Thomas White] for the magnificent tribute which he has paid to the great worth of the illustrious dead. The tribute is so full, so comprehensive, so complete, so just, that indeed very little is left to be added to it. It would rather spoil the effect of what has been said so well and moulded so completely to try to add very much to it.

Nevertheless, Mr. Speaker, it comes home to me, as the deskmate of our late revered leader, and for so many years his friend, that we should from this side of the House join with the Honourable Leader of the Government in saying something about our departed friend. I stand, Mr. Speaker, by the vacant chair, a chair that will never so worthily be filled in this House or in any other Canadian House within my lifetime and perhaps not within the lifetime of the youngest man here. The leadership of the Opposition and of the Liberal Party will someday be filled, but it is no disparagement to whoever may fill that position to say that we have not the mould, nor the man to fill the place of the departed Chieftain of the Liberal Party.

As to the love and affection which the people of this country had for him, may I remind you, Mr. Speaker, and my Honourable Friends, of that great pattern of human love that has been held out to us and which we used to read in our school books and in the Sacred Book itself about David and Jonathan of old; held out to us as the greatest human evidence of love between two men. When David and Jonathan were parting, Jonathan, his brother-in-law, took him fervently by the hand and said: David, I will never see your face again; we are parting now and forever; but to-morrow you will be missed, for your seat will be empty."[199]

The great dead is missed in this House today, because his seat is empty and it can never be filled. His place in this House is empty, his place in his home is empty, but his memory shall never fade. We as his friends, have reason to be thankful, and we are thankful, that his great worth has been appreciated by the people of Canada and presented to this House today in such a magnificent manner by the hon. gentleman who is leading the Government.

I am sorry that the duty of paying this tribute to the departed statesman has not fallen upon someone more capable than I. One cannot help thinking on an occasion of this kind of the masterly eulogies which our late leader has pronounced, and one is apt to say, with the poet: "O, for the touch of a vanished hand, and the sound of a voice that is still!"[200]

The acting leader of the Government has pointed to the many things Sir Wilfrid Laurier had done for the development of this nation, and it is no disparagement to others to say that in bringing this country of ours up to the full measure of nationhood, in bringing it vividly to the attention of the Mother Country and of the home Government, in securing for it as a nation and as a dominion the high position we hold in the commercial and political world, none has done so much as Sir Wilfrid Laurier. Canada has risen to her rightful place as a nation within the great Empire to which we belong. The position which Sir Wilfrid Laurier took at the time of the diamond jubilee of Her late Majesty Queen Victoria, and again at the coronation of King Edward VII and of King George V and at the various imperial conferences of the great statesmen of the Empire, did more to bring Canada before the world and to secure for us the position which we now occupy than anything hitherto done by any other Canadian. We have therefore much to be thankful for, both for his life, and for the memories he has left behind not only in Canada but throughout the Empire.

Sir Wilfrid Laurier rose to the very highest position in the gift of the people of this country. As he had often himself said, he was a democrat to the hilt. He was capable of realizing and anticipating every feeling of the people and almost of every individual in the community, for he had gone through the various stages of life within Canada, and he could see what was necessary for the true welfare of his native land, of which he was so proud. Sir Wilfrid Laurier, I repeat, occupied the very highest position in the gift of this country and I submit that had he lived in any other country of the civilized world he would have occupied a similarly high position. Had he lived in the great republic to the south, with its hundred millions of people, he would have shared in the hearts of the people of that country a place with Washington, Lincoln and Grant. Had he lived in France, the home of his ancestors, I submit that he would have been President of France. Had he lived in our own beloved Mother Country of Great Britain and Ireland, I have no doubt, and I have often heard it said, that he would have occupied a similar position to that held by Lord Chatham, John Bright, Gladstone and Disraeli. It has often been stated by men in this Chamber, and not by those in sympathy with him politically, that if Sir Wilfrid Laurier had lived in Great Britain, nothing could have prevented him from becoming its Prime Minister. So we have reason to believe that his talents, although afforded plenty of scope in Canada, did not reach the full limit of their possibilities here, and that he was fully capable of performing higher and more exacting duties if fate had placed those duties as his task.

I think it is sometimes justifiable to use the language of others when it exactly expresses one's own sentiments, and what I am about to quote I would adopt as the language of this side of the House as well as adopting the sentiments so ably expressed by the Minister of Finance. This newspaper was not a supporter of Sir Wilfrid Laurier, and therefore I quote from it with the greater freedom. It says:

"Another Link with the Glorious Days of Canada's Making is Broken by Laurier's Death.

In the passing of Sir Wilfrid Laurier yet another link with the spacious days of Canada's making has gone. There are great names in Canadian history – Baldwin and LaFontaine, Brown, Galt and Tupper, Blake, Macdonald and Laurier," and rightly indeed does the *London Daily Chronicle*, in its tribute to the dead statesman, say:

"Laurier's name will be permanently associated with some of the most important phases in the development of the British Commonwealth. Not only will Canada always rank him among the great builders of her nationhood, but he will hold his niche in the temple of world history."

Apart altogether from the political views which he held, and advocated, the testimony is universal that Sir Wilfrid Laurier in the truest sense was a great man. He belonged to the Empire, and for many years he was the most considerable figure in Greater Britain. A French Canadian with unquestioned devotion to that race and its traditions, he yet accepted as his task the establishment of a better understanding and closer union of the two races of the Dominion, and though it was a task which has not yet been completed, Sir Wilfrid had the satisfaction of achieving a marked advance. No need of Canada has been greater and none has lain nearer to the statesman's heart than the removal of discord between the different races and tongues and creeds which comprise the Canadian Confederacy. To have attempted a task of such magnitude and hedged with tremendous and critical difficulties, is in itself an eloquent testimony to his essential greatness.

Former political opponents are one today in voicing their ungrudging admiration and unqualified recognition of his undoubtedly great gifts. Though not blind to his political failings and to views which they believed to be detrimental to Canada's truest welfare, yet as one man they express the highest regard of Sir Wilfrid's strict personal probity, his untarnished character and the years of strenuous and devoted service to the Dominion.

As an orator Sir Wilfrid Laurier occupied a unique position. As one writer in the English press has said – "He was gifted with unusual personal advantages. His appearance alone was worth a handsome fortune. His figure, lithe and straight as a larch; his face unwrinkled; his glance clear and searching, made up a personality that wielded a strange fascination for his hearers. He spoke as well in English as he did in French – his mother-tongue." Among the many gems of Sir Wilfrid's oratory, the following, delivered in Paris in 1897, is considered one of his finest utterances – "a speech touched with a prophetic fire":

The citation from the speech referred to by this writer, I quote:

"It may be that here in France the memories of the ancient struggles between France and England have lost nothing of their bitterness, but as for us, Canadians of whatever origin, the days we hold glorious are the days when the colours of France and of England, the tri-colour and the Cross of St. George, waved together in triumph on the banks of Alma, the heights of Inkerman, the ramparts of Sebastopol.[201] Times change; other alliances are made, but may it be permitted to a son of France, who is at the same time a British subject, to salute those glorious days with a regret which will perhaps find an echo in every generous mind on either side of the Channel."

This quotation which I have taken the liberty to read, conveys to you, Sir, and to the House, my own views, and perhaps puts them better and more concisely than I myself could. Let me conclude by saying that we appreciate what has been done in the country, and what is now being done, to honour the memory of the great departed chieftain. We acknowledge, with thankfulness, what has been done by the Government in honouring his mortal remains, and we are thankful for the tribute that has been paid to his memory by the leader of the Government today. We on this side of the House, and his friends generally, particularly those of his own party, might say, as has been said by a wise man of old, "Our Father, our Father, the chariots of liberalism and the horsemen thereof,"[202] and may I say, with one of old, to my friends and the public at large, "Know ye not that this day there has fallen in Canada a prince and a great man."[203]

Honourable Rodolphe Lemieux (Maisonneuve and Gaspé):[204] Mr. Speaker, the Shadow of Death has stalked through this Chamber; a chair stands vacant. As we gaze upon the flowers strewn about us, which, by the morrow, will have withered away, more deeply than ever do we understand the baffling brevity of this life's span, the specious vanity of each and every thing. Sir Wilfrid Laurier is no more.

The mellow voice which for so long enthralled this assembly and stirred the enthusiasm of all who heard it, is silent.

"The trumpet's silver voice is still
The warder silent on the hill."[205]

The last survivor of a great generation, he whose imposing stature, whose eagle eye and whose white plume recalled those noblemen of the eighteenth century, such as we meet them still in medallions of olden times, is sleeping his last sleep.

An illustrious ancestor has passed away. Let us incline our heads with respect in the presence of this grave: its closing writes "finish" to a whole epoch of our history.

Death is a law and not a punishment. No one better understood this profound truth than the eminent statesman whose loss we mourn. He had long since made his preparations for the voyage from Time into Eternity. Without bitterness the old gladiator saw himself disarmed as he was about to descend once more into the arena. His spirit passed gently, serenely, as though "midst the darkening shadows of life's falling night the Faith of his forefathers had already revealed the gleam of dawn, passage of Eternal Day."[206]

Speaking here in the name of my colleagues of the old French province who counted him her most distinguished son, and whose idol he became, it does the heart good to recall that throughout his entire career he was ever faithful to his origin and to the finest traditions of his race.

"I love," he was wont to say, "I love France who gave us birth, I love England who gave us liberty, but the first place in my heart belongs to Canada, my country, my native land."

This striking formula was, if I may speak thus, the Ideal, the Polar Star which guided his public life. Affectionate gratitude towards the nation, resplendent among all nations – whose sons we have the honour to be – the splendour of whose glory lights up the highest summits; unswerving loyalty towards that great and generous nation who inherited the administrative genius of the Romans and of whom Tennyson could say that hers was the classic land of liberty.

But, first and foremost, Laurier was a Canadian. To his French inheritance he owed his golden tongue, his keen intellectual vision, the boldness and the grandeur of his conceptions. To his contact with the great English school, the school of Burke, Fox, Pitt, O'Connell, Gladstone, he owed his deep practical knowledge of British institutions, and it may be said without exaggeration that it was by assimilating the teachings of these parliamentary leaders that Sir Wilfrid Laurier made for himself a lasting niche in the Hall of Fame.

At the time when he stepped through the threshold of Parliament, the memory of the great Papineau still hovered over the country. And the image of Lafontaine, whose profound wisdom had saved many rights from the wreckage of a storm-tossed sea, was becoming greater as time went by.

In those days Cartier and Dorion represented the two different channels of opinion in our province. The one, dashing, impetuous, disdained all obstacles; the other calm, of proverbial integrity, possessing a mind of very high attainments, trusted to time to dispel hoary prejudice. If it be true that, in a certain way, Laurier was the disciple of Dorion, events made him the fortunate successor, rather the direct heir, of Lafontaine's policy – the policy which strives to soothe all hurts, the better to build on a solid foundation; the policy of conciliation for the sake of unity; the policy of the golden mean; the best, the true, the sole policy which can obtain in our country.

Sprung from a vanquished people, but a people who, in their turn had themselves made the conquest of Liberty, his dream was to unite the two races on the only rational basis: equality of rights, mutual respect and tolerance. His political vision moved him to seal anew the pact entered into by Lafontaine and Baldwin in days gone by and so bring fresh strength to the work of the Fathers of Confederation.

Was this majestic vision too ambitious? History, that impartial judge of men and events, will say whether or not he brought it to realization, but what we of his time may uphold from this moment is his untiring perseverance, his steadfast courage, his invincible faith in the ideal he set out to attain from the very start of his career. However, he was too well versed in psychology not to realize the difficulties which beset his path.

In 1887, hardly a year after that historical debate when, at one flight, he had risen to the greatest heights of parliamentary eloquence, when the English-speaking press had acclaimed him as the "silver-tongued orator," the Liberal Party, helpless after the retirement of Edward Blake, was casting about for a leader. The French Liberals formed a minority in this party, as they formed a minority in the country. Let it be said to the honour of the English Liberals, it was Edward Blake, it was Sir Richard Cartwright, it was David Mills, who selected the leader, and the unanimous choice fell upon Wilfrid Laurier. What was the answer of the young member for Quebec East? Ah, Mr. Speaker, our great countryman, despite his marvellous endowments, did not covet the honour offered him. He well knew the burden he was assuming; already he could catch a glimpse of the obstacles which lay in wait for him, and the answer of this man who, beneath a stolid exterior, hid very deep emotions, his answer was a sob.

Thus, unable to escape the earnest entreaties of his English-speaking friends, he undertook to lead the Liberal Party, determined to steer the ship of state towards progress and liberty, to bind together, by conciliation in both word and deed, the heterogeneous elements which go to make up Canada. He had often said that the national sentiment of a country is worth no more than the pride which it inspires in its sons. He knew this country was overflowing with strength and vigour, full of activity, of ambition.

He loved its distant childhood; its history, every page of which he knew; its legends; its fertile, majestic natural beauty; he loved this country especially for its ethnic duality which showed him the children of two greatest races of Europe, henceforth fellow-wayfarers towards a common destiny in the boundless spaces of the New World.

By healing the wounds of days-gone-by and rallying all for the development of our immense resources, he opened a new era, he anticipated the day when he could declare in the presence of his Sovereign: "Sir, Canada is a nation. The nineteenth century belonged to the United States; but the twentieth century will witness the expansion of Canada."

The twenty-third of June, 1896, was a memorable date in our political annals. The member for Quebec East had just been borne into power by a majority of the electorate. He became Prime Minister of a Dominion which had been guided by the genius of Macdonald. The old Tory chieftain had passed from the stage some five years before and the memory of his bewitching magnetism bordered on the legendary. People anxiously wondered if the orator from Quebec would reveal himself a statesman of sterling worth.

Would he have the necessary firmness? Could he grapple with our intricate problems? Would he prove himself an experienced helmsman and steer the ship safely through shallow shoals, flinging into the teeth of the gale, to ride at anchor in the port beyond?

My answer to all these apprehensions, already distant and, mayhap, forgotten, is that which John Morley made, one day, regarding Gladstone. The occasion was the unveiling of the statue erected in honour of the Grand Old Man, but a step or two from Lincoln's Inn. "The stalwarts of finance, of the City, looked with misgiving upon the idealism of Gladstone and smiled at his supposed incompetence in matters of money and business. I wonder," added Morley – and I still see him, his finger pointing to the monument – "I wonder, whether after Gladstone's long and brilliant career, the Bank of England itself would not feel honoured by the presence and strengthened by the counsel of the orator?"

As I have just said, it is only in the cold, calm light of impartial history that the part played by men in the great events of their time, can be duly appreciated. But I think I am within the mark of stating now that in Laurier's optimism, in his power of assimilation, in his incessant and untiring toil, in his boundless faith in the future of our country, may be seen and reflected in the powerful impulsion given to Canada from 1896 to 1911, her wonderful ascent towards economic progress, her marvellous development. How often have I not heard him whenever grappling with some difficult problem repeating the lines penned by André Chénier, the great French poet:

"*L'illusion féconde habite dans mon sein,*
J'ai les ailes de l'espérance!
"In my bosom dwells fruitful Illusion
On the wings of hope I soar!"

He had to the fullest extent mastered the sense of the Constitution; he had an insight into its jurisprudence and genius, and he loved it.

He ever advocated adherence to the federal pact, in its integrity. To his mind, any change, any departure or new orientation involved a danger. He was an apostle of autonomy, like Blake and Mowat.

His political creed borrowed its inspiration from British liberalism. He believed in progress grounded on order; he believed in the advent of democracy through evolution, not through revolution, but never did he allow himself to be carried away by his love of liberty beyond those two limits laid down by conscience and human reason, that is to say, rights and duties.

From the national standpoint, none of the two great ethnical elements of the country was to predominate or to be domineered. Equal justice, equal rights for all such, was his motto. He deprecated isolation, because as he said, for an ethnical group to isolate itself is tantamount to stagnating in inferiority. Let me add that he always advocated harmonious relations between religions and liberty, by means of a loyal alliance. In a country like ours so hard to govern, and owing to the fact that the opinions and creeds of the various ethnical groups have to be taken into consideration – policy of exclusiveness is not properly speaking a policy but a blunder which must prove fatal to minorities. Love of justice and of freedom, tolerance, loyalty grounded upon autonomy, patriotism, such were his ideals. And with what mastery did he expound them!

Those who will read his speeches in which the scholar always controls the tribune, checks his outburst, chastens his language, will no doubt find in them the luster of fancy coupled with the magic of style, but they will first of all discover loftiness of thought combined with an unerring judgment, and the intuition of the right course to steer through the winds of Canadian politics. And this constitutes a lofty ideal, and it was this ideal which fashioned Laurier into the Great Canadian that he was. But in appreciating his career, it is on his firm and dignified attitude in the relations of Canada and the Mother Country that our attention must be focused.

None more than Laurier admired the majestic institutions of the British Empire, where liberty wrought this miracle of a Gavan

Duffy, a Wilfrid Laurier, a Louis Botha, respectively governing Australia, Canada, Africa, with intense loyalty and devotedness to the interests of the Crown.[207]

In this connection may I be allowed to add that after the Transvaal war, Sir Wilfrid Laurier was consulted in turn by [Henry] Campbell-Bannerman[208] and by General Botha as to the contemplated South African Union and that both these statesmen benefited by vast experience. I shall never forget the words uttered in my presence at Cape Town, in November, 1910, by the Boer General: "In South Africa, two names are particularly dear to us, that of Campbell-Bannerman and that of Wilfrid Laurier. To those two men we owe an eternal debt of gratitude."

At the several Imperial conferences which he attended – and we all know what a brilliant role he played in them – Sir Wilfrid Laurier, whose fiscal policy had tickled the pride of the Mother Country, had nevertheless to withstand the new wave which was just then beginning to roll from London into the Dominions. This brilliant dream of a vast Empire, whose centre of action would be Westminster, could, forsooth, seduce the leaders of British politics, but Laurier was a Canadian first and last. Our country having disentangled itself from the bonds of Colonialism had gradually conquered its political freedom, through the extension of the principle of autonomy. Knowing the exact extent of our rights and duties, he boldly and sincerely proclaimed the principle of Imperial unity based upon local liberties.

That virile attitude was to him, no doubt, the source of disappointment. But the old Premier was too much of a philosopher not to realize that impulses cannot play the part of reason, and that popularity is a poor substitute for arguments.

Were I called upon to define the outstanding qualities of Sir Wilfrid Laurier as a statesman, I would say that his moderation was a driving power in itself, his gift of expression a shining light, and that, with this master of oratory, sound judgment and common sense outweighed his very eloquence.

His worthy manner of living, his thorough honesty, his perfect equanimity through the worst ordeals, his devouring intellectual activity, his unimpeachable righteousness, his home life imbued with such charm and beauty, his loyalty to friends, his discreet charity, but, above all, his eloquence exerted in behalf of the downtrodden, all these recall in many respects some distinctive characteristics of Gladstone and Lincoln.

We shall no longer have before our eyes those refined and aristocratic features of Laurier, whose most amiable smile went to the plebeian, the needy, the humble, the lowly and the feeble; but his memory made immortal in works of bronze and marble will pass on to coming generations as one of the greatest embodiments of virtue in public and private life, as one of the finest products of human-kind in the last century.

We, as his followers, his admirers, find solace in the thought that he died in the way he had wished to die. As the Norman knights of old, it was clothed in his armour that he appeared before the Supreme Judge. Death, the soother of all suffering, was to him like the declining hours of a beautiful day.

Before closing his eyes to things terrestrial, he had the supreme joy of seeing the Allies victorious. Enamoured of freedom and justice, he witnessed the downfall in Europe of autocracy and its instrument, militarism, and the founding on their ruins of the League of Nations.

As of yore at Inkerman and at Sebastopol, he saw our two great mother countries clasping hands and joining their forces on the battlefield, and our sons rushing with a light heart to meet together a glorious death and take their full share of sacrifice and victory.

Yes, he was granted that supreme consolation of seeing France,

France which was branded as frivolous, because she was cheerful, standing before the whole world as an example of endurance and fortitude, and showing herself to the oppressed what she had ever been, the shield of civilization, the champion of right. He beheld England, that country deemed cold and self-seeking, set out all her sails, spend lavishly of her wealth; call to arms all her children to rescue the world from oppression.

The alliance of these two great powers, sealed by the purest of blood, was especially dear to his heart. To him it appeared like the rainbow which breaks through the clouds, and which is described in the Holy Writ as a messenger of peace, a presage of better days to all men of good will.

O Laurier! Should there remain something to be done towards the fulfillment of that triumph of harmony and goodwill which you have so persistently striven to bring about, then those younger Canadians, whose teacher you were, will in turn take up the work and carry it to its full completion. They will pride themselves in following in your footsteps along the rugged and endless path of duty which you have opened and pointed out to them.

And now, with this last farewell, allow us to mingle the expression of our deep sense of gratitude. We are thankful to you, Laurier, for having ever remained worthy of the part entrusted to you by Providence, since from the palaces of our sovereigns and from the most humble farmhouse, from the towering cathedral as well as from the smallest country church, there ascends towards heaven the same hymn of gratitude.

We say farewell and we thank you. We thank you for having thus gathered around you your own people, the descendants of those Canadians of old, the last to give up the fight in that last battle, who, with souls anguished by defeat, escorted the Marquis of Montcalm from the gates of Old Quebec to the Château Saint-Louis, on the night following the battle on the Plains of Abraham. We thank you for having lifted them up to you and invited them to share your glory.

We say farewell and we thank you. We thank you for the shining memento which you bequeathed to the historian at large. Its brilliancy will not fade. It will be a guiding light which the tempest-beaten mariner will look to. It will be as a pillar of fire which will guide, on their march towards the promised land of a better Dominion, all sections of the Canadian people, reconciled at last to one another and linked together by the bonds of an "Union sacrée."

Farewell. Close to your resting place, amid maples and poplars, adorned by the coming spring with luxuriant foliage, we shall, many of us, congregate to pray in the tongue of your ancestors. The field wherein you lie, whose tender embrace you received, will be light to you. For it is part of that native land whose history is three centuries old and whose motherly womb will some day cover our meanness with its vastness and shroud our nothingness with its perennity. Adieu!

By David Lockhart

Few words are as likely to evoke anxiety in a speechwriter as, "I'll need you to draft the eulogy." Blame Pericles. Ever since his funeral oration for the fallen of the Peloponnesian War in the fifth century B.C., there has been an expectation that the death of worthies should be marked with an appropriate eulogy.

Few succeed. Lincoln came closest with his Gettysburg Address – a speech that leaned heavily, in structure and theme, on Pericles's masterpiece.

With the passing of Wilfrid Laurier in 1919, the challenge of providing a fitting tribute was compounded by the fact that he had himself set the gold standard with his eulogies of Sir John A. Macdonald and Queen Victoria. Any eulogy of him, in other words, would be measured against the eulogies by him. No pressure.

And yet . . .

All three speakers rose to the occasion with thoughtful, eloquent speeches. The language in every case is grand and glorious. Their sentences proceed at their own dignified pace. Their themes move inexorably from the particular to the universal, setting Laurier's life against the larger ideas of principles, values, and history.

Could such speeches be delivered today? Probably not. Certainly the style of speaking would be different. Today's speeches are informal, even conversational. You'd never get away with, "No need of Canada has been greater and none has lain nearer to the statesman's heart than the removal of discord between the different races and tongues and creeds which comprise the Canadian Confederacy."

It's a beautifully crafted sentence, but it reflects the style of its time. In 1919, oratory was still prized and attention spans were longer. Politicians didn't speak in sound bites, and audiences were used to following long, complex arguments through meandering sentences and extended speeches.

Speakers of the early twentieth century were also able to refer freely to history, poetry, literature, and the Bible, confident that their audience would know exactly what they were talking about. Today? If a speaker wants to be sure that their listeners will get a cultural reference, it probably has to be about "The Simpsons." (D'oh!)

To be sure, today's political leaders can rise to the occasion in times of deep emotion and high patriotism. We saw them do so after the shootings on Parliament Hill and in the tributes to the Honourable Jim Flaherty.[209]

Even in these cases, however, there were important differences. Reading the tributes to Flaherty, for example, one is struck by the apparent relief felt by members of Parliament, from all sides, in being able to speak without partisanship. In 1919, at such moments of national import, neutrality was a given.

Today's tributes are also much more self-referential. If the eulogies to Laurier were exhortations to idealism, today's speeches are exercises in association. Members recount their own interactions with Flaherty. This insertion of one's self into a eulogy would have been deemed unseemly in 1919. Indeed, the only such reference in these earlier speeches is to declare the speaker's own inadequacy to pay the required tribute.

In our age, obsessed with self-image, self-regard, and self-actualization, it seems that even tributes to others are, ultimately, still about us.

It is also affecting to see how the long shadow of Sir John A. Macdonald extends over Laurier even in death. All three speakers refer to the Old Chieftain. While the comparisons are always favourable, and Laurier would no doubt have appreciated the association, it would also have been nice for Laurier to be remembered for his own merits, rather than for his relationship with Macdonald.

The three eulogies also connect Laurier to his place in history, with an almost elegiac acknowledgment that his passing marks the closing of an age – an age when Canada was born, fought its first wars, welcomed new provinces and took its place on the world stage.

Today, the setting of events in their historical context is rare, perhaps because that history is less well known or perhaps because our perspective, like our attention span, is more limited.

But if the speeches reflect the tone and tenor of their time, they also express ideals that should inspire us still. In light of current debates over "reasonable accommodation" and the integration of immigrants, we might benefit by remembering D.D. McKenzie's articulation of Laurier's aim: ". . . to bind together, by conciliation in both word and deed, the heterogeneous elements which go to make up Canada."

In her latest book, History's People: Personalities and the Past, *historian Margaret MacMillan writes of the relationship between history and biography, of the role of individuals in shaping events. Tributes like those offered on Laurier's death remind us of the difference one person can make and of the example he or she can set for those who follow.*

To modern ears, these speeches can sound stilted, archaic, grandiose. But to those who love words, to read them is to luxuriate, if only for a few moments, in the kinder temper of earlier times. And to recall that language used to matter in politics.

It still should.

Veteran Ottawa speech writer David Lockhart, who has worked with the Right Honourable John Turner, the Right Honourable Paul Martin, and numerous other public figures, leads Lockhart Communications.

DEDICATION OF LAURIER'S
PARLIAMENT HILL STATUE

OTTAWA, ONTARIO
AUGUST 3, 1927[210]

Sir Robert Borden: I am grateful for the privilege of paying my sincere tribute to the great Canadian we honour today. It was in 1881 that I first saw Sir Wilfrid Laurier during his tour of Nova Scotia with Edward Blake, then leader of the Liberal Party. Ten years later I listened with rapt attention in the Gallery of the House of Commons while there fell from his lips a moving tribute to Sir John Macdonald who had just passed away. In another ten years, as Leader of the Liberal–Conservative Party, I stood opposite to him in the House of Commons and for eighteen years thereafter we led the respective parties that had honoured us with their confidence.

Upon Sir Wilfrid's magnetic personality, his wonderful intellect, imagination and compelling eloquence I need not dwell, nor upon the splendid distinction of his great career. Rather would I speak of his remarkable personal charm, which recalled the poet's words: *Such grace befell not every man on earth as crowns this one.*[211]

He was indeed endowed with infinite grace both in speech and action. Like Sir John Macdonald he inspired his party with the deepest emotion of love and devoted loyalty; even strong political opponents cherished for him a feeling of warm affection. To me it is a happy memory that although we differed on most questions of public policy, our personal relations were never disturbed, and that from first to last, although I was obliged to own him as a political foe. I was proud to hold him as a personal friend, and perhaps this personal friendship may have assisted not only to maintain, but to increase the amenities of political conflict in the federal arena.

Although he was designated as a Liberal in his public activities, Sir Wilfrid Laurier was a Conservative in all that concerned the upholding of the best traditions of parliamentary government. He sometimes described himself as a Liberal of the Gladstone school, but I have heard him say that in methods of parliamentary government he had been brought up in the school of Sir John Macdonald, and that he would always maintain the principles which he had thus learned.

For more than ten years I led the Opposition, while he was in power, and in all that concerned the maintenance of the wholesome traditions of Parliament and the principles of parliamentary government I am glad to acknowledge that I was a disciple of Sir Wilfrid Laurier. He had a remarkably thorough grasp of constitutional practice and procedure which were always safe in his hands. His attitude to the party in Opposition was not only fair, but generous and considerate.

His profound faith in the high destiny of Canada never faltered for a moment. The years of his Premiership were attended with many events and developments of the greatest importance, and with questions of exceptional difficulty. All these he approached with a keen sense of public trust, and when the storm of war burst upon the Empire in 1914 he gave to the Administration of the day his unstinted support in making Canada's effort worthy of the cause and our country.

To me the House of Commons was never the same after his gracious presence no longer moved among us. Without distinction of race or party his countrymen hold him in happy memory, and accord him a final fame that will overcome, that shall overbear reluctant time.

By Hugh Segal

Every leader and prime minister brings with him or her to high office aspects of inspiration, determination, hard work, and personal style. Each is unique in the particular mix and tone of what is brought and portrayed. Some of these qualities are rewarded by our politics and the voters and media who shape its dynamic. In some cases, because of the broader competitive frame, the rewards are illusory.

For Sir Wilfrid Laurier, icon of post-Confederation Liberalism, founder of the Royal Canadian Navy, defender of both francophone rights and the British connection, there was a particular magic to the way his eloquence, stature, decency, and personality not only shaped his career, but became a formative cornerstone not only for Canadian Liberalism, but for the core duality and federalist spirit at the centre of the Canadian idea and experience. Always, his breadth of outlook eschewed the small or parochial, and embraced instead the higher purpose and longer view for Canada, its domestic purpose and global linkage.

This mix of vision and balance, coherence and intellectual integrity not only shaped the deepest of loyalties among his co-partisans, and the deepest of respect and regard by those who were formally in Opposition, as our Westminster system of parliamentary government provides.

Part of this abiding respect and affection was engendered by the brand of "liberalism" he avowed. He clearly rejected the Lord (Radical Jack) Durham approach, which sought to subsume Canadian institutional and political norms to a global brand of British liberalism, which set aside acquired collective respect for identity, language, and the accommodation implicit in the core underpinnings for language and identity in the premises of Confederation itself.

Instead, he embraced very much the style and form of Sir John A.'s Conservative frame, wherein different groups worked with each other because they were comfortable about the accommodation on which they depended. This central theme of accommodation drove Confederation itself. It drove Sir Wilfrid's mastery of the Manitoba Schools crisis, and the electoral success it engendered. It drove his championing, with Robert Borden his Tory successor, of the creation of the Canadian Navy over a century ago. It was a characteristic Laurier response to an imperative to support the British Navy and the mother country's defence of free passage on the seas in the face of other countries' naval expansion. Canada would begin its own navy, loyal to the mother country, but an independent and Canadian force.

He supported Canadian deployment in the Boer War. His French-Canadian nationalism and pride embraced the full gambit of the Imperial connection. This tonality and sensibility underlined his brand of liberal nationalism – and made Canada a stronger bi-cultural and bilingual home for millions.

There are political leaders who live within their own partisan traditions, show little courage and less breadth of vision in ways that broaden their version of inclusive politics. There are others, less numerous, who reach out to build a bigger tent – one in which not only their partisans feel comfortable. Sir Wilfrid was this latter style of leader and prime minister. The country he inherited and helped make was made incalculably stronger as a result.

Hugh Segal, a former senator and past chief of staff to Prime Minister Brian Mulroney, is Master of Massey College in the University of Toronto and honorary chair of the Navy League of Canada.

AFTERWORDS

THE CANADA THAT
LAURIER BUILT

BY THE RIGHT HONOURABLE JEAN CHRÉTIEN

The first French-Canadian prime minister. A tireless champion of national unity. A visionary who opened Canada's doors to the world and who settled the West. A pioneer of Canadian independence. An avatar of Canadian values. The captain who steered a young nation into the promise of a new century.

Sir Wilfrid Laurier is certainly all these things and more. It's hard to imagine what our country would be today without his singular contribution.

Like every Canadian, I owe him a debt. But all through my life Laurier has had an even deeper and more personal influence on me.

He was close to a secular saint in our household. As a young man, my father, Wellie, had shaken Laurier's hand – an experience he cherished for the rest of his long life. For me, a young boy growing up in rural Quebec, a unilingual francophone growing up in a country whose power structure was decidedly – and almost uniquely – English-speaking, Laurier was an inspiration and an ideal. Much in the same way that the election of Barack Obama inspired all young children to dream of exciting and unlimited opportunities, Laurier, a rural francophone, who rose to lead an overwhelmingly Anglo-Saxon Canadian society, was an example to me.

And throughout my forty years in public life, he was a guiding light and constant presence. No more so than during the decade that I was privileged to lead our country as prime minister.

Canada was envisioned by the Fathers of Confederation as a partnership between the English and French founding cultures. That vision truly became a reality in the 1896 election. Laurier, the rural Quebecer from Saint-Lin, became Canada's first French-speaking prime minister. Laurier was a flesh-and-blood symbol to French-Canadians that they had a place of respect in Canada, even if they were and would remain a minority.

Laurier truly believed in the promise of Canada, and he inspired Canadians to make that promise a reality by calling on them to look beyond their particular region, language, or religion. Laurier believed that Canadian unity could be built on diversity, rather than sameness.

Laurier took over a country torn apart by divisions between English and French, Catholics and Protestants, over the Manitoba Schools question. On this issue and many others, he rejected the extreme views on both sides because he understood that a nation as diverse and far-flung as Canada could not survive that kind of polarization. He believed, as do I, that our country is better served by pragmatism rather than ideology, by compromise rather than conflict. This approach earned him many followers, but also many detractors, notably those among Henri Bourassa's nationalists and in the Protestant Orange Order. As he said in 1911, "I am branded in Quebec as a traitor to the French and in Ontario as a traitor to the English. . . . [But] I am a Canadian."

From 1993 to 2003, the desk in my office on Parliament Hill was Laurier's own. His portrait hung on the wall. I often found myself wondering, when facing the difficult questions of the day, how to apply his lessons and wisdom. Many of Laurier's ideas remain as relevant as ever to today's politics. His wisdom, now a century old, is surprisingly modern.

Laurier was ahead of his time in recognizing the emancipating and lifting power of liberalized trade. Just as he crashed barriers in his own life, he worked hard to bring down the walls and fences of protectionism. He understood that Canada's true economic promise could only be achieved by opening itself to the world.

But at the same time, he was a fierce and courageous advocate of Canadian independence. For a young country, still very much in the shadow of the British Empire, that was a daunting and audacious stance. In his time many – if not most – English-speaking Canadians felt themselves more British than

Canadian. But Laurier resisted attempts, both at home and abroad, to weave Canada ever more tightly with the Empire. He put it simply, clearly, unmistakably: "Canada first, Canada last, Canada always."

Laurier saw a positive role for government in nation-building. He built Canada's second transcontinental railroad to strengthen the ties that bind us together. He created two new provinces, Saskatchewan and Alberta, in 1905. He opened up the West to settlers, including French Quebecers such as my maternal grandfather, who went out to a farm north of Edmonton in 1907. He also encouraged immigration to Canada to inhabit our sparsely populated country. Faced with the current market downturn, Laurier would ask what government can do through smart policies on infrastructure, regulation, and immigration to strengthen our economy.

People often forget that Laurier had opposed Confederation at first, but once he became convinced of the merits of the new arrangement, he became the most ardent Canadian of his era. It's no wonder that Laurier often called Canada the inspiration of his life. Just as he transformed Canada, so too was he transformed by it.

Laurier imagined Canada as a strong, independent country whose voice would be heard on the international stage, and the first modern nation to celebrate diversity, tolerance, and generosity. He built a country in this image through his four terms as prime minister.

It's often said that we stand on the shoulders of those who came before us. I know that as a Canadian, and as someone who has had the honour of serving our country in so many capacities, including its highest elected office, I thank fortune that Wilfrid Laurier's shoulders were so broad and solid.

The Right Honourable Jean Chrétien was Canada's twentieth prime minister.

LAURIER'S ECHOS

BY THE RIGHT HONOURABLE STEPHEN J. HARPER

One of the greatest privileges I had as prime minister was retracing Sir Wilfrid Laurier's footsteps in travelling to London to honour a Queen on her Diamond Jubilee.

While times had changed in world and Canadian politics, I still felt and heard the echoes of Sir Wilfrid's Diamond Jubilee visit of so long before while I was in London in 2012.

It was there, at Queen Victoria's Diamond Jubilee in 1897, that our Canada took her first steps, under Laurier's gifted leadership, onto the world stage. Canada has remained on Laurier's confident path ever since.

Sir Wilfrid Laurier took office in 1896, not long after the death of Canada's Father of Confederation, Sir John A. Macdonald. The Laurier Years (1896 to 1911) were ones of great promise and growth for Canada. My own province, Alberta, along with Saskatchewan, joined Confederation on his watch; the entire West was settled by thousands from beyond our shores, and Canada's stature, both continentally and internationally, heightened substantially.

Laurier's speeches remind us today that he spent decades in elected politics before becoming prime minister. Sitting opposite his greatest opponent, Sir John A. Macdonald, he participated in the discussions that defined and shaped the young Dominion in which he lived. Provincial rights, the events involving Louis Riel, minority languages, the building of the CPR, French–English relations and the quest for freer trade with the United States: these were debates he engaged in with vigour and unmatched eloquence.

As a Conservative I note the constant themes that emerge when reading Laurier's speeches. He believed in low taxation and government economy. The seventh prime minister also kept a watchful eye on incursions by the federal government into areas of provincial jurisdiction, and, sought to reduce trade barriers between Canada and the United States. He also carried within him a passionate belief in parliamentary government and her institutions, such as the monarchy.

A study of Laurier also reminds us what a ground-breaking political innovator he proved to be. It was at his direction, for example, that his party became the first in post-Confederation Canada, in 1893, to hold a national convention. His addresses also demonstrate the attention he paid throughout his career to party organization. There are lessons for all political leaders, at all levels of government, in these speeches today.

Politics was his calling, craft, and profession. And he was a master.

Despite the ups and downs of his career and the all too frequent moments when Canadian unity was tested, Sir Wilfrid Laurier never lost his faith in Canada and her peoples.

His challenge and example, like Macdonald, is so very relevant today. Sir Wilfrid Laurier stands as one of our greatest prime ministers.

<u>He always will.</u>

We are correct to continue to celebrate his legacy. And I am confident that prime ministers and Canadians will always do so as Canada grows and prospers.

Just as Laurier, like Macdonald before him, predicted our nation would.

The Right Honourable Stephen J. Harper was Canada's twenty-second prime minister.

ENDNOTES

1. John Willison, *Sir Wilfrid Laurier and the Liberal Party*, vol. II (Toronto: George N. Morang and Company, 1903), 388.

2. According to the Library of Parliament, Laurier served forty-four years, ten months, and seventeen days in the Commons, from January 22, 1874 to February 17, 1919. When combined service in both the House of Commons and Senate is taken into account, Laurier's contemporary, fellow prime minister Sir Mackenzie Bowell, bested Laurier, serving in the Commons from 1867 until 1892, and then in the Senate from 1892 until his death in 1917.

3. I owe a special debt of gratitude to my long-time friend Peter O'Malley, and also my colleague from the Prime Minister's Office, Evan Silver, for encouraging me to utilize the Internet and look beyond traditional methods in my research.

4. "Well Under Stress of Traveling," *Vancouver Daily World*, December 16, 1917.

5. Augustus Bridle, *The Masques of Ottawa* (Toronto: Macmillan, 1921), 48.

6. John Willison, *Sir Wilfrid Laurier and the Liberal Party*, vol. II (Toronto: George N. Morang and Co., 1903), 387-88.

7. Ulric Barthe, *Wilfrid Laurier on the Platform: 1871–1890* (Quebec: Turcotte and Menard, 1890).

8. Laurent-Oliver David (1840–1926) was a respected Quebec journalist, politician, and friend of Laurier's. He was made a senator, on Laurier's advice, in 1903.

9. Barthe, *Wilfrid Laurier on the Platform: 1871–1890*, v.

10. Richard Clippingdale, *Laurier: His Life and World* (Toronto, McGraw Hill, 1979), 9.

11. Quoted in "Grandest meeting Toronto ever had," *Toronto Daily Star*, October 15, 1904.

12. "Canada's Royal Citizen unveils bronze statue to Canada's great son," *Toronto Globe*, August 3, 1927.

13. Quoted in Joseph Schull, "Laurier: The First Canadian" (Toronto: Macmillan, 1966), 8.

14. Schull, "Laurier: The First Canadian," 6-7.

15. Quoted in Réal Bélanger, "The Right Honourable Sir Wilfrid Laurier," in *The Prime Ministers of Canada* (Ottawa: New Confederation House, 2005), 32.

16. Source: *Proceedings of the Annual Convocation of the McGill University, Montreal, held on Tuesday, the 3rd, and Wednesday, the 4th of May, 1864* (Montreal: M. Longmoore & Co., Gazette Steam Press, 1864), 35-39. Laurier's speech was read in French and appears in the original in the *Proceedings*. This is its first complete translation. I am most grateful to Michel W. Pharand for his generous assistance in both translating and annotating this important speech.

17. An allusion to Romans 2:6.

18. Barristers John Scott, 1st Earl of Eldon (1751–1838), and Thomas Erskine, 1st Baron Erskine (1750–1823), became lord chancellors.

19. Henry Peter Brougham, 1st Baron Brougham and Vaux (1778–1868).

20. Jules Favre (1809–1880), Émile Ollivier (1825–1913), Adolphe Billault (1805–1863), Eugène Rouhers (1814–1884).

21. "Perhaps even this will one day be a pleasure to recall." Virgil, *The Aeneid*, Book I, line 203.

22. André Pratte, *Wilfrid Laurier* (Toronto: Penguin Group, 2011), 13.

23. Pratte, *Wilfrid Laurier*, 5.

24. Public Archives of Canada, Laurier Papers, 92017, Laurier to W. Gregory, November 11, 1904, quoted in H. Blair Neatby, "Laurier and Imperialism," *Report of the Annual Meeting of the Canadian Historical Association* 34.1 (1955), 24.

25. Source: Barthe, *Wilfrid Laurier on the Platform: 1871–1890*, 1–8.

26. Cokayne is the mythical land of luxury and endless comforts and pleasures from medieval lore.

27. The Greek mythological figure punished in Tartarus, in the Underworld, by standing in a pool of receding water near a fruit tree whose branches forever eluded his grasp.

28. Narcisse-Fortunat Belleau (1808–1894), lieutenant governor of Quebec 1867–73.

29. Louis-Joseph Papineau (1786–1871), the great *Patriote* leader during Lower Canada's rebellion.

30. Pierre-Joseph-Olivier Chauvreau (1820–1890), Quebec's first post-Confederation premier, later served for less than a year as speaker of the Canadian Senate and, after politics, was a professor of law at Laval University.

31. See "La Barbe bleue," in Charles Perrault, *Histoires ou contes du temps passé* (1697).

32. Source: from Ulric Barthe, *Wilfrid Laurier on the Platform: 1871–1890*, 21-40.

33. Louis Riel (1844–1885), the famed Canadian Métis leader whose leadership of the Métis, particularly during the Rebellions (so-called) in Manitoba and later Saskatchewan, continues to inspire hope for his people and among all Canadians – and to arouse controversy. Issues surrounding Riel proved crucial during the early years of Laurier's participation in politics.

34. Luther Hamilton Holton (1817–1880), a veteran Quebec Liberal politician who served both provincially and federally after Confederation.

35. Granville Leveson-Gower, 1st Earl Granville (1773–1846), a leading British Whig parliamentarian and diplomat.

36. John Sadleir (1813–1856), an Irish nationalist and British parliamentarian who committed suicide after his involvement in a financial scandal.

37. Sir Mackenzie Bowell (1823–1917), Canadian prime minister 1894–96.

38. Thomas Scott (1842–1870) was a Protestant government surveyor whose execution by Louis Riel's Provisional Government in 1870 inflamed Protestant and Orange public opinion, leading to the dispatch by Ottawa of a military force to what would become Manitoba.

39. Louis Riel spent these years in exile in the United States.

40. Alexandre-Antonin Taché (1823–1894), at this time bishop of the diocese of St. Boniface.

41. Father Joseph-Noël Ritchot (1825–1905), who negotiated with the Government on behalf of the Métis during the troubles at Red River, Manitoba.

42. Sir George-Étienne Cartier (1814–1873), Father of Confederation and Quebec's key player in Confederation and in Sir John A. Macdonald's Conservative Party.

43. Source: Barthe, *Wilfrid Laurier on the Platform: 1871–1890*, 51-80.

44. *History of England*, Macaulay, Vol. 1. [Barthe's note]

45. Junius is the pseudonym of the anonymous author of a series of famous letters to the London *Public Advertiser* in 1869–1872.

46. In Greek mythology, Argus is the famed giant with one hundred eyes.

47. In Greek mythology, Sisyphus is condemned to spend eternity rolling a boulder up a hill and retrieving it when it rolls back down.

48. Charles James Fox (1749–1806) was an important British Whig who spent decades in Parliament.

49. Daniel O'Connell (1775–1847) was a famed Irish political leader who fought for equal rights for Catholics in British-ruled Ireland.

50. Charles Grey, 2nd Earl Grey (1764–1845), Whig prime minister considered the architect of the great 1832 Reform Bill; Henry Brougham (see note 19) served as lord chancellor of Great Britain; John Russell, 1st Earl Russell (1792–1878), a Whig who twice served as prime minister; Francis Jeffrey, Lord Jeffrey (1773–1850), famed Scottish Whig writer, jurist, and politician.

51. The Representation of the People Act 1832 vastly extended the franchise and reformed Britain's electoral system.

52. *The Life and Letters of Lord Macaulay*, by Trevelyan. [Barthe's note]

53. Sir Louis-Hippolyte Lafontaine (1807–1864), the important French-Canadian politician who, with Robert Baldwin, brought responsible government to Canada East and Canada West in the critical pre-Confederation era.

54. From "La curée," by French poet Henri Auguste Barbier (1805–1882).

55. Alfred Tennyson, 1st Baron Tennyson (1809–1892), the most famous British poet of the Victorian age. He completed his poem (quoted by Laurier), "In Memoriam A.H.H.," in 1849.

56. The orator has confounded J.B. Rousseau with Lefranc de Pompignan; but the two great lyric poets are so often cited together in collections of literature that the lecturer, who was quoting from memory, may easily be pardoned for this *qui pro quo*. [Barthe's note] Jean-Baptiste Rousseau (1671–1741) was a famous French poet.

57. Source: Barthe, *Wilfrid Laurier on the Platform: 1871–1890*, 141–46.

58. Edward Blake (1833–1912) was Laurier's predecessor as leader of the Liberal Party. Briefly premier of Ontario, Blake played a leading role in promoting provincial rights. As a young MP, Laurier, in effect, had acted as Blake's secretary.

59. "The winning cause pleased the gods, but the losing cause pleased Cato." Lucan, *Pharsalia*.

60. On August 6, 1870, at the beginning of the Franco-Prussian War, German forces defeated the French at the Battle of Wörth (also called the Battle of Reischoffen). Hundreds of French cavalry were mowed

down at close range after a desperate counterattack aimed to cover the French retreat.

61. Source: Barthe, *Wilfrid Laurier on the Platform: 1871–1890*, 171–91.

62. Alexander Mackenzie (1822–1892), Canada's second prime minister.

63. Princess Louise, Duchess of Argyll (1848–1939), daughter of Queen Victoria, lived in Canada while her husband, John Campbell, Marquess of Lorne (1845–1914), was governor general in 1878–1883.

64. Henry Du Pré Labouchère (1831–1912), noted British politician, writer, and newspaper publisher.

65. Otto Eduard Leopold, Prince of Bismarck (1815–1898), was the famed Prussian leader who is credited with uniting Germany in the nineteenth century.

66. Spencerwood (built 1854) was the official residence of lieutenant-governors of Quebec from the 1870s until destroyed by fire in 1966.

67. Luc Letellier de Saint-Just (1820–1881) was Quebec's third lieutenant governor; for Sir Narcisse-Fortunat Belleau, see note 28.

68. A small commune in northern France. Laurier was surely referring to one of the poems by noted author Pierre-Jean de Béranger (1780–1857), who satirized in verse the tiny community's past monarchy. See https://archive.org/stream/onehundredsongso00beraiala/onehundred songso00beraiala_djvu.txt.

69. When Sir John A. Macdonald's government fell in late 1873 due to the Pacific Scandal, Alexander Mackenzie was invited to form Canada's first-ever Liberal administration. He and his party were then victorious in the general election in early 1874.

70. Sir Charles Tupper (1821–1915), a Father of Confederation and briefly prime minister in 1896.

71. Georges Jacques Danton (1759–1794), a leading figure during the French Revolution, served as president of the infamous Committee on Public Safety.

72. Although he remained in the Commons, Mackenzie had been stricken by paralysis and by this time had great difficulty speaking.

73. Sir Richard Cartwright (1835–1912) was one of the leading Liberals of his day. Known for his advocacy of reciprocity with the United States and for his dislike of fellow Kingstonian Sir John A. Macdonald, Cartwright would later serve in Laurier's cabinet.

74. Source: Barthe, *Wilfrid Laurier on the Platform: 1871–1890*, 353–88.

75. François de Gaston, Chevalier de Lévis (1719–1787), Montcalm's second-in-command.

76. Quoted in Richard Gwyn, *Sir John A. Macdonald: His Life, Our Times. Volume II: 1867–1891* (Toronto: Random House Canada, 2011), 589.

77. Quoted in Gwyn, *Sir John A. Macdonald*, 292.

78. Source: Barthe, *Wilfrid Laurier on the Platform: 1871–1890*, 525–31.

79. Laurier alludes to France's defeat in the Franco-Prussian War of 1870–1871.

80. Honoré Mercier (1840–1894), one Quebec's leading political figures, would become premier of Quebec in 1887.

81. Major Charles John Short and his colleague Stg. George Wallick gave their lives attempting to stop the flames during the great fire that destroyed much of the Quebec City community of St. Sauveur on May 16, 1889. Their heroism is commemorated by a statue that still stands in Quebec City.

82. William Pitt, 1st Earl of Chatham (1708–1778), Britain's famed Whig leader and distinguished parliamentarian, collapsed while speaking in the House of Commons and died soon afterwards.

83. Sir Antoine-Aimé Dorion (1818–1891) was co-premier of the Province of Canada and later served as minister of justice under Prime Minister Alexander Mackenzie. He was later appointed chief justice of the Court of Queen's Bench of Quebec.

84. Source: Willison, *Sir Wilfrid Laurier and the Liberal Party*, vol. II, 363–71.

85. Alexis-Charles-Henri Clérel de Tocqueville (1805–1859), the French politician and thinker, is most famous for his two-volume study, *Of Democracy in America* (1835, 1840).

86. John Neilson (1776–1848) was a Quebec printer, writer, and politician who proved a crucial early ally of Papineau's, though the two later fell into dispute. Fluently bilingual, Neilsen spent his life seeking accommodation and mutual respect between the French and English populations of Quebec. Edmund Bailey O'Callaghan (1797–1880) was a journalist and politician who became a key partner of Papineau's. After the Rebellion in Lower Canada of 1837, O'Callaghan, a doctor, fled British North America and never set foot on British soil again.

87. Wolfred Nelson (1791–1863), a doctor and political leader, was a reformer allied with Papineau.

88. At the famous Battle of Saint-Charles (November 25, 1837), British forces overcame those of the Lower Canada rebels.

89. Thomas Storrow Brown (1803–1888), a journalist and military official, was another crucial supporter of Papineau's during the events surrounding 1837 Rebellion.

90. William Ewart Gladstone (1809–1898), famed Liberal who served four times as prime minister of the United Kingdom.

91. Charles Forbes René de Montalembert (1810–1870) was a French intellectual, politician, and writer known for his liberalism. Jean-Baptiste Henri-Dominique Lacordaire (1802–1861), another famous French liberal, made a tremendous impact in the movement to free his country's educational system from official Church influence.

92. Protestant Protective Association: Based in Ontario, the notoriously anti-Catholic and anti-French Protestant Protective Association was affiliated with the Orange Order. It fought against the presence of French-Canadians in politics and the extension of French educational rights in Ontario and Manitoba.

93. French novelist and poet Victor Marie Hugo (1802–1885), the most famous and prolific writer of his era.

94. Source: *Official Report of the Liberal Convention Held in Response to the Call of the Hon. Wilfrid Laurier, Leader of the Liberal Party of the Dominion of Canada, Ottawa, Tuesday, June 20th, and Wednesday June 21st, 1891* (Budget Printing and Publishing Co., 1893). Accessed at https://archive.org/stream/cihm_09048/cihm_09048_djvu.txt.

95. Sir Oliver Mowat (1820–1903), a Father of Confederation, remains Ontario's longest-serving premier. He later entered Laurier's cabinet and was appointed lieutenant governor of Ontario. William Stevens Fielding (1848–1929) was premier of Nova Scotia before entering Laurier's cabinet. He served as minister of finance throughout Laurier's premiership and held the same post under Prime Minister Mackenzie King in the 1920s. Andrew George Blair (1844–1907), a premier of New Brunswick, joined Laurier's first cabinet but later resigned over disagreements about railway policy. Arthur Peters (1854–1908) was a premier of Prince Edward Island. Sir Clifford Sifton (1861–1929), at this time Manitoba's attorney general, went on to become a key member of Laurier's cabinet; he was known for his work in attracting thousands of European immigrants to western Canada. He resigned from cabinet in 1905 due to disagreements with Laurier and in 1911 campaigned against his former leader's policy of reciprocity with the United States. Sir Henri-Gustave Joly de Lotbinière (1829–1908) was premier of Quebec before entering federal politics and joining Laurier's cabinet. He was one of the founders of the Canadian Forestry Association; Laurier would appoint him British Columbia's lieutenant governor.

96. Thomas White (1830–1888) was a journalist and politician who served in Sir John A. Macdonald's cabinet.

97. Nathaniel Clarke Wallace (1844–1901), a leading member of the Orange Lodge, served as a Conservative cabinet minister, first under Sir John A. Macdonald.

98. Sir George Eulas Foster (1847–1931), one of the leading Conservative politicians of his era, served in the cabinets of seven prime ministers, from the days of Sir John A. Macdonald to Arthur Meighen. He was Canada's minister of finance under Macdonald, Sir John Abbott, Sir John Thompson, Sir Mackenzie Bowell, and Sir Charles Tupper.

99. Sir Auguste-Réal Angers (1837–1919) served in the cabinets of three prime ministers: Sir John Thompson, Sir Mackenzie Bowell, and Sir Charles Tupper.

100. Sir John Carling (1828–1911), of the famous brewing family, served with distinction as Macdonald's minister of agriculture and was later named to the Senate of Canada.

101. On June 20, 1877, a fire swept through Saint John, N.B., killing twenty people and destroying more than 1,500 structures.

102. Sir John Sparrow David Thompson (1845–1894), prime minister 1892–94.

103. Arthur Rupert Dickey (1854–1900), a Nova Scotia MP, was a leader in the temperance movement and Conservative cabinet minister under prime ministers Sir Mackenzie Bowell and Sir Charles Tupper.

104. Joseph-Israël Tarte (1848–1907) was a leading Quebec journalist and provincial and federal politician. While elected to the Commons as a Conservative, he later joined Laurier's cabinet and later severed ties with him. In the end, they reconciled and Tarte wrote articles in the popular press supporting his former leader. Dalton McCarthy (1836–1898), notoriously anti-French and anti-Catholic, was elected to the Commons as a Conservative but later broke with his party and was elected as an independent. His was a prominent voice during the Manitoba Schools Crisis, calling for the curtailment of rights of French-Canadian Catholics in Western Canada.

105. David Mills (1831–1903), one of the leading Liberals of his generation, served in the cabinets of both Mackenzie and Laurier, the latter appointing him to the Supreme Court of Canada. Sir Louis Henry Davies (1845–1924), a premier of Prince Edward Island and a federal Liberal cabinet minister under Laurier, was later elevated to the Supreme Court of Canada, becoming chief justice. John Charlton (1829–1910) was a businessman and Liberal MP who held his Ontario riding for a commanding thirty-two years. William Paterson (1839–1914) was a veteran Liberal

Ontario MP who became a member of Laurier's cabinet. Sir William Mulock (1843–1944) was an Ontario Liberal MP for decades before entering Laurier's cabinet. He was later appointed to senior positions on Ontario's Bench. He is often remembered today as the cabinet minister who brought a young William Lyon Mackenzie King into public life as his deputy minister. Sir James David Edgar (1841–1899) was a Liberal MP known for his strong support of French-Canadian minority rights. He was named speaker of the House of Commons by Laurier and died in office.

106. George Brown (1818–1880), the Reform leader who played a key role (with Sir John A. Macdonald) in making Confederation a reality, had organized the Clear Grit (Liberal) Party in 1857. He was founder and editor of the *Globe* newspaper.

107. Source: "Future prime minister Wilfrid Laurier visited Pembroke in 1894," *Pembroke Observer*, February 25, 2010, and "Laurier's eloquent words," *Winnipeg Tribune*, May 18, 1894, at www.newspapers.com/image/44187108/?terms=.

108. Source: "At Winnipeg: Mr. Laurier's first speech in Manitoba," *Globe*, September 4, 1893.

109. Thomas Mayne Daly (1852–1911), the first mayor of Brandon, Manitoba, served in Conservative cabinets in Ottawa between 1892 and 1896, becoming Manitoba's first federal cabinet minister.

110. Richard Cobden (1804–1865), British Liberal politician and businessman famous for his support of free trade; John Bright (1811–1889), famed British Liberal politician known for his oratory.

111. Sir Robert Peel (1788–1850), a Conservative, was twice prime minister of Great Britain.

112. Thomas McGreevy (1825–1897) was a scandal-plagued contractor and MP who enjoyed close ties with leading Quebec members of Sir John A. Macdonald's cabinet. Nicholas K. Connolly (d. 1901) was a principal in the firm of Larkin, Connolly & Co.

113. Christopher Finlay Fraser (1839–1894) was a leading Catholic member of Ontario's Legislature under Sir Oliver Mowat. He supervised the re-construction, as minister of public works, of the Legislative Assembly at Queen's Park, dying the year it was completed.

114. Thomas Greenway (1838–1908), a long-time MP, was Manitoba's seventh premier. It was his government's anti-French and anti-Catholic educational reforms that led to the Manitoba Schools Crisis.

115. Source: "Two Great Speeches: Laurier Defines His Attitude on the School Question," *Vancouver Daily World*, October 16, 1895.

116. The Lines of Torres Vedras were a remarkably successfully set of military fortifications, ordered built by the Duke of Wellington in Portugal during the Peninsular War (1807–1814), which protected British, Spanish, and Portuguese armies from the superior French forces.

117. André Masséna (1758–1817) was the leader of Napoleon's forces during French invasion of Portugal.

118. Willison, *Sir Wilfrid Laurier and the Liberal Party*, vol. II, 371–72.

119. Oscar Douglas Skelton, *Life and Letters of Sir Wilfrid Laurier*, vol. 2 (Toronto: Oxford University Press, 1922), 162; quoted in Patrice Dutil and David MacKenzie, *Canada 1911: The Decisive Election That Shaped the Country* (Toronto: Dundurn, 2011), 23–24.

120. For the full membership of Laurier's first cabinet, go to http://faculty. marianopolis.edu/c.belanger/quebechistory/encyclopedia/The Cabinetofalltalents.html.

121. Quoted in Joseph Schull, *Laurier: The First Canadian* (Toronto: Macmillan, 1966), frontispiece.

122. Source: "Brilliant speech by Sir Wilfrid Laurier," *Western Star and Roma Advertiser* (Toowoomba, Queensland) August 25, 1897. Accessed at http:// trove.nla.gov.au/ndp/del/article/97481114?searchTerm=%22Laurier%22 +and+%22Dominion+Day%22+%22London%22.

123. The so-called Trent Affair arose after a British vessel, the RMS *Trent*, was boarded by U.S. naval personnel from the USS *San Jacinto* in November 1861 and Confederate diplomats on the British ship were taken into Union custody. British public opinion viewed the incident as a serious affront to Britain's neutrality rights during the American Civil War and a strike against Britain's national honour. The incident could have seen the British entering the war but, as alluded to by Laurier, cooler heads prevailed.

124. Camillo Paolo Filippo Giulio Benso (1810–1861), Count of Cavour, of Isolabella, and of Leri, played a key role in Italy's push for unification.

125. Louis Jean Joseph Charles Blanc (1811–1882) was a leading French socialist and politician.

126. Gladstone's controversial pamphlet, *Bulgarian Horrors and the Question of the East* (1876), became an instant best-seller.

127. Sources: Lewis Copeland, Lawrence W. Lamm, and Stephen J. McKenna, eds., *The World's Great Speeches*, 4th enlarged ed. (Mineola, NY: Dover, 1999), 381–83, and "McKinley and Laurier make telling speeches," *San Francisco Call*, October 10, 1899, at http://cdnc.ucr.edu/cgi-bin/cdnc?a=d &d=SFC18991010.2.21.1&srpos=23&e=-------en--20--21-byDA-txt-txIN-Wilfrid+Laurier--1001----.

128. The Great Chicago Fire of October 8 to 10, 1871, left approximately 300 people dead and destroyed nine square kilometres.

129. John Greenleaf Whittier (1807–1892), "To Englishmen" (1862).

130. Whittier, "To Englishmen."

131. Library and Archives Canada, Diary of William Lyon Mackenzie King, January 21, 1901. Accessed at www.bac-lac.gc.ca/eng/discover/politics-government/prime-ministers/william-lyon-mackenzie-king/Pages/diaries-william-lyon-mackenzie-king.aspx#a.

132. Source: "Presentation to Premier," *Ottawa Journal*, May 16, 1902.

133. William Samuel Calvert (1859–1930) was an Ontario Liberal MP from 1896 to 1909.

134. King Edward VII (1841–1910).

135. John Colin Forbes (1846–1925) was a Canadian visual artist; a number of his portraits are part of the House of Commons Heritage Collection.

136. Nova Scotia's Robert Laird Borden (1854–1937), later Sir Robert Borden, served as Canada's Conservative leader from 1901 until 1920 and prime minister from 1911 to 1920.

137. Laurier was as good as his word and donated this painting in 1906; it remains part of the National Gallery of Canada's collections. See www.gallery.ca/en/see/collections/artwork.php?mkey=13100.

138. Source: "Welcomed home by fellow citizens, " *Ottawa Journal*, October 20, 1902.

139. Source: "Grandest meeting Toronto ever had," *Toronto Daily Star*, October 15, 1904.

140. Source: "The Premier of Ontario pleads his party's cause," *Ottawa Journal*, January 21, 1905.

141. Sir George William Ross (1841–1914), Ontario's premier between 1899 and 1905, is remembered for the advances in Ontario's education system he led as minister of education under Premier Sir Oliver Mowat. He was named to the Senate on the advice of Laurier in 1907.

142. I am grateful to the Rt Hon. Stephen J. Harper for drawing my attention to this address. It was accessed at www.ourroots.ca/e/page.aspx?id=245091.

143. Albert Henry George Grey, 4th Earl Grey (1851–1917), governor general of Canada 1904–1911.

144. George Hedley Vicars Bulyea (1859–1928), the first lieutenant governor of Alberta.

145. On March 27, 1907, the *Fredericton Gleaner* published a story stating that a federal cabinet minister had been ejected from a Montreal hotel after being found there in the company of two women of "ill repute."

The minister was later identified as H.R. Emmerson (1853–1914), whose struggles with alcohol were well known in official Ottawa. Emmerson sued the *Gleaner* for libel, but the case was thrown out. See *Ottawa Journal*, May 30, 1907, for details of the libel trial.

146. Wendell E. Fulton, "Henry Robert Emmerson," Dictionary of Canadian Biography Online. Accessed at www.biographi.ca/en/bio/emmerson_henry_robert_14E.html.

147. Emmerson family, "Hon. Henry Robert Emmerson, 1853–1914," undated compilation of biographies and obituaries assembled by the Emmerson family.

148. E-mail exchange between Jacques Poitras and Steve Scott, July 30, 2015.

149. Fulton, op. cit.

150. Emmerson family, op. cit.

151. Source: *The British and American constitutions. An address by Rt. Hon. Sir Wilfrid Laurier, K.C.M.G., P.C. LL.D., to the Women's Canadian Club of Montreal, 27 October, 1909.* Accessed at https://ia802606.us.archive.org/19/items/cihm_74909/cihm_74909.pdf.

152. From Lord Tennyson, "You Ask Me, Why."

153. Daniel Webster (1782–1852), one of the leading American political figures of his age. He served under three U.S. presidents as secretary of state and was a veteran senator known for his oratorical skills.

154. William Howard Taft (1857–1930), twenty-seventh U.S. president 1909–1913. William Jennings Bryan (1860–1925), one of the most famous orators of his age, was a three-time Democratic presidential candidate. He lost to Republican Taft at the November 1908 election.

155. Horace Greeley (1811–1872), famed American newspaper editor and politician who ran for president in 1872.

156. The Rt Hon. Kim Campbell would like to acknowledge the research assistance for this essay provided by Arthur Milnes.

157. See "Ethel Roosevelt enjoys secret visit to Canada," *San Francisco Call* 112.86, August 25, 1912.

158. Quoted in "Canadian Newspapers Reflect Bitter Feeling Stirred Up in Dominion by Reciprocity Fight," *Brooklyn Daily Eagle*, September 17, 1911, 27.

159. Oscar Douglas Skelton, *Life and Letters of Sir Wilfrid Laurier*, vol. 1, 107–08.

160. Quoted in *Debates*, House of Commons, Ottawa, Canada, May 26, 1898.

161. Quoted in *Brooklyn Daily Eagle*, September 17, 1911, 27.

162. Source: "Sir Wilfrid Laurier welcomed by thousands at head of Lakes," *Manitoba Morning Free Press*, July 11, 1910.

163. Source: Arthur Morton, *Written in Letters of Gold. A.S. Morton's History of the University of Saskatchewan's First 25 Years.* Accessed at http://library. usask.ca/archives/campus-history/pdfs/Essays2006_Morton.pdf.

164. Robert Stevenson (1772–1850), Scottish civil engineer known in particular for his design of coastal lighthouses.

165. Source: "British Columbia to Sir Wilfrid Laurier," *Vancouver Daily World*, August 16, 1910.

166. Sources: "East and West work together," *Chilliwack Progress*, September 7, 1910, and "Sir Wilfrid Laurier and the Motherland," *The Times* (London), September 5, 1910.

167. Source: quoted in Dutil and MacKenzie, *Canada 1911*, 228–29.

168. Henri Bourassa (1868–1952), the Quebec politician and journalist, is considered one of the most important nationalist figures in the province's history. He and Laurier often clashed.

169. Frederick Debartzch Monk (1856–1914) was a veteran federal Conservative leader in Quebec who formed a close alliance with Henri Bourassa, particularly over Canada's naval question, even breaking with his own party in opposing the navy. He later served in Sir Robert Borden's cabinet but became disillusioned with the Conservative government's policies, particularly those on French–English relations.

170. Source: quoted in Dutil and MacKenzie, *Canada 1911*, 228–29.

171. Quoted in Dutil and MacKenzie, *Canada 1911*, 34.

172. Richard Bedford Bennett (1870–1947), Canada's eleventh prime minister (1930–35), is now credited with advancing Canadian autonomy within the British Empire and, while a member of Britain's House of Lords in the 1940s (as Viscount Bennett), often invoked Laurier's name.

173. Albert Sévigny (1881–1961), a leading Conservative from Quebec first elected in 1911, rose to become speaker of the House of Commons and later joined Sir Robert Borden's cabinet. In 1921 Prime Minister Arthur Meighen appointed him to the Quebec Superior Court, where he served with distinction for decades.

174. Source: "Speech Delivered by Rt. Hon. Sir Wilfrid Laurier, P.C., G.C.M.G., M.P., on the occasion of a Banquet tendered by the Montreal Reform Club at the Windsor Hotel, Montreal, Wednesday, May 29, 1912." Accessed at https://ia802703.us.archive.org/20/items/cihm_75073/ cihm_75073.pdf.

175. "My Orders" by poet and journalist Ethelwyn Wetherald (1857–1940).

176. Laurier refers to Lincoln's famous Second Inaugural Address of 1864.

177. The white feather is the traditional symbol of cowardice, especially in the British army.

178. Sir Francis Hincks (1807–1885), a journalist and leading pre-Confederation voice, was Premier of the United Province of Canada. Sir Allan MacNab (1798–1862), an important railway businessman, was co-Premier of the United Province of Canada.

179. Sources: "Sir Wilfrid – 1893–1913," *Winnipeg Tribune*, December 2, 1913, and "Policy of Liberal Party Is for Free Food," *Ottawa Journal*, November 27, 1913.

180. The Rt Hon. Arthur Meighen (1874–1960) served as prime minister of Canada in 1920–1921 and 1926.

181. Sir Alexander Tilloch Galt (1817–1893) was one of the leading Fathers of Confederation. He later served as Canada's first minister of finance under Sir John A. Macdonald and was Canada's first-ever high commissioner to the United Kingdom.

182. Samuel Leonard Tilley (1818–1896) was a leading Father of Confederation from New Brunswick and a firm supporter of Confederation, entering Sir John A. Macdonald's cabinet after July 1, 1867, and serving as minister of finance.

183. Joseph Howe (1804–1873) was a leading journalist and political leader from Nova Scotia who served as premier before 1867. Originally opposed to Confederation, he entered Sir John A. Macdonald's cabinet and was later appointed Nova Scotia's lieutenant governor. He is considered today to be one of Nova Scotia's most significant early citizens.

184. Source: "Fight the strong . . . Be merciful to the weak: Laurier at London," *The Globe*, October 12, 1916.

185. *Macbeth* V.v.19-21, slightly misquoted.

186. Robert Rogers (1864–1936) was an important Manitoba Conservative politician at both the provincial and federal levels. He served as Manitoba's minister of public works for more than a decade. Between 1911 and 1917 he served in Sir Robert Borden's federal cabinet.

187. The correct version is "Parcere subiectis et debellare superbos," "show mercy to the conquered and subdue the proud." Virgil, *Aeneid* VI.853.

188. Source: *Sir Wilfrid Laurier's Manifesto to the Canadian People, Ottawa Evening Journal*, November 5, 1917, 9. Undated typescript accessed at http://images.ourontario.ca/Partners/WLU/0028356801T.PDF.

189. The resort to an older legal tradition that defers to the Crown, or State authority, may also reflect a more general Canadian cultural trait that

shows "reverence for law and order and authority." See Graham Parker, "Canadian Legal Culture," in Louis A Knafla, ed., *Law and Justice in a New Land* (Toronto: Carswell, 1986), 24.

190. See Philip Girard, "Politics, Promotion and Professionalism: Laurier's Judicial Appointments," in *Essays in the History of Canadian Law: A Tribute to Peter N. Oliver*, ed. J. Philips, Roy McMurtry and John T. Saywell. See also Joseph Swainger, "Judicial Scandal and the Culture of Patronage in Early Confederation 1867–78," in *Essays in the History of Canadian Law* 10 (Toronto: Osgoode Society and University of Toronto Press, 2008), 240.

191. One British court declared that "war cannot be carried on according to the principles of the *Magna Carta*." See *Ronnefeldt v Phillips* (1918), 35 TLR 46 (CA).

192. Arthur Lower, *Colony to Nation: A History of Canada* (Toronto: McClelland & Stewart, 1969), 473.

193. (1914) 5 Geo v, c 2 (Can).

194. This resulted in widespread prosecution and "severe" penalties. See Gregory S. Kealey, *State Repression of Labour and the Left in Canada: 1914–1920* (Toronto: University of Toronto Press, 1992), 301.

195. *British North America Act* (1916) 6-7 Geo v, c 19 (UK).

196. Source: *The Eastern Ontario Liberal Association, formed January 14th, 1919: constitution and officers and advisory council and executive committee: resolutions, addresses by the Right Hon. Sir Wilfrid Laurier and others.* Accessed at https://archive.org/details/cihm_74525.

197. Sir Thomas White (1866–1955), Sir Robert Borden's minister of finance, served from November 1918 to May 1919 as Canada's acting prime minister while Borden represented Canada at the peace talks in Europe.

198. Daniel Duncan McKenzie (1859–1927) served as interim leader of the Liberal Party and leader of the Opposition from the time of Laurier's death in February 1919 until August 1919, when William Lyon Mackenzie King was elected the party's leader.

199. Samuel 1:20.

200. Lord Tennyson, "Break, Break, Break" (1842).

201. The Battle of Alma took place in the Crimea on September 20, 1854, and the joint Anglo–French forces proved victorious; the Battle of Inkerman (November 5, 1854) was another victory for the French and British Forces, joined by the Ottoman Turks, over the Russian army; the Allies laid siege at Sebastopol for a year after Inkerman.

202. See 2 Kings 2:12.

203. See 2 Samuel 3:38.
204. Rodolphe Lemieux (1866–1937) held various positions in Laurier's cabinet and was a close ally. He later became speaker of the House of Commons.
205. Sir Walter Scott, "Patriotism, Nelson, Pitt, Fox."
206. Proverbs 4:18.
207. Sir Charles Gavan Duffy (1816–1903) was a famed Irish nationalist who became a significant political figure in Australia; Louis Botha (1862–1919) was the first prime minister of the Union of South Africa.
208. Sir Henry Campbell-Bannerman (1836–1908) served as prime minister of the United Kingdom from 1905 to 1908.
209. James Michael "Jim" Flaherty (1949–2014) was Prime Minister Stephen Harper's popular minister of finance (2006–2014), whose death at age sixty-four was mourned by politicians of all parties. On October 22, 2014, there occurred a series of shootings on Parliament Hill in Ottawa perpetrated by Michael Zehaf-Bibeau. After fatally shooting Corporal Nathan Cirillo at Canada's National War Memorial, Zehaf-Bibeau entered the Centre Block, where he was shot and killed by security forces. There were moving tributes from all party leaders in the Commons.
210. Source: "Canada's Royal Citizen unveils bronze statue to Canada's great son," *Toronto Globe*, August 3, 1927.
211. Algernon Charles Swinburne, "On the Monument Erected to Mazzini at Genoa."

INDEX

514